Sri Lanka

a travel survival kit

John Noble
Susan Forsyth
Tony Wheeler

Sri Lanka – a travel survival kit

5th edition

Published by
Lonely Planet Publications
Head Office: PO Box 617, Hawthorn, Vic 3122, Australia
Branches: PO Box 2001A, Berkeley, CA 94702, USA
10 Barley Mow Passage, Chiswick, London W4 4PH, UK
71 bis rue du Cardinal Lemoine, 75005 Paris, France

Printed by
Colorcraft, Hong Kong

Photographs by
Richard I'Anson (RI'A)
John Noble (JN)
Paul Steel (PS)
Paul Tracey (PT)
Tony Wheeler (TW)

Front cover: Sigiriya Damsels – frescoes at Sigiriya, D & J Heaton, Scoopix
Back cover: Buddha & boy monk, Polonnaruwa (PS)

First Published
February 1980

This Edition
May 1993

National Library of Australia Cataloguing in Publication Data

Noble, John, 1951 Oct.11 –
Sri Lanka – a travel survival kit.

5th ed.
Includes index.
ISBN 0 86442 169 9.

1. Sri Lanka – Guide-books. I. Forsyth, Susan. II. Wheeler, Tony, 1946–
(Series: Lonely Planet travel survival kit).

915.493043

John Noble & Susan Forsyth

John, from the Ribble valley, England, and Susan, from Melbourne, Australia, met at Unawatuna, Sri Lanka in 1986, where John was researching for the previous edition of this book and Susan was taking a much-needed beach break from a one-year stint as a volunteer teacher-trainer in a small, nondescript town in Sri Lanka's hill country. Both of them spent nearly all that year delving into the island's quaint nooks and crannies. Previously John had pursued a newspaper journalism career from the Ribble valley's *Clitheroe Advertiser* to the *Jakarta Post* via London's *Observer*, *Times* and *Guardian*, while Susan taught English to high school students and adult migrants around Melbourne. Since '86 John has co-authored Lonely Planet's *Mexico* and *USSR* guides and John and Susan together have worked on *Australia* and *Indonesia* updates. They have also squeezed in a wedding and produced children Isabella and Jack, who both accompanied their parents back to the serendipitous isle for this edition, although Jack was still waiting to see the light of day at the time. Current home base for all of them is the sunny Ribble valley.

Tony Wheeler

Tony was born in England but grew up in Pakistan, the Bahamas and the USA. He returned to England to do a university degree in engineering at Warwick University, worked as an automotive design engineer, returned to university to complete an MBA in London, then dropped out on the Asian overland trail with his wife, Maureen. Eventually settling down in Australia they've been travelling, writing and publishing guidebooks ever since, having set up Lonely Planet Publications in the mid-1970s. Travel for the Wheelers is considerably enlivened by their daughter Tashi and their son Kieran.

This Edition

Tony Wheeler wrote and researched the first three editions of this book, the first on a lengthy investigation with Maureen, the second as a high-speed solo expedition, and

the third a more leisurely circuit of the country accompanied by their children Tashi and Kieran. John Noble tackled the fourth edition, in 1986, but not long afterwards Sri Lanka's ethnic troubles became so acute that travellers almost stopped going there altogether. When things calmed down, in the south and centre of the island at least, and travel and tourism revived, John and Susan made a detailed six-week research trip for this edition. Information on parts of the island which travellers normally can't visit, or can visit only with difficulty or risk, has been cut back this time. Let's hope there's reason to expand it for the next edition.

From the Authors

John and Susan would specially like to thank Eva & Co and Faiesz & Sue (all of Kandy), Asoka of Unawatuna, Batty Weerakoon of Luton, and Jessica Watkin for help on this edition.

From the Publisher

This edition was edited by Sally Steward, with thanks to Sue Mitra for guidance and proofreading. Jacqui Schiff was responsible for design and layout, map drawing and illustrations. Margaret Jung designed the cover. Michelle Stamp and Trudi Canavan assisted in map drawing and Ann Jeffree provided invaluable assistance with Ventura.

Thanks to all the readers whose letters helped us with this update. Their names are listed at the back of this book.

Warning & Request

Things change – prices go up, schedules change, good places go bad and bad places go bankrupt – nothing stays the same. So if you find things better or worse, recently opened or long since closed, please write and tell us and help make the next edition better.

Your letters will be used to help update future editions and, where possible, important changes will also be included in a Stop Press section in reprints.

We greatly appreciate all information that is sent to us by travellers. Back at Lonely Planet we employ a hard-working readers' letters team to sort through the many letters we receive. The best ones will be rewarded with a free copy of the next edition or another Lonely Planet guide if you prefer. We give away lots of books, but, unfortunately, not every letter/postcard receives one.

Contents

THE ANCIENT CITIES 159

EAST COAST BEACHES 188

JAFFNA & THE NORTH 195

GLOSSARY 198

INDEX 202

Map Legend

BOUNDARIES

—·—·—·—	........International Boundary
—··—··—	...............Internal Boundary
++++++++++	....National Park or Reserve
— — — — —	.........................The Equator
················	.........................The Tropics

SYMBOLS

◉ NATIONAL	........................National Capital
● PROVINCIAL	........Provincial or State Capital
● Major	...............................Major Town
● Minor	...............................Minor Town
■	.........................Places to Stay
▼	.........................Places to Eat
⊠	..................................Post Office
✈	....Airport
i	....................Tourist Information
⊖	.............Bus Station or Terminal
66	............Highway Route Number
⚲☦⛪⛪	......Mosque, Church, Cathedral
∴	..........................Temple or Ruin
✚	....................................Hospital
※	....................................Lookout
⚑	...........................Camping Area
⊓	...............................Picnic Area
⌂	...............................Hut or Chalet
▲	.........................Mountain or Hill
↦▬↤	.... Railway Station
═══	..............................Road Bridge
↦┼┼↤	..........................Railway Bridge
⇒ ⇐	...........................Road Tunnel
↦⟩ ⟨↤	..........................Railway Tunnel
⌒⌒	...................Escarpment or Cliff
⌣⌢	....Pass
⊓⊔⊓	............Ancient or Historic Wall

ROUTES

──────	.......Major Road or Highway
– – – – –	.... Unsealed Major Road
────	.... Sealed Road
– – – – –	..... Unsealed Road or Track
═══	...........................City Street
+++++++++	.................................Railway
━●━━	.... Subway
··················	..........................Walking Track
– – – – –	.... Ferry Route
┼┼┼┼┼┼┼┼	.... Cable Car or Chair Lift

HYDROGRAPHIC FEATURES

	......................River or Creek
	.............Intermittent Stream
	........Lake, Intermittent Lake
	..........................Coast Line
	..................................Spring
	.... Waterfall
	.... Swamp
	.... Salt Lake or Reef
	.............................Glacier

OTHER FEATURES

	Park, Garden or National Park
	.... Built Up Area
	... Market or Pedestrian Mall
	.........Plaza or Town Square
	............................Cemetery

Note: not all symbols displayed above appear in this book

Introduction

It's easy to think of Sri Lanka as a tropical island offshoot of India – with the difference that the majority of people are Buddhist, not Hindu, and there aren't so many of them, but their quarrels are bloodier. In fact Sri Lanka is totally different from India and has its own qualities which, recent political and ethnic problems apart, make it hard to disagree with Marco Polo's impression that this is the finest island in the world. No matter what you want Sri Lanka is likely to have it. Beaches? – the coastal stretch south of Colombo has beach after beach as beautiful as anywhere in the world. Culture? – try the Kandyan dances, a procession of elephants or the demon mask dances for size. Ruins? – if you like ruins you'll find your fill in the ancient cities of Anuradhapura and Polonnaruwa. Scenery? – head for the hill country where the heat of the plains and the coast soon fade away. Wildlife? – Sri Lanka has its own subspecies of elephant which you can see wild in the national parks. All this comes with friendly people, good food, pleasant places to stay and reasonably low costs in a handy, compact package.

> On leaving the Island of Andoman and sailing a thousand miles, a little south of west, the traveller reaches Ceylon, which is undoubtedly the finest Island of its size in all the world.
>
> **Marco Polo**

CEYLON OR SRI (OR SHRI) LANKA?

Changing the country's name from Ceylon to Sri Lanka in the 1970s caused considerable confusion, but in fact it has always been known to the Sinhalese (the majority people of Sri Lanka) as Lanka, or to the Tamils as

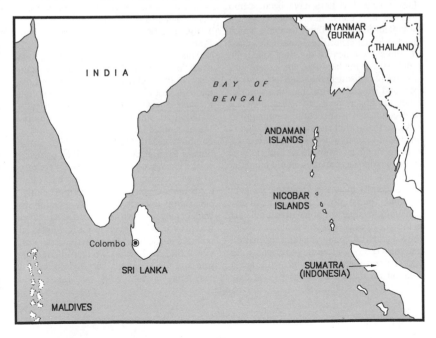

Ilankai. Indeed the 2000-year-old Hindu epic, the *Ramayana*, tells of Rama's beautiful wife being carried away by the evil king of Lanka. Later, the Romans knew it as Taprobane and Muslim traders talked of the island of Serendib, from which was derived the word serendipity – the faculty of making happy and unexpected discoveries by accident. The Portuguese called it Ceilão, a corruption of the native name Sinhala-dvipa. In turn, the Dutch altered this name to Ceylan and the British to Ceylon. In 1972 the original Lanka was restored with the addition of Sri, which means 'auspicious' or 'resplendent' in the Sinhalese language. At least 'Sri' was how the Sinhalese letter ශ්‍රී was normally rendered in our Roman alphabet, until the 1990s when 'Shri', which is said to be much closer to the pronunciation, started growing in popularity.

IS IT SAFE?

Many potential visitors have been scared away from Sri Lanka in the past decade by the violent Sinhalese-Tamil troubles, which have rendered the north and east of the island off limits for much of the time since the mid-1980s. In the late '80s, when there was a Sinhalese uprising in the south too, tourism collapsed altogether. But since that was put down, the government and tourist industry have conducted a successful campaign to persuade the world that most of the island is again safe to visit. Tourists began returning in large numbers from 1990 and, it was hoped, would pass previous record numbers in the mid-'90s.

The security picture is liable to change at any time. Tourist offices and anyone in any kind of responsible position will naturally err on the side of caution if you ask their advice. They'd much rather put you off a destination than run a risk of you coming to grief testing it out. All travellers must sound out the latest situation for themselves. Perhaps one day,

somehow, a lasting peace will break out and the whole east coast and the north will be safe again. The ferry to India may even start again. Unfortunately, at the time of writing such things seem as far away as ever and basically anywhere north of Anuradhapura (including Wilpattu National Park) or east of Polonnaruwa remains risky. The government currently controls Trincomalee town and the occasional traveller who heads there tends to be allowed through the road blocks. But the town still can't be called 100% safe and nor can the countryside around Trincomalee be regarded as absolutely secure. Batticaloa town too is back in government hands but the hinterland here is the main centre of Tamil Tiger activity outside the north, and attempting to reach Batticaloa is definitely not recommended at present. In just one incident, in July 1992, a train on the Batticaloa-Colombo line was attacked in the Batticaloa district and 40 people were killed. A few travellers venture to Arugam Bay, further down the east coast, but there are also occasional attacks on vehicles on the road to Arugam Bay, through Monaragala and Pottuvil.

This leaves the southern half of the west coast (including Colombo and all the main resorts), the south, the hill country and the main ancient city sites – more than enough to make a visit worthwhile – as basically trouble-free, although there's still the occasional isolated incident such as the two big bombings near Colombo in April 1992, at the time of the Sinhalese and Tamil New Year.

The closure of some parts of the country to visitors is an incentive to explore other areas more closely. One of the most enjoyable things to do in Sri Lanka is simply to walk or bicycle down a side road to wherever it takes you. Here, even just a few hundred metres from some of the main tourist towns, you'll find Sri Lanka's wonderful countryside and the people as friendly, polite and easy going as ever.

Facts about the Country

HISTORY

Sri Lanka is one of those places where history seems to fade into the mists of legend. Is not Adam's Peak said to be the very place where Adam set foot on earth, having been cast out of heaven? Isn't that his footprint squarely on top of the mountain to prove it? Or is it the Buddha's, visiting an island halfway to paradise? And isn't Adam's bridge (the chain of islands linking Sri Lanka to India) the very series of stepping stones which Rama, aided by his faithful ally the monkey god Hanuman, skipped across in his mission to rescue Sita from the clutches of the evil demon Rawana, king of Lanka, in the epic *Ramayana*?

It is probable that the story of the *Ramayana* actually does have some frail basis in reality, for Sri Lanka's history recounts many invasions from the south of India. Perhaps some early, punitive invasion provided the background for the story of Rama and his beautiful wife, a story which is recounted over and over again all around Asia. Whatever the legends, the reality points towards the first Sinhalese people – who probably originated in north India – arriving in Sri Lanka around the 5th or 6th century BC, and gradually replacing the prior inhabitants, the Veddahs, only a few of whom linger on today.

The Rise & Fall of Anuradhapura

The Sinhalese kingdom of Anuradhapura developed in the dry, northern plain region of the island in the 4th century BC. Later, other Sinhalese kingdoms arose in the south and west, but Anuradhapura remained the strongest. In the 3rd century BC the great Buddhist emperor, Ashoka, reigned in India and his son, Mahinda, came to the island with a retinue of monks to spread the Buddha's teachings. He soon converted the Anuradhapura king and his followers to Buddhism, and his sister planted a sapling of the sacred bo-tree under which the Buddha

attained enlightenment in Bodh Gaya in northern India. It can still be seen flourishing in Anuradhapura today. Buddhism went through a rejuvenation in Sri Lanka and it was here that the *Theravada* or *Hinayana* or 'small vehicle' school of Buddhism developed, later spreading to other Buddhist countries. Even today, Buddhists of the Theravada school in Myanmar (Burma), Thailand and other countries look to Sri Lanka for spiritual leadership.

Buddhism gave the Sinhalese people a sense of national purpose and identity, and also inspired the development of their culture and literature – factors which were to be important in the tumultuous centuries that followed. Anuradhapura was the centre of Sinhalese kingdoms for well over 1000 years, from around the 4th century BC to the 10th century AD. But it suffered from its proximity to south India, where Hinduism continued to flourish. There were repeated invasions and takeovers of Anuradhapura by south Indian kingdoms, and self-defeating entanglements in south Indian affairs by Anuradhapura's rulers.

A number of Sinhalese heroes arose to repel the invaders, two of the most famous being Dutugemunu (2nd century BC) and Vijayabahu I (11th century AD). It was Vijayabahu I who finally decided to abandon Anuradhapura and make Polonnaruwa, further south-east, his capital. Today the majestic ruins of these two cities are not the only reminders of this period of Sri Lankan history. Scattered over the country are enormous 'tanks', artificial lakes developed for irrigation purposes in the dry regions of Sri Lanka. Even today they would be amazing engineering feats.

The Rise & Fall of Polonnaruwa

Polonnaruwa survived as a Sinhalese capital for over two centuries and provided two other great kings, apart from Vijayabahu I. His nephew Parakramabahu I (1153-86 AD),

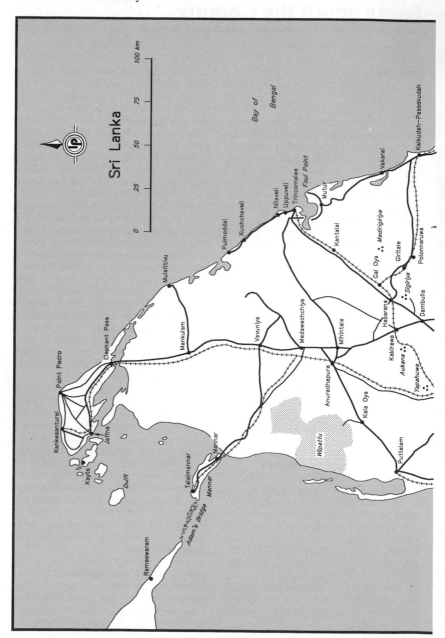

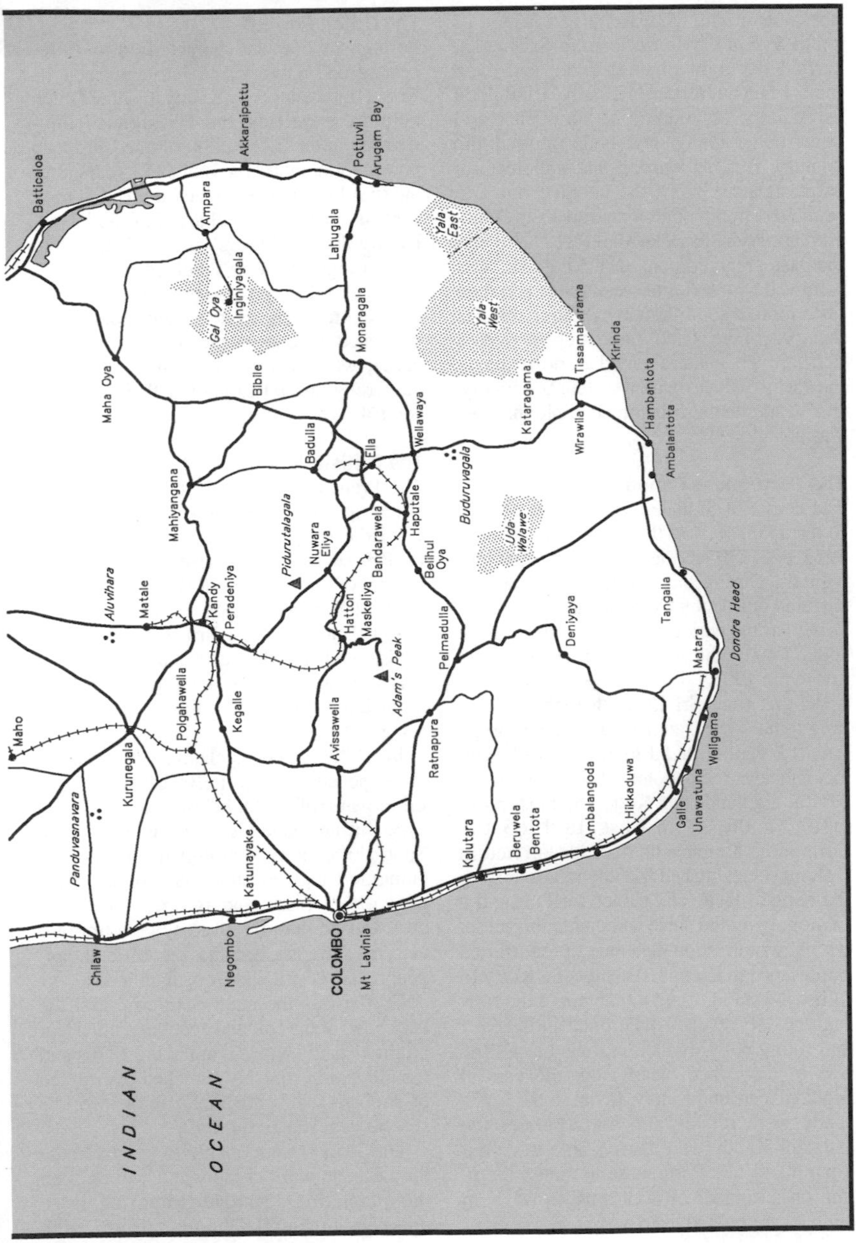
Batticaloa
Akkaraipattu
Pottuvil
Arugam Bay
Ampara
Lahugala
Yala East
Gal Oya
Inginiyagala
Monaragala
Yala West
Tissamaharama
Kirinda
Maha Oya
Bibile
Kataragama
Wellawaya
Wirawila
Hambantota
Badulla
Ella
Buduruvagala
Ambalantota
Mahiyangana
Haputale
Bandarawela
Nuwara Eliya
Pidurutalagala
Uda Walawe
Belihul Oya
Aluvihara
Matale
Kandy
Peradeniya
Hatton
Maskeliya
Pelmadulla
Deniyaya
Tangalla
Dondra Head
Matara
Adam's Peak
Maho
Polgahawella
Kegalle
Avissawella
Ratnapura
Weligama
Kurunegala
Panduvasnavara
Unawatuna
Galle
Hikkaduwa
Ambalangoda
Beruwela
Bentota
Kalutara
Katunayake
Chilaw
Negombo
COLOMBO
Mt Lavinia
INDIAN
OCEAN

not content with Vijayabahu's expulsion of south Indian Chola rulers from Sri Lanka, carried the fight to south India and even made a raid on Burma. Internally he indulged in an orgy of building at his capital and constructed many new tanks around the country. But his warring and architectural extravagances wore the country out and probably shortened Polonnaruwa's lifespan. His successor Nissanka Malla (1187-96) was the last great Polonnaruwa king. He was followed by a series of weak rulers and then once more a south Indian kingdom arose in the north of the island. Tanks were neglected or destroyed, malaria started to spread due to the decay of the irrigation system and finally, like Anuradhapura before it, Polonnaruwa was abandoned.

The Portuguese Period

The centre of Sinhalese power now shifted to the south-west of the island and between 1253 and 1400 AD there were five Sinhalese capitals. During this period Sri Lanka also suffered attacks by Chinese and Malaysians as well as the periodic incursions from south India. Finally the colonial European powers arrived in 1505.

At this time Sri Lanka had three main kingdoms – the Tamil (south Indian-originated) kingdom of Jaffna in the north, and the Sinhalese kingdoms of Kandy in the central highlands and Kotte, the most powerful, in the south-west. In 1505 the Portuguese, Lorenço de Almeida, arrived in Colombo, established friendly relations with the King of Kotte and gained for Portugal a monopoly on the spice and cinnamon trade, which would soon become of enormous importance in Europe. Attempts by Kotte to utilise the strength and protection of the Portuguese only resulted in Portugal taking over and ruling not only their regions but all the rest of the island, apart from the central highlands around Kandy. Because the highlands were remote and inaccessible, the kings of Kandy were always able to defeat attempts by the Portuguese to annex them, and on a number of occasions drove them right back down to the coast.

The Dutch Period

Portuguese rule was characterised by European greed, cruelty and intolerance at its worst, but attempts by Kandy to enlist Dutch help in expelling the Portuguese only resulted in the substitution of one European power for another. By 1658, 153 years after the first Portuguese contact, the Dutch took control over the coastal areas of the island. During their 140 years' rule the Dutch, like the Portuguese, were involved in repeated unsuccessful attempts to bring Kandy under their control. The Dutch were much more interested in trade and profits than the Portuguese, who spent a lot of effort spreading their religion and extending their physical control.

The British Period

The French revolution resulted in a major shake-up among the European powers and in 1796 the Dutch were easily supplanted by the British, who in 1815 also managed to win control of the kingdom of Kandy, becoming the first European power to rule the whole island. Until 1802 the British administered Sri Lanka from Madras in India, but in that year it became a Crown Colony and in 1818 a unified administration for the island was set up.

In 1832 sweeping changes in property laws opened the doors to British settlers – at the expense of the Sinhalese, who in British eyes did not have clear title to their land. Soon the country was dotted with coffee, cinnamon and coconut plantations and a network of roads and railways was constructed to handle this new economic activity. English became the official language, and is still widely spoken today.

Coffee was the main cash crop and the backbone of the colonial economy, but a leaf blight virtually wiped it out in the 1870s and the plantations quickly switched over to tea or rubber. Today Sri Lanka is the world's second largest tea exporter.

The British were unable to persuade the Sinhalese to work cheaply and willingly on the plantations, so they imported large numbers of Tamil labourers from south

Rubber

Rubber is grown as an intermediate crop – between the high-country tea plantations and the low-country coconut belt. Its arrival in Sri Lanka has a distinct flavour of Victorian industrial espionage. Rubber was once a Brazilian monopoly but in 1876 Sir Henry Wickham quietly departed from the Amazon with 700,000 rubber tree seeds. They were whisked across the Atlantic and taken to Kew Gardens in London, where all the flowers had been removed from the greenhouses in readiness for this illicit crop.

From these seedlings a rubber tree nursery of 2000 plants was set up 30 km from Colombo in the Henerathgoda Botanic Gardens; all the rubber trees in Sri Lanka, and later Malaysia, came from this first planting. You can still see the very first rubber tree planted in Asia. Today Sri Lanka is one of the world's leading rubber producers. ■

India. Sinhalese peasants in the hill country lost land to the estates, and today friction between the hill country Tamils and their Sinhalese neighbours still leads to occasional violence – although so far the hill country has kept out of the conflict that has engulfed the north and east of the country.

Sri Lanka's first government after independence deprived the hill country Tamils of citizenship; eventually deals in the 1960s and '80s between Sri Lanka and India allowed some of them to be 'repatriated' to India while others were given Sri Lankan citizenship.

Independence

Between WW I and WW II, political stirrings started to push Sri Lanka towards eventual independence from Britain – but in a considerably more peaceful and low-key manner than in India. At the end of WW II it was evident that independence would come very soon, in the wake of Sri Lanka's larger neighbour. In February 1948 Sri Lanka, or Ceylon as it was still known, became an independent member of the British Commonwealth. The first independent government was formed by D S Senanayake and his United National Party (UNP). His main opponents were Tamil parties, from the north of the country or from the tea plantations, and Communists. At first everything went smoothly. The economy remained strong; tea prices, running at a high level from WW II, were further bolstered by the Korean conflict. The government concentrated on strengthening social services and weakening the opposi-

tion. By disenfranchising the hill country Tamils, they certainly helped the latter programme.

In 1952 D S Senanayake was killed in an accident and was succeeded by his son Dudley Senanayake. His first of four periods as prime minister was very short. One of the first policies instituted after independence had been free rations of rice to every Sri Lankan and also subsidies for imports of this staple. But worldwide the price of rice had started to escalate and the balance of payments started to run the wrong way. An attempt in 1953 to increase the rice price resulted in mass riots, many deaths and the declaration of a state of emergency. Dudley Senanayake resigned – he was not the last Sri Lankan leader to be brought down by the 'rice issue'.

Sir John Kotelawala, his uncle, took his place, and the UNP earned the nickname 'Uncle Nephew Party'. Kotelawala was heavily defeated in the 1956 general election by the Mahajana Eksath Peramuna (MEP) coalition led by Solomon Bandaranaike.

Solomon Bandaranaike

Bandaranaike defeated the UNP primarily on nationalistic issues which harked back to the Dharmapala movement of the late 19th century (see the Religion section in this chapter). Nearly 10 years after independence English remained the national language and the country continued to be ruled by an English-speaking, mainly Christian elite. Many Sinhalese thought that the elevation of their language to 'official' status, to be used in government and official work, would increase their power and job prospects. The Tamils, whose mother tongue was Tamil, were caught in the middle of this English *vs* Sinhala and Christian *vs* Buddhist disagreement, and when Bandaranaike enacted the 'Sinhala-Only' law, making Sinhalese the official language of the country, Tamil protests were followed by violence and deaths. The Tamils now put their weight behind the Federal Party, pressing for a federal system of government, with greater local autonomy in the main Tamil-populated areas, the north and east.

Sri Lanka's serious Sinhalese-Tamil difficulties really date from this time, although they had started simmering with the jockeying for position as the end of colonial rule came in sight. From the mid-1950s, as the economy slowed, competition for wealth and work – intensified by the high expectations created by Sri Lanka's fine education system – exaggerated Sinhalese-Tamil jealousies. The main political parties, particularly when in opposition, played on Sinhalese paranoia that their religion, language and culture could be swamped by the Hindu, non-Sinhala-speaking peoples of India, whose natural allies the Tamils in Sri Lanka were thought to be. The Tamils began to see themselves as a threatened minority.

Bandaranaike launched a huge programme of nationalisation and state monopolies. The most visible of these was the Ceylon Transport Board (CTB) which took over every private bus line in the country and managed to make bus travel an uncomfortable and thoroughly chaotic experience everywhere. (Private buses were reintroduced a couple of decades later but by then everyone had forgotten that bus travel *could* be comfortable.)

Bandaranaike was assassinated by a Buddhist monk in 1959, and to this day is looked upon as a national hero who brought the government of Sri Lanka back to the common people.

Sirimavo Bandaranaike

In the mid-1960 general election the Sri Lanka Freedom Party (SLFP), led by Solomon Bandaranaike's widow Sirimavo, swept to power. She was the first female prime minister in the world.

Mrs Bandaranaike pressed on with her husband's nationalisation policies and soured relations with the USA by taking over the Sri Lankan oil companies. But the economy was running from bad to worse and an attempt to abolish the rice policy led to massive opposition. In the 1965 election Dudley Senanayake scraped back into power with the support of the Federal Party – but his reluctance to turn back the clock on the SLFP's nationalisation programme soon lost him much support. The UNP was massively defeated in the 1970 elections.

JVP Uprising Mrs Bandaranaike again failed to come to grips with the economic crisis. In 1971 a Sinhalese Marxist insurrection broke out, led by students and young people under the banner of the Janatha Vimukthi Peramuna (JVP, People's Liberation Army). The poorly organised rebels were quickly and ruthlessly eradicated by the army, at a cost of many thousand lives. North Korea was accused of aiding the revolt.

The revolt handed the government a mandate for sweeping changes including strengthened armed forces, a new constitution, and a new, Sinhalese name – Sri Lanka – for the country. But still the economy continued to deteriorate. Attempts to continue the supply of free rice at all costs led to drastic shortages of almost everything else. Long queues became commonplace at shops all over the country and in the 1977 elections the SLFP (in its new guise of the ULF – the United Left Front) went down to a stunning defeat at the hands of the UNP.

Tamil Unrest Meanwhile the Tamils were growing more alienated, with two pieces of legislation causing particular grievance. One, in 1970, was designed to cut their numbers in universities – previously Tamils had tended to win a higher proportion of university places than their percentage in the population. The second was the new 1972 constitution's declaration that Buddhism had the 'foremost place' and that it was the state's duty to 'protect and foster' Buddhism. When unrest grew among northern Tamils, a state of emergency was imposed on their areas for several years from 1971. Since the police and army who enforced the state of emergency now contained few Tamils (partly because of the 'Sinhala-Only' law), and were often ill-disciplined and heavy-handed, they came to be seen more and more as an enemy force by Tamils. In the mid-'70s some young Tamils, mostly left-wing, started to take to violence, fighting for an independent Tamil state, 'Eelam'. On the political front, the Tamil United Liberation Front, founded in 1976, also campaigned for Eelam.

J R Jayewardene
Economic Change The new UNP prime minister elected in 1977, Junius Richard (J R) Jayewardene, back-pedalled on the Bandaranaike nationalisation programmes and made an all-out effort to lure back some of the foreign investment chased away by Mrs Bandaranaike. He cut subsidies, devalued the rupee to help exports, opened the country up on a large scale to tourism and foreign imports and investment (especially by setting up a free trade zone north of Colombo around Katunayake airport), and speeded up the Mahaweli Project, in which a series of dams have been constructed on Sri Lanka's longest river to provide hydro-electricity and more irrigation. Other steps were taken to improve agricultural output, and some state companies were sold off to the private sector.

These measures yielded some successes: unemployment was halved by 1983, Sri Lanka became self-sufficient in rice in 1985, and tourism and the large numbers of Sri Lankans working in the Middle East brought in lots of foreign currency. On the other hand, inflation rose until it peaked at 40% in 1979-80 (though it had been brought down below 10% by 1986); prices of major exports like tea and rubber were unstable; and while some people made a lot of money fast from

tourism and trade, others' incomes stood still or were eaten into by inflation.

Political Developments Jayewardene took a number of steps said to be aimed at achieving the political stability needed to counter left-wing subversion, but which were also criticised as undemocratic. In 1978 he introduced a new constitution which, among other things, conferred greatest power on the new post of president, to which he himself was elected by Parliament. In 1980 Parliament found Mrs Bandaranaike guilty of 'abuse of power' while in office, and her civic rights were removed for seven years. This meant she could no longer be an MP. (Jayewardene restored her rights in 1986.)

In 1982 Jayewardene was re-elected president in national polls (after amending his own constitution to bring the voting forward two years) and then the same year won a referendum to bypass the 1983 general election and leave the existing parliament in office until 1989. As usual there were allegations of electoral skullduggery.

The Tamil Rebellion
Jayewardene promoted Tamil to the status of a 'national language', to be used in official work in Tamil-majority areas, and introduced greater local control in government, but couldn't stop the clashes between Tamil 'boys' and the security forces from growing into a pattern of killings, reprisals, reprisals for reprisals, etc. All too often the victims were civilians.

The 1983 Riots The powder keg finally exploded in 1983. The spark was an ambush and massacre of an army patrol by Tamil 'Tiger' secessionists in the northern Jaffna region, the heartland of the island's Tamil population. For several days afterwards Sinhalese mobs and gangs indulged in an orgy of killing, burning and looting against Tamils and their property in towns all over the island. Between 400 and 2000 Tamils were killed and some areas with a large Tamil population – such as Colombo's Pettah district or the business districts of some hill country towns – were virtually levelled. The government, the police and the army were unable, and in some cases unwilling, to stop it. There had been similar, smaller-scale, anti-Tamil outbursts in 1958, 1977 and 1981, but this was the worst and for many marked the point of no return. Tens of thousands of Tamils fled to safer, Tamil-majority areas while many others left the country altogether. Sinhalese started to move out of Jaffna and other Tamil-dominated areas.

Escalation Both sides grew more violent and there were several large-scale massacres – probably the worst being the May 1985 Anuradhapura massacre in which about 150 mainly Sinhalese people were gunned down. The government was condemned by Amnesty International and others over torture and disappearances, but for its part pointed to the intimidation and violence against civilians (including Tamils) by the Tamil fighters, and the help and training India allowed them to receive in its own Tamil areas. The Indian government was reluctant to clamp down on this for fear of losing Indian Tamils' votes.

The area claimed by the Tamil militants for the independent state of Eelam was Sri Lanka's northern and eastern provinces – roughly speaking, the region north of Vavuniya plus a strip all the way down the east coast. This amounted to about one-third of Sri Lanka's land area, which the government couldn't even contemplate conceding, given the strength of Sinhalese feeling. While Tamils were the overwhelming majority in the northern province, in the east Muslims, Sinhalese and Tamils were all present in nearly equal numbers (although Tamils argued that the Sinhalese numbers had only been bumped up to this level in recent years by newcomers settled on lands opened by the Mahaweli irrigation schemes). The limited self-government the Tamils were offered in the mid-'80s was too little, too late. Tamil feeling had hardened and the militants' grip over the Tamil population had tightened. At the same time, the

sometimes ill-disciplined government forces alienated many moderate Tamils.

By the end of 1985 fighting had spread not only throughout the north but also down most of the east coast, where the strongest and most hard-line Tamil armed group, the Tigers (officially the Liberation Tigers of Tamil Eelam or LTTE), attacked Sinhalese villages, leading of course to reprisals on Tamil inhabitants. Clashes also began between Tamils and Muslims in the east. Around 50,000 people (Tamils, Sinhalese and Muslims) were in refugee camps in Sri Lanka, according to the government, and about 100,000 Tamils were in camps in India. Thousands more Tamils had left for other countries.

The violence also had great costs for Sri Lanka's economy. Many businesses were destroyed and tourism slumped badly after 1983. The government had to put crippling amounts of money into defence; aid-giving countries threatened to cut assistance because of the ill-treatment of Tamils; and just to add to the woes, tea prices dived.

Indo-Sri Lankan Accord
In 1987 government forces pushed the LTTE back into Jaffna city, only to provoke increasingly serious threats of Indian intervention on the Tamil side. Jayewardene turned round and struck a deal with India by which the Sri Lankan army would return to barracks while an Indian Peace Keeping Force (IPKF) would disarm Sri Lanka's Tamil rebels and keep the peace in the north and east. A single provincial council would be elected to govern the east and north with substantial autonomy for a trial period. Opposition to the deal came not just from the secessionist LTTE – which complied initially, but only because India gave it no choice – but also from the ranks of Muslims and Sinhalese, including the SLFP, a reviving JVP, and a number of important Buddhist monks, who feared Indian influence and considered the deal a sell-out of non-Tamils in the east. Colombo was hit by Sinhalese riots and the LTTE carried out some savage

attacks on Sinhalese villages in the east. The IPKF laid into the LTTE and took Jaffna city with hundreds dead on both sides.

JVP Rebellion

Just as the lid was put on the Tamil insurgency, a Sinhalese rebellion broke out in the south and centre of the country. In 1987 and 1988 the Marxist JVP, which had threatened Mrs Bandaranaike's government in 1971, re-emerged under the leadership of a dropout from Moscow's Lumumba University, Rohana Wijeweera, to launch a series of political murders and strikes enforced on pain of death. By late 1988 the centre and south of the country were terrorised and the economy crippled. At one critical point tourists were flown out of the country in their thousands, killing the tourism industry stone dead. The military had to force employees of essential services to go to work at gunpoint.

At the end of 1988 Jayewardene retired. His successor as UNP leader, Ranasinghe Premadasa, defeated Mrs Bandaranaike in the new presidential election, and the UNP went on to win a general election in February 1989. Premadasa's ruthless answer to the JVP, after both Jayewardene and he had failed to persuade it to join mainstream politics, was death squads which went round killing JVP suspects. Finally, in late 1989, Wijeweera and most of the rest of the JVP leadership were killed or captured. JVP activity tailed off in 1990 but the method of eliminating it brought pressure from aid-giving Western countries for improved human rights in Sri Lanka. Estimates of the number killed in its three-year insurrection go up to 17,000.

Indian Withdrawal

One of Premadasa's main electoral promises, which had won him the support of Sinhalese nationalists, had been the removal of the IPKF from Sri Lanka, despite the fact that it had seemingly almost eliminated the LTTE. Premadasa soon set about securing his goal. The LTTE, desperate to see the back of the IPKF, agreed a ceasefire with the government to help speed up the Indian withdrawal, but at the same time began to gear up for another war.

The IPKF completed its pull-out in March 1990. At its peak it had numbered 80,000 men. In three years it lost over 1000 lives, as the LTTE merged with the civilian population and harassed it with landmines and small arms.

As the IPKF's departure drew near, the Eelam People's Revolutionary Liberation Front (EPRLF), an Indian-backed Tamil group that had won the 1988 elections for the joint provincial council in the north and east, unilaterally declared an independent Tamil state in the north and east. In June the LTTE attacked several police stations in the east, and, it's thought, massacred hundreds of police. The war between the LTTE and the Sri Lankan government began all over again. By the end of 1990, while the LTTE held much of the north, the east was largely back under government control, though still subject to LTTE attacks on Sinhalese and Muslim villagers aimed at diverting government forces from the north.

New War in the North

The new war reached a peak in mid-1991 – soon after the assassination of India's prime minister, Rajiv Gandhi, by a suspected Tamil Tiger – with a series of set-piece battles around Jaffna, but then tailed off as the LTTE suffered some reverses. The LTTE's support among Tamils was declining. By early 1992 it seemed ready to consider some kind of federal arrangement, giving a united north and east self-control within a unitary Sri Lankan state. The mood among Tamil and Sinhalese people alike seemed to favour peace. But Sinhalese nationalists, who thought the Tigers were simply buying time, blocked any chance of the government coming to talks.

In mid-1992 the army, which had doubled in size in nine years to 75,000 and was better armed and trained than ever before, launched a big new assault in the north. It was also reportedly conducting a 'hearts and minds' effort in areas it captured by giving protection to the Tamil inhabitants – an important change, if genuine, because it still had a reputation for senseless killings of Tamil civilians. The LTTE, relying increasingly on women fighters after heavy losses of its 'boys', declared that even if it lost a conventional war it would fight on as an urban guerrilla army. By now at least 20,000 people had died in the decade of the Tamil insurrection and 700,000 people had been displaced. Over 200,000 Sri Lankans were living in the Indian state of Tamil Nadu, about half of them in refugee camps. There were also large numbers of refugees within Sri Lanka.

GEOGRAPHY

Sri Lanka is shaped like a teardrop falling from the southern end of India. It's just 353 km long from north to south and only 183 km at its widest. Its area of 66,000 sq km is about the same as Ireland or Tasmania.

The central hill country rises a little south of the centre of the island and is surrounded by a coastal plain. The flat north-central and northern plain extends from the hill country all the way to the northern tip of the island and this region is much drier than the rest of the island. The best beaches are on the south-west, south and east coasts.

The highest mountain in the spectacularly beautiful hill country region is Piduratalagala, which rises to 2524 metres above Nuwara Eliya. Adam's Peak, at 2224 metres, is far better known and much more spectacular. The Mahaweli, Sri Lanka's longest river, has its source close to Adam's Peak and runs into the sea at Trincomalee. In the north-west of the country Mannar Island, joined to the mainland by a bridge, is almost connected to Rameswaram in southern India by the long chain of sandbanks and islets called Adam's Bridge.

CLIMATE

Sri Lanka is a typically tropical country in that there are distinct dry and wet seasons, but the picture is somewhat complicated by the fact that it is subject to two monsoons. From May to August the south-west monsoon brings rain to the southern and western coastal regions and the central hill country. This season is called Yala. The dry season in these regions is from December to March. The north-east monsoon blows from October to January, the Maha season – bringing rain to the north and east of the island. This peculiar monsoon pattern means that it is always the 'right' season somewhere on the island – though that advantage has been undermined by the troubles in the east for much of the past few years. Don't count on the weather following the rules though – it often seems to be raining where it should be sunny and sunny where it should be raining, and like many other parts of the world Sri Lanka has suffered some unusual weather conditions in recent years, with a serious drought in 1992.

In the low-lying coastal regions the temperature is uniformly high year round – Colombo averages 27°C. The temperatures rapidly fall with altitude, so if you don't feel like cooling off in the sea you have simply to go up into the hill country. At Kandy (altitude 450 metres) the average temperature is 20°C and at Nuwara Eliya (at 1890 metres) you're down to 16°C. The climate is generally like an eternal spring up in the hills but you should come prepared for chilly evenings.

The highest temperatures are usually from March to June but the mercury rarely climbs above 35°C. November to January is usually the coolest time of the year. The sea can be counted upon to remain at around 27°C year round, although it is much less suitable for swimming during the monsoon period when it can be choppy and murky.

There is also an inter-monsoon period in October and November when rain and thunderstorms can occur in many parts of the island. The south, south-west and central highlands are much wetter than the northern and north-central regions. In the latter area annual rainfall averages only 100 cm and the many 'tanks', built over 1000 years ago to provide irrigation water, indicate that this is by no means a new problem. In the wetter part of the country annual rainfall reaches 400 cm or more.

FLORA & FAUNA

Sri Lanka has not only an exciting and varied range of animal and plant life – with elephants and leopards to the fore – but also an impressive national parks and reserves system, with some 10% of the island under protection.

The following descriptions of Sri Lanka's flora, fauna and reserves are largely based on an account by Constance S Leap Bruce and Murray D Bruce.

Flora

The south-western Wet Zone is tropical rainforest with characteristic dense undergrowth and a tall canopy of hardwood trees, including ebony, teak and silkwood. Here also are some of the most spectacular orchids and many of the plants used in Ayurvedic (traditional) medicine. The central Hill Zone, such as on Horton Plains, is typical of cool, damp highland areas with hardy grasslands, rhododendron and elfin (stunted) forests, and trees often draped in sphagnum moss. The remainder of the island forms the arid Dry Zone, with a sparser cover of trees with shrubs, and grasslands that may erupt into bloom with the first rains. Only 25% to 35% of the island is still under forest cover and a large amount of this has been threatened by the massive Mahaweli Development Project in the east. Fortunately, the system of protected areas is considered an important priority, and four new national parks are being created on and near the Mahaweli.

Fauna

The animals of Sri Lanka are some of the most unusual and varied anywhere.

Mammals The 86 mammal species include the famous elephant, a unique subspecies seen in all national parks (notably Gal Oya and Lahugala), and leopard (notably Wilpattu). Many species of deer are in all the national parks. Monkeys, especially the long-tailed grey langur and the toque macaque, are common throughout the island. Other interesting mammals include the sloth bear, loris, porcupine, jackal, dugong and flying fox (roosting in huge treetop colonies during the day, such as at Peradeniya Gardens near Kandy). The wild boar is one beast that hunters are still welcome to take a shot at, since the Sri Lankans reckon there are far too many of them!

Birds Birdlife is a major attraction of Sri Lanka, with about 450 species recorded, including around 250 found throughout the year, and 21 unique to Sri Lanka. As there is no land between Sri Lanka and Antarctica, the island is a very important seasonal home for migrants escaping from northern winters as far away as western Europe and Siberia. From August to April these can be seen in their hundreds and thousands at tanks, lagoons and other wetland areas. Sri Lanka's network of bird sanctuaries not only plays host to the thousands of visitors, but also forms important breeding grounds for many other species. The best time to see birds is from January to April, when visibility and field conditions are good everywhere.

Perhaps the showiest bird is the flamingo, arriving in large numbers. Other residents and migrants include hornbills, flycatchers, bee-eaters, minivets, orioles, woodpeckers, pelicans, fishing eagles, ducks, storks, herons, egrets, spoonbills and other waterbirds.

Fish & Reptiles Some 54 species of fish are found in the waterways and marshlands, including many highly prized aquarium varieties such as the red scissortail barb and the ornate paradise fish. The British introduced several kinds, including trout, which are still common around the Horton Plains. Then there are the myriad colourful tropical seafish.

Also present are 40 species of frogs and toads, and the large variety of reptiles includes two species of crocodile (so watch where you swim!) and five of turtles. Most reptiles, however, are land dwellers, including the beautiful star tortoise and the infamous cobra. Of the 83 species of snakes recorded, only five are poisonous (cobra, Russell's viper, Indian and Sri Lankan krait and the saw-scaled viper) – but these five are relatively common.

PARKS & RESERVES

The early edicts of the country's Buddhist leaders and the Sinhalese culture itself have kept much of the island's natural richness undisturbed for centuries. Sri Lanka can boast the world's first wildlife sanctuary, created by King Devanampiya Tissa in the 3rd century BC. One proclamation carved in Polonnaruwa for King Nissanka Malla (1187-96 AD) called for a ban on killing all animals within seven *gaw* (39 km) of the city. These rulers were also aware of the importance of undisturbed forests and set aside large *Thahanankalle* (Forbidden Forests) as wilderness areas and watersheds. Some of these ancient reserves are still in existence today, including the spectacular Sinharaja Rainforest Reserve and the Udawattakelle Sanctuary.

Today's system of reserves is mostly a synthesis of traditionally protected areas and those established by the British, who were also responsible for clearing large tracts of forest for their coffee, tea and rubber plantations and the slaughter of 'big game'. Nearly 100 protected areas are acknowledged by the government.

Sadly, owing mainly to the ethnic violence, only three – Yala West, Horton Plains and Uda Walawe – of the 11 national parks are open to visitors at the time of writing. Some information on other parks is included in this book in the hope that they'll reopen in the not-too-distant future.

National Parks

In national parks visitors' movements are restricted and you must be accompanied by an official tracker, whom you can pick up on entering the park. (In the recently created Horton Plains national park, regulations are easier and it seems acceptable to wander round without a tracker.) In most parks – though again not Horton Plains – you need a vehicle to get around, and for Yala West and (when it was open) Wilpattu, squads of jeeps lurk around the nearest sizeable towns ready for 'safari' hire, which is the most common method of visiting.

Wilpattu Wilpattu, 176 km north of Colombo, is Sri Lanka's largest park and most famous for its leopards, bears and birdlife. See the Ancient Cities chapter.

Yala West (Ruhuna) Yala West, 305 km south-east of Colombo, is conveniently approached from the south coast or the hill country. Its open, undulating country is studded with rocky formations and lagoons, and it's famous for its elephants. See the West Coast Beaches chapter.

Yala East Divided from Yala West by a strict natural reserve, where visitors aren't allowed, Yala East contains the Kumana mangrove swamp, with a large variety of waterbirds in spectacular numbers. Access is by a 25 km jeep road from Arugam Bay. See the East Coast Beaches chapter.

Horton Plains Horton Plains are in the south-central hill country. The forests at this altitude (over 2000 metres) have unusual plant and animal life adapted to a cooler climate. The spectacular World's End precipice is just one feature of a highly unusual landscape. See the Hill Country chapter.

Gal Oya North of Yala and 312 km from Colombo, this isolated park near Inginiyagala surrounds a large tank, the Senanayaka Samudra, and protects an important sanctuary for elephants and a large variety of other wildlife. See the East Coast Beaches chapter.

Uda Walawe This is about the same size as Gal Oya and features a smaller tank. Elephants may be seen. The park is about 200 km south-east of Colombo, close to the southern end of the highlands, and can be reached from Ratnapura or Embilipitiya. See the Hill Country chapter.

Lahugala This small park near Pottuvil protects tanks which attract good numbers of elephants. It's also very good for birdlife. See the East Coast Beaches chapter.

New Eastern National Parks Four new national parks being created in the central east will help counter the effects of the Mahaweli Development Scheme. These are Maduru Oya, around the reservoir of the same name west of Batticaloa; Wasgomuwa, south of Polonnaruwa; and Floodplains and Somawathiya, along the Mahaweli River east and north-east of Polonnaruwa.

National Park Accommodation
The Department of Wildlife Conservation (☎ 01-567083), at 82 Rajamalwatte Rd, Battaramulla, near Colombo, has visitor bungalows sleeping up to 10 people each in Yala West (seven bungalows), Horton Plains (one), Wilpattu (seven) and Yala East (two). Normally water, fridge, toilet, shower, cutlery, crockery, lamps and a cook are provided, but you have to take your own bedding and food. Sometimes you also need to bring kerosene. The charge for non-Sri Lankans is usually around Rs 100 each a night, with a minimum booking of five persons. Bookings through the department in Colombo are necessary and can be made two to three months in advance. But you need to make inquiries as early as possible – maybe even before you go to Sri Lanka – for certain dates get booked up immediately they become available.

There are campsites, too, in one or two parks, and the Wildlife & Nature Protection Society of Ceylon (☎ 01-25248), opposite the lighthouse on Marine Drive, Colombo Fort, maintains bungalows just outside Yala West, Wilpattu and Lahugala parks, which visitors can rent. Near the main parks there's also a selection of hotel and guest house accommodation in all price ranges.

Other Reserves
Some of the other protected areas are Strict Natural Reserves, where no visitors are allowed – they're for nature only. Others are Nature Reserves, which can be populated by humans as well as other flora and fauna.

Sinharaja Rainforest Reserve This most important reserve in the south-west is just south of Pelmadulla near Ratnapura. It's Sri Lanka's last remaining patch of virgin rainforest and the richest in endemic flora and fauna. It has spectacular rainforest scenery and associated wildlife (the highest concentration of animals unique to Sri Lanka is found here). Entry has, to date, only been by permits issued by the Forest Department (☎ 01-566631), 82 Rajamalwatte Rd, Battaramulla, near Colombo. If anyone from the Forest Department is planning a visit to Sinharaja, you may be able to accompany them.

Peak Wilderness Sanctuary The forest around Adam's Peak offers a spectacular variety of birds, butterflies and other wildlife. The pilgrimage season, from December to April, is also the best time for wildlife. Entry is unrestricted. See the Hill Country chapter.

Udawattakelle Sanctuary This ancient reserve now surrounded by Kandy offers pleasant walking as well as opportunities to see birds and other wildlife. You may not have to go far to see the monkeys here (toque macaques) as they usually come to you first – we had them stealing fruit from our hotel room. See the Hill Country chapter.

Knuckles Range Entry is not restricted in this reserve east of Kandy. As seen from Kandy, the profile of the hills forming the range looks like the knuckles on a closed fist.

Chundikkulam & Kokkilai Lagoon Bird Sanctuaries These two sanctuaries on the north-east coast are on Sri Lanka's eastern migration route and attract spectacular numbers of birds on the spring and autumn days when the birds are passing through. At other times there are still large numbers of birds and other wildlife. The sanctuaries are currently off limits because of the ethnic violence.

Wirawila-Tissa Bird Sanctuary If you stay at Tissamaharama during a visit to Yala, you cannot miss the extensive network of bird-covered lagoons that form this sanctuary. It is centred on the Wirawila tank, where cattle can wade far out when the water is low, and many parts are carpeted in lily or lotus flowers. It's such places as this that can start people off on the bird-watching trail. See the West Coast Beaches chapter.

Bundala Sanctuary Bundala, on the south coast between Hambantota and Tissamaharama, is the end of the line for migratory birds. The concentrations which can build up make it one of the best places to watch birds, with flamingos a star attraction. Bundala can also be good for elephants. See the West Coast Beaches chapter.

Malabar Pied Hornbill

ECONOMY

Prior to independence it was a constant complaint that the British had forced a typical colonial economy upon Sri Lanka. All effort was concentrated on a limited number of commodities – tea, rubber and coconuts – whose production was probably more beneficial to the coloniser than the colonised. While these (especially tea) remain important, other products and businesses have finally gained comparable importance in recent years. Textiles and garments, which are strongly represented in the free trade zone set up in the 1970s north of Colombo, have finally overtaken tea as export earners, with sales worth US$629 million in 1990 against US$495 million for tea – though a lot depends on the price of tea, which is subject to big swings. The third big foreign currency earner is tourism. In 1982, 407,000 foreign tourists visited Sri Lanka, but tourism sagged in the mid-'80s as the Tamil rebellion took root, and collapsed altogether in 1988 during the JVP rebellion. Since then things have taken a big upturn: 317,000 tourists came in 1991, and the 1982 peak looks likely soon to be passed.

The UNP governments in power since 1977 have taken a radically different economic approach from the previous Bandaranaike governments, reducing state control and encouraging private enterprise, and opening up to more international trade, investment and tourism. Rice production improved markedly and by 1985 Sri Lanka was more or less self-sufficient in this staple, no longer having to spend crippling amounts of money on importing it. Work on the large irrigation and hydro-electric schemes such as the Mahaweli Project has been accelerated and they are helping both agriculture and industry, though some of their environmental effects are worrying.

Production has picked up after the debilitating JVP rebellion in the late '80s which almost brought the economy to a complete halt. But the Tamil war is increasingly costly: Sri Lanka's armed forces have tripled in size since 1983, and there's also the cost of providing for hundreds of thousands of refugees. Fortunately for Sri Lanka, foreign aid has kept coming despite complaints from donors about its human rights record.

While there's currently an overall air of optimism in the non-war-torn parts of the country, life remains basic for the average Sri Lankan, and particularly so for rural workers, like the hill-country Tamils and others, whose living conditions are primitive and whose wages are low.

POPULATION & PEOPLE

Sri Lanka has a population of around 17 million; the resulting population density of around 260 people per sq km is one of the highest in Asia. In 1948 the population was only seven million. Nearly two-thirds of the people are under 30 years old; 79% of them live in the rural areas.

The welfare policies of most post-independence governments have given Sri Lanka a creditable literacy and health record. Adult literacy in 1981 was 86%, compared with 36% in India, 69% in China, and 78% in Portugal. Life expectancy at birth in 1989 was 71, and infant mortality 19 per 1000 live births, both creditable figures.

Ethnic Groups

You can hardly fail to notice that Sri Lanka's ethnic jigsaw is currently its biggest problem. But despite claims that the Sinhalese and Tamils have been fighting each other for 2000 years and are 'natural enemies', there was little trouble between them during the colonial years and in the first few years after independence. Indeed, the distinction between them is fuzzy. Although the first Sinhalese settlers in Sri Lanka almost certainly came from north India, and the ancestors of most Tamils came from south India, their ranks have been mixed over the centuries with each other and others of Sri Lanka's ethnic groups. The leading Sinhalese politician Sirimavo Bandaranaike, for instance, lists a Tamil and a European in her family tree. From outward appearance you certainly can't do more than guess whether a person is Sinhalese or Tamil. Language and religion however are two important aspects in which the two groups do differ.

Sinhalese The Sinhalese constitute about 74% of the population. They speak Sinhala, are predominantly Buddhist and have a reputation as easy-going. Their forebears probably came from somewhere round the northern Bay of Bengal: their chronicles state that the first Sinhalese king, Vijaya, arrived in Sri Lanka with a small band of followers in the 6th century BC. The Sinhalese have a caste system although it is nowhere near as important as in India. Sinhalese see themselves as either 'Low Country' (about seven million) or 'Kandyan' (about five million), and the Kandyan Sinhalese have a pride – some would say snobbishness – which stems from the time when the hill country was the last bastion of Sinhalese rulers against European colonists.

Tamils The Tamils are the second largest group, constituting about 18% of the population. They may claim that the percentage is higher and that there is a Sinhalese plot to underestimate their numbers. Tamils are predominantly Hindu and speak Tamil. Many million more Tamils – far more than the whole population of Sri Lanka – live across the Palk Strait in India.

There are two distinct groups of Tamils in Sri Lanka. The origins of the so-called Sri Lanka or Ceylon Tamils go back to the southern Indians who started coming to Sri Lanka during the centuries of conflict and intrigue between Sinhalese and south Indian kingdoms 1000 or more years ago. These Tamils are concentrated in the north, where they now form nearly all the population, and down the east coast, where they are present in roughly equal numbers with Sinhalese and Muslims.

The other group is the 'Hill Country' or 'Plantation' Tamils whose ancestors were brought from India by the British to work on the tea plantations in the 19th century. The hill country Tamils and the Sri Lanka Tamils are separated by geography, history and caste (the hill country Tamils come mainly from lower Indian castes and have largely kept out of the bloody conflict with the Sinhalese over the last 10 years). Caste distinctions among the Tamils are more important than among the Sinhalese, although nowhere near as important as in India.

Muslims Muslims comprise about 7% of the population. Most of them are so-called 'Sri Lanka Moors', whose presence goes back to Portuguese times and who are probably the descendants of Arab or Indian Muslim traders. They are scattered all over the island, perhaps more thinly in the south and north, and are still particularly active in trade and business. Tamil is the mother tongue for most of them. They have largely steered clear of the Sinhalese-Tamil troubles, though there has been some conflict between Tamils and Muslims in the east. A smaller group of Muslims is the Malays, many of whose ancestors came with the Dutch from Java. They still speak Malay and there's a concentration of them in Hambantota. A second small group is the 'Indian Moors' who are more recent Muslim arrivals from India or Pakistan.

Others The Burghers are Eurasians, primarily descendants of the Portuguese and Dutch – more frequently the former than the latter. For a time, even after independence, the Burghers had a disproportionate influence over the political and business life of Sri Lanka, but growing Sinhalese and Tamil nationalism has reduced their advantage and many Burghers have moved abroad. Nevertheless, names like Fernando, de Silva or Perera are still very common. There are also small Chinese and European communities and a small, down-trodden group of low-caste south Indians brought in to perform the most menial tasks.

The society of the Veddahs, the aboriginal people who inhabited Sri Lanka before the Sinhalese came on the scene, has been all but destroyed by government settlement schemes and latterly by tourism. The few small Veddah groups still inhabiting the east are best left alone.

RELIGION

Buddhism is the dominant creed of the dominant ethnic group, the Sinhalese, and is followed by 70% of the population. It plays an extremely important role in the country both spiritually and culturally. Sri Lanka's literature, art and architecture is to a large extent a product of its Buddhist basis. About 15% of the population, mainly Tamils, are Hindu. Muslims and Christians account for

about 7.5% each. The Christians include both Sinhalese and Tamil converts.

Buddhism

Strictly speaking, Buddhism is not a religion, since it is not centred on a god, but is rather a system of philosophy and a code of morality. It covers a wide range of interpretations of the basic beliefs which started with the enlightenment of the Buddha in north India around 2500 years ago. Siddhartha Gautama, born a prince, is said to be the fourth Buddha ('enlightened one'), and is not expected to be the last. Since Buddhists believe that achieving enlightenment is the goal of every being, eventually we will all reach Buddhahood.

The Buddha never wrote his *dhamma* (teachings) down, and a schism later developed so that today there are two major schools of Buddhism. The Theravada, Hinayana, 'doctrine of the elders' or 'small vehicle' school, holds that to achieve *nirvana*, the eventual aim of every Buddhist, you must 'work out your own salvation with diligence'. In contrast the Mahayana, or 'large vehicle', school holds that its belief is enough eventually to encompass all humankind and bear it to salvation.

The Mahayana school has not rejected the Theravada teachings but claims that it has extended them; the Theravada school sees the Mahayana as a corruption of the Buddha's teachings. It is true that the Mahayana offers the 'soft option' – have faith and all will be well – while the Theravada is more austere and ascetic and harder to practise. In the Buddhist world today Theravada Buddhism is practised in Sri Lanka, Thailand, Myanmar (Burma), Vietnam, Laos and Cambodia; Mahayana Buddhism is followed in Japan, Vietnam and among Chinese Buddhists. The 'large' and 'small' vehicle terms were coined by the Mahayana school. There are also other, sometimes more esoteric, divisions of Buddhism such as the Hindu-Tantric Buddhism of Tibet, also practised in Nepal, or the Zen schools of Buddhism of Japan.

The Buddha taught that life is suffering, and that although there may be happiness in life this is mainly an illusion. To be born is to suffer, to live and toil is to suffer, to die is to suffer. The cycle of life is one of suffering but humanity's suffering is caused by its ignorance, which makes it crave things which it feels could alleviate its pain. This is a mistake, for only by reaching a state of desiring nothing can one attain true happiness. To do this one must turn inward, master one's own mind and find the peace within.

The Buddha preached the four noble truths:

1 all life is suffering
2 this suffering comes from selfish desire
3 when one forsakes selfish desire suffering will be extinguished
4 the 'middle path' is the way to eliminate desire

The middle path to the elimination of desire and the extinction of suffering is also known as the 'eight-fold path' which is divided into three stages: *sila* – morality; *samadhi* – equanimity of mind; *panna* – wisdom and insight. The eight 'right' actions are:

1 right understanding
2 right thought
3 right speech
4 right action
5 right aspiration
6 right exertion
7 right attentiveness
8 right concentration

This is an evolutionary process through many states of spiritual development until the ultimate goal is reached – death, no further rebirths, entry to nirvana.

The Buddha taught that all things are part of the whole: 'In the beginning is the One and only the One is. All things are One and have no life apart from it; the One is all things and incomplete without the least of them. Yet the parts are parts within the whole, not merged in it.'

Supreme enlightenment is the only reality in a world of unreality, the teachings continue. All else is illusion and there is no unchanging soul which is reborn after life, but a consciousness which develops and evolves spiritually until it reaches the goal of nirvana or oneness with the all. Central to the doctrine of rebirth is *karma*, the law of causation; each rebirth results from the actions one has committed in the previous life. Thus in Buddhism each person alone is responsible for their life. The Buddha did not claim that his way was the only way, since in the end all beings will find a path because the goal is the same for all.

Ashoka, the great Indian emperor who was a devout Buddhist, sent missions to all the known world, and his son Mahinda brought Buddhism to Sri Lanka. It took a strong hold on the country almost immediately and Sri Lanka has been looked upon as a centre for Buddhist culture and teaching ever since. It was in Sri Lanka that the Theravada school of Buddhism first developed and was later passed on to other countries.

Buddhism emphasises love, compassion and gentleness. This tolerant outlook has often resulted in its absorption into other religions (as eventually happened with Hinduism in India) or its absorption of already extant beliefs. On a personal level, the general experience one has of Buddhism remains largely the same from country to country despite local adaptations, changes, amalgamations and inclusions – it's an overriding impression of warmth and gentleness; a religion practiced by friendly people who are always eager to explain their beliefs. In

Sri Lanka however, Buddhism's institutionalisation and politicisation have given rise to one or two less agreeable aspects.

Modern Sri Lankan Buddhism Since the late 19th century a strand of 'militant' Buddhism has developed in Sri Lanka, centred on the belief that the Buddha – who according to tradition visited Sri Lanka three times – charged the Sinhalese people with the task of making the island a citadel of Buddhism in its purest form. This more campaigning, less tolerant Buddhism, perhaps taking its cue from the type of Christianity practised by the British colonial power, emerged around the turn of the century under the inspiration of Anagarika Dharmapala. It sees threats to Sinhalese Buddhist culture in both European Christianity and Tamil Hinduism. Sri Lankan Buddhism has become increasingly intertwined with politics, to the point where the clergy can exert great pressure on politicians by accusing them of failing to look after Buddhism. Some Buddhist monks are among the country's least tolerant people when it comes to compromise with the Tamils. Nor are all monks anything like as pure, virtuous and unworldly as you might imagine! On the other hand, many monks are genuinely dedicated to the personal and sprirítual side of Buddhism and many of the people still practise it in a simple, gentle way.

Books on Buddhism A good book to start with is Christmas Humphrey's *Buddhism* (Pelican). There are many books on Buddhism available in Sri Lanka; a particularly good place to look is the Buddhist Publication Society in Kandy. There is also a Buddhist Information Centre & Bookshop (☎ 01-23079) at 50 Ananda Kumaraswamy Mawatha (Green Path), Colombo 7; and a library of Buddhism at the Gangaramaya Bhikku Training Centre, 61 Sri Jinarathana Rd, Colombo 2. For more information on practising and studying meditation and Buddhism, see Kandy in the Hill Country chapter.

LANGUAGE
It's easy to get by in Sri Lanka with English.

Although Sinhala is the official national language, Sri Lanka's unique brand of English – 'You are having a problem, isn't it, no?' – is still widely spoken, particularly among the middle and upper classes, and you'll find people who can speak it almost everywhere. Off the beaten track knowledge of it thins out so it's nice to know a few words of Sinhala – and it's pleasant to be able to greet people in their own language anyway. Remember that Sinhala is not the only local language; a substantial minority (including nearly all Muslims) speak Tamil as their first language.

The Sinhalese alphabet has about 50 letters so you're unlikely to find yourself able to read signposts from just a short stay in Sri Lanka! Sinhalese is somewhat simplified by the use of many 'eka words'. *Eka* is used more or less similarly to the English definite article 'the', *ekak* is used like 'a' or 'any'. English words for which there is no Sinhalese equivalent have often been incorporated straight into Sinhalese with the simple addition of *eka* or *ekak*. Thus if you're in search of a telephone it's simply *telifoon ekak* but if it's a specific telephone then you want *telifoon eka*. Similarly, specifically English definitions of people have been included in Sinhala simply by adding *kenek* – if you hire a car the driver is the *draiwar kenek*.

There's a Lonely Planet *Sri Lanka phrasebook* as part of our language survival kit series.

Greetings & Civilities
As in many other Asian countries, in Sri Lanka our multitude of greetings – hello, good morning, how are you, goodbye – simply don't exist. Saying *aaibowan* more or less covers them all. Similarly there isn't really a Sinhalese word for 'thank you'. You could try *bohoma stutiy* but it's a rather awkward thing to say – better to smile. Appreciation of a meal could be covered by *bohoma rahay* which serves as appreciation and a compliment – sort of 'that was good'. *Hari shook* covers our expressions like 'wonderful, terrific' or even 'fine'. Remember that, as in India, a side-to-side wiggle of the head, not unlike our shake meaning 'no', can often mean 'yes' or 'OK'.

Personal Terms

In Sinhalese there are over 20 ways to say 'you' depending on the person's age, social status, sex, position and even (as in French and German) how well you know him or her. It's best to simply avoid saying you! The word for Mr is *mahatteya* and Mr Jayewardene is Jayewardene mahatteya since the word comes after the name, not before. Similarly, Mrs is *noona*. Any non-Eastern foreigner is defined as white, so a male foreigner is a *suda mahatteya*.

Useful Words & Phrases

Yes.	*ou*
No.	*naa*
OK.	*hari honday*
Certainly/Of course.	*nattan*
Really?	*habaata?*
So so?	*itin itin?*

room	*kaamare*
bed	*anda*
food	*kaama*
tea	*tea*
eggs	*bittara*
vegetables	*eloolu*
fish	*maalu*
hoppers	*aappa*
rice	*bhat*
milk	*kiri*
sugar	*sini*
glass	*widuru*
bank	*bankuwa*
post office	*tapal kantooruwa*
this/that	*mee/oya*
what/where	*mokadda/koheda*

Wait a minute.	*poddak inna*
How much?	*kiiyada?*
My name is ...	*ma-ge nama ...*
What is this?	*meeka mokadda?*
When is the bus?	*bas-eka kiiyata da?*
Where is the hotel?	*hootale koheda?*
How much is this?	*meeka kiiyada?*
How are you?	*kohomada?*
Getting down.	*bahinawa*
(from bus or train)	
Don't want.	*epa*

Two useful little Sinhalese words are *da* and *ge*. *Da* turns a statement into a question – thus if *noona* means a lady then *noona-da* means 'This lady?' or 'Is this the lady?'. *Ge* is the Sinhalese equivalent of an apostrophe indicating possession; thus 'Tony's book' in Sinhala would be *Tony-ge pota*. *Ta* is like the English preposition to – if you want to go 'to the beach' it's *walla-ta*.

Numbers

1	*eka*
2	*deka*
3	*tuna*
4	*hatara*
5	*paha*
6	*haya*
7	*hata*
8	*ata*
9	*namaya*
10	*dahaya*
20	*wissai*
50	*panahai*
100	*siiya*
1000	*daaha*
8.30 (time)	*ata amarai*

Place Names

Sri Lanka's often fearsome-looking place names become much simpler with a little analysis. *Pura* or *puram* simply means town – as in Ratnapura (town of gems) or Anuradhapura. Similarly *nuwara* means city and *gama* means village. Other common words that are incorporated in place names include *gala* or *giri* (rock or hill), *kanda* (mountain), *ganga* (river), *oya* (large stream), *ela* (stream), *tara* or *tota* (ford or port), *pitiya* (park), *watte* (garden), *deniya* (rice field), *gaha* (tree), *arama* (park or monastery) and *duwa* (island).

Not surprisingly, many towns are named after the great tanks – *tale*, *wewa* or *kulam*. The same word can appear in Sinhala, Sanskrit, Pali and Tamil! Finally *maha* means great. Put it all together and even a name like Tissamaharama makes sense – it's simply '(King) Tissa's great park'.

Facts for the Visitor

VISAS & EMBASSIES

Tourists from 24 countries including Australia, New Zealand, the USA, Canada, everywhere in western Europe (except Portugal and Iceland), Israel, Japan, Singapore and Hong Kong don't need visas to enter Sri Lanka. Automatic entry for 30 days is given on arrival and that can be extended for two one-month periods. You may be asked to show 'sufficient' funds for your stay, and an onward ticket or the funds to buy one. 'Sufficient' is officially US$30 a day but it's very much up to the discretion of the individual immigration officer – US$500 would probably be enough, and quite possibly less. A major credit card is also acceptable.

To extend your initial 30-day stay you need to go in person, with your passport, to the Department of Immigration & Emigration (☎ 01-29851, 421509) on Marine Drive, Colombo 1, which is open from 8.30 am to 3.30 pm Monday to Friday. Enter the building by the sign that says 'Department for Registration of Persons of Indian Origin' and turn right into the visa room. It usually takes just an hour or two to complete the fairly straightforward process of filling in a form and having a quick interview – but don't leave it too late in the day or you'll have to come back and finish it off next morning.

To get the extension, you're supposed to show three things (though in practice you might not be asked for any of them):

- a ticket out of the country (the funds to buy one would probably do if you don't have one)
- 'sufficient' funds for your stay – again 'sufficient' is officially US$30 a day or a credit card, but if the individual immigration officer can be happy that you'll lead a respectable life on US$10 a day you'll be OK
- bank receipts to prove you have changed US$30 into rupees for each day you've been in Sri Lanka. Many people manage to avoid this requirement simply by saying they didn't know about it and threw away their receipts. In any case, you can change the required amount and change it back again afterwards if you want.

The price you have to pay for the extension varies wildly and is related to the prices Sri Lankans have to pay for visas to other countries. Australians, New Zealanders and US citizens pay nothing, Germans Rs 275, French Rs 390, Italians Rs 720, Britons Rs 1640 and Canadians Rs 1760. You pay in cash at a counter (open till 3 pm) in the immigration office.

Extensions of stay beyond three months are very difficult, if not impossible, if you haven't got a special reason. But going out of the country (to India, for instance) for a couple of weeks usually entitles you to re-enter for another month or more.

Sri Lankan Embassies

Sri Lankan missions abroad include:

Australia
  High Commission, 35 Empire Circuit, Forrest, Canberra ACT 2603 (☎ (062) 239 7041/2)
Canada
  High Commission, 85 Range Rd, Sandringham, Suites 102-104, Ottawa, Ontario KLM 8J6 (☎ 233 8440)
Germany
  Embassy, Rolandstrasse 52, 5300 Bonn 2 (☎ (0228) 332055)
India
  High Commission, 27 Kautilya Marg, Chanakyapuri, New Delhi 110021 (☎ 3010201)
  Consulate, 9D Nawab Habibullah Ave, Anderson Rd, Madras 600006 (☎ 470831)
  Consulate, Sri Lanka House, 34 Homi Mody St, Bombay 400023 (☎ 2045861)
Singapore
  High Commission, 51 Goldhill Plaza, 1307-1312 Newton Rd, Singapore 1130 (☎ 2544595)
Thailand
  Embassy, 48/3 Soi 1, Sukhumvit Rd, Bangkok (☎ 251 2788)
UK
  High Commission, 13 Hyde Park Gardens, London W2 2LU (☎ (071) 262 1841)
USA
  Embassy, 2148 Wyoming Ave NW, Washington DC 20008 (☎ 483 4025)

Foreign embassies in Colombo are listed in the Colombo chapter.

MONEY

A$1	=	Rs 31
US$1	=	Rs 43
UK £1	=	Rs 74
I Rs 1	=	Rs 1.6
DM1	=	Rs 30
FFr 1	=	Rs 9.0
Lire 100	=	Rs 3.6

The Sri Lankan currency is the rupee (Rs), divided into 100 cents (c). There are coins of 5, 10, 25 and 50c and of Rs 1, 2, 5 and 10. Notes come in denominations of Rs 10, 20, 50, 100, 500 and 1000. The usual Asian rules apply to Sri Lankan money. First, break down larger notes when you change money – it can sometimes be a problem to change a large note. Second, don't accept very dirty or torn notes as they are often difficult to dispose of, except to a bank. Again this is not as big a problem as in some other Asian countries.

Travellers' cheques get a slightly better rate of exchange than cash in Sri Lanka. You can change cheques at almost any branch of the Bank of Ceylon or the People's Bank, and every town has at least one of these. Banking hours are from Monday to Friday, 9 am to 1 or 3 pm. See the Colombo and Kandy sections for places where you can change money outside normal bank hours.

Major credit cards like American Express, Visa, MasterCard and Diners Club are widely accepted in Sri Lanka. See the Colombo chapter for American Express, Visa and MasterCard bureaus there. Recent letters have reported that Visa cards can now be used to make cash withdrawals at major Bank of Ceylon branches – at an even better exchange rate than travellers' cheques – and that the Bank of Ceylon can replace stolen Visa travellers' cheques.

You can change rupees back to foreign currency at the airport on departure but you must have proof that you changed money into rupees in the first place.

A few operators hang round Colombo Fort offering black market exchange rates. Just how real their offers are is open to question, but what is absolutely certain is that many of them are superb sleight-of-hand tricksters who will perform 'folded money' or 'cash in the envelope' tricks quicker than you can shout 'rip off'.

Sri Lanka is not the best place for getting money sent to – if you have to, ask your home bank to send it by telegraphic transfer and specify one of the commercial banks such as Grindlays.

Costs

Sri Lanka is still a pleasantly economical country to travel around. Accommodation prices have, on average, roughly doubled since the previous edition of this book but, to balance that, the rupee has almost halved in value. Competition for tourist custom means that prices are kept in check. Restaurant prices have slightly more than doubled, but transport costs have risen only marginally.

Almost anywhere in the country pleasant shoestring doubles can be found for Rs 200 (about US$5) and in many places for much less. If you really want to economise you can get a single or dormitory bed for Rs 50 to Rs 75 in most places, sometimes less. You'd be very hard pressed to spend more than Rs 50 on a day's bus travel. Up the scale a bit Rs 350 is a typical price for a double in one of Sri Lanka's delightful rest houses or a more comfortable guest house. There are also many top end hotels where Rs 1000 a night can be the start and the sky the upper limit.

Prices given in this guide generally refer to high-season (from December to February/March) rates. When things aren't busy, room rates come down – sometimes spectacularly – and in many places you can bargain them down at any time of year.

Two-Level Costs Sri Lanka is no exception to the worldwide phenomenon of locals trying to overcharge tourists for anything from a bus fare to a gemstone necklace, but what really irritates some visitors is that for some things there is an *official* policy of charging visitors a much higher price than local residents. This applies at places like Colombo Zoo, the ancient cities, Wildlife Department lodges in national parks, even the Peradeniya Botanic Gardens at Kandy. The charges for overseas visitors here can be five or 10 times what local residents pay! 'Plain racism!', wrote one disgruntled traveller. The alternative view is that the prices still aren't that bad and that tourists, who are well off compared to the average Sri Lankan, might as well do some subsidising.

Service Charge & Tipping Nearly every accommodation or eating place in the middle and top ranges, and even the odd one at the bottom end, loads a service charge of 10% on to its bills now, and they don't always tell you about it when they quote you a price. So be aware of it or you may find everything is costing you more than you expected. When you're paying the 10% there's no need to tip, even though the people who serve you are unlikely to see much of it. Nor is there any need to top up taxi or three-wheeler fares. Hotel porters normally get Rs 5 or Rs 10 per heavy bag.

Prices in this book are almost always quoted without the 10%.

WHEN TO GO

Climatically the driest and best seasons are from December to March on the west and south coasts and in the hill country, and from May to September on the east coast. December to March is also the time when most foreign tourists come, the majority of them escaping the European winter. Out of season travel has its advantages – not only do the crowds go away but many airfares and accommodation prices go right down. Nor does it rain *all* the time. Reefs may protect a beach area and make swimming quite feasible at places like Hikkaduwa, which during the monsoon can be quite pleasant.

WHAT TO BRING

Not too much! Apart from the hill country,

where the temperatures can sink surprisingly low at night, Sri Lanka is definitely a place for high-summer gear only. In the hill country, and Nuwara Eliya in particular, you'll need a sweater or light coat for the evenings. If you intend to make the pre-dawn ascent of Adam's Peak you'll need all the warm gear you can muster – wearing a T-shirt, shirt, sweater and ski-jacket Tony still found it bitterly cold until the sun rose, when the temperature became comfortable almost immediately. At times in the hill country it can also get very wet.

The usual Asian rules of decorum apply – you should be decently dressed if you do not wish to risk offending the locals. Shorts on women are really only for the beach. Topless bathing by women may cause offence or attract unwanted attention, except on a few beaches such as Hikkaduwa where it's widely practised. Sri Lanka is not as staunch as Myanmar (Burma) in insisting that visitors barefoot it in Buddhist temples, but you should be prepared to discard your footwear; it therefore makes sense to wear sandals or thongs if you expect to visit a temple. Some sort of head cover is also a wise precaution when you're exploring the ruins in the dry, hot, ancient cities area of Sri Lanka – but your head must be uncovered in temples.

You'll find all the usual Asian ethnic gear on sale in Sri Lanka, particularly at Hikkaduwa, so if you want a new blouse, shirt, lightweight trousers or whatever, you'll have no problem finding it. Sri Lankan tailors will make clothes quickly and cheaply if you can't find what you want ready-made.

If you're a snorkelling fan then bring your mask and snorkel with you. It's easy enough to rent them in Hikkaduwa and one or two other places, but not so simple elsewhere.

Soap, toothpaste (some terrible local brands but also most Western brands) and other toiletries are fairly readily available. However it's advisable to bring some tampons and condoms if you need them. Bring a towel, too, because many cheaper hostelries don't provide them. A small torch is very handy for finding your way along dark or wet streets and paths at night – and

Top: Monks, Anuradhapura (PS)
Bottom: Fruit Vendor (PS)

Top: Boats, Trincomalee (TW)
Middle: Sunset, Matara (TW)
Bottom: Dutch built canal in Negombo, West Coast (TW)

for finding candles when the electricity fails! A sink plug can be useful, as can a padlock for securely locking cheap hotel rooms. See the Health section in this chapter for a suggested small medical kit.

TOURIST OFFICES

The headquarters and main information office of the Sri Lanka (Ceylon) Tourist Board (SLTB) is at 78 Steuart Place, Galle Rd, Colombo 3 (☎ 01-437059, 437060), opposite the Oberoi Hotel. See the Colombo chapter for its opening hours. There's also an SLTB info desk at the airport (☎ 01-452411). These offices can help with hotel bookings as well as answer queries and hand out booklets and leaflets. In Colombo the Railway Tourist Office at Fort Station is also helpful, often with non-railway info too.

In Sri Lanka the only one other tourist office is in Kandy. The Sri Lanka Tourist Board runs some overseas offices which may, among other things, be able to tell you about possible cheap flight agents. In other countries Sri Lankan embassies or high commissions should be able to supply tourist information. The SLTB offices are:

France
    19 Rue du 4 Septembre, 75002 Paris (☎ 42 60 49 99)
Germany
    Allerheiligentor 2-4, D-6000 Frankfurt/Main 1 (☎ (069) 28 77 34)
Japan
    Dowa Building 7-2-22, Ginza Chuo-Ku, Tokyo (☎ (03) 289 0771)
Thailand
    1/7-1/8 Soi 10, Sukhumvit Rd, Bangkok (☎ 251 8062)
UK
    53-54 Haymarket, London SW 1Y (☎ (071) 925 0177)

Among the publications the tourist offices both in and outside Sri Lanka can provide is an *Accommodation Guide*, updated every six months or so. Establishments have to pay to appear in this, but it's a fairly thorough listing of middle and upper range places to stay, with reasonably accurate prices.

Another publication is the only moderately useful *Official Tourist Handbook*.

BUSINESS HOURS & HOLIDAYS

The working day in offices is usually from Monday to Friday, 8.30 am to 4.30 pm. Some businesses also open Saturdays till about 1 pm. Shops normally stay open from Monday to Friday till about 7 pm, and 3 pm on Saturdays.

Sri Lanka has a very wide range of Buddhist, Hindu, Christian and Muslim festivals, helping create nearly 30 public holidays a year. A full five-day working week is a comparative rarity! Many of the holidays are based on the lunar calendar so they vary in date from year to year by the Gregorian calendar. The Muslim festivals Id-ul-Fitr (the end of Ramadan), Id-ul-Alha (the Haji festival) and Milad-un-Nabi (Mohammed's birthday) vary each year, coming 11 to 12 days earlier with subsequent years. In 1993 they were late March, early June and late August; in 1994 mid-March, mid-June and mid-August; in 1995 early March, mid-June and early August; in 1996 mid-February, late April and late July.

January
    On the full moon day in January the Duruthu Perahera is held at the Kelaniya Temple in Colombo. Second in importance only to the huge Kandy Perahera, this festival celebrates a visit by the Buddha to Sri Lanka. On 14 or 15 January the Thai Pongal harvest festival is held by Hindus in honour of the Sun God.
February
    National Day on 4 February, celebrating independence from Britain, features parades, dances and national games all over the country. At the February full moon, Navam, a perahera which was first held only in 1979 but is already one of Sri Lanka's biggest, is held around Viharamahadevi Park and Beira Lake in Colombo, starting from the Gangaramaya Temple. About 100 elephants take part and this is now bigger than the Kelaniya Perahera.
    In late February or early March the Hindu festival of Maha Sivarathri commemorates Parvati's winning of her consort, Lord Shiva.
April
    A month of festivals and holidays with not only the Christian Good Friday holiday usually falling in April, but also both the Sinhalese and Tamil New Year's Days on 14 April. New Year's Eve,

the 13th, is a holiday too. This is an occasion for hospitality and it also coincides with the end of the harvest season. The New Year also marks the start of the south-west monsoon and the end of the Adam's Peak pilgrimage season. During the New Year period it can be difficult to find transport and some hotel restaurants even shut down. An Easter passion play is performed on the island of Duwa off Negombo.

May

May Day (1 May) is a holiday as in other parts of the world, and 22 May is celebrated as National Heroes' Day, but Wesak is the important holiday this month. This two-day holiday – full moon day and the day after – celebrates the birth, enlightenment and death of Lord Buddha. Villages are decorated with huge panels showing scenes from the Buddha's life; puppet shows and open-air theatre performances take place. The temples are crowded with devotees bringing flowers and offerings. The high point of Wesak is the lighting of countless paper lanterns and oil lamps which turn the island into a fairyland.

June

The Poson full moon day in June is a celebration of the bringing of Buddhism to Sri Lanka by Mahinda. Anuradhapura and Mihintale, where Mahinda met and converted the Sinhalese king, are the main sites for this celebration. Thousands of white-clad pilgrims climb the stairs to the summit of Mihintale.

July & August

On the Esala full moon – usually in July but occasionally early August – the Kandy Esala Perahera, the most important and spectacular festival in Sri Lanka, climaxes 10 days and nights of increasingly frenetic activity in Kandy. This great procession honours the Sacred Tooth Relic of Kandy. Thousands of dancers, drummers and temple chieftans take part in the parade, which also features 50 or more magnificently decorated elephants including the most splendid of them all, the mighty Maligawa Tusker which carries the golden relic casket. Smaller peraheras are held at other locations around the island.

The Hindu Vel festival is held in Colombo at the same time. The gilded chariot of Skanda, the God of War, complete with his *vel* (trident), is ceremonially hauled from a temple in Sea St, Pettah to another at Bambalapitiya.

Another important Hindu festival is held at Kataragama, where devotees put themselves through the whole gamut of ritual masochism. Some thrust skewers through their tongues and cheeks, others tow heavy carts or suspend weights from hooks piercing their skin. The grand finale is the fire-walking ceremonies, as the devotees prance barefoot across beds of red-hot embers. A pilgrimage from Batticaloa to Kataragama takes place. A host of Hindu festivals is held in the Jaffna area in July-August.

October

Deepavali, the Hindu festival of lights, takes place in late October or early November. Thousands of flickering oil lamps celebrate the triumph of good over evil and the return of Rama after his period of exile, and welcome Lakshmi, the Goddess of Wealth.

December

The pilgrimage season to climb Adam's Peak starts during this month. The full moon day commemorates Sangamitta, Ashoka's daughter who accompanied Mahinda to Sri Lanka and brought a sapling from the sacred bo-tree. The tree grown from that sapling still stands in Anuradhapura today. Christmas Day is a holiday.

Poya

Every full moon *(poya)* day is a holiday. Especially if it falls on a Friday or Monday, poya causes people to swarm all over the island and accommodation, buses and trains fill up. No alcohol is supposed to be sold in hotels, restaurants, bars or stores on poya days, and some establishments close down. If you're likely to be thirsty, stock up in advance! Many hotels and guest houses discreetly provide their needy guests with a bottle of beer 'under the table'.

POST & TELECOMMUNICATIONS
Postal Rates

A letter or postcard up to 10g costs Rs 13 to Europe or Australia, Rs 15 to North America. Each additional 10g is Rs 6 and Rs 8 respectively. An aerogram is Rs 9. There's an international express mail service (EMS), available at major post offices like Colombo, Kandy and Galle, which guarantees delivery of anything from 10g to 500g in two days: to Australia for Rs 1000, Britain for Rs 1170 or the USA for Rs 1350.

Sending & Receiving Mail

Delivery of letters and cards from or to Sri Lanka is pretty reliable. Expect them to take about 10 days to or from Western countries. But get them franked before your eyes in a post office, to ensure that no one removes and resells the stamps! Mail posted in mailboxes has a reputation for disappearing. Sri

Lanka has both regular government post offices (virtually every village has at least a sub-post office) and agency post offices which have sprung up in recent years in most sizeable towns. Agency post offices are privately run but perform most of the same functions as ordinary post offices, sometimes noticeably quicker.

Sri Lanka has a good poste restante system and the poste restante at Colombo GPO is particularly efficient. It holds mail for two months and accepts parcels and telegrams as well as letters. You can call it on 01-26203 to ask if there's anything awaiting you, or 01-448482 to get mail forwarded to poste restante in another town.

Mail addressed c/o American Express is held for collection on the 2nd floor of Steuart House, 45 Janadhipathi Mawatha, Colombo Fort, even though the address to have it sent to is MacKinnons Travels, PO Box 945, 4 Leyden Bastion Rd, Colombo 1.

Telephone
Phone calls within Sri Lanka are cheap and you can usually book accommodation ahead by phone if you wish. Apart from Colombo numbers in the Colombo chapter, the phone numbers in this book are generally shown with their long-distance codes. This initial code is dropped when you are dialling locally. For directory inquiries dial 161. You can nearly always phone from post offices and often from police stations. In sizeable towns, agency post offices, and the 'communications centres' which are starting to spring up, also have telephone services, usually slightly more expensive than ordinary post offices but quicker. The greatest concentration of them is in Colombo Fort.

From private lines, local calls cost Rs 3.70 for the first three minutes and Rs 2.70 for each succeeding three-minute period. Long-distance calls within Sri Lanka are between Rs 6.40 and Rs 25.30 (depending on the distance) for the first three minutes, Rs 5.40 to Rs 24.30 for following three-minute periods. Post offices and communications centres charge a bit more; a hotel may double these figures to make a call for you.

Area Codes

Aluthgama	034	Jaffna	021
Ambalangoda	09	Kalutara	034
Anuradhapura	025	Kandy	08
Badulla	055	Kataragama	047
Bandarawela	057	Kurunegala	037
Bentota	034	Matara	041
Beruwela	034	Mt Lavinia	01
Colombo	01	Negombo	031
Dambulla	066	Nuwara Eliya	052
Dehiwela	01	Polonnaruwa	027
Ella	057	Ratnapura	045
Galle	09	Sigiriya	066
Giritale	027	Tangalla	047
Habarana	066	Tissamaharama	047
Hambantota	047	Trincomalee	026
Haputale	057	Unawatuna	09
Hikkaduwa	09	Weligama	041

International Calls There's international direct dialling (IDD) to many countries from Colombo and an increasing number of other towns. The international access code is 00; follow this with the country code. If you can't dial direct you have to book the call, for a minimum of three minutes, through the international operator (100 in Colombo, 161 elsewhere) or at the post office. You then usually have to wait an hour or so, and maybe longer if it's collect, though you can save waiting by booking it a few hours ahead.

IDD calls from private lines are 40% cheaper off-peak (from 10 pm to 6 am). Full rates per minute are Rs 50 to India, Rs 72 to Australia, Rs 94 to Europe and Rs 105 to North America. Prices from post offices are a bit higher (Rs 324 for three minutes to Europe, for example). From agency post offices and communication centres they're higher still (about Rs 360 for three minutes to Europe), but you're more likely to find one of these open at night and therefore able to give you an off-peak rate.

Collect calls to some countries including Britain, Canada and New Zealand are only allowed on a person-to-person basis, which costs extra.

Fax, Telex & Telegraph
Domestic and international telegrams can be

sent from post offices: to Europe, Australia or the USA it's Rs 8.70 a word. Faxes and telexes can be sent from communications centres.

TIME

Sri Lankan time is 5 hours 30 minutes ahead of Greenwich Mean Time. When it is noon in Sri Lanka the time is 4.30 pm in Sydney, 6.30 am in London, 1.30 am in New York and 10.30 pm the previous day in San Francisco. Make allowances for summer time changes in other countries.

ELECTRICITY

The electric current in Sri Lanka is 230-240 volt, 50 cycles, alternating current.

BOOKS

Colombo is well endowed with bookshops, and in the other sizeable towns there are usually one or two with at least a few English-language books. The major hotels in tourist centres often have interesting bookshops – and those in Colombo's top-end hotels are some of the best stocked in the country, though their prices are usually marked up heavily. In many of these places you'll find a range from English classics and serious Sri Lankan historical, cultural or political works (there are numerous publications on the recent ethnic troubles), to lighter novels, travel guides, coffee-table books, and so on. In the Colombo hotels and other tourist centres there'll usually be books in German and other European languages too. Hikkaduwa has a couple of 'tourist libraries' where you pay a small fee to borrow a book.

History & Politics

An Historical Relation of Ceylon by Robert Knox (Tisara Prakasakayo, Colombo) is a fascinating book. Robert Knox was an Englishman captured near Trincomalee in the 17th century and held captive by the King of Kandy for nearly 20 years. His captivity was relatively loose and he had considerable freedom to wander around the kingdom and observe its operation. When he eventually escaped and returned to England his descrip-

tion of the kingdom of Kandy became an instant bestseller. It's equally readable today and is far and away the best book on pre-European Sri Lanka.

Dr K M De Silva's monumental *A History of Sri Lanka* (Oxford University Press, 1981) brings Sri Lankan history up to modern times. Until its publication there had been something of a gap for a book covering the country's post-independence history. *The Story of Ceylon* by E F C Ludowyk (Faber, London, 1962) and *The Modern History of Ceylon* by the same author (Praeger, New York, 1966) provide good introductions to Sri Lankan history.

Only Man is Vile: The Tragedy of Sri Lanka by William McGowan (paperback, Picador, 1993) is an excellent recent account of the modern ethnic troubles, mixing travelogue, history and reporting. It lays the blame on the Sinhalese elite and the legacy of British colonialism. *Ethnic & Class Conflicts in Sri Lanka* by Kumari Jayawardena (Centre for Social Analysis, Colombo) is a readable short book which links the current troubles to nearly a century of incidents between the different groups in Sri Lanka. *Sri Lanka, Island of Terror* by E M Thornton & R Niththyananthan (Eelam Research Organisation, London, 1984) is a readable account of the 1940s to mid-1980s from a Tamil point of view.

Guidebooks

The excellent *Handbook for the Ceylon Traveller* (Studio Times Publications, Colombo, 1983) covers almost every place of historic or cultural interest in Sri Lanka in considerable (and poetic!) detail. *The Thorana Guide to Sri Lanka* (Lever Brothers Cultural Conservation Trust, Colombo, 1979) has some interesting material on temples and buildings not found elsewhere. There's a series of useful booklets produced by the Ministry of Cultural Affairs including *A Guide to Polonnaruwa, A Guide to Anuradhapura* and one titled simply *Kandy*. For those in search of unusual guides there's even *A Guide to the Waterfalls of Sri Lanka* by Eberhard Kautzsch (Tisara Prakasakayo, Dehiwala, 1983).

The *Insight Guide Sri Lanka* (Apa Productions, Singapore, 1983) is a beautiful coffee-table paperback on the country. One to read before you go and to remind yourself of the country after your return.

Wildlife

A Guide to the Birds of Ceylon by G M Henry (Oxford University Press/K V G De Silva, Kandy) is a detailed hardback which will help you identify any bird you see. *A Selection of the Birds of Sri Lanka* by John & Judy Banks (published by the authors) is a slimmer, well-illustrated introduction, on sale in Sri Lanka for Rs 250. The Banks have also produced good books on the island's animals and butterflies for the same price.

General

Running in the Family by Michael Ondaatje (Penguin) is the Canadian writer's humorous account of returning to Sri Lanka in the 1970s after growing up there in the 1940s and 1950s. It includes some superb sketches of upper-class life in Ceylon in the first half of this century, and captures precisely many of the little oddities that life in Sri Lanka often seems to be made up of.

Ceylon, History in Stone by R Raven-Hart (Lake House, Colombo, 1973) is a description of a lengthy visit to Sri Lanka. *Seeing Ceylon* by R L Brohier (Lake House, Colombo, 1965) is a surveyor's account of his wanderings around the island. *Born to Labour* by C V Vellupillai (Gunasena, 1970) tells of the hard lives of the Tamil labourers on the tea estates.

Sri Lanka is a photogenic place and many coffee-table books take it as their subject. One of the best is *Sri Lanka* by Tim Page (Lake House).

'A must for anyone who goes to the Kataragama fire-walking festival', suggested one visitor, is *Medusa's Hair* by Gannanath Obeyesekere. 'It explains a lot about society which is not readily apparent to the passing visitor'. First published in 1913 and now available in paperback from

Oxford University Press (1981), Leonard Woolf's *The Village in the Jungle* is a readable, but depressing, story set in a small, backward village of Sinhalese *chena* (slash-and-burn) farmers around the turn of the century. Woolf went on to become a leader of the literary Bloomsbury set between the world wars.

Sri Lanka's best known writer is Arthur C Clarke, who has spent many years on the island. His science fiction novel *The Fountains of Paradise* (Pan, 1980) is set on an imaginary island called Taprobane and features places remarkably like Adam's Peak and Sigiriya. A good book to read while you're on the spot!

MAPS

One of the best foreign-produced maps is the Nelles Verlag 1:450,000 *Sri Lanka* which includes a few town plans.

The Sri Lanka government Survey Department's *Road Map Sri Lanka* at 1:500,000 (one cm to five km) is an excellent overall map, clear to read and priced at only about Rs 50. You can buy it at the Survey Department Map Sales Centre (☎ 01-35328) on York St, Colombo Fort, open from Monday to Friday, 9 am to 4 pm, and (usually more expensive) at various bookshops and bookstalls around the island. At the Map Sales Centre you'll also find maps of Colombo, historical maps, ancient city maps, and other maps showing things like the distribution of tea estates or national parks.

The Survey Department has mapped the whole country in British Ordnance Survey style at three scales: one inch to one mile, 1:10,000 and 1:5000. Unfortunately these excellent maps and the town plans also produced by the department are not currently on general sale for security reasons, but you can consult them at the Map Sales Centre. If you really want to buy them you must seek the permission of the national Surveyor General at the Survey Department head office (☎ 01-585111) on Kirula Rd, Narahenpitiya, in south Colombo!

Lake House of Colombo publishes a *Pictorial Tourist Map of Sri Lanka*. The

Serendib Gallery at 100 Galle Rd, Colombo 4 often has some interesting old maps of Ceylon.

MEDIA
Newspapers & Magazines

Sri Lanka has a number of daily and Sunday English-language papers. The widest circulated and most professional is the government-controlled *Daily News*, which gives quite good coverage of foreign news (including sports) but whose version of events in Sri Lanka is a bit lopsided. It reports in loving detail virtually every word uttered in public by the president! It also goes into amazing detail about leaning telegraph poles, stray cattle and other items considered important by its correspondents in remote country districts. *The Island* tends to back the Sinhalese opposition party, the SLFP, and has a habit of being a day or two late with the news! The *Lanka Guardian* is a fortnightly magazine containing some of the country's most intelligent and independent journalism for Rs 7.50. All these journals are written in the unique Sri Lankan brand of English, worth reading for its style alone. There's no formal press censorship but journalists say they are forced to exercise self-censorship because of the government's control of newsprint imports and valuable amounts of advertising.

This Month in Sri Lanka, available from some tourist offices and hotel receptions, is a booklet with all sorts of info of use to tourists. It comes out monthly but isn't updated thoroughly. *Time* (Rs 60), *Newsweek* and foreign newspapers a few days old are readily available in Colombo, particularly in the top-end hotels. The clearest analysis of Sri Lankan politics and economics is to be found in the weekly Hong Kong-published *Far Eastern Economic Review* (Rs 70), but it carries a Sri Lankan item only every few weeks so check the contents.

TV & Radio

There are two government-controlled TV channels, Rupavahini and ITV, with a commercial channel called MTV due to start any time. The government channels show news (censored) in all three languages. News in English is at 9.30 pm on Rupavahini and 10 pm on ITV. MTV is expected to steer clear of local politics but to concentrate on foreign affairs, entertainment and educational TV. Although Sri Lanka has quite a few locally produced programmes, including its very own soaps, there are a lot of Western-made series too. Every major cricket match is broadcast live on TV and radio – you'll see crowds of men gathered round the sets, especially when Sri Lanka are winning!

The Sri Lanka Broadcasting Corporation has radio news and other programmes both with and without commercials, in English, Sinhala and Tamil. There's also an English-language FM stereo service in the evenings, Studio STX.

Cinema

Tamil and Sinhalese films offer an entertaining insight into the peoples' culture and they're easily comprehensible. Outside Colombo '1st-class seats' are Rs 10 or less. Western films tend to be rather scratched and old by the time they reach Sri Lanka.

FILM & PHOTOGRAPHY

It's wise to bring film and batteries with you rather than count on buying them in Sri Lanka. Supplies are plentiful, especially in Colombo, Kandy and the major tourist resorts, but you can't always be sure of quality. Millers, on the corner of Mudalige Mawatha and York St in Colombo Fort, is one of the best photography shops and one of the few places where you can get Kodachrome 64 slide film (Rs 600 for 36 exposures). Its price for 36-exposure Kodacolor 100 print film is Rs 170. For camera repairs try Studio Durst, 95A Chatham St, Colombo Fort.

The usual Asian and tropical rules apply to photography in Sri Lanka – ask people's permission before taking pictures; and better results are obtained earlier in the morning or later in the afternoon, before the sun gets too high and everything looks washed out.

HEALTH

Overall Sri Lanka is a remarkably healthy country and if you're only slightly careful you should suffer no stomach problems. Pharmacies usually stock a fairly wide range of proprietary drugs but be aware of possible brand name changes from the West. Sri Lanka also has an indigenous system of herbal treatments, known as Ayurvedic medicine. There are Ayurvedic stalls in most markets.

Books

A detailed, well organised and compact travel health guide is Dirk Schroeder's *Staying Healthy in Asia, Africa & Latin America*. If you can't find it write to Moon Publications, 722 Wall St, Chico, CA 95928 USA. *Travel with Children* by Maureen Wheeler (Lonely Planet) is full of basic advice on travel health for young people.

Pre-Departure Preparations

Insurance A policy covering theft, loss, flight cancellation and medical problems is a good idea. Your travel agent will have recommendations. Check the small print. A clause that pays the cost of an emergency flight home is worth considering. If you have to stretch out you'll need two seats and somebody has to pay for it!

Medical Kit A small kit for routine problems might include tweezers, scissors, a thermometer (mercury thermometers are prohibited by most airlines), aspirin, antiseptic, bandages, plasters, and something for diarrhoea (such as a kaolin preparation like Pepto-Bismol, or Imodium or Lomotil). A rehydration mixture is a good idea in case of severe diarrhoea, especially in children.

Sunscreen or suntan lotions are worth taking with you as they'll be more expensive locally. Insect repellent will help keep particularly vicious or numerous mosquitoes away, but normally covering your skin or, when you're in your room or otherwise stationary, using a mosquito net or mosquito coils, which are available widely in Sri Lanka for Rs 20 a box, should be just as effective. Wearing white clothes also discourages mozzies, Sri Lankans say. Mosquitoes are more numerous in the wet season.

A broad-spectrum antibiotic like tetracycline or penicillin can be useful but it must be prescribed, and you should carry the prescription with you. Take only the recommended dose at the prescribed intervals and continue the course for the prescribed period.

Considering the potential for contamination through dirty needles, some travellers carry a sterile pack of disposable syringes, available from medical supply shops.

Immunisations Vaccination certificates for yellow fever or cholera are only required if you have recently visited an infected area. Yellow fever basically only applies to South America and Africa. Cholera outbreaks do happen in Sri Lanka but tend to be widely reported and therefore avoidable. Since the cholera vaccination only lasts six months, and that with limited success, you may not consider it worth having routinely. It's not recommended if you're pregnant. In Sri Lanka cholera vaccinations are available for Rs 20 at the Assistant Port Health Office (☎ 01-697421), 385 Deans Rd, Colombo 10.

You should, however, take precautions against malaria, which is certainly present in parts of the country and is spread by mosquito bites. Symptoms include headaches, fever, chills and sweating which may subside and recur. Without treatment malaria is potentially fatal. Anti-malarial drugs don't prevent the disease but suppress the symptoms. Chloroquine, which comes under various brand names, is the usual drug and is taken as a tablet weekly from one or two weeks prior to arrival in the area, to five or six weeks after you leave. It has minimal side effects and can be taken by pregnant women. Because of the existence of chloroquine-resistant strains of malaria you may be recommended to supplement chloroquine with a drug containing proguanil (which has to be taken daily), or Maloprim (weekly), or another anti-malarial. Fansidar is not recommended because of dangerous side effects, though it may be used as a treatment for known cases.

Protection against polio, tetanus and typhoid is also advised, with a gammaglobulin injection against hepatitis-A optional.

Basic Rules

The number one rule is *don't* drink the water – and that includes ice – unless you are certain it has been thoroughly boiled (ideally this means for 10 minutes). Take care with fruit juice too, as water may have been added to it. On the other hand you must make sure you drink enough in the heat – see the Drinks section for substitutes for water. Don't become paranoid about food risks – you'll be missing out on a key element of Sri Lankan life if you do – but take care with things like ice cream from street vendors, shellfish, and food that has been left to cool then reheated. If an eatery is clean and its workers look clean and healthy then the food is probably safe. Places packed with travellers or locals are usually OK.

Keep your diet balanced. Eggs, beans and lentils are all safe protein sources. Fruit you can peel is always safe and a good vitamin source. Don't forget grains (such as rice) and bread.

Wash your hands frequently and if possible treat any cuts with antiseptic solution and mercurochrome. Bandages and band-aids can hinder wounds from drying. Coral cuts are notoriously slow to heal and can be avoided by wearing shoes.

Take great care in the sun – a hat makes a big difference. Cover up as soon as you feel you might be burning. If you don't take in enough liquids, you may suffer dehydration, salt deficiency or even heat exhaustion. To avoid fungal infections wear loose, comfortable, natural-fibre clothes, wash often and dry carefully. Remember that you can get worm infections through bare feet.

If you get one of those virulent Sri Lankan colds, coriander tea and lots of pineapple will help set you right.

Medical Treatment

If you need medical attention, your embassy or one of the top-end hotels are the best places to seek a recommendation – though they're quite likely to send you to someone with top-end prices (which is where your medical insurance comes in handy!). If you need hospitalisation it's probably best to hightail it for Colombo – see the Colombo chapter for some suggestions there. One traveller wrote of the unwanted 'adventure' of being hospitalised in Haputale – you have to do a fair amount of the work yourself and it's useful to have someone handy to make sure you get food, drugs and other attention!

Diseases of Insanitation

Diarrhoea A few desperate dashes to the loo with no other symptoms are nothing to worry about but moderate diarrhoea, with half a dozen loose movements a day, needs watching. Dehydration is the main danger, particularly for children, so fluid replenishment is essential. Weak black tea with a little sugar or soft drinks allowed to go flat are good. Some Sri Lankans recommend hot lime juice, or black coffee with lime juice. In severe cases a rehydrating solution is necessary to replace minerals and salts. If you didn't bring one with you, add a few pinches of salt and a teaspoon of sugar to a litre of purified water and sip it slowly all day. Stick to a bland diet as you recover.

Lomotil or Imodium plugs you up but doesn't cure you. Use it only if absolutely necessary – if you *must* travel, for instance. Don't use it if you have a fever or are severely dehydrated. An Ayurvedic treatment for minor stomach ailments is the beli fruit, obtainable from the Ayurvedic stall at your local market. You eat it fresh to tackle diarrhoea, or boiled for constipation. Get a local to choose one for you. It tastes a bit like a fig, and it works!

Dysentery The main symptom of this serious illness, caused by contaminated food or water, is severe diarrhoea, often with traces of blood or mucus. Bacillary (or bacterial) dysentery shows rapid onset, a high fever, headache, vomiting and stomach pains. It generally doesn't last more than a week, but it's highly contagious. Amoebic dysentery develops more gradually, has no fever or vomiting but is more serious. It will persist until treated and can recur and cause long-term damage. Only a stool test can reliably distinguish the two, and they must be treated differently. Tetracycline can be used for bacillary dysentery, metronidazole for amoebic.

Viral Gastroenteritis This intestinal infection caused by a virus is characterised by cramps, diarrhoea, and sometimes by vomiting or a slight fever. Rest and drink lots of fluids until it goes away.

Hepatitis The more common hepatitis-A, or infectious hepatitis, is spread by contaminated food or water. Symptoms are fever, chills, headache, fatigue, weakness, aches and pains. These are followed by loss of appetite, nausea, vomiting, abdominal pain, dark urine, light-coloured faeces and jaundiced skin. The whites of your eyes may turn yellow.

There isn't much you can do but rest, drink lots of fluids, eat lightly and avoid fatty foods. You must forego alcohol for six months afterwards, since the disease attacks the liver.

Hepatitis-B, or serum hepatitis, is spread through sexual contact, especially male homosexual activity, and through the use of dirty needles. Avoid injections where you have doubts about sanitation. Symptoms and treatment are much the same as for type A.

Typhoid Typhoid fever is a gut infection from contaminated water or food. Vaccination isn't totally effective, and it's a very serious disease. At first you may feel as if you have a bad cold or flu, with headache, sore throat, and a fever that rises a little each day to 40°C or more. The pulse may be abnormally slow and gets slower as the fever rises (in a typical fever it speeds up). There may also be vomiting, diarrhoea or constipation.

In the second week pink spots may appear on the body, along with trembling, delirium, weakness, weight loss and dehydration. If there are no complications, the fever and symptoms can disappear in the third week but medical help is essential before this, as common complications are pneumonia or burst appendix, and typhoid is very infectious.

The victim should be kept cool and made to drink a lot of fluids. Chloramphenicol is the recommended antibiotic but there are fewer side effects with ampicillin.

Worms These are more common in rural areas. Worms can be present on unwashed vegetables or in uncooked meat, and you can pick them up through your skin by walking barefoot. Infestations may not show up for some time, and if left untreated may cause severe health problems. A stool test pinpoints the problem.

Diseases Spread by People & Animals

Tetanus Tetanus, or lockjaw, is potentially fatal but preventable by immunisation. It occurs when a wound is infected by a germ from animal faeces, so clean all cuts or bites. The first symptom may be discomfort in swallowing, followed by stiffening of the jaw and neck, then painful convulsions of the jaw and whole body.

Rabies Rabies is caused by a bite or scratch from an infected animal. Dogs are noted carriers but cats, bats, monkeys, cattle and other mammals can also spread it. Any bite, scratch, or even a lick at the site of a cut or scratch should be scrubbed immediately with soap and running water and, if possible, cleaned with an alcohol solution. If there is any chance that the animal is infected, medical help should be sought immediately. Rabies that is not treated before the onset of symptoms is fatal. A rabies vaccination is now available.

Sexually Transmitted Diseases Abstinence is the only sure preventative for diseases spread by sexual contact, but use of a condom is very effective. Gonorrhoea and syphilis are the most common diseases; symptoms include sores, blisters or a rash around the genitals, discharge or pain when urinating. They may be less marked or absent in women. Syphilis symptoms eventually disappear but the disease continues and can cause severe problems in later years. Treatment of gonorrhoea or syphilis is by antibiotics.

There is currently no cure for Acquired Immune Deficiency Syndrome (AIDS). Condoms and abstention are the most effective protection. AIDS can also be spread through blood transfusions or by dirty needles; vaccinations, acupuncture, tattooing, even dental work are potentially as dangerous as intravenous drug use if the equipment is not clean.

Women's Health
Gynaecological Problems Poor diet or lowered resistance from the use of antibiotics or even contraceptive pills can pave the way for vaginal infections. Keeping the genital area clean, and wearing cotton underwear and skirts or loose-fitting trousers will help to prevent them.

Yeast infections, characterised by a rash, itch and discharge, can be treated with a vinegar or lemon juice douche, or with yoghurt. Nystatin suppositories are the usual medical prescription. Trichomonas is a more serious infection with a discharge and a burning sensation when urinating. Male sexual partners must also be treated and if a vinegar-water douche is not effective, medical attention should be sought. Flagyl is the prescribed drug.

Pregnancy Most miscarriages occur during the first three months so this is the riskiest time to travel. The last three months should also be spent within reach of good medical care. Pregnant women should avoid unnecessary medication, but vaccinations and malarial prophylactics should still be taken if they're not contraindicated. Extra care should be taken to prevent illness, and good diet and rest are doubly important.

WOMEN TRAVELLERS
The more modestly you dress, the less unwanted attention you'll attract, but even so you may not completely avoid some of the pests who like to latch on to or follow Western women. Beaches in relatively remote places, in particular, are places where a woman alone might have to cope with some annoyance. Stray hands on crowded buses are something else to watch out for. The sight of Western women even seems to make a few men masturbate on the spot. Fortunately such behaviour rarely escalates to threatening. Some women find Sri Lanka a lot easier to handle than India, others find it harder.

But don't imagine travelling in Sri Lanka is one long hassle. Such unpleasant incidents are the exception not the rule, and if you try to keep your sense of humour and treat them with a pinch of salt, they shouldn't unduly bother you.

Shops in the main towns have a basic supply of Western toiletries, and in Colombo you can find most things you'd want, but if there's anything you're particularly attached to you should bring it with you.

DANGERS & ANNOYANCES
Touts
Undoubtedly most travellers' biggest headache in Sri Lanka is touts. These individuals, mostly young males who misleadingly call themselves guides, latch on to you pretending to offer help or friendliness. Their real aim is to steer you into a guest house, hotel, gem shop or other place where they hope you'll spend money and they'll get a commission. Often they'll plausibly but dishonestly make out that it's their 'own' place they're taking you to and that it's all as much a matter of hospitality as business.

In some towns touts demand such high commission from guest house owners that the guest house has to charge *you* extra. If a guest house refuses to pay touts commission, they will often spread tales that it is infested with rats or cobras, or plagued by thieves, or washed away by the monsoon, or that the owner has died, to scare off potential customers. Some touts, even though rebuffed by travellers, may still follow them to their accommodation, sneak round the back, tell the owner that they have 'brought' the travellers, and claim a commission! You'll be much more popular with hotel and guest house proprietors if you turn up without a tout in tow. Some places will claim 'house full' if you arrive with a tout; others will pick you up if you call from the station to avoid the touts.

The tout's usual tactic is to lurk around bus or rail stations or other places where travellers are to be found, effect a 'casual' meeting, then cling on like a leech until either the traveller has followed his 'advice', or been rude enough to shake him off. The lengths to which some of them go are amazing. Some from Kandy or Hikkaduwa will even travel all the way to Colombo with the sole aim of picking up travellers on the train back. They can be unbelievably clever at disguising their intentions, and by the time you've tumbled to them it may be too late.

It's not generally in the Sri Lankan nature to be intrusive and anyone who seems to be even slightly forcing the pace of a casual meeting or conversation is likely to be up to something. So being curt with such people, unless they show that their motives are clean, is a good defence against touts. If you know where you want to go, go there no matter what you are told. Saying you have a reservation, whether true or not, is a good ploy. If the tout continues with unnecessary questions, you can tell him it's none of his business.

Taxi drivers are not immune to the touting disease. So if one starts telling you that the place you've hired him to take you to is no good, and he knows somewhere much better, tell him to keep his mind on his driving!

'Tourist = $$$'

Touts are perhaps the most prominent example of an attitude among some Sri Lankans that really disenchants some visitors. This is the attitude – contrasting with the genuine friendliness and hospitality displayed by many Sri Lankans – that Westerners exist solely in order to be milked for dollars. It may well involve dishonestly professing friendship, hospitality and equality while all along scheming for some profit. While it's entirely understandable that citizens of a poor country should see Westerners as a possible source of funds, the cunning and devious lengths to which some people go can be amazing and hurtful. The following from a reader is an extreme case but shows how Sri Lanka rubs some people up the wrong way:

The people are not to be trusted. They are very sly and insincere. Ninety-nine per cent of times a Sri Lankan approaches a tourist is for money. They invent the most extraordinary lies to get this money. The tourist is not welcomed in Sri Lanka. The people believe that tourists are responsible for all the evil in the world and they behave as if you owe them all the money you have on you. Sri Lanka is a very beautiful country but the soul of the people who live in it is not affected by this beauty. In the end their hustling takes all the nice memories away.

In reality the Sri Lankans who try to prey on tourists are just a minority, and in any case many travellers will be able to handle this kind of thing with a shrug of the shoulders. But if you're aware from the start of the possible economic angles in almost any contact with Sri Lankans, you may avoid some unpleasant surprises.

Theft

Theft is always something to be guarded against in Sri Lanka, whether you're on the move or staying in a guest house or hotel. Pickpockets are active on crowded buses, notably in Colombo along Galle Rd. They often work together – one to jostle you and the other to pick your pocket or slit your bag with a knife, often as you board the bus. All you can do is try to keep a little space around you and hold tight to what you're carrying. It's often unwise to sleep with your windows open – particularly if you're on the ground floor. Even if the windows are barred, thieves may use long poles with hooks on the end to lift out your bags, camera, etc.

One thieves' trick reported by a number of travellers is to take the bottom one or two of a block of travellers' cheques, so that you don't notice anything missing until much later.

If you do get robbed go to the police – you won't get your money back but passports and tickets are often jettisoned later. One Australian actually got her passport back from her embassy after the pickpockets had dropped it in a mailbox!

Traffic

The quality of some Sri Lankan driving – above all, by drivers of private buses – has deteriorated to the point where it has to be ranked a real danger. It seems to be acceptable for a bus, car or lorry to overtake in the face of oncoming smaller road-users – who sometimes simply have to get off the road or get hit. To announce that they are overtaking, or want to, drivers use a series of blasts on loud, shrill horns. If you're walking or cycling along any kind of main road keep all your senses on alert in every direction – even (or especially) if you're walking on the side of oncoming traffic, when you could be collected from behind by a crazed overtaker.

ACCOMMODATION

Sri Lanka is very seasonal, particularly along the beach strips. Prices quoted in this guide are generally the high-season rates (without the 10% service charge that's common in middle and top-end places), but you can often find spectacular bargains in the off-season. Additionally the 'season', and its prices, have a more-or-less official starting date – 15 December on the west and south coasts, 1 April on the east – and the monsoon may have ended well before the season starts. You can, of course, often bargain prices down at any time of the year. Many places have a variety of rooms at different prices, and it's often worth asking, after they have shown you their first room or quoted you their first price, if there are any cheaper rooms available. If there are more than two of you, some places have three- or four-

person rooms, which bring the cost per person well down.

Most room prices in this book are quoted in Rs, but some are in US$ if a hotel quotes them that way – which some do to ensure that they get the same number of dollars whatever the fluctuations in the rupee/dollar exchange rate.

See the preceding Dangers & Annoyances section for information on touts, who are a sadly important aspect of the accommodation scene.

Guest Houses

These are often the best deals in Sri Lankan accommodation. Sometimes just a couple of rooms in a house are rented out like English bed & breakfast establishments. Other times they're like small hotels. You'll find some very cheap places to stay in this category, plus some in the medium-price bracket and even the occasional more expensive place. It's a good idea to pin down exactly what you're getting for your money, or be prepared in some places for an unpleasant surprise when you find out how many cups of tea you've had and how much each of them has cost!

In the family-style guest houses you'll also often find very good food – better Sri Lankan food, in fact, than in almost any of the restaurants and many of the more expensive hotels. The Sri Lankans are proud of their cuisine and asking for seconds is the best compliment you can give. They will usually be only too happy to show you round the kitchen and explain how dishes are prepared. Apart from the low cost, the 'meeting people' aspect is the big plus of guest house accommodation.

Rest Houses

Originally established by the Dutch for travelling government officials, then developed into a network of wayside inns by the British, the rest houses now mostly function as good small middle-range hotels. They're found all over the country, in little out-of-the-way towns (where they may be the only regular accommodation) as well as in the tourist centres. Many of the more popular ones now come under the wing of the government-sponsored Ceylon Hotels Corporation, which has a booking office in the arrivals hall at Katunayake Airport and another (☎ 01-23501) at 63 Janadhipathi Mawatha, Colombo Fort. In the main December to March tourist season, it's often worth booking ahead as tour groups tend to fill rest houses up quickly. We have also received some complaints from disgruntled travellers about reservations not being honoured, or of having to move rooms, or check out altogether, because preference was given to groups at some more popular rest houses, so bear that in mind.

Although they vary widely in standards and prices, many rest houses offer the most pleasant accommodation in town – attractively old fashioned, with big rooms, well kept and usually very well situated. Wherever you go, you'll find that the rest houses enjoy the view from the highest hill, along the best stretch of beach or in some other way have grabbed the best position going. Prices in rest houses vary from the lower middle price range to the bottom end of the upper price range. A room-only double generally costs around Rs 350 or 400.

Hotels

The borderline between lower-price hotels and upper-range guest houses is a blurred one, not least in name since some 'hotels' are really guest houses, while some small hotels call themselves inns, lodges, villas and so on. You'll rarely find a double in a hotel for less than Rs 250. There are places going all the way up the price scale to US$100 or more. For Rs 450 you'll usually get a spacious, clean double with attached toilet and shower.

The larger hotels are of two basic types: modern resort hotels and older colonial-style places. The latter definitely have the edge when it comes to atmosphere, and their facilities are often just as good. The newer places pride themselves on luxury facilities like tennis courts, windsurfing instruction, nightclubs and prime beach, riverside or hilltop sites, and are mostly geared to package tourists. West coast resort hotel doubles go from around US$25 up to US$100-plus, while the upper-bracket colonial-type places are rarely much over US$30 – excellent value compared to the West.

FOOD

Sri Lanka does not have one of the great Asian cuisines but it's certainly enjoyable and the food quality is generally quite high. The staple meal is rice and curry. If you insist on eating just like back at home, the Sri Lankans also manage to make a very reasonable stab at cooking Western-style, unlike some nationalities who are most definitely best left to their own cuisines. There are even quite a few restaurants specialising in foreign cuisines – Chinese, of course, but also German, Italian and even some places that haven't forgotten how the British like their food! In the main traveller centres there are plenty of places serving travellers' standard fare like pancakes, omelettes, fried rice, noodles, salads, yoghurt and so on. A Sri Lankan taste treat not to be missed is fruit. Sri Lanka rates right up there with the best places in South-East Asia when it comes to finding the knock-out best of tropical fruits.

Rice & Curry

Like many other aspects of Sri Lankan life, the food is closely related to that of India – but Sri Lankan rice and curry has many variations from Indian. Curries in Sri Lanka can be very hot indeed but adjustments will often be made to suit sensitive Western palates! If you find you have taken a mouthful of something that is simply too hot, relief does not come from a gulp of cold water. That's like throwing fuel on a fire. Far better is a fork of rice, or better still some cooling yoghurt or curd (buffalo yoghurt) or even cucumber. That's what those side dishes are for. Of course if it's not hot enough the solution to that is there too – simply add some *pol sambol*, a red-hot, grated coconut, chilli and spice side dish. *Sambol* is the general name for any spicy-hot dish.

Sri Lankan rice and curry usually includes a variety of small curry dishes – vegetable, meat or fish. Sri Lankans say, and it's true, that only by eating with the fingers can you fully enjoy the flavour combinations from the different curries. To eat Sri Lankan style, start by ladling a heap of rice on to your plate, followed by the desired quantities of the different curries. Then delve the ends of the fingers of your right hand in and mix things up a bit to mingle the flavours. With the aid of your thumb you then mix a mouthful-sized wad of food, combining whichever elements you choose, in the same finger-ends, slightly cupped, and push it into your mouth with the thumb. Add more of the curries, or more rice, to your plate as the fancy takes you. A finger bowl appears for you to wash your fingers when you have finished. Eating with the fingers may seem messy and inelegant at first but it gets a lot easier with a little practice. If you don't fancy it – and in smarter restaurants many people feel embarrassed – fork and spoon are provided.

Disappointingly, for the amount of rice eaten in Sri Lanka, the rice is not always so special. Cheaper rice often has a musty, 'old' taste to it. Certainly not of the same standard as Thai rice. The spices used to bring out the subtle flavours of Sri Lankan curry (and remember that 'curry powder' is purely a Western invention) are all from Sri Lanka. It was spices, particularly cinnamon, that first brought Europeans to the island, and even today a selection of Sri Lankan spices is a popular item to take home when you leave.

The usual Indian curry varieties are also available of course: south Indian vegetarian *thali*, or the delicate north Indian *biriyani*. From the northern Jaffna region comes *kool*, a boiled, fried and dried-in-the-sun vegetable combination.

Fish & Seafood

Coastal towns have excellent fish (often served with chips and salad); prawns too are widespread, and in Hikkaduwa, Unawatuna and Trincomalee, to name but a few places, you can find delicious crab. In the south of the island a popular dish is *ambul thiyal*, a pickle usually made from tuna, which translates literally as 'sour fish curry'.

Other Specialities

Unique Sri Lankan foods include hoppers, which are usually a breakfast or evening snack. A regular hopper is rather like a small pancake: with an egg fried into the middle of it you have an egg hopper; with honey and yoghurt in the middle it's a honey and yoghurt hopper. String hoppers are quite different – they're tangled little circles of steamed noodles; used as a curry dip instead of rice they make a tasty and filling meal. Another rice substitute is *pittu*, a mixture of flour and grated coconut which is steamed in a bamboo mould so that it comes out as a cylinder. *Lamprai* is a popular Sinhalese dish of rice boiled in meat stock, then added to vegetables and meat and slowly baked in a banana-leaf wrapping.

At lunchtime you can dine lightly on a plate of 'short eats'. A selection of spring rolls, vegetable patties, meatballs and other snacks is placed in the middle of the table. You eat as many as you feel like and the bill is added up according to how many are left. At the Pagoda Tea Room in Colombo Fort, a favourite place for short eats, they even follow it up with what you could call 'short desserts'.

A filling snack which crops up mainly in streetside huts devoted to it is the *rotty*, a small parcel of anything you fancy wrapped up in a sort of elasticated, doughy pancake. Fillings can range from chilli and onion to bacon and egg!

Desserts & Snacks

The Sri Lankans also have lots of ideas for desserts, such as *watalappam*, a Malay-originated egg pudding, vaguely caramel-like in taste. Curd and honey, or curd and treacle (which often seems to get misspelt 'trickle') is good at any time of day. Curd is yoghurt made from buffalo milk – it's rich and tasty but certainly does not come in a handy plastic container. A street stall curd container is a shallow clay pot, complete with a handy carrying rope and so attractive you'll hate to throw it away. The treacle *(kitul)* is really palm syrup, a stage on from toddy! If it's dried into hardened blocks you have *jaggery*, an all-purpose Sri Lankan candy or sweetener.

Like the Indians, the Sri Lankans waste no opportunity to indulge their sweet tooth – sweets are known as *rasa-kavili*. You could try *kavun*, spiced flour and treacle battercake fried in coconut oil. Or *aluva*, rice flour, treacle and cashew nut fudge. Coconut milk, jaggery and cashew nuts give you dark and delicious *kalu dodol*.

Fruit

After travelling in Asia and trying rambutans, mangosteens, jackfruit and durians how could anybody live with boring old apples and oranges again? Well, if you're already addicted, Sri Lanka is a great place to indulge. If you've not yet developed a taste for tropical fruits then it's a great place to get into it. Here are just a few favourites.

Rambutan The name (it's Malay) means 'spiny' and that's just what they are: fruit about the size of a large walnut or small tangerine, covered in soft red spines. You peel the spiny skin off to reveal a very close cousin to the lychee. The cool and mouthwatering flesh is, unfortunately, often rigidly attached to the central stone.

Pineapple In season Sri Lanka seems to be afloat in pineapples. They're generally quite small and very thirst quenching.

Mangosteen One of the finest tropical fruits, the mangosteen is about the size of a tangerine or small apple. The dark purple outer skin breaks open to reveal pure-white segments shaped like those of an orange – but with a sweet-sour flavour which has been compared to a combination of strawberries and grapes. Queen Victoria, so the story goes, offered a considerable prize to anybody able to bring a mangosteen back intact from the east for her to try.

Mango The Sri Lankans claim that it is the mango which grows best on their island. It comes in a large variety of shapes and tastes, although generally in the green-skinned, peach-textured variety like that found around Jaffna – Sri Lanka's mango-capital.

Custard Apple The custard apple that grows in Australia is not the real thing (to Asian-inclined tastes) whereas the Sri Lankan variety definitely is. Actually there are a number of custard apple types with a variety of flavours. The refreshing, slightly lemon/tart flavour is one some people particularly love. Outwardly custard apples are about the size of a grapefruit but more pear shaped. The thin skin is light green and dotted with little warts but a custard apple isn't ready for eating until it has gone soft and squishy, and the skin is starting to go grey-black in patches.

Jackfruit This watermelon-size fruit hangs from trees. It breaks up into hundreds of bright orange/yellow segments with a slightly rubbery texture. It's also widely used as a vegetable, cooked with rice or curries. While ripening on the tree jackfruits are often shrouded in sacking to protect them from birds.

Coconut The all-purpose coconut palm provides far more food value than the obvious coconut itself would suggest. For a refreshing drink, you can't go far wrong with a *thambili*, the golden king-coconut. Anywhere in Sri Lanka there will be some lad sitting with a huge pile of coconuts, machete at the ready to provide you with a thirst-quenching drink for Rs 5 or so.

Other Fruit There is a wide variety of bananas which are often referred to as plantains. And there are papayas (pawpaw), that best known of tropical fruits with the golden-orange, melon-like flesh – a delicious way to start the day with a dash of lemon. And woodapples, a hard, wooden-shelled fruit which is used to make a delicious drink, a creamy dessert topping or a uniquely Sri Lankan jam. And melons, passion fruit, avocados, guavas (particularly the little pink variety, like crispy pears) and many others to be discovered. Not to mention the famous durian – a big, green hand-grenade of a fruit which breaks open to emit a smell like a disgustingly blocked-up sewer! But what a taste!

DRINKS
As in most Asian countries you're advised not to drink water unless you're certain that it has been thoroughly boiled. Of course you've got no way of telling if that really has been done, should a restaurant tell you so. Plus you get awfully thirsty at times. Safe substitutes? There's Sri Lanka's famous tea, and Sri Lankans are generally a bit better at making a cup of the stuff than their Indian neighbours. If you order a pot, it will probably come with warm milk and sugar in separate bowls or jugs to be added as you please. The tea itself may be fresh, even fragrant, or it may be stewed black. Or you can get a glass of 'plain tea' (you must specify with or without sugar); also, there's the concoction called 'milk tea' in which tea, hot milk and sugar are mixed together before being poured into the cup. This can warm you up in the cool hill country or after a long spell in the sea. Coffee is something of a lottery – after days of drinking dishwater you'll come across a place that provides good, strong, real filter coffee!

The other side of the drinks menu will usually be labelled 'cool drinks', which simply means the sort of drinks that could possibly (if there was a fridge, and it was working) be served cool! There'll often be lime juice, excellent but made from the questionable water, and a range of bottled soft drinks. Coca-Cola is widely available in Sri Lanka but usually rather more expensive than the local brands. Most widespread of the Sri Lankan soft drinks are Elephant House – a wide variety of flavours (including a not

very good cola), generally quite palatable, in big 400 ml bottles and reasonably cheap at about Rs 4 to Rs 10 depending on where you buy it and whether it's cold or not. The supposed legal maximum price is printed on the label.

Alcoholic Drinks
The Lion Pilsner and Royal Pilsner beers produced by Nuwara Eliya Breweries are, to our taste, more palatable than Three Coins from McCallums of Negombo, but all are OK, though none will win many prizes. In the hill country you'll even come across a couple of varieties of stout. Beer is an expensive drink by Sri Lankan standards, at around Rs 50 a bottle in the shops and up to Rs 90 depending where else you drink it. Once again there is a legal maximum price. You can buy all manner of imported grog too. Note that alcohol cannot be sold on the monthly full moon poya holiday.

Sri Lanka also has two extremely popular local varieties of intoxicating beverage. Toddy is a natural drink, a bit like cider, produced from one or other of the palm trees. Getting the tree to produce toddy is a specialised operation performed by people known as 'toddy tappers'. Your typical toddy tapper will have as many as 100 trees in his territory, and his daily routine involves tightroping from the top of one tree to another on shaky ropeways to remove full buckets of toddy, lower them to the ground and replace them with empty buckets. Toddy tapping is not a particularly safe occupation, although fewer toddy tappers manage to fall out of the trees than you'd expect.

Fermented and refined toddy becomes arrack. It's produced in a variety of grades and qualities – some of which are real firewater. Proceed with caution! A bottle costs from about Rs 100 to Rs 200. Kalutara, 40 km south of Colombo on the road to Bentota and Hikkaduwa, is the toddy and arrack capital of Sri Lanka. Annually Sri Lanka produces five million gallons of toddy and 7½ million bottles of arrack. With a soft-drink mixer arrack is very pleasant.

SPORTS

Although Sri Lankans play volleyball, netball, soccer, tennis and a few other sports, the most popular, and the only one where they can compete with the best internationally, is cricket. Radio commentaries of big games are broadcast down streets, boys play the game on the roadside or in forest clearings, and Sri Lankans whose knowledge of English is otherwise limited can tell you: 'First innings, two hundred and twelve, eight wickets, declared'. Sri Lankans have a thoughtful and subtle approach to the game and even when there are just five or six boys playing on a scrap of waste ground, they will go through the whole panoply of innings, overs, tactical field placings, etc.

The teams of other main cricketing nations like India, Pakistan, Australia and England all visit Sri Lanka from time to time. It's usually easy to see a big match and the main stadiums are CCC, NCC and SSC, all in Colombo 7, south-east of Viharamahadevi Park; Moratuwa, a few km down the coast from Colombo; Asgiriya, in Kandy; and Kettarama, the newest and biggest (40,000 capacity) in north Colombo. The main cricket season is from January to April.

One entirely sedentary sport enjoyed by large numbers of Sri Lankans is betting – on British horse and dog racing! With racing in Sri Lanka frowned upon by the Buddhist establishment, you'll see people in hole-in-the-wall betting shops throughout the land avidly studying the day's runners and riders from Aintree, Ascot and Hackney. Commentaries on the races are beamed over from Britain starting about 6 pm Sri Lankan time.

THINGS TO BUY

Sri Lanka has a wide variety of very attractive handicrafts on sale, most of which you can find in shops and street stalls in Colombo although you will, naturally, find greater variety 'at source'. The government-run Laksala shop in Colombo has a very representative collection of items from all over the country and will give you a good idea of what to look for and how much to pay. Its stuff is generally of reasonably good quality and at reasonable prices. It doesn't, however, seem to get the really excellent pieces.

Masks

Sri Lankan masks are a very popular collectors' item for visitors. They're carved at a number of places, principally along the south-west coast, and sold all over the island, but the town of Ambalangoda, slightly north of Hikkaduwa, is the mask-carving centre. You can visit a number of showroom-workshops here.

If you'd like to know a lot more about masks, there are some expensive coffee-table quality books and a rather haphazard booklet, *The Masks of Sri Lanka* by M H Goonatilleka (Department of Cultural Affairs, 1976), which is very scathing on the 'tourist' masks, which are all you really see on sale today, outside museums.

There are three basic types of mask. One is the *kolam* mask; the name literally means a mask or form of disguise and these are used in rural dance-dramas where all the characters wear masks. Kolam masks generally illustrate a set cast of characters but although these masks are still made for dance performances, with some new characters being introduced, they are not produced for tourist consumption. The second type, *sanni*, is the devil-dancing mask where the dancers wear masks in order to impersonate disease-causing demons and thus exorcise them. Thirdly, *raksha* masks are used in processions and festivals. There are about 25 varieties, including the widely seen *naga raksha* (cobra) masks, where a demonic face complete with protruding eyeballs, lolling tongue and pointed teeth is topped with a 'coiffure' of writhing cobras. Legend has it that Sri Lanka was once ruled by a race called the Rakshasas, whose king was Rawana of the Ramayana story. The Rakshasas could assume the form of cobras to terrify and subjugate their enemies. Their victims, however, would sometimes plead for help from the *gurulu*, a bird which preys on snakes, and today the *gurulu raksha* is another frequently seen type of mask.

The masks you see on sale, apart from the

raksha masks, are the '18 disease' sanni masks. A demon figure, clutching one or more victims and often with another clenched in his teeth, is flanked by 18 faces, each used to exorcise a different disease ranging from rheumatism, earache or boils, to blindness or the 'morbid state of wind, bile and phlegm'. The whole ensemble is bordered by two cobras and others sprout from the demon's head. Most masks are made from a light balsa-type wood locally called *kaduru* (Latin *nux vomica*), which is smoke-dried before the mask is cut out of it.

Touristic or not, the masks are remarkably well made, low in cost and look very nice on the wall back home. They're available from key-ring size for a few cents, up to big, high-quality masks over Rs 2000.

Batik

The Indonesian art of batik making is a relatively new development in Sri Lanka but one it has taken to with alacrity. You'll see a wide variety of batiks made and sold around the island and some of the best and most original are the batik pictures made by Upali Jayakody in Kandy, and Fresco Batiks on the Peradeniya road outside Kandy. '...Kandy batiks were very poor compared with the superb ones at the batik village of Mahawewa beyond Negombo', wrote a visitor. Batik pictures start from Rs 50 or Rs 100, and go up to well over Rs 1000. Batik is also used for a variety of clothing items.

Leather

You can also find some very low-priced and good quality leatherwork – particularly bags and cases. Look in the leatherwork shops and shoe shops around Colombo Fort. The bazaar on Olcott Mawatha, beside Fort Station, is cheaper than the Laksala for similar-quality goods. Hikkaduwa is also a good place for leather bags.

Gems

Sri Lanka's famous gemstones remain an important (and interesting!) facet of the economy. Initially gems were found mainly around Ratnapura and this remains one of the most important areas for gemming, but they are now also found in many other localities.

There are countless showrooms and private gem dealers all over the country. In Ratnapura everybody and their brother is a spare-time gem dealer! In Colombo there's a big concentration of them in the Gem Exchange at 310 Galle Rd, Kollupitiya, Colombo 3. In the same building, on the 2nd floor, is the State Gem Corporation's testing laboratory, where tourists can get any stone tested free from 8.30 am to 12.30 pm or 1.15 to 4.30 pm, Monday to Friday. (But if you want a certificate, that'll cost you Rs 100.) The State Gem Corporation has its own showroom next door, too. The only snag with the testing service is that it's not always easy, or practical, to 'borrow' a stone to take it in for testing before you buy it. However one reader wrote that a reputable dealer, at least from Colombo, would accompany you to the State Gem Corporation for a testing.

For more information on gems see Ratnapura in the Hill Country chapter. High quality though Sri Lanka's gemstones may be, the jewellery settings are often abysmal – stones often simply fall out.

John Brotherton and Bobbie Rubin of Britain wrote:

The very best stones go to the Gem Corporation for sale to foreign merchants, who pay good prices quickly and that's what it's all about. Most of the good stones that are left go to the more upmarket jewellers – they too can afford to pay and carry good stocks (the quality of the premises is a good guide to the quality of the stones). Stones are marked up 33% to 50% before sale. As a tourist, if you can bargain the price down 15% to 20% it's the best you'll get – if any more, be suspicious.

There have also been a number of letters from readers to whom Sri Lankans have tried to sell large amounts of gems with the promise that they can be resold for a big profit in other countries. Strict export regulations are apparently given as the reason why the Sri Lankans can't trade the stones themselves. Galle seems to be the epicentre of this sort of activity and our advice is to be extremely careful. Even if it is legal, the only people who make money on that sort of deal are usually people who really know what they are about.

Other Souvenirs

There are countless other purchases waiting to tempt your travellers' cheques out of your moneybelt. The ubiquitous coconut shell is carved into all manner of souvenirs and useful items. Like the Thais and Burmese, the Sinhalese also make lacquerware items like bowls and ashtrays – layers of lacquer are built up on a light framework, usually of bamboo strips. Kandy is a centre for jewellery and brassware, both antique and modern. There are some nice chunky silver bracelets, as well as some rather dull stuff. The brass suns and moons are attractive – or try a hefty brass elephant-head door knocker for size.

Coir, a rope fibre made from coconut husks, is made into baskets, bags, mats, and many other useful items. Weligama on the south coast turns out some attractive earthenware pottery. All the usual travellers'-style clothes are available, particularly in Hikkaduwa. Although the quality is often low the prices are even lower. Tortoise-shell and ivory are best left on the backs of turtles or in the tusks of elephants, especially as Sri Lanka's unique sub-species of elephant is threatened by illegal hunting. One reader requested people to avoid ebony, from which many wooden elephants are carved, for similar reasons.

Cargill's Department Store in Fort, Colombo, will pack items in cardboard or wooden boxes – they do a good job at reasonable prices.

Getting There & Away

Unless you're on a cruise, the only way into Sri Lanka at present is to fly, which you can do direct to Colombo (Sri Lanka's only international airport) from around 30 cities in Europe, Asia, Australia and the Middle East. There are currently no direct flights from the Americas or Africa – you have to change planes en route from those continents. The number of airlines serving Sri Lanka declined when tourism slumped in the late 1980s but is picking up again. The national carrier, Air Lanka, has more flights to Sri Lanka than any other airline. Though it has a reputation for overbooking and delays (the joke goes that its flight code, UL, stands for 'Usually Late'), its service on board is good, with free drinks and good food. Bear in mind the steady increase in airfares when you read the details that follow.

The ferry between Rameswaram in south India and Talaimannar in Sri Lanka has been a casualty of the Sinhalese-Tamil troubles, but will probably restart if the war ends.

AIR

Sri Lanka Tourist Board offices – or where they don't exist, Sri Lankan embassy or high commission tourism sections – may be able to tell you of some air ticket outlets. See the Tourist Offices section in Facts for the Visitor.

To/From the UK

Discounted tickets are readily available from London 'bucket shop' travel agents for around UK£300 one way or UK£450 to UK£500 return (a bit more if you want to stay longer than three months). At the time of writing the cheapest are with Air Lanka, Balkan Bulgarian Airlines, Aeroflot, Gulf Air and Emirates. Air Lanka is the only airline actually flying from London to Colombo: with the others you must make a connection en route. There is seasonal variation in the price of some tickets: if you fly outside the peak mid-December to March period, or even just avoid mid-December to about 10 January with some airlines, you can make savings. The potential savings are least on tickets which are already cheap.

Sri Lanka is quite a good place to break a journey between London and Australia, being on a fairly direct route between the two places and not too expensive. A London-Melbourne ticket with Colombo stopovers can be bought for about UK£480 one way or UK£700 12-month return at the time of writing.

To find agents for cheap tickets check the travel ads in London magazines like *Time Out, City Limits, Southern Cross* or *TNT*, or the travel pages of national newspapers. Trailfinders (☎ (071) 938 3366) at 46 Earls Court Rd, London W8, and STA (☎ (071) 581 4132) at 74 Old Brompton Rd, London SW 7 and 117 Euston Rd, London NW1 (☎ (071) 465 0484) are two reliable agents for cheap tickets. STA has offices in other British cities too. *Sri Lankans Monthly* magazine (☎ (081) 952 9527) of PO Box 110, Edgware, Middlesex HA8 5RG, advertises some particularly cheap fares.

To/From Continental Europe

KLM, Lufthansa, the French airline UTA, Aeroflot and Balkan Bulgarian fly direct from Europe to Sri Lanka, as does Air Lanka from Amsterdam, Berlin, Brussels, Frankfurt, Paris, Rome, Vienna, and Zurich. The cheapest fares will be with Air Lanka, Aeroflot, Balkan and some Middle Eastern airlines such as Emirates, with which you change planes on the way. A typical return-trip fare from Germany to Sri Lanka is DM 1600 or DM 1700, or from Holland 1400 to 1500 florins, though you can save by avoiding the peak seasons. From some countries, including Germany, there are also possibilities of cheap places on charter flights – contact discount ticket agents.

To/From Australia

Air Lanka is the only airline flying direct between Australia (Sydney or Melbourne) and Sri Lanka. Flights depart twice a week. You can get return tickets for around A$1360, or one way for A$915 – watch out for reduced fares during the off-peak season (from April to November). Tickets on Singapore Airlines or MAS involve a change of plane on the way and are usually more expensive.

Return fares to Europe with Colombo stopovers can be found for A$1700 or so, while Air Lanka offers flights to India with a stopover in Sri Lanka for A$1530 return, around A$1000 one way.

STA is usually good for discounted tickets out of Australia, but you can also check the travel pages of the main dailies for travel agent advertisements.

To/From North America

Cities like San Francisco, Los Angeles and New York have specialist agents dealing in discounted tickets, just like the 'bucket shops' of London. Scan the travel section of a Sunday paper to find adverts for these agents. STA and Council Travel, two student travel operators with lots of offices around the country, are good agents for discounted tickets.

There are no direct flights from Canada or the USA to Sri Lanka. Tickets from the west coast of North America involve at least one stop somewhere else in Asia. Singapore and Bangkok, at around US$550 one way or US$850 return from San Francisco or Los Angeles, are the obvious transit points. Returns from Singapore or Bangkok to Colombo can be found for around US$350. Hong Kong is little cheaper than Bangkok or Singapore to reach from North America but significantly dearer to reach Sri Lanka from. From the Canadian or US east coast it would be cheaper to fly to London and connect there.

To/From India

Air Lanka and the Indian domestic carrier, Indian Airlines, between them now fly to/from Madras at least twice daily, Trivandrum daily, and Trichy (Tiruchirappalli) and Bombay four times weekly. Trivandrum is the cheapest route, closely followed by Trichy. The two airlines' fares are about the same but at the time of writing it's cheaper to fly India-Colombo-India than Colombo-India-Colombo. One-way fares from Colombo are Trivandrum US$50, Trichy US$53, Madras US$75, Bombay US$160, all including tax. From India to Colombo, you pay about 30% less. Return fares are double the single fares in both countries. Book ahead as all these flights can be pretty full at times, particularly around Christmas, New Year and the Sinhalese-Tamil New Year in mid-April.

Indian Visas The Indian High Commission in Colombo has to send a telex (for which you pay Rs 240) to the Indian High Commission in your own country, and get a reply, as part of the visa process. It says you should allow six working days for this – although some travellers have reported that you can persuade them to do it much quicker if there's special urgency, or you have some even vaguely official connection or reason for your trip. Three photos and a fee of Rs 213 for one-month visas or Rs 1064 for longer visas, are required with the application. The high commission (☎ 01-421604, 422788) is at 36-38 Galle Rd, Colombo 3, and is open for visa business from Monday to Friday 9.30 am to noon, and for visa collection from 4.30 to 5.20 pm.

To/From Elsewhere in Asia

Apart from connections with India there are direct flights between Colombo and Bangkok, Hong Kong, Karachi, Kuala Lumpur, Male (Maldives) and Singapore, on Air Lanka and a few other airlines. Discount tickets can be bought in Singapore, Hong Kong and Bangkok, but take care who you deal with as there are a few fly-by-nights. Count on around US$200 one way or US$350 return from Bangkok, a little more from Singapore, and about US$350 one way or US$600 return from Hong Kong.

The Air Lanka Colombo-Male fare is US$81 one way, US$162 return.

Stopovers & Round-the-World Tickets

If Sri Lanka is just one stop on a longer Asian/Australasian or round-the-world trip, Air Lanka and the Dubai-based Emirates are probably the two most interesting airlines to look into, as they fly both east and west of Sri Lanka. Most other airlines basically fly from their home countries to Colombo and back again. Emirates has flights from Sri Lanka to Male (Maldives), Singapore and the Middle East, where you can connect for Europe. Discount ticket agents can put together combined tickets using different airlines for different sections of your trip.

SEA

The ferry between Rameswaram in southern Tamil Nadu, India, and Talaimannar in north-west Sri Lanka was suspended in 1984, when it was believed to be a conduit for arms and other aid to the Tamil rebels. It's highly unlikely to reopen as long as there's any significant trouble going on in northern Sri Lanka. It used to operate three days a week in each direction except during the worst of the monsoon (usually November and December), and the crossing took about 3½ hours. Fares were less than a quarter of the cheapest Colombo-India airfare at the time. From Talaimannar there is a railway through Anuradhapura to Colombo.

TOURS

The majority of visitors to Sri Lanka come on package tours – mainly from Europe – which typically divide their time about equally between touring the hill country (and maybe the ancient cities) and relaxing in beach hotels. The Sri Lanka part of such trips usually costs between US$200 and US$400 a week, to which you must add the airfare, which will be at discount rates. On some holidays it's possible to stay on at your own expense for an extra week or two before flying home. This is worth considering for people who fancy some independent travel but would like a guiding hand to start with. Sri Lanka Tourist Board offices (see Tourist Offices in Facts for the Visitor) can supply names of tour companies running Sri Lanka trips.

LEAVING SRI LANKA

Colombo is not like Bangkok or Singapore for hunting out cheap flights, and it's often cheaper to book your onward flight before you go, in conjunction with your inward flight. But there are a few agents in Colombo offering some savings on regular fares. George Travel (☎ 01-422347, 423447) on the 2nd floor at 29 Bristol St, Colombo Fort (the entrance is in the side of the Ex-Servicemen's Institute), is one of the most-used cheap agents. Another recommended by a reader is Gabo Travels (☎ 01-447559) at 59 Chatham St. Fares from Colombo quoted by George include: Singapore one way US$240, Singapore one-year return US$395, Darwin or Perth one way US$540, London one way US$480, Bangkok/Singapore-Hong Kong-Frankfurt/Amsterdam one year US$695, Bangkok-Jakarta-Singapore one year US$450, Bangkok-Athens-western Europe one year about US$650.

Booking & Reconfirming

When tourism is doing well, flights out of Sri Lanka can be heavily booked at the busiest times of year, particularly January, and if you do not have a reservation you could find yourself waiting some time for a flight out. Equally important, if you do have a reservation, reconfirm at least 72 hours ahead. Otherwise your seat confirmation may be cancelled. Air Lanka now has an office in Kandy as well as a few in Colombo, with others in Anuradhapura, Galle and Matara due to open soon.

Departure Tax

There is a Rs 500 airport tax on departure.

Getting Around

There are no internal passenger flights in Sri Lanka so public transport is a choice between buses and trains. Both are cheap but often overcrowded. At least there's enough public transport to enable everyone to move around the island fairly easily. On the whole, trains are a bit slower than buses, but a seat on a train is preferable to standing on a bus. Even standing on a train is better than standing on a bus, come to that.

A comfortable seat on a bus is often the best of all possibilities, but you won't know whether you'll get one till you're on board. If you think you won't, 2nd or even 3rd class on the train will probably leave you a lot less bedraggled at the end of the journey. Price-wise, a bus fare is usually between the 2nd and 3rd-class fares on a train. Railways don't reach some places, so then you have no choice but the bus.

All public transport gets particularly crowded around poya days and their nearest weekends, so it's good to avoid travelling then if you can.

BUS

There are now three kinds of bus in Sri Lanka, all cropping up on both long-distance and local routes. One is the old red 'government buses', run by what is officially called the Sri Lanka Transport Board (SLTB) but still universally known as the CTB – Central (formerly Ceylon) Transport Board. The second is the 'peoplised' buses – former CTB buses from depots which have been handed over to their workers' control under a privatisation programme which is ultimately intended to dissolve the CTB altogether. Some peoplised buses are repainted yellow, others remain red. Either way the only real difference seems to be that the service has deteriorated a little.

The third category of bus – which you'll probably use most often – is private buses. These range from the modern, quite large coaches used on some inter-city runs to decrepit old minibuses that limp along some city streets or on short inter-town or village runs. Private buses were reintroduced in the early 1980s when the CTB – a state monopoly created in the 1950s – had become inefficient, unreliable, and horrendously overcrowded.

In many cases private buses run parallel services in competition with the CTB or peoplised buses. There is very little difference in fares between the various types of bus. Typical fares from Colombo include Rs 16 for the two to 2½ hour trip to Hikkaduwa, Rs 25 to Kandy (2½ to three hours) and Rs 32 to Anuradhapura (five hours). CTB conductors seem less likely than private bus conductors to try to overcharge unwary travellers. To ensure you're not overcharged, check the price before you get on and make sure you get a ticket. The only buses which are significantly more expensive are the few 'express' private buses which run between Colombo and a few main towns.

Private buses are usually quicker than CTB services. Theoretically they should also be more comfortable than the bumpy, noisy CTB vehicles. In practice, however, their operators' desire for as much profit as possible results in some appalling overcrowding – such as routinely squeezing five people into four seats and allowing far too many standing passengers for safety, let alone comfort – and really dangerous driving as they race their rivals and pack as many journeys as possible into one day. Some of them are unfit to be on the roads and they are involved in far more than their fair share of the country's road accidents. As a result some people prefer CTB buses which, though slower, can be much more comfortable.

On buses and trains certain seats are reserved for women. Like the 'smoking prohibited' sign, this injunction is completely ignored; it's first come, first served.

On the other hand the first two seats are always reserved for 'clergy' (Buddhist monks) and this is never ignored – a pregnant woman would probably have to stand if a strapping teenage monk hopped on!

One traveller described this uniquely Sri Lankan experience:

A crowd of passengers wrestled for the best seats at the terminus where a CTB bus began its journey, only for the bus to pull in a few minutes later at a stop where no less than 11 monks were waiting – and 11 occupants of hard-won seats looked resignedly at each other and stood up.

We leave the final word on Sri Lankan buses to reader George Wright, who took a true busman's holiday:

One of my main reasons for going to Sri Lanka was to find the old Routemaster double decker London buses which formed part of a British aid package in 1988. I drive one in London and had this inexplicable urge to see them in their tropical home. Alas, I found out that 37 of the 40 are broken down – but my search for them took me to wacky and wonderful outposts of Colombo such as Maharagama, Kadawatha and Moratuwa. Being a rare white face arriving in these places, I was frequently mobbed by locals. How true it is that Sri Lankans are hospitable, friendly people.

I travelled every day on the buses and naturally preferred the CTB ones. As the 'boy' in my guest house said, 'Private buses...crazy men!'. Being a fan of public transport I was sad to see the dilapidated state of all their vehicles, and sadder still to see the Routemasters dumped in depots. Sri Lanka desperately needs *more* buses!

TRAIN

Train travel in Sri Lanka can be pretty good. It's generally nowhere near as crowded as in India and the simple act of buying a ticket involves none of the Indian-style bureaucratic hassles. Although the trains are quite slow, with badly deteriorated track in some places, the distances are short so there are few overnight or all-day ordeals to contend with. Generally a train ride is a more relaxed experience than a bus ride.

Life does not revolve around the railway stations to anything like the same extent as it does in India. Railway station restaurants are generally terrible in Sri Lanka, whereas they're little havens of safe, reasonable-quality food in India. But there are railway retiring rooms at certain stations, including Galle and Kandy, which are worth remembering for accommodation when all else fails.

Be a little cautious on the trains, particularly at night. The Talaimannar-Colombo service used to be notorious for thieves relieving sleepy travellers of their belongings. One traveller wrote of a far more frightening incident as he sat in an open doorway on a train approaching Colombo one night. Somebody simply pushed him out. Luckily he landed from the slow-moving train with nothing more than cuts and bruises but, of course, all his possessions were gone.

Information

There's a Railway Tourist Office (☎ 01-435838) at Fort Station, Colombo, which is one of the most helpful and knowledgeable information places in the country. Its staff can sell you the useful publication *This Month in Sri Lanka* which includes the main train services and fares. National rail timetables can be bought at some stations, but tend to be a bit out of date.

As in India, station masters often have considerable discretionary powers. When the seats are all 'booked out' a polite request will often find a seat for a foreign visitor.

Routes

There are three lines of most importance to travellers. One is from Colombo down the west coast to Aluthgama, Hikkaduwa, Galle and Matara. The second is from Colombo east up through Nanu Oya (the station for Nuwara Eliya) and Haputale in the hill country, to Badulla, with a branch for Kandy. The third goes north from Colombo to Anuradhapura. There are branches from the Anuradhapura line to Trincomalee and Batticaloa on the east coast, and continuations from Anuradhapura to Talaimannar, Jaffna and Kankesanturai, but services on all these are subject to the security situation. The line into Jaffna has reportedly been pulled up by Tamil Tiger rebels.

Classes & Fares

The cost of train travel depends on which class you go in. Third class, with wooden benches for seating, is economical by any standards. Second class has more comfortable seats and is generally less crowded, though you can't be certain of a seat on some busy services. First class, which is nearly double the cost of 2nd class, means either a seat in an observation saloon (pulled at the rear of the train, with all-round glass and comfortable seats) or a 1st-class sleeping berth. At the time of writing only three trains, all on the Colombo-Badulla line, have 1st-class accommodation.

Fares on the roughly 250-km, nine-hour Colombo-Haputale run, for instance, are Rs 203.50 in 1st class, Rs 116.75 in 2nd class, and Rs 42.25 in 3rd class. All sleeping berths are an extra Rs 50 in 1st class or Rs 30 in 2nd, and sleeperettes Rs 15 2nd or Rs 12 in 3rd. The 2nd and 1st-class sleeping berths are individual twin-bunked rooms which are the last word in Asian train comfort – if you've just come from India, anyway.

CAR & MOTORBIKE

Motorbike and self-drive car hire are not as popular in Sri Lanka as in some Asian countries, but they're becoming more so. More common is renting a car with a driver – in effect a long- distance taxi – for a day-trip or a few days' tour of a region. If you're on a relatively short visit to Sri Lanka with a middle-range budget, the cost of this can be quite reasonable.

Being Driven

You can find drivers in all the main tourist centres who will happily become your chauffeur for a day or a few. Guest house owners will probably be able to put you in touch with a driver. Or you can ask taxi drivers or, probably more expensive, travel agents, the big hotels or the self-drive car hire firms in Colombo, which also have chauffeur-driven vehicles. The advantages of being driven rather than taking public transport include door-to-door travel, stops of your own choosing, easy baggage handling, and

greater comfort and speed. You also have a ready-made guide. And you don't have the responsibilities that go with driving yourself such as looking after the vehicle and avoiding the dangers on the road.

Prices depend to a large extent on distance. One day typically costs Rs 1500 or Rs 2000. For longer periods the daily rate should come down, and shared between a few passengers this doesn't seem so bad, especially when you remember that some taxis are minibuses which can easily take six or eight passengers. The price of petrol – Rs 30 a litre at the time of writing – is an aid to working out a fair price. But remember that some vehicles run on diesel, which is much cheaper at Rs 11 a litre. The supposedly fixed rates for long-distance taxis from some towns could function as a top-end bargaining level: for example, from Hikkaduwa it's supposed to be Rs 1400 to Colombo or Rs 3500 to Kandy. Drivers will usually find their own accommodation and meals and you normally won't have to pay any extra for these, but it's wise to check on this at the outset. On a one-way journey you should expect to account for the driver's return petrol in the price. If you're offered what seems an amazingly low price, think twice as there may be some rip-off in store.

The biggest disadvantage of going by car (with or without a driver), even if the cost is not a consideration, is that you lose some of the day-to-day contact with Sri Lankan life and the Sri Lankans which public transport always provides.

Self-Drive Car Rentals

The major car hire companies operating in Sri Lanka are:

Quickshaw's Ltd
    8 York St, Colombo 1 (☎ 01-28511) and 3 Kalinga Place, Colombo 5 (☎ 01-583133-5); representing Hertz
Mackinnons Travel Ltd
    4 Leyden Bastion Rd, Colombo 1 (☎ 01-29881); representing Avis
Mercantile Tours (Ceylon) Ltd
    568 Galle Rd, Colombo 3 (☎ 01-500578/9, 500687/8)

Mackinnons is probably in the lead when it comes to self- drive rates. A Datsun Sunny, for which it's advisable to book ahead, is Rs 550 per day or Rs 3300 per week plus Rs 4 per km. With unlimited km it's Rs 4900 a week. A Mitsubishi Colt with air-con is Rs 650 per day or Rs 3900 per week plus Rs 5 per km, or Rs 6000 a week with unlimited km. These prices include fully comprehensive insurance. In addition, you must pay a refundable deposit of Rs 3000, or a non-refundable collision damage waiver of Rs 125 a day. With any of the firms, if you're paying by cash as opposed to a credit card you may need to surrender your outward air ticket to them for the rental period as a guarantee. See the following Driving Yourself section for licence requirements.

There's a minimum age of 23 with Mackinnons, 25 with Quickshaw's, and a maximum of 65 with either. Generally you're not allowed to take the car into national parks, wildlife sanctuaries or jungle, or along other unmade roads.

There are also one or two less formal car rental places around the island, with rates comparable to Colombo. See the Negombo section for info on one outfit.

Driving Yourself

While researching an earlier edition of this guide Tony rented a Daihatsu Charade for 15 days, during which time he covered 2710 km. A small car like a Charade – comparable in size to a Honda Civic, Austin Metro or VW Polo – is really all you need for Sri Lanka. The distances are not great and despite your slow speed you won't be cooped up in it for too long.

Finding your way round the country is no problem at all; there are milestones or km markers on all the major roads and Sri Lankan maps indicate where these are, so you can always tell exactly where you are and how far it is to the next town or junction.

Paperwork You must obtain a temporary Sri Lankan driving licence, for which you need to show your home country driving licence and preferably an International Driving Permit too. If you have an International Driving Permit, all you need do is get it endorsed by the Automobile Association of Ceylon (☎ 01-421528/9), 40 Sir Macan Markar Mawatha, Galle Face, Colombo 3 (next to the Holiday Inn). The process takes only a few minutes and the association is open from Monday to Friday except holidays. If you hire a car, the renter will probably obtain the endorsement for you for a small fee. If you turn up with only your home country driver's licence, however, you'll have to pay Rs 600 for a special permit from the Registrar of Motor Vehicles on Elvitigala Mawatha in Colombo 5.

On the Road Speed limits are 55 kp/h in built up areas and 70 kp/h in the country. Petrol is widely available. The Automobile Association of Ceylon can supply information on road conditions and answer other driving queries.

Although you may see a number of accidents during your time on the road, driving seems fairly safe overall if you take care. You have to watch out for sudden unexpected manoeuvres by other road users, particularly private bus drivers. Whenever you meet an oncoming car you have to slow right down because the road is usually not wide enough and each car will have to pull part way off. Also watch out for the unpredictable nature of pedestrians and cyclists. Any cyclist may suddenly decide to make a completely unannounced U-turn at any time and for no apparent reason. Apart from the Colombo-Kandy, Colombo-Negombo and Colombo-Galle roads, which are crowded, traffic is usually quite light. But you don't travel at any great speed for the roads are narrow and potholed, and there is often much pedestrian, bicycle and animal traffic to navigate around. Even on the odd stretch where the road is clear you still have to proceed cautiously and slowly because bumps, dips and severe potholes can appear almost anywhere.

Punctures seem to be a way of life – the roads are hard on tyres and the tyres are not always in A1 condition to start with. During

Tony's circuit of Sri Lanka he had three punctures, two of them through picking up nails. Every little village seems to have a puncture-repair specialist who will do an excellent, though rather time-consuming, repair using decidedly primitive equipment. A tube patch will be vulcanised on by attaching a metal container to the appropriate place, filling it with kerosene and setting the kerosene aflame!

Mechanical repairs, should you be so unfortunate as to need them, are likely to be equally ingenious. 'Our jeep broke down three times', wrote another wheeled traveller. 'Twice with a broken axle! Every time there was willing, constructive help available.'

Motorbike

Motorcycles are a reasonable alternative for intrepid travellers. Distances are relatively short and some of the roads are simply a motorcyclist's delight – other drivers sometimes excepted! There are lots of places renting bikes in Hikkaduwa and Negombo, with daily rental rates ranging from about Rs 200 to Rs 300 for 125 cc machines, or Rs 275 to Rs 350 for 250 cc. On top of that you'll be spending about Rs 3 a km on petrol. Helmets may be extra too. You can get discounts for periods of a few days or longer – but check the insurance position and the bike itself carefully before you agree on a deal. Get a bike that will cope well with bumpy roads. In Colombo you can enquire at the tourist office, or try Two Wheel Tours (☎ 01-553757) at Mirihana, Nugegoda, also contactable through Mackinnons Travel at 4 Leyden Bastion Rd, Fort.

BICYCLE

Keen round-the-world cyclists will probably find Sri Lanka a joy, apart from the uphill sections of the hill country, but hiring a bike in Sri Lanka is often far from that. We have hired bikes in Anuradhapura, Polonnaruwa, Kalkudah, Hikkaduwa and Negombo, and with a few exceptions they ranged from barely reasonable to diabolical. You cer-

tainly wouldn't use them for any long-distance riding.

Flat tyres come with alarming regularity and if one brake works with 25% efficiency you're doing well (one bike Maureen was handed in Polonnaruwa had absolutely no brakes at all; ever tried stopping a bike with your feet on the ground in an emergency?).

Bringing your own bicycle to explore the country is quite a different story. The following account comes from Ian Anderson, England:

As a cyclist I would recommend Sri Lanka because its size means it can easily be covered in six weeks or so. The usual advantages that a cyclist has in mobility and independence are emphasised when you look at crowded trains and minibuses.

There are disadvantages. Number one is the state of the roads, which range from very poor to appalling, especially around the monsoon period. I was able to go on flooded roads that no four-wheeled transport could use but this required a combination of wading, swimming, wheeling the bike along handy railway lines and, when necessary, hiring a canoe! It all adds to the interest.

I would recommend bringing a good supply of spare tyres and tubes as these can suffer excessively from the poor road surface. The normal size bicycle tyre in Sri Lanka is 28" x 1½". Some imported 27" tyres for our 10-speed bikes are available but only in a few shops in Colombo and at high prices. Suriyages Ltd (☎ 01-91505), 524 Maradana Rd, Colombo 10 is a possible source of parts.

A second problem with bicycling in Sri Lanka is the driving of some bus drivers. Few Sri Lankans can resist sounding their horns at every opportunity – it usually means 'Look what a big vehicle I am' or 'I'm coming through regardless'! On the other hand, outside the towns traffic is very light and as long as you keep your wits about you and accept a certain lack of signals or predictable behaviour by other road users or pedestrians, you should be OK.

I recommend a good lock when your bike is out of sight or else constant vigilance, particularly in small villages. Early starts are essential due to the heat. The distances you cover will be limited by the state of the roads and a large amount of 'eyes down' cycling will be necessary. Brings lots of sunblock. You can take your bike on the trains but at 'parcel rate' it costs about twice the 3rd-class passenger fare.

Gilles Rubens of the Netherlands adds:

We found that from Hikkaduwa to Colombo the traffic was too busy to enjoy riding, which implies getting involved with the Sri Lankan railway bureau-cracy. Every part of the bicycle has to be described on the travel documents (even bells, lights and pad-locks). Therefore you should deliver the bicycle at least half an hour before the departure of the train.

LOCAL TRANSPORT

Many Sri Lankan towns are on a small enough scale to walk around but when they aren't you have a choice, in ascending price order, between buses, three-wheelers, and taxis.

Bus

Buses go to most places including villages outside towns. They may be CTB, peoplised or private, and they may be real buses or old minibuses designed for a dozen people but holding three dozen. Their signboards are usually in Sinhala, so you have to check by asking which is your right bus. Fares are low – for instance the five km, 15-minute trip from Galle to Unawatuna is usually Rs 3.

Three-Wheeler

These vehicles – known in other parts of Asia as tuk-tuks, bajajs or auto-rickshaws – have increased markedly in numbers in recent years, a welcome development as they're much more convenient than a bus and cheaper than a taxi. They're usually painted yellow. You must agree on the fare before you get in. A two-km journey should cost about Rs 30. Curiously, bicycle rickshaws are nowhere to be seen in Sri Lanka. Three-wheelers and taxis waiting outside tourist hotels and similar places expect higher than usual fares.

Taxi

Sri Lankan taxis often used to be quaint old British Morris Minors, but in recent years these have mostly been replaced by more modern vehicles, including some minibuses. They're common enough in all the sizeable towns and even some villages will be able to dig out a taxi from somewhere. Only a few are metered and even with them it can be advisable to agree on the fare before you get in, as you never know how fast a meter will tick over. A two-km trip should cost Rs 50 or Rs 60.

Colombo

Sri Lanka's easy-going biggest city (around one million population) holds less of obvious interest than many other parts of the island – but it's a colourful enough place and, as the country's political, economic and cultural centre, worth a visit if you want to understand a little of what makes Sri Lanka tick. The odds are high that you'll pass through Colombo at some time during your visit, and you'll find yourself there in any case if you need to extend your entry permit, or perhaps if you need to buy flight tickets or conduct some other business. Colombo is by no means overwhelming and its centre (known as 'Fort', although there is little sign of that today) is distinctly handy and very easy to get around on foot.

If Colombo doesn't appeal to you, you need hardly touch it. If your flight arrives in the morning you can travel straight from the airport (30 km north of the city) to another destination the same day, perhaps just changing transport in the city; if not, you could stay near the airport or make the resort-cum-fishing town of Negombo, 10 km north of the airport, your first stop.

Kotte, on the south-east fringe of Colombo, was the capital of a major Sinhalese kingdom in the pre-colonial era. Today, under the name Sri Jayawardenepura-Kotte (which bears a trace of ex-presidential ego!) it's again the administrative capital, with a 1980s purpose-built parliament. Colombo itself, which was the capital under the British and in the first four independence decades, rose to prominence in the 19th century. Until its harbour was created in the 1870s, Galle had been a bigger port.

ORIENTATION

Once you've got a few directions down, you'll find Colombo relatively easy to find your way around. From the visitor's point of view it's virtually a long coastal strip extending 10 or 12 km south from the central area, Fort or Colombo 1. The spine of this strip is Galle Rd – which eventually leaves Colombo far behind and ends up in Galle. But first, if you head straight inland from Fort you quickly come to the Pettah, Colombo 11. Colombo's main railway station, Fort, is actually in the Pettah, and so are the main bus stations – all 10 or 15 minutes' walk from Fort itself.

Travelling down Galle Rd, south from Fort, you come first to Galle Face Green, inland from which is Slave Island (Colombo 2), which isn't really an island at all since only two of its three sides are surrounded by water. (But it really was used for keeping slaves in the Dutch era.) The Galle Face Green area and neighbouring Kollupitiya are Colombo 3. Next along Galle Rd are Bambalapitiya (Colombo 4) and Wellawatta (Colombo 6), followed by Dehiwala and the old beach resort Mt Lavinia, which aren't officially part of Colombo at all but are definitely within its urban sprawl. Finding addresses along Galle Rd is slightly complicated by the street numbers starting again at one as you move into each new district. Thus there will be a 100 Galle Rd in Colombo 3, again in Colombo 4, again in Colombo 6, again in Dehiwala, and again in Mt Lavinia.

If you turned inland (east) along Dharmapala Mawatha in Kollupitiya you'd soon find yourself in Cinnamon Gardens (Colombo 7) – home for the art gallery, museum, university, Viharamahadevi Park (the city's biggest), the most exclusive residential quarters, and many embassies. Some Colombo streets have an old name and a new name, both in common use. The road running through Viharamahadevi Park is called both Ananda Kumaraswamy Mawatha and Green Path; R A De Mel Mawatha, which runs parallel to Galle Rd for a few km, is also still known as Duplication Rd. Some alternative names are given in brackets in this chapter.

Maps

The tourist offices give out a leaflet with a reasonable map of the city. If you're going to be spending any time in Colombo the Survey Department's *Tourist Map of Colombo* or the handy little *A to Z Colombo* street directory will come in useful. The A to Z does not extend as far south as Dehiwala and Mt Lavinia but it does include info on city buses and where you can board them in the centre. Both the Tourist Map and the A to Z are available from the Survey Department Map Sales Centre on York St, open from Monday to Friday 9 am to 4 pm (Rs 100 for the A to Z). Pavement sellers and hotel bookshops may sell them too, at a mark-up.

INFORMATION
Tourist Offices

The Sri Lanka Tourist Board has information desks at the airport (☎ 452411) and at its head office (☎ 437059, 437060) on Galle Rd at 78 Steuart Place, Colombo 3, opposite the Lanka Oberoi hotel. They cover not just Colombo but the whole island, and can help with hotel bookings as well as answer queries and hand out the accommodation guide and leaflets. Opening hours of the Galle Rd office are from Monday to Friday 8.30 am to 4.45 pm, Saturday 8.30 am to 12.30 pm, and closed Sunday.

The helpful Railway Tourist Office (☎ 435838) at Fort Station can often help with non-railway info too – open from Monday to Friday 8.30 am to 4.30 pm.

The Tourist Police (☎ 26941, or 21111 extension 218) are in the New Secretariat Building on Sir Baron Jayatillake Mawatha just round the corner from the main post office in Fort.

Money

Most of the main banks are in Fort. There are also several exchange offices open outside normal banking hours. One is the Bank of Ceylon Bureau de Change on York St, Fort, just down from the Grand Oriental Hotel, which is open from Monday to Friday 9 am to 6 pm, Saturday and Sunday 9 am to 4 pm. Others include the People's Bank, 27 Bristol St, Fort (from Monday to Friday 9 am to 3 pm, Saturday 9 am to 1 pm); Thomas Cook, 15 Sir Baron Jayatillake Mawatha, Fort (from Monday to Friday 8.30 am to 4.30 pm, Saturday 10 am to 12.30 pm); and several bank branches in the arrivals hall at the airport (open for all flight arrivals). You can change money or travellers' cheques at reduced rates in the main hotels.

The American Express representative is MacKinnons Travels (☎ 29881) in the MacKinnons Building at 4 Leyden Bastion Rd, Fort, but the customer service section – including card services – is 10 minutes' walk away on the 2nd floor of Steuart House, 45 Janadhipathi Mawatha. Visa and MasterCard holders can get cash or travellers' cheques with their cards at the Hongkong & Shanghai Bank (☎ 25435), 24 Sir Baron Jayatillake Mawatha.

Post & Telecommunications

Colombo General Post Office is on Janadhipathi Mawatha in Fort. It's open for stamp sales and domestic phone calls 24 hours, seven days a week; for poste restante from 8 am to 5 pm daily; for telegrams from Monday to Saturday 7 am to 7 pm, and Sunday 8 am to 1.30 pm; and for international phone calls Monday to Saturday 8 am to 7 pm, and Sunday 8 am to 5 pm. The efficient poste restante holds mail for two months, and accepts parcels and telegrams as well as letters: you can call 26203 to ask if there's anything awaiting you. Stamp collectors may want to visit the Sri Lanka Philatelic Bureau, 4th floor, Ceylinco House, Janadhipathi Mawatha, Fort.

International phone calls from the main post office are operator-connected, with a one hour or so wait. Quicker, but a bit more expensive, are the private enterprise communication centres littered around Fort and on Galle Rd, such as Unique Communication Service in Mudalige Mawatha, or the agency post offices like Salaka in the bazaar next to Fort Station. These also offer regular post office services plus fax, telex and photocopying.

Mail addressed c/o American Express is

held for collection on the 2nd floor of Steuart House, 45 Janadhipathi Mawatha, even though the address to have it sent to is MacKinnons Travels, PO Box 945, 4 Leyden Bastion Rd, Colombo 1.

Colombo phone numbers are often changed – you can get info on new numbers by calling 575211.

Foreign Embassies
Consulates and embassies in Colombo include:

Australia
    High Commission, 3 Cambridge Place, Colombo 7 (☎ 698767-9)
Austria
    Consulate, 424 Union Place, Colombo 2 (☎ 691613)
Bangladesh
    High Commission, 286 Bauddhaloka Mawatha, Colombo 7 (☎ 502198)
Canada
    High Commission, 6 Gregory's Rd, Colombo 7 (☎ 695841-3)
Denmark
    Consulate-General, 264 Grandpass Rd, Colombo 14 (☎ 447806)
Finland
    Embassy, 81 Barnes Place, Colombo 7 (☎ 698819, 699568)
France
    Embassy, 89 Rosmead Place, Colombo 7 (☎ 699750)
Germany
    Embassy, 40 Alfred House Ave, Colombo 3 (☎ 580431-4)
India
    High Commission, 36-38 Galle Rd, Colombo 3 (☎ 421604, 422788)
Italy
    Embassy, 55 Jawatha Rd, Colombo 5 (☎ 588622, 588388)
Japan
    Embassy, 20 Gregory's Rd, Colombo 7 (☎ 693831-3, 698628-9)
Malaysia
    High Commission, 87 Horton Place, Colombo 7 (☎ 694837, 696591)
Maldives
    Embassy, 25 Melbourne Ave, Colombo 4 (☎ 586762, 500943)
Myanmar (Burma)
    Embassy, 17 Skelton Gardens, Colombo 5 (☎ 587607/8)

Nepal
    Consulate-General, 5th Floor, 52 Galle Rd, Colombo 4 (☎ 583536, 502139)
Netherlands
    Embassy, 25 Torrington Ave, Colombo 7 (☎ 589626-8)
New Zealand
    Consulate, 185 Fife Rd, Colombo 5 (☎ 581385)
Pakistan
    Embassy, 211 De Saram Place, Colombo 10 (☎ 696301-2)
Russia
    Embassy, 62 Sir Ernest De Silva Mawatha, Colombo 7 (☎ 573555, 573657)
Spain
    Consulate, 36 D R Wijewardene Mawatha, Colombo 10 (☎ 434446, 447789)
Sweden
    Embassy, 315 Vauxhall St, Colombo 2 (☎ 435870, 540479)
Switzerland
    Embassy, 1st Floor, Baur's Building, 7 Upper Chatham St, Colombo 1 (☎ 447157, 447663)
Thailand
    Embassy, 43 Dr C W W Kannangara Mawatha (Alexandra Place), Colombo 7 (☎ 697406)
UK
    High Commission, 190 Galle Rd, Colombo 3 (☎ 437336-9)
USA
    Embassy, 210 Galle Rd, Colombo 3 (☎ 421271, 448007)

Cultural Centres & Libraries
The British Council (☎ 581171) is at 49 Alfred House Gardens, Colombo 3, just inland of R A De Mel Mawatha, two blocks south of the Hotel Empress. It puts on regular free cultural events including films (usually Fridays and Saturdays), exhibitions and lectures. It has a library, open from Tuesday to Saturday 8.30 am to 6 pm, for which there's a minimal membership fee.

The American Center (☎ 691461, 694662) at 39 Sir Ernest De Silva Mawatha, Colombo 7, also puts on films, seminars and so on. Its library – open from Tuesday to Saturday 10 am to 6 pm, membership free – includes news videos and newspapers. You don't have to be American to use it. The Alliance Française (☎ 694162) is located at 11 Barnes Place, Colombo 7, just east of Viharamahadevi Park, has similar events (film night Wednesday) and another library.

The German Cultural Institute (☎ 694562) is at 39 Gregory's Rd, Colombo 7.

The Colombo Public Library (☎ 696156) on Ananda Kumaraswamy Mawatha (Green Path) at the west end of Viharamahadevi Park, Colombo 7, has a reference section and a wide selection of foreign periodicals. It's open daily except Wednesdays and holidays from 8 am to 6 pm.

Books & Bookshops

The *Colombo Handbook* published by the American Women's Association is a 240-page reference book telling you where to locate anything from medical care to a one-girl orchestra. You can buy it in some city bookshops for up to Rs 350. One of the widest ranges of books in English is at Lake House Book Shop at 100 Sir C A Gardiner Mawatha in Colombo 2. Other good Colombo bookshops include K V G De Silva (Kandy) in the YMBA Building at the corner of Sir Baron Jayatillake Mawatha and Lotus Rd, Fort; K V G De Silva (Colombo) at 415 Galle Rd, Colombo 4; and the bookshops in most of the major hotels. Hotel bookshops have some of the best ranges but tend to mark prices up. Cargill's on York St, Fort, also has books.

Some interesting finds are likely to turn up in second-hand bookshops like Bibliomania, 32 Hospital St, Fort, or Asoka Trading at 183 Galle Rd, Colombo 4, which has a marvellous collection of tatty old books. Serendib Gallery at 100 Galle Rd, Colombo 4, sells antiquarian books.

Medical Services

If you have to go to hospital, the private sector (where a consultation is at least Rs 150) is likely to offer better care. Nawaloka Hospital (☎ 544444, 546258) at 23 Sri Saugathodaya Mawatha, Colombo 2, has emergency care and an English-speaking doctor available 24 hours a day. Durdans Hospital (☎ 575205/6) at 3 Alfred Place, Colombo 3, also has a doctor available 24 hours. The Joseph Fraser Nursing Home (☎ 588466, 588385-6) on Joseph Fraser Rd, Colombo 5, is run on the lines of a British

nursing home and has its own operating rooms, but you have to arrange your own physician.

The main public hospital, Colombo General (☎ 691111) on Regent St, Colombo 8, has few in-patient facilities, though its intensive care unit is reportedly adequate. Its accident ward is on Ward Place at De Soysa Circus (Lipton Circus), Colombo 7 (for an ambulance call 422222). For a Red Cross Society ambulance call 691905 or 695434. Other public and private hospitals and clinics are listed in the *Official Tourist Handbook* and *This Month in Sri Lanka*. The state-run pharmacy Osu Sala (☎ 694716) at De Soysa Circus is open 24 hours.

Buddhism

The Buddhist Information Centre (☎ 23079) at 50 Ananda Kumaraswamy Mawatha (Green Path), Colombo 7, has a good selection of books on Buddhism. The Gangaramaya Bhikku Training Centre at 61 Sri Jinarathana Rd, off Sir James Peiris Mawatha, Colombo 2, has a library on Buddhism and other religions – ask at the temple office if you want to visit it. Meditation classes are sometimes held in English, German and French.

Left Luggage

There are left-luggage facilities at the airport (see the Colombo chapter, Getting There & Away) and in the cloakroom on platform 3 of Fort Station, open daily from 5 am to 8 or 9 pm, where the daily charge is Rs 2 a bag.

THINGS TO SEE & DO
Fort

During the Portuguese and Dutch periods 'Fort' was indeed a fort. Today it is simply the commercial centre of Sri Lanka, with most of the major offices and big hotels, and many of Colombo's top shops – not to mention airline offices, banks, the main post office, immigration office, travel agents, restaurants, and countless street hustlers ready to sell you anything from a padded bra to a carved mask. The government-run Laksala (in the Australia Building on York St) has a

Top: Masks, Ambalangoda (TW)
Bottom: Elephants, Navam Perahera, Colombo (JN)

Top Left: Ruvan Welijiya, Anuradhapura (TW) Top Right: Diyaluma Falls, Haputale (JN)
Middle: Palm Paradise Cabanas, Tangalla (TW)
Bottom Left: Temple of the Tooth, Kandy (JN) Bottom Right: Tangalla (JN)

Top: Offerings Stall, Kataragama (JN)
Middle: Dancers, Kandy (TW)
Bottom: Stilt Fishermen, Weligama (PT)

Top: Wewurukannala Vihara, near Matara (PS)
Bottom: The Temple of the Tooth, illuminated at night, Kandy (TW)

complete exhibition of Sinhalese handicrafts expertise; far more than just a shop. On the same street Cargill's and Millers are two delightfully old-fashioned department stores with ancient brass signs and wooden display cabinets. But in the main it's Fort's street life which attracts attention. Here you'll see everything from briefcase-toting city workers to Buddhist monks, apprentice snake charmers to uniformed young school-girls.

A good landmark in Fort is the clock tower at the junction of Chatham St and Janadhipathi Mawatha (once Queen St), which 140 years ago was a lighthouse. It's almost exactly midway between the big Ceylon Intercontinental Hotel and the main post office. Other sights in Fort include the president's residence (known as 'Queen's House') opposite the main post office, the busy port area, and, just up Marine Drive from the immigration office, a large white dagoba perched about 20 metres off the ground on stilts – a major landmark for those approaching by sea – which you can ascend by a staircase if you first remove your shoes and socks.

Fort now has a cluster of high-rise hotels and banks, but colonial-era office buildings also give it an air of great Victorian cities like Melbourne and Manchester. St Peter's Church near the Grand Oriental Hotel was converted from the Dutch governor's banquet hall and first used as a church in 1804.

Galle Face Green

Immediately south of Fort is Galle Face Green – a long expanse of grass by the seafront. Life goes on round the clock on the green whether it's an early morning cricket match, a lovers' midday meeting beneath a discreet umbrella, or a late evening stroll. Galle Face Green is at its busiest on Saturday and especially Sunday evenings when dozens of food stalls gather here. Facing each other from opposite ends of the green are the delightful old Galle Face Hotel and the contemporary Ceylon Intercontinental. Beware of people who strike up a conversa-tion while walking beside you along the green and eventually ask for money for a blind school or some such cause – they are con artists.

Galle Rd

Galle Rd is noisy, polluted and little pleasure to walk along, but it's dotted with some of Colombo's better restaurants, shops and shopping centres and, near the north end, one or two other places of note like the Indian and British high commissions, the US Embassy, and the prime minister's official residence 'Temple Trees', opposite the UK High Commission. The 1842 St Andrew's Scots Kirk stands a long way from the bonny Highlands on Galle Rd in Kollupitiya, next to the Lanka Oberoi hotel.

Pettah

Adjacent to Fort and immediately inland from it is the Pettah, Colombo's bustling bazaar area. You name it and some shop or street stall will be selling it in the Pettah. Each street seems to have its own speciality. Colombo's bus and railway stations are on the south and east fringes of the Pettah.

Places of Worship The Pettah harbours many mosques and Hindu temples – see the later sections with those headings. The 1749 Wolvendaal Church on Wolfendhal St is Colombo's oldest Dutch church, and still holds services – in English and Tamil – on Sunday mornings. Its floor is made of tombstones from a Dutch church in Fort, moved here in 1813.

Museum The Dutch Period Museum at 95 Prince St, Pettah, has at various times been the Dutch town hall, a residence, an orphan-age, a hospital, a police station and a post office. Now restored to its former glory, with a pleasant garden-courtyard, it's open from Monday to Friday, 9 am to 5 pm.

Cinnamon Gardens

Cinnamon Gardens, or Colombo 7, is Colombo's ritziest address, full of large res-idences and embassies, four or five km south

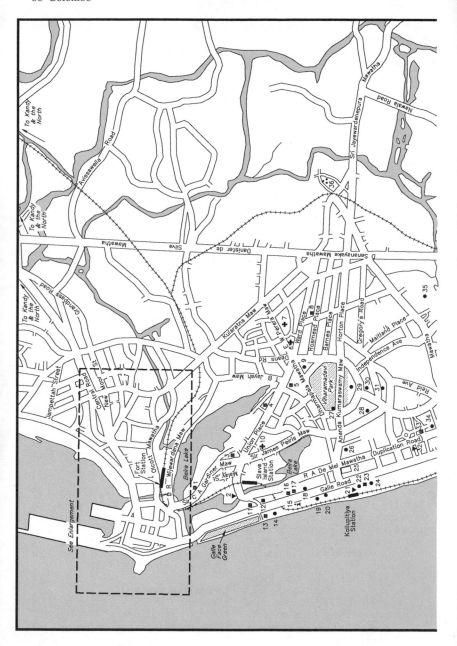

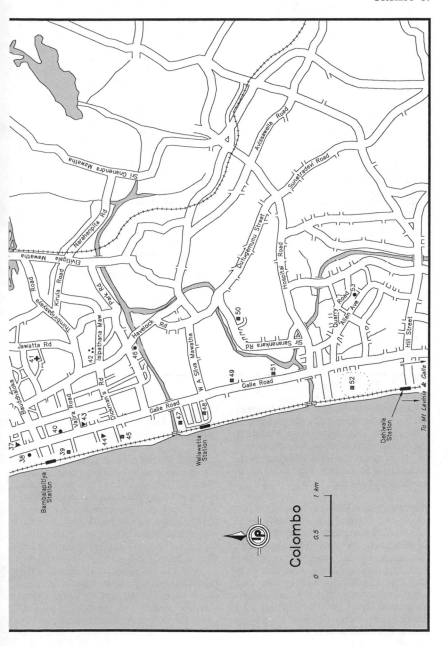

■ PLACES TO STAY

1	Ramada Renaissance Hotel
3	Hotel Nippon
4	YWCA International
5	Hotel Galaxy
8	A Wayfarer's Inn
11	Taj Samudra Hotel
12	Holiday Inn
13	Galle Face Hotel
16	Lanka Oberol
17	YWCA National Headquarters
23	Hotel Renuka
33	Hotel Empress
39	Youth Hostel
45	Ottery Inn
47	Island Pride Beach Inn
48	Chanuka Guest House
49	Hotel Sapphire
50	Star Inn
51	Hotel Ceylon Inns
52	Dehiwala Cheap Accommodation

▼ PLACES TO EAT

2	Fountain Cafe
21	Restaurant Ginza Araliya
32	Saras
37	Green Cabin
43	Sapid Restaurant
44	Greenlands Hotel

OTHER

6	Colombo General Hospital Accident Ward
7	Colombo General Hospital
9	Town Hall
10	Nawaloka Hospital
14	Indian High Commission
15	Sri Lanka Tourist Board
18	Temple Trees
19	British High Commission
20	US Embassy
22	Sri Lanka Gem & Jewellery Exchange
24	PIA
25	Liberty Plaza
26	Buddhist Information Centre
27	Library
28	American Center
29	National Museum
30	Australian High Commission
31	Lionel Wendt Centre
34	British Council
35	Bandaranaike Conference Hall
36	Gotami Vihari
38	Barefoot
40	Sri Lanka Handlooms Emporium
41	Joseph Fraser Nursing Home
42	Isipathanaramaya Temple
46	Lumbini Theatre
53	Zoo

of Fort and one to three km inland. A century ago it was covered in cinnamon plantations. Today, as well as elegant tree-lined streets and the mansions of the wealthy and powerful, it harbours the city's biggest park, several sports grounds and a cluster of museums and galleries.

Viharamahadevi Park The focus of the area is Colombo's biggest park, originally called Victoria Park but renamed in the 1950s after the mother of the early Sinhalese leader, Dutugemunu. It's notable for its superb flowering trees in March, April and early May. Cutting across the middle of the park is the broad avenue Ananda Kumaraswamy Mawatha (Green Path). North of this are a funfair and mini-zoo. Colombo's big white domed Town Hall overlooks the park from

the north-east. Working elephants sometimes overnight in the park, happily chomping on palm branches.

National Museum Housed in a fine colonial-era building on Albert Crescent, just south of Viharamahadevi Park, the museum has a good collection of ancient royal regalia, Sinhalese artwork (carvings, sculptures, and so on), antique furniture and china, and ola-leaf manuscripts. There are fascinating reproductions of English paintings of Ceylon from 1848 to 1850, and an excellent collection of antique demon masks. But the high point, leaving culture totally to one side, would have to be the superbly awful collection of presents that heads of state feel obliged to shower upon other heads of state! Upstairs is a children's section with a good puppets of the world display and live shows at weekends.

Admission to the museum is Rs 40 and it is open daily except Friday, from 9 am to 5 pm. Get there on a bus No 114 or 138 from Fort Station.

Other Museums & Galleries The national Art Gallery at 106 Ananda Kumaraswamy Mawatha (Green Path) is just across the road from Viharamahadevi Park. It's open daily from 8 am to 5 pm, except poya days. The permanent collection is mostly portraits but there are also temporary exhibits of Sri Lankan artists. The Natural History Museum next door, open daily from 9 am to 5 pm, includes a display on the Mahaweli hydro-power-cum-irrigation scheme. For a view of Sri Lankan art since the 1920s, visit the Sapumal Foundation at 32/4 Barnes Place, which houses the Harry Peiris collection – open from Thursday to Saturday, 10 am to 1 pm, admission free. The Lionel Wendt Centre at 18 Guildford Crescent puts on contemporary art and craft exhibitions.

The Bandaranaike Museum in the Bandaranaike Conference Hall on Bauddhaloka Mawatha, Colombo 7, tells of the life, times and assassination of the 1950s Prime Minister Solomon Bandaranaike. It's open daily from 9 am to 4 pm, except Mondays and poya days.

Buddhist Temples
Colombo is a relatively young city so there are no great religious monuments of any age. The most important Buddhist centre is the Kelaniya Raja Maha Vihara seven km east of Fort, a short distance off the Kandy road. The Buddha is reputed to have preached here on a visit to Sri Lanka over 2000 years ago. The temple later constructed on the spot was destroyed by Indian invaders, restored, destroyed again by the Portuguese, and restored again in the 18th and 19th centuries. The dagoba, which is unusual in being hollow, is the focus of a major perahera (procession) in January each year. There is a very fine reclining Buddha image here. To reach the temple take bus No 235 from in front of the police barracks on Olcott Mawatha, to the east of the main CTB bus station.

Detail of carving, Kelaniya Raja Maha Vihara

Other important Buddhist centres in Colombo include the Isipathanaramaya temple in Havelock Town, which has particularly beautiful frescoes. The Vajiraramaya temple at Bambalapitiya is a centre of Buddhist learning from where monks have taken the Buddha's message to countries in the west. The modern Gotami Vihara at Borella, six km south-east of the centre, has impressive murals of the life of the Buddha.

Hindu Temples

Hindu temples, known as *kovils* in Sri Lanka, are numerous. On Sea St, the goldsmiths' street in the Pettah, the Kathiresan and the old Kathiresan kovils, dedicated to the war god Skanda, are the starting point for the annual Vel Festival (see Festivals in Facts for the Visitor). The huge Vel chariot is dragged to kovils on Galle Rd in Bambalapitiya.

The Sri Ponnambalam-Vaneswaram Kovil, in Kochchikade, three km north of Fort, is built of south Indian granite. Other kovils are blessed with equally unpronounceable names, such as the Sri Bala Selva Vinayagar Moorthy Kovil, with shrines to Shiva and Ganesh, off D R Wijewardena Mawatha, Colombo 10; the Sri Shiva Subramania Swami Kovil on Kew Rd, Slave Island; and the Sri Muthumariamman Kovil on Kotahena St.

Mosques

The most important of Colombo's many mosques is the Grand Mosque on New Moor St in Pettah. In Pettah you'll also find the decorative 1909 Jami-Ul-Alfar Mosque, on the corner of 2nd Cross St and Bankshall St, with its candy-striped red and white brickwork. There are many mosques on Slave Island, dating from the British days when it was the site for a Malay regiment from which an alternative name for part of Slave Island – Kompanna Veediya (Company Street) – is derived.

Dehiwala Zoo

By Asian standards the zoo at Dehiwala, 10 km south of Fort, treats its animals well – although the big cats and monkeys are still rather squalidly housed. The major attraction is the 5.15 pm elephant show – they troop on stage in true trunk-to-tail fashion and perform a whole series of feats of elephantine-agility. They dance around with bells on their legs, stand delicately on little round platforms, balance momentarily on their front feet, one picks up his keeper in his trunk, and finally they all troop out, the leader tootling merrily on a mouth (trunk?) organ.

The zoo has a wide collection of other creatures, including a fine range of birds and an aquarium. It's open from 8 am to 6 pm daily; entry is Rs 60. You can get there on a 132 bus from Galle Rd or Janadhipathi Mawatha in Fort.

Swimming & Diving

The only Colombo beach where you'd consider swimming is Mt Lavinia, a somewhat faded resort area 11 km south of Fort – and even that's borderline, with severe undertow at times and some foul waterways issuing into the ocean not too far north. But outsiders can use the pools at several top-end Colombo hotels for a fee. One of the best deals is the outdoor saltwater pool right by the seafront at the Galle Face Hotel, which costs Rs 99 for non-residents. A dip in the magnificently sited Mt Lavinia Hotel pool will set you back Rs 250.

Underwater Safaris (☎ 694012, 694255) of 25 Barnes Place, Colombo 7, runs diving trips and courses, and may be able to rent out diving gear. Its courses, reportedly leading to the PADI certificate, involve eight to 10 hours of pool tuition plus four sea dives.

PLACES TO STAY – BOTTOM END

Around the city centre, basically it's a choice between hostels in Fort and a few downmarket hotels and guest houses in Pettah. There are a couple more hostels and a few guest house bargains scattered just off Galle Rd as far along as Mt Lavinia, 11 km south of Fort. Insect repellent or mosquito coils help you sleep in most of these places.

Fort & Pettah

The *Sri Lanka Ex-Servicemen's Institute* at 29 Bristol St in Fort – 10 to 15 minutes' walk from Fort Station – is a basic but friendly place, nothing like as austere as its name sounds. A bed (not a bunk) with one sheet in a 10-person mixed-sex dormitory costs Rs 93.50 – generally non-Sri Lankans are put in a separate dorm from the locals. The dorms have fans and nearly as many lockers as beds (though you need your own padlock). There are also small single/double rooms at Rs 165/297. The whole place, including the shared bathrooms, is kept pretty clean. The *Central YMCA*, almost next door at 39 Bristol St, has options ranging from cramped 16-bunk dorms with very little locker space at Rs 70 a person, up to double rooms with fan, attached bath and hot water for Rs 385. Sharing a fanless room and its locker with one other person costs Rs 90. Singles/doubles with fan and shared bath are Rs 150/255. There's a Rs 5 daily membership charge and a reasonable cheap cafeteria.

The *Mettro Inn* on Bodhi Raja Mawatha, just off Olcott Mawatha in the Pettah, is well situated within a couple of minutes' walk of both Fort Station and all the main bus stations – OK for a night if you arrive in Colombo late. Box-like, bare but adequately clean rooms with fans go for Rs 200 single or double with shared bath, Rs 300 with attached bath. There are a few even more basic places dotted along Olcott Mawatha and in the Pettah streets behind – such as the *Ajantha Hotel* at 125 Olcott Mawatha, virtually opposite Fort Station, with small singles/doubles at Rs 150/225 with shared bath – but many of them tend to be full with locals.

The *Lodgings*, near the Wolvendaal Church on the east edge of the Pettah at 41 1/1 Mahavidyalaya Mawatha (Barber St), Colombo 13, has 18 basic but reasonably clean rooms with attached bath, at prices ranging from Rs 130 without fan to Rs 200 with fan, table, chair and washbasin. It's 1½ km from Fort Station. If you don't fancy the colourful walk through the Pettah to reach it, a three-wheeler from the station should cost Rs 25.

Inland

The *YWCA International* (☎ 24181, 24694) at 393 Union Place, Colombo 2, two km inland from Galle Rd, is right at the top of the bottom end in price. It has 20 large clean bare rooms, all with fans, mosquito nets, and attached bath, at Rs 200 or Rs 250 per person depending on the size. Prices include breakfast and the meals are good. The Y is well back from the road, with a flowery garden, and fairly quiet.

Mrs D Peiris' small guest house at 62/2 Park St, Colombo 2, has received some good reports. It's close to Viharamahadevi Park and the price for singles/doubles with bathroom is Rs 200/250. A good breakfast costs Rs 50 and Mrs Peiris is a helpful host.

Along Galle Rd

Kollupitiya The hostel at *YWCA National Headquarters* (☎ 28589, 23498), 7 Rotunda Gardens, Kollupitiya, Colombo 3, has two five-bed dormitories at Rs 150 plus singles with shared bathroom at Rs 200 and doubles with attached bathroom at Rs 400 (all including breakfast). It's a clean, secure-feeling place with a nice garden, but there aren't always vacancies. Men are allowed if with a woman. Rotunda Gardens is the second, very narrow, lane east off Galle Rd south of the Lanka Oberoi.

Bambalapitiya Off Galle Rd five km south of Fort at 50 Haig Rd, Bambalapitiya, Colombo 4 the *Youth Hostel* (☎ 581028) has 30 bunks in very basic separate-sex dormitories at Rs 55 for YHA members, Rs 60 for non-members. Sheets cost Rs 6.50 for three days. The bunks are squeezed in with little space to spare, and the few lockers have very flimsy locks – but at least it's a fairly friendly, cheap place to lay your head. The showers and toilets are clean enough.

Half a km further south, the *Ottery Inn* (☎ 583727) at 29 Melbourne Ave has eight fairly well kept rooms with singles/doubles, some with attached bath, at Rs 175/300 including breakfast. It's on a quiet street within sight of the sea and all in all is fair

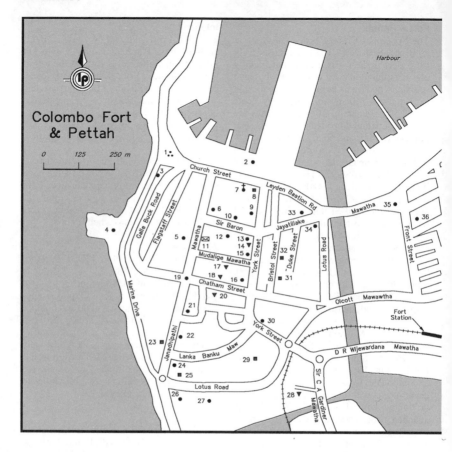

Colombo Fort & Pettah

Harbour

0   125   250 m

Church Street
Leyden Bastion Rd
Galle Buck Road
Flagstaff Street
Sir Baron Mawatha
Mawatha
York Street
Bristol Street
Jayatillake
Duke Street
Lotus Road
Front Street
Mudalige Mawatha
Chatham Street
Marine Drive
Janadhipathi
Lanka Banku Maw
York Street
Olcott Mawawtha
Fort Station
D R Wijewardana Mawatha
Sir C A Gardiner Mawatha
Lotus Road

■ PLACES TO STAY	42 Mettro Inn	OTHER
8 Grand Oriental Hotel	45 The Lodgings	1 Dagoba
23 Ceylon Intercontinental Hotel	▼ PLACES TO EAT	2 Passenger Harbour Terminal
25 Le Galadari Meridien Hotel	14 Casamara Restaurant	3 Immigration Department
29 Colombo Hilton	17 Soya City Restaurant	4 Lighthouse
31 Central YMCA	18 Pagoda Tea Room	5 President's Residence
32 Sri Lankan Ex-Servicemen's Institute	20 Orchid Restaurant	6 Tourist Police
41 Ajantha Hotel	28 Seafish Restaurant	7 Church of St Peter
		9 Bank of Ceylon/ Bureau de Change

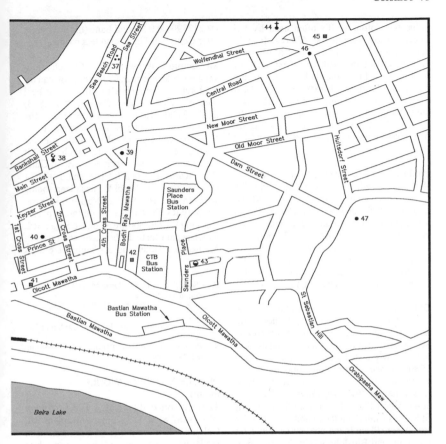

10	Thomas Cook	24	Bank of Ceylon	38	Jami-Ul-Alfar Mosque
11	Main Post Office		Headquarters	39	Old Town Hall
12	Air Lanka	26	Secretariat	40	Dutch Period Museum
13	Singapore Airlines	27	Finance Ministry	43	Buses to Airport
15	Cargill's	30	Map Sales Centre	44	The Wolvendaal
16	Laksala	33	Indian Airlines		Church
19	Fort Clock Tower	34	YMBA Building	46	Clock Tower
21	Air Lanka	35	Khan Clock Tower	47	Courts of Justice
22	Ceylinco House	36	Old Dutch Cemetery		
		37	Sea Street Temples		

value for Colombo. It's often used by US Peace Corps volunteers. Almost directly across Galle Rd from the top of Melbourne Ave is Dickman's Rd, and first left off Dickman's Rd is Bethesda Place, where the *Perpetual Tourist Lodge* (☎ 582419), at No 8A, has rooms with attached bath at Rs 200 single or double, plus a couple of little self-contained apartments for longer stayers. Six new rooms with balconies were being added in 1992.

Wellawatta The next suburb south is Wellawatta, where at 26 Charlemont Rd (turn by the Savoy cinema) you'll find the *Island Pride Beach Inn* (☎ 583250, 508584), affiliated to the Sri Lanka National Youth Hostels Association. It has 37 rooms at Rs 175 or 200 for singles with shared bath, Rs 250 for doubles with shared bath, Rs 300 for doubles with attached bath. There's a Rs 50 discount if you have a YHA card.

Dehiwala The next suburb after Wellawatta, Dehiwala, used to be a major shoestring accommodation centre, with cheap rooms available in numerous private houses, but only a few places hung on through the late 1980s tourism slump. Some may reopen as visitor numbers grow – ask around. One long-time standby is *Big John's* (☎ 715027) at 47 Albert Place. If you get off the bus at St Mary's Church on the inland side of Galle Rd, Albert Place is the next street down on the right, and Big John's is at the bottom, a few metres from the sea. Small singles are Rs 50, bigger ones with fan Rs 75, doubles with shared bathroom Rs 100, with attached bathroom Rs 125. Meals are available. Big John's changed hands a few years ago and has had mixed reviews since – 'dingy, flea-ridden, money up front' complained one traveller, but since then the new owner has started renovations and the finished rooms we saw were fair value.

At 37 Campbell Place, the foot of the next street along from Albert Place (a few steps along the railway from Big John's) *Seabreeze* (☎ 717996) has two rooms with bath at Rs 125 or 175 double. *Gehan Villa*

(☎ 717390) at 9 Second Lane (the next street after Campbell Place) also lets rooms.

Mt Lavinia If you want a bit of beach atmosphere while you're in Colombo, you can try Mt Lavinia, although it's a bit down-at-heel these days. The *Seaview Tourinn* (☎ 714893) at 174/3 Galle Rd is down a little lane by the Odeon Cinema, almost in Dehiwala. It's a friendly, family-run place with singles/doubles at Rs 100/150. To reach the Mt Lavinia resort area proper, you turn off Galle Rd towards the beach. The small *YMCA* (☎ 713786) at 55 Hotel Rd has clean rooms with fans for Rs 200/250. Breakfast is extra, but only Rs 25. The following larger places charging Rs 250/300 are all on De Saram Rd, which is parallel to the beach north of the big Mt Lavinia Hotel and a couple of blocks inland:

Blue Seas Tourist Guest House (☎ 717279), 9/6 De Saram Rd, 12 rooms
Mt Lavinia Holiday Inn (☎ 717187), 17 De Saram Rd, 27 rooms
Ranveli Beach Resort (☎ 717385), 56/9 De Saram Rd, 28 rooms
Sea Breeze Tour Inn (☎ 714017/8), 22/5 De Saram Rd, 23 rooms

PLACES TO STAY – MIDDLE
Inland
The old, once dilapidated *Hotel Nippon* (☎ 431887/8) at 123 Kumaran Ratnam Rd, Colombo 2, a km south of Fort, has been modernised, with tasteful decor and white cane furniture, and is now reasonable value at US$15 single or double. Half the 30 rooms have air-con and those with balconies over the street are a good size. There's a restaurant on the spot. Take a 138 bus from Fort, or it's about Rs 25 by three-wheeler.

A km south-east of the Nippon at 388 Union Place, Colombo 2, the friendly *Hotel Galaxy* (☎ 699320) has good-sized air-con rooms of variable cleanliness for Rs 700/800, plus a restaurant, coffee shop and rooftop pool.

Another km east at 77 Rosmead Place in Colombo 7 (Cinnamon Gardens), you'll find *A Wayfarer's Inn* (☎ 693936) with rooms at

US$11, or US$13 with air-con, including breakfast. It has a pleasant garden and is located in a peaceful area. A three-wheeler from Fort is about Rs 50.

Along Galle Rd

Kollupitiya The *Hotel Renuka* (☎ 573598, 573602) at 328 Galle Rd, Colombo 3, 2½ km south of Fort, is good value with clean, well modernised air-con rooms for which it asks Rs 550/600 in high season. There's also a good restaurant, the Palmyrah, here. A few yards north of the Renuka a sign points inland to the nearby *Sea View Hotel* (☎ 573570), which certainly doesn't have a view of the sea but is down a quiet lane at 15 Sea View Ave, with 23 quite spacious double rooms with fans, mosquito nets and attached bath at Rs 425.

A km further south and a block inland from Galle Rd at 383 R A De Mel Mawatha (Duplication Rd), Colombo 3, the *Hotel Empress* has comfortable and clean enough rooms, all air-con, at Rs 650/800, plus a restaurant/bar open till 2 am.

Wellawatta The *Hotel Sapphire* (☎ 583306) at 371 Galle Rd, Colombo 6, has 40 doubles with private bath at Rs 400 with fan, Rs 500 or 600 with air-con. The dearest are well renovated but at the noisier road end. The *Hotel Ceylon Inns* (☎ 580474-6), at 501 Galle Rd, also Colombo 6, looks grubby outside but inside there's a nice courtyard garden with a swimming pool. The rooms are nothing special – moderately sized with ageing air-con – but clean enough, and cost Rs 500 a double.

Mt Lavinia The *Palm Beach Hotel* (☎ 717484, 712771) at 52 De Saram Rd has 50 rooms at Rs 400 (air-con extra). The *Hotel Riviras* (☎ 717786, 717731) at 50/2 De Saram Rd has 16 rooms at Rs 700. The *Sea Spray Beach Resort* (☎ 716304) at 45 Vihara Rd, a few metres down the track from Mt Lavinia railway station, has 10 modernised rooms with balconies overlooking the sea. These cost Rs 500/590, Rs 170 extra with air-con.

PLACES TO STAY – TOP END

Colombo has seven top-bracket modern international hotels, all in Fort or not far south of it, typically with elegant, spacious public areas, large swimming pools, shops, several restaurants, and fully air-conditioned. Their 2000 rooms are far more than Colombo needs and several of them will – unofficially – offer much cheaper room rates than the US$70-plus that they're supposed to charge according to Tourist Board agreements. At any of them it's worth asking if there are any US$40 rooms available.

But if you're in the US$40 range, consider a much older hotel with more character than any of the 'big seven' – the 1864 *Galle Face Hotel* (☎ 541010) at the south end of Galle Face Green. It was the superior establishment during the British colonial era and, though now showing its age, still has loads of colonial charm – from creaking barefoot waiters ambling along the terrace by the oceanside garden to some truly vast rooms whose toilets alone have as much acreage as the average room in a modern 'luxury' hotel. The Galle Face displays boards listing famous people who've stayed there, so you'll know you have at least one thing in common with Bo Derek, Yury Gagarin, Prince Philip and John D Rockefeller! It also has antique air-conditioning and plumbing, and the rooms on the Galle Rd side are noisy. Still, if you like Raj-era hotels of the Raffles type you'll love the Galle Face. The 60 rooms range from US$35 to US$55 (with US$5 off for non-smokers). Have a look at different prices before deciding: some of the US$45 rooms, for instance, are much bigger and better than the US$35 ones.

Another top hotel of an older generation, now given a new lease of life, is the *Grand Oriental Hotel* (☎ 20391, 448734), formerly the Taprobane, at 2 York St, Fort, across the street from the harbour. It's elegantly refurbished, with quite spacious rooms from US$32/42 (though the best with harbour views are US$60 a double), and fine views from its 4th-floor Harbour Restaurant, but lacks the open spaces that make the Galle Face and some other top hotels so attractive.

Of the modern hotels, newest and glitziest is the *Colombo Hilton* (☎ 544644) on Lotus Rd, Fort, with 387 rooms at US$90/100 and upwards, a sports centre, special Japanese, non-smoking and executive floors, secretarial services and most else you could imagine you need. 'Terrific service and a fabulous swimming pool,' raved one happy, and obviously not penniless, reader.

The *Ceylon Intercontinental* (☎ 421221) is beautifully located at 48 Janadhipathi Mawatha, facing the sea on one side and the north end of Galle Face Green on another. Its 250 rooms are US$75/80 and upwards. They're very comfortable but, like many of their competitors', disappointingly small for the money. Across the street at 64 Lotus Rd is *Le Galadari Meridien Hotel* (☎ 544544) with 494 rooms at, officially, US$80/90. In the inland direction from the Hilton the elegant 350-room *Ramada Renaissance Hotel* (☎ 544200) at 115 Sir C A Gardiner Mawatha, Colombo 2, charges from US$75 single or double. The food is reportedly excellent but one traveller described the rooms as unkempt.

Facing the sea across the south end of Galle Face Green is the *Taj Samudra Hotel* (☎ 446622) at 25 Galle Face Centre Rd, with 400 rooms at US$85/90, some particularly beautiful public areas and a large, well-tended garden. A short walk from the Taj Samudra is the *Holiday Inn* (☎ 422001) at 30 Sir Mohamed Macan Markar Mawatha, with 100 rooms at a minimum US$70/80, but, like the price, this is a step down from other top bracket hotels. All mod cons, but smaller and simpler.

The *Lanka Oberoi* (☎ 20001, 437437), on Galle Rd a short distance from Galle Face Green (though its address is 77 Steuart Place), has 600 rooms at US$75. Externally it's a rather unexciting cube, but internally it's a hollow atrium hotel with gigantic batik banners hanging from top to bottom of the airy lobby, where a string quartet plays in the evenings.

Eleven km south of Fort, the magnificently marbled and barbled *Mt Lavinia Hotel* (☎ 715221-3), once the ostentatious residence of the British governor, is on the waterfront and very close to Mt Lavinia railway station. Though there's a private sandy beach, a 24-hour coffee shop, and a beautifully sited pool and terrace, the 320 rooms ranging from US$15/20 in the old wing to US$55/65 in the new wing aren't especially big. We found the staff haughty and readers have commented that it's worth a visit but not very good value to stay in. The *Mount Royal Beach Hotel* (☎ 714001) at 36 College Ave, Mt Lavinia, has 60 rooms from US$30/35.

PLACES TO STAY – AIRPORT AREA

Colombo airport at Katunayake is 30 km north of the city, and while transport there from the city – and indeed from elsewhere on the island – isn't difficult, there are several accommodation options in the vicinity if you want to stay close at hand.

Side by side, a km from the airport terminal on Canada Friendship Rd, which runs up to the airport from the Colombo-Negombo road, are the *Hotel Goodwood Plaza* (☎ 452561-3) with 32 rooms at Rs 825 single or double, and, similarly equipped with a swimming pool, air-con, etc, the *Orient Pearl Hotel* (☎ 452356) charging Rs 660. Buses between the airport and Colombo, or the airport and Negombo, pass the doors of these hotels.

The *Airport Garden Hotel* (☎ 452951) at 234 Negombo Rd, Seeduwa, two km south on the main road towards Colombo, is a bigger, more luxurious lagoonside place with rooms at US$60/75, while the little *Airlink Rest Inn* (☎ 030-3607), a further three km towards Colombo at 580 Colombo-Negombo Rd, Seeduwa, has rooms with attached bath at Rs 300 single or double – and offers a free lift to the airport if you stay 24 hours.

Further south, about halfway to Colombo, is the *Palm Village Hotel* (☎ 530766) on the beach at Uswetakiyawa. It has 50 air-con rooms at US$22/25. *Pegasus Reef Hotel* (☎ 530205, 530208) on Santha Maria Mawatha, Hendala, Wattala, is about 20 km from the airport and 10 km from the city. It too is on the beach, with 150 air-con rooms at US$45/60. Taxi is the easiest way to get to the Pegasus. The cheapest accommodation of all near the airport is at Negombo, about 10 km north – see the West Coast Beaches chapter.

PLACES TO EAT

Colombo has as good a selection of restaurants as anywhere in Sri Lanka, and is also one of the better places for finding real Sri Lankan food. Don't neglect the hotels, many of which have good restaurants. Some of the all-you-can-eat hotel buffets, while more expensive than an average restaurant meal, are worth the money because they supply limitless quantities of often excellent food.

Fort & Pettah

A Colombo favourite of nearly everybody is the *Pagoda Tea Room* on Chatham St. It's a big, old-fashioned, crowded place, a mile away from your average run-of-the-mill Asian cheapie. You can choose between a self-service section or waiter service. In either case the food is of good quality and remarkably low in price. There's a variety of Asian and Western food. Basic rice and curry is Rs 25 and there are different big lunch specials daily (for example, on Fridays mixed vegetable fried rice, sweet and sour prawns, fish chop suey and shredded beef) for Rs 60. Alternatively you could have bacon and eggs (Rs 35) for breakfast or steak and vegetables (Rs 50) for lunch. On hot days the lemon squash and ice cream are knockouts, but the Pagoda is mainly a breakfast and lunchtime place as it shuts at 6 pm weekdays and 2.30 pm on Saturdays (it's closed Sunday). Incidentally, former Duran Duran fans may once have seen the Pagoda in one of their heroes' videos!

Almost opposite the Pagoda at 70 Chatham St, the *Orchid Restaurant* is a clean, fan-cooled, slightly superior Chinese place with most main dishes around Rs 60 to Rs 70, but fried rice and noodle dishes at Rs 30 to Rs 40. Also better-than-average is the *Casamara Restaurant* on York St, underground and air-conditioned, with omelettes

at Rs 30, curries up to Rs 60, and fish, chips and veg for Rs 60 to Rs 80.

A pleasant surprise for health foodies is the *Soya City Restaurant*, a small café on Mudalige Mawatha doling out original snack lines like tofu rotty (Rs 7.50), soya burgers (Rs 8) and choc-flavour sour milk (Rs 3.50). It closes at 5.30 pm.

The *Akasa Kade Restaurant* on the 12th floor of Ceylinco House on Janadhipathi Mawatha has a lunchtime Sri Lankan buffet where you can fill up pretty well for Rs 50 or Rs 60.

Just south of Fort is the *Seafish* (☎ 26915), behind the Regal cinema at the north end of Sir C A Gardiner Mawatha, with excellent seafood. Most main courses cost Rs 75 to Rs 110; there are also good salads at Rs 20 to Rs 50.

Basic, cheaper Fort eateries include the *Taj Restaurant* at 99 Chatham St almost next to the Pagoda; the *Risan Restaurant* on the corner of Chatham St and Janadhipathi Mawatha; the self-service *Nectar Café* on the corner of York St and Mudalige Mawatha (rice and curry Rs 13 to Rs 30) and the *Fort Restaurant* up the same steps as the Sri Lanka Ex-Servicemen's Institute on Bristol St. The *Central YMCA* on Bristol St has a cheap self-service cafeteria, good for an early breakfast when most of Colombo is still asleep.

Over in the Pettah, *Woodlands* at 192 4th Cross St is a good cheap vegetarian restaurant where a lunch of rice, vegetable curry, papadam, pickle, rasam, buttermilk and sago pudding, eaten with the hand off a banana leaf or stainless steel plate, is yours for Rs 20. Go at 1 pm or after when the crowds have thinned out.

For good coffee, croissants (Rs 10), cakes and pastries in air-conditioned cool, the *Patisserie* in Le Galadari Meridien Hotel is a good bet. If you want to move well upmarket the big hotels all have multiple restaurants and coffee bars. The *Ceylon Intercontinental's* Rs 200 breakfast buffet in its ground-floor restaurant is well worth a splurge; also here are a pizzeria and the reportedly good rooftop *Palms Restaurant*.

Buffets in *Le Galadari Meridien's* coffee shop (lunch Rs 250, dinner Rs 295) feature a different cuisine – French, Sri Lankan, Chinese, etc – each day of the week.

Galle Face Green & Around You could do a lot worse than start a day with the all-you-can-eat Rs 200 breakfast buffet at the *Ports of Call* restaurant in the Taj Samudra Hotel. If you're staying across the road at the Galle Face Hotel it's almost a necessity since the food there is poor. The Taj Samudra also has a good Indian restaurant. If you just want to sample the Galle Face's colonial atmosphere, drop in for a pot of tea (Rs 40) or lime soda (Rs 65) on the verandah. The nearby *Holiday Inn* has a terrific Moghul buffet on Friday and Saturday evenings if you can afford Rs 275.

A five-minute walk inland from the Holiday Inn is the clean, air-conditioned *Fountain Café* at 1 Justice Akbar Mawatha, something of a showpiece for Ceylon Cold Stores (bottlers of Elephant House soft drinks). It does good Western and Sri Lankan meals from Rs 25 to Rs 85, plus terrific ice cream and iced coffee, and stays open in the evenings.

Opposite the Galle Face Hotel, in Galle Face Court, the *Alt Heidelberg German Restaurant* does decent German food – main dishes Rs 150 to Rs 200 – as well as draft German beer. It's open at lunch and from 6 to 10 pm. A little further down Galle Rd, the *Hotel Lanka Oberoi* has an all-you-can-eat lunchtime salad buffet for Rs 125, plus more expensive evening buffets at Rs 290.

Kollupitiya Near the Hotel Renuka at 286 Galle Rd, Colombo 3, the clean, air-conditioned *Restaurant Ginza Araliya* does a mixture of good Sri Lankan and Western food at good prices from 11 am to 10 pm. Fish and seafood, at around Rs 70 to Rs 100, are among its specialities. Rice and four tasty veg curries at lunchtime costs just Rs 30. Local residents speak highly of the *Palmyrah Restaurant* in the Hotel Renuka itself, and the *Curry Bowl* 300 metres further south at 24 Deal Place, an upmarket rice and curry

place. Across the road from the Ginza Araliya at 265 Galle Rd is the *Chinese Lotus Hotel*, doing crab dishes at about Rs 75 and other things a little cheaper.

A block inland from the Ginza Araliya and Chinese Lotus, the *Zanshi Palace*, open till 11 pm at 263 R A De Mel Mawatha (Duplication Rd), near the Liberty Plaza shopping centre, has good, though not cheap, Chinese food, while about 700 metres further south at 450E R A De Mel Mawatha, on the corner of Alfred Place, *Saras* does excellent, though again pricey, Indian food. It's air-conditioned and specialises in vegetarian fare, although it also does meat dishes including tandoori food.

If you like the Pagoda Tea Room in Fort then the *Green Cabin* at 453 Galle Rd, Colombo 3 will appeal just as much – it's run by the same people. It's smaller than the Pagoda but the food is of equal quality and you can also eat in a small garden. Unlike the Pagoda, the Green Cabin stays open in the evenings. A lunchtime rice and curry is Rs 25 to Rs 40.

Bambalapitiya A particularly good-value place is the *Greenlands Hotel* in Shrubbery Gardens, on the seaward side of Galle Rd about 300 metres north of Dickman's Rd. It has no pretensions to anything except serving good Indian vegetarian food, with most items costing under Rs 12. Masala dosa, slightly dearer at Rs 16, is delicious. Ice cream is served, and good milk coffee too. *Sapid Restaurant* on the corner of Galle Rd and Vajira Rd has fairly good Sri Lankan food – rice and curry Rs 30 to Rs 55, fish and prawn dishes Rs 50 to Rs 80 – plus Indian and Western options. It has some pleasantly breezy upstairs rooms.

Opposite Dickman's Rd in Colombo 4, the *Chinese Dragon Café* at 231 Galle Rd has good, fairly cheap food (fried rice or noodles Rs 35, other main dishes Rs 50 to Rs 100). About a km inland at 65 Havelock Rd, Colombo 5, *Ristorante Italiano Guido* (☎ 33815) does authentic Italian food prepared by Italians, and has good wines.

Dehiwala The clean, fan-cooled little *Hot Rock Restaurant* at 63 Galle Rd almost next to St Mary's Church will do you fish and chips for Rs 60, a fair plateful of veg noodles for Rs 26, or rice and curry for Rs 18 (vegetable) or Rs 30 (chicken). The *Hotel Concord* at 139 Galle Rd has a Sri Lankan and Western restaurant.

Places to Drink

The bar of the *Sri Lanka Ex-Servicemen's Institute* at 29 Bristol St serves bottles of beer at Rs 52 – about the cheapest you'll get it outside a shop. Reader Joe Neal tells us there's also non-inflated beer in the upstairs bar at *British India*, 13 Mudalige Mawatha, which also does simple, tasty rice and curry lunches (the downstairs bar is for 'gulpers' and may get rowdy – but even in the upstairs bar a woman alone would provoke comment). The *White Horse* at the clock tower end of Chatham St is relaxed and holds no problems for women.

ENTERTAINMENT

Colombo is not the place to head for if you're looking for the excitement of Asia after dark – it's distinctly sleepy. The big hotels usually have nightclubs and/or casinos. The Mt Lavinia Hotel has nightly cultural performances, such as Kandyan dancing or low country devil dancing, for Rs 250. Other hotels sometimes have similar shows and *This Month in Sri Lanka* gives details. Occasionally medium or big-name musicians or other entertainers pass through on tour – such as The Wailers who staged an open-air concert in Viharamahadevi Park during our last visit. Keep an eye on the local papers for info on any such events.

Cinemas showing English-language films are mainly along Galle Rd. Western films are often not in great shape by the time they reach Sri Lanka, having been unreeled on the projection room floor a few times too many. Indian films and locally produced films in Sinhala are generally simple enough in their plot to make language comprehension unnecessary. And they're very cheap.

There is quite an active Sinhala language theatre, particularly at the Lumbini Theatre in Havelock Town, the Lionel Wendt Centre at 18 Guildford Crescent, Colombo 7, and the John De Silva Memorial Theatre, 3 Ananda Kumaraswamy Mawatha (Green Path), Colombo 7.

The foreign cultural institutes put on films, lectures and other events – see Colombo Information.

THINGS TO BUY

The government-run Laksala in Fort is a good place for all the usual handicrafts and local items. Two places with more individual Sri Lankan crafts, not far apart on Galle Rd, are Barefoot at 704 Galle Rd, Colombo 3, and the Sri Lanka Handlooms Emporium, run by the government Department of Small Industries, at 71 Galle Rd, Colombo 4. Barefoot has quality local handloom-woven fabrics in original designs, some made into clothes, toys, cushion covers, and so on. Brightly patterned cushion covers cost around Rs 500 each. The Handlooms Emporium has more handloom work but also above-average wooden elephants, light earthenware pottery from Weligama, and other crafts. Not very much further south, the Serendib Gallery at 100 Galle Rd, Colombo 4, sells old maps and prints, and sometimes rare books on Sri Lanka, as well as modern crafts.

Colombo's greatest concentration of gem dealers is at the Sri Lanka Gem & Jewellery Exchange at 310 Galle Rd, Colombo 3, a few doors north of the Hotel Renuka. The State Gem Corporation has its testing centre upstairs and a showroom next door. A block inland from here at the junction of R A De Mel Mawatha (Duplication Rd) and Ananda Kumaraswamy Mawatha (Green Path) is Liberty Plaza, Colombo's prime shopping mall. Here are lots of imported goods, along with Keells Super, probably the biggest Western-style supermarket in the capital, with all sorts of Western goods from baked beans to disposable nappies (diapers).

When the Pettah shops are closed on Sundays, Main St, Pettah, becomes an open-air bazaar. There's also a bazaar on Olcott Mawatha beside Fort railway station.

For unadulterated spices try the YWCA Spice Shop at 393 Union Place.

GETTING THERE & AWAY

Colombo is the gateway to Sri Lanka from abroad, and also the centre of the island's bus and rail networks. See the Getting Around chapter for general info on buses and trains. Initially you may find that leaving Colombo by train is easier than by bus, though trains are usually less frequent and a little more expensive than bus services. There's more order (fairly dependable timetables, posted prices, ticket windows, sensible queues) at the railway station than at the bus stations, and often less overcrowding on board.

More info on transport to/from particular towns is given in the relevant regional sections.

Air

Info on flights in and out of Colombo is given in the Getting There & Away chapter. The airport is at Katunayake, 30 km north of the city and two km east of the Colombo-Negombo road. After a bout of reconstruction in the 1980s the terminal is quite modern and efficient. There are bank counters where you can change money round the clock. When leaving, save Rs 500 for the departure tax but change back *all* your other rupees before you go through passport control – you can't spend them after that. In the arrivals section are a Ceylon Tourist Board info desk, a left-luggage counter (Rs 60 a day per item), and booking desks for hotels, guest houses and the Ceylon Hotels Corporation which runs several rest houses – as well as numerous accommodation and transport touts who buzz around claiming to be 'official'. Shake them off.

Once you have cleared passport control on departure there's an expensive duty-free shopping complex – complete with charity collecting boxes waiting for the rupees that unwary travellers saved for a final drink in the café here, but found were useless because it only accepts foreign currency!

For arrivals, departures and other airport information, call 452911 or 452281, or 546175 for Air Lanka only.

Accommodation near the airport is dealt with under Colombo Places to Stay; transport to/from the airport (including to/from Negombo and further afield) is under Colombo Getting Around.

Airline offices in Colombo (in Fort unless stated) include:

Air India
    108 YMBA Building, Sir Baron Jayatillake Mawatha (☎ 25832, 422249)
Air Lanka
    55 Janadhipathi Mawatha (☎ 27564, 28331-4)
    14 Sir Baron Jayatillake Mawatha (☎ 421291)
    600 Galle Rd, Colombo 3 (☎ 581131-4)
Aeroflot
    79/81 Hemas Building, York St (☎ 25580, 433062)
Emirates
    Le Galadari Meridien Hotel, 64 Lotus Rd (☎ 544544, 438978/9)
Gulf Air
    11 York St (☎ 26633, 434662)
Indian Airlines
    95 Sir Baron Jayatillake Mawatha (☎ 23136, 29838, 23987)
KLM
    67 Dharmapala Mawatha, Colombo 7 (☎ 25984-8)
Kuwait Airways
    Ceylinco House, Janadhipathi Mawatha (☎ 445531-3, 438832/3)
Lufthansa
    273 Galle Rd, Colombo 3 (☎ 574227)
MAS
    51 Janadhipathi Mawatha (☎ 445410-2)
Pakistan International
    342 Galle Rd, Colombo 3 (☎ 573475, 575052)
Saudi Arabian Airlines
    51-53 Janadhipathi Mawatha (☎ 436725, 27506, 27911)
Singapore Airlines
    30 Sir Baron Jayatillake Mawatha (☎ 422711-9)
Thai International
    Ceylon Intercontinental Hotel, 48 Janadhipathi Mawatha (☎ 438050-3)
UTA
    5 York St (☎ 27605/6)

Bus

Colombo has three main bus stations, or rather yards, all on the south edge of the Pettah, a few minutes' walk east of Fort railway station. Most important, most chaotic, utterly shadeless and alternately dusty and muddy is the Bastian Mawatha station, where you must go for private buses to, among other places, Kandy, Nuwara Eliya, Trincomalee, Ambalangoda, Hikkaduwa, Galle, Matara, Tangalla and Kataragama. Private buses to Negombo, Ratnapura, Kurunegala, Haputale, Badulla, Anuradhapura and Polonnaruwa go from Saunders Place, while the CTB bus station is on Olcott Mawatha. Private buses are generally quicker and more frequent. The Bastian Mawatha and CTB stations have info kiosks, but always double check anything they tell you. The Saunders Place and CTB stations have posted timetables which are even less reliable, though they can serve as a general guide to rough frequency of service.

Buses to main towns are frequent – for instance, to Kandy there are private buses (Rs 25) every few minutes from about 6 am to 8 pm, plus fairly frequent CTB buses which supposedly continue hourly all night. To Galle there are private buses until midnight and CTB buses timetabled round the clock. To lesser or more distant places there are fewer buses – for instance to Tangalla or Anuradhapura there are a dozen or so private buses daily, plus four or five CTB buses – though buses going beyond these places (such as to Hambantota or Kataragama for Tangalla) will take you too. Many of the buses to distant places like these (four to five hours or more away) leave by 9 or 10 am.

Train

The main railway station, Colombo Fort, is within easy walking distance of the city centre. See the introductory Getting Around chapter for general information on train services, and the regional chapters for info on trains to specific places. At the station, beware of porters who will grab your bags and then demand an extortionate fee if you're not careful. Either negotiate before you let go or carry them yourself.

The helpful Railway Tourist Office, at the front of the station where taxis pull up, open from Monday to Friday 8. 30 am to 4.30 pm,

can tell you most of what you need to know about schedules, booking and so on. There are separate sets of ticket windows for second and third class, a special window for the inter-city trains to Kandy, and another for sleeping berth reservations.

There are also accommodation touts at the station, and on the trains going to major tourist destinations, who try to persuade you to go with them to 'their' place in Hikkaduwa, Kandy, and so on. However plausible they sound, they're best firmly rebuffed. Saying you have a room reservation helps shake them off.

GETTING AROUND
To/From the Airport

Bus Private and CTB buses (Rs 7) run to/from Colombo every 15 to 30 minutes from about 4.30 am to 10 pm. The trip takes about 45 minutes. To reach the bus stops, walk out on to the road outside the arrivals terminal building and turn left. Ignore any touts who try to distract you on the way. Private buses park in an area now straight ahead of you. For CTB buses turn right shortly before you reach the private buses, and go out through the airport perimeter gate. The stop for buses to Colombo is about 50 metres along the road to the left. The stop to the right from the gate is for buses heading inland, including the daily bus to Kandy. Buses have no right to charge you for luggage. The Colombo terminus for private buses is at the corner of Saunders Place and Beira Rd, a short distance south of the Saunders Place bus yard.

See the Kandy section for direct buses to/from Kandy.

Taxi The taxi counter in the airport arrivals building operates a fixed-price ticket system which removes the need for bargaining blind on arrival – although you might get a lower fare by asking around on the road outside the terminal. The fixed price depends on the distance: to Colombo Fort it's Rs 450, but you can also take one much further afield, for example to Kandy for Rs 1600, or Hikkaduwa for about Rs 1800. At the counter you are given a ticket which you hand over to a driver outside. Going back to the airport you can use these prices as top end bargaining levels.

Negombo Transport Negombo, the beach resort/fishing town about 10 km north of the airport, is used by some travellers as a last base in Sri Lanka before flying out. There are buses (No 270, Rs 5) roughly every 15 to 30 minutes between about 4.30 am and 10 pm, to/from Negombo bus station. A taxi costs Rs 200 to Rs 300 (depending on which end of Negombo you want), a three-wheeler about half that.

City Transport
Bus & Train The *A to Z Colombo* street atlas (see Colombo, Orientation) has useful info on bus routes and where to pick buses up in Fort. Although you can use the railway for reaching the suburbs dotted along Galle Rd – Bambalapitiya, Kollupitiya, Dehiwala and Mt Lavinia – it's usually easier to take a bus. CTB and private buses operate parallel services. A timetable is not necessary – the buses can hardly be described as running to one. Buses going down Galle Rd from Fort, which include Nos 100, 101, 102, 106, 133

and 134, can be picked up at Fort Station or on Janadhipathi Mawatha, or Sir C A Gardiner Mawatha. Not all go all the way out, so check the suburb you want with the conductor before getting on. While there are supposedly fixed fares on buses, you may come across minor variations in price. From Fort to Dehiwala down Galle Rd should be Rs 4. Train fares are fixed and usually marginally lower than bus fares.

Three-Wheelers These are numerous and useful. Bargain for the fare before you get in: as a tourist you'll have difficulty in getting a local price but you can be satisfied if you pay Rs 20 from Fort Station to Fort clock tower, or from the clock tower to the Galle Face Hotel, Rs 50 from Fort to Bambalapitiya, or Rs 80 from Fort to Dehiwala. You'll often get a better price hailing one on the street than using one that's waiting outside a hotel.

Taxi Some taxis are metered but often you'll find the driver won't use it and you must bargain for the fare – do this *before* you get in. A taxi from Fort Station to the Galle Face Hotel – a little over two km – should be no more than Rs 60.

West Coast Beaches

The west coast is the major sea-and-sand tourist area of Sri Lanka and with very good reason. There can hardly be a coastline anywhere in the world endowed with so many beautiful beaches. Round every bend you seem to come upon yet another inviting tropical vista – the appropriately beautiful palm trees, bending over the appropriately gold sands, lapped by the appropriately blue waves.

The beach region extends for about 270 km starting at Negombo (about 36 km north of Colombo), and then runs south of Colombo through Kalutara, Beruwela, Bentota, Ambalangoda, Hikkaduwa, Galle, Unawatuna, Weligama, Matara, Tangalla and Hambantota, where the road finally turns inland and north towards the hill country, with a branch to Tissamaharama, Kataragama and Yala National Park, and another to Monaragala and the coast at Pottuvil near Arugam Bay. The west coast road also runs north of Negombo but this region is not of such great interest.

The bulk of Sri Lanka's beach resort development is concentrated on the west coast, but beaches are not all the coast has to offer. You can visit the mask carvers at Ambalangoda, explore Galle, Sri Lanka's most historically interesting town, and find many other attractions. The coast is at its best from around November to April. From May the south-west monsoon makes it less palatable than the east. Most accommodation is concentrated in a handful of towns along the coast, but there are also many small guest houses and hotels scattered in quiet, secluded places between the larger centres.

Anywhere on this coast you have to watch out for dangerous currents, undertow and rip tides. These may be more likely with the bigger seas in the wet season from April/May to October/November but at any time of year take care. Watch where other people are swimming and if in any doubt keep asking. Pollution is another deterrent to swimming in some places – the further you are from town centres, and from Colombo, the better.

NEGOMBO

After Hikkaduwa, Tangalla and other fine beaches on the west coast, or Passekudah and Nilaveli on the east, Negombo's beach is a disappointment. It's long but often narrow and grubby. One of the better stretches of beach is in the Browns Beach Hotel area – and with the sea rarely clean enough for a swim, outsiders can use the good pool at this hotel for Rs 44. Negombo town, bustling and historically interesting, the lagoon islands to its south, and the road northward make for much more interesting exploring than the untidy hotel strip that backs the beach.

Many people make Negombo their last stop in Sri Lanka before flying out, as it's conveniently close to the airport. It has a reputation for gay prostitution, and Sri Lankans think of it as their AIDS capital, although numbers of AIDS cases on the island are relatively low.

Things to See

The Dutch captured the town from the Portuguese in 1640, lost it again the same year, then captured it again in 1644; but the British took it from them in 1796 without a struggle. During the Dutch era Negombo was one of the most important sources of cinnamon, and there are still reminders of the European days. Close to the seafront near the lagoon mouth are the ruins of the **old Dutch fort** with its fine gateway inscribed with the date 1672. Also here are a Dutch cemetery and a green, with a magnificent banyan tree, where cricket matches are a big attraction.

Several old Dutch buildings are still in use, including the lagoon rest house. The Dutch also revealed their love of canals here, as nowhere else in Sri Lanka. **Canals** extend from Negombo all the way south to Colombo and north to Puttalam, a total of over 120 km.

You can easily hire a bicycle in Negombo and ride the canal-side paths for some distance.

The people of Negombo, the Karavas, fisherfolk of Indian descent, take their outrigger canoes or *oruvas* out each day in search of the fish for which Negombo is well known. Sweeping home into the lagoon after a fishing trip, they're a fine sight. Fish auctions on the beach and fish sales in the market are common. The shark catch is brought in on the beach in the early afternoon. Nor is the catch all from the open sea. Negombo is at the northern end of the 12-km lagoon between Katunayake airport and the sea, which is famous for its harvest of lobsters, crabs and in particular, prawns.

All of Negombo is dotted with churches – so successfully were the Karavas converted to Catholicism that today the town is often known as 'little Rome'. A Fishers' Festival is held here in late July. **St Mary's Church** in the town centre has very good ceiling paintings by a local artist. The island of **Duwa**, joined to Negombo by the lagoon bridge, is famed for its annual passion play which involves the whole village.

Small villages dot the coast to the north and south; you can reach them by bicycle. Just across the lagoon bridge there's a second fish market, a good place to visit in mid-afternoon or at sunset as the fishing boats return. The road over the lagoon bridge continues along a small coastal road between lagoon and ocean almost all the way to Colombo.

Thirty km up the coast from Negombo, the village of **Mahawewa** is renowned for its batiks.

Places to Stay – bottom end & middle

Most places to stay in Negombo are on or just off Lewis Place, which runs for a few km parallel to the beach, starting about 1½ km north of the town centre. There are several places with rooms below Rs 200.

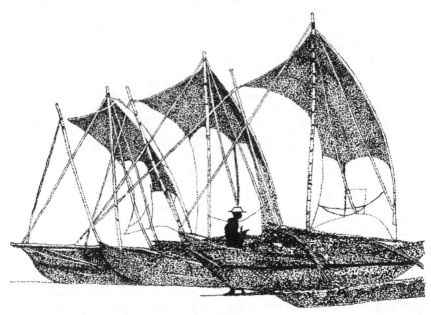

Oruva Boats

One of the best and longest running cheapies is inland on Anderson Rd, which runs alongside the canal. *Dil-wood* (☎ 031-2810), at No 71, has four well-kept rooms with fans and attached bath, and prices from Rs 100 to Rs 125 a single, Rs 175 to Rs 200 a double. Breakfast is available at Rs 70. Dil-wood refuses demands for extortionate commission from taxi and three-wheeler drivers and touts, who in revenge put about false tales of it being closed, cobra-infested and similar rubbish.

Over near the beach on Bolonghe Mawatha, which runs down to the sea from the south (the scruffier) end of Lewis Place, the *Sun Shine Guest House* at No 16 has singles/doubles with net, fan and attached bath which are fair value at Rs 100/175. Breakfast is available for Rs 50 and the helpful people here will store luggage for you. *Sea Drift* (☎ 031-2601), a short distance north at 2 Carron Place, is on the corner of Lewis Place but not far from the beach. It's very friendly, family-run, clean and cool, with fans and nets provided. Rooms are Rs 150 single or double. There's no guest house sign but the house name is on view. There are several other establishments in Carron Place, including the *Interline Beach Hotel* (☎ 031-2350) with a nice bit of garden fronting the beach and rooms, all with sea view, at Rs 200/250 or Rs 250/300.

A little further north, at 104 Lewis Place on the inland side of the road, the *Ocean View Guest House* has clean doubles with attached bath for Rs 150. On the beach side of the road, the friendly *Dephani Guest House* (☎ 031-3225) at 182 Lewis Place is good if you're prepared to pay a little more. Its eight clean rooms with nets, fans and private bath are Rs 300 single or double. It has its own good beachside restaurant. A couple of doors north, the *Catamaran Beach Hotel* (☎ 031-2342) is a typical middle-range hotel with two double-storey lines of sizeable rooms facing each other across a narrow garden, at the end of which is a beachfront pool. Rooms are Rs 550 single or double.

Nearly opposite the turning into Perera

Place, the next street north, the *Hotel Silver Sands* (☎ 031-2880) fronts the beach with 15 rooms all with their own balcony or patio and private bath for Rs 300 or 350. The beds are particularly comfortable and there's good food.

Much cheaper is the *Travellers' Halt* at 26 Perera Place, about 300 metres inland. It's very basic but clean, and has five rooms with attached baths and sometimes net and/or fan, at Rs 100/150. The people who run it are friendly but are only around from 8 am to 5 pm – so make sure you lock up securely at night.

Some of the small hotel-type places dotted between the big establishments towards the northern end of the beach strip are fair value. Here you have left Negombo behind and entered Ethukala, and Lewis Place has become Porutota Rd. The *Sea-Sands Guest House* (☎ 031-3154) next to the Topaz Beach Hotel has clean medium-sized rooms at Rs 175 single or double downstairs, Rs 250 upstairs with balconies to catch the breeze. On the inland side of the road at 20A the *Village Inn* (☎ 031-2423) is special value for Rs 330. Its three 'rooms' are in reality spacious, comfortable, modern, clean three-room suites each with a big double bed and mosquito net, and separate bath and sitting/dressing rooms. The *Beach View Guest House*, just south of the Blue Oceanic Beach Hotel, has clean and pleasant rooms on three floors, and its own beachside restaurant, but maintains a guest house feel. Singles/doubles with fan and private bath are Rs 200/300.

South of the beach strip, near the town, Negombo has two rest houses, both fairly pleasant – the *New Rest House* (☎ 031-2299) close to the seafront, with big rooms at Rs 350/440 with fan, Rs 550 air-con; and the *Lagoon View Rest House* (☎ 031-2199), by the lagoon bridge, without air-con, costing Rs 220 single or double. In the town itself, one traveller recommended *Mrs Ratnayake's* guest house at 49 Main St, next to the post office at the junction of Fifth Cross St, with a nice garden, reasonable doubles for Rs 150, and good meals for Rs 50.

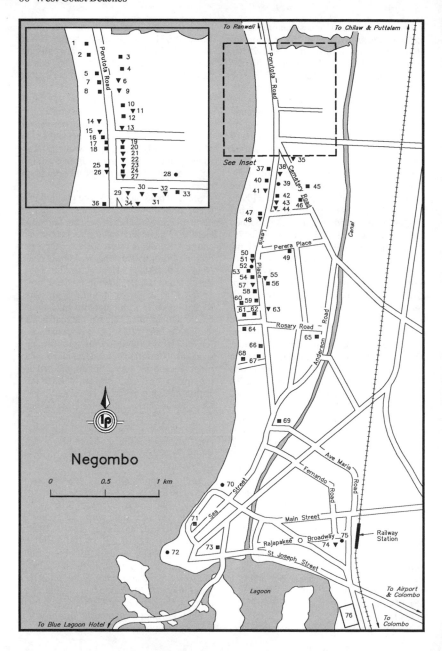

Negombo

0   0.5   1 km

■ PLACES TO STAY			
1	Goldi Sands Hotel	47	Sunflower Beach Hotel
2	Royal Oceanic Hotel	49	Traveller's Halt
3	Club Oasis Beach Hotel	50	Silver Sands Hotel
4	Jet Wing Travels Hotel	53	Catamaran Beach Hotel
5	Blue Oceanic Beach Hotel	54	Dephani & Starbeach Guest Houses
7	Hotel Sea Garden	56	Ocean View Guest House
8	Beach View Guest House	58	Golden Star Beach Hotel
10	Windmill Beach Hotel & The Spice Restaurant	59	Sea Drift
12	Village Inn	60	Aquarius Beach Hotel
16	Sea-Sands Guest House	61	Interline Beach Hotel
17	ABC Guest House	62	Rainbow Guest House
18	Topaz Beach Hotel	64	Beach Villa
20	Four Seasons Restaurant & Guest House	65	Dil-wood
24	Silva's Beach Restaurant & Guest House	66	Ceylonica Beach Hotel
25	Halcyon Beach Restaurant & Guest House	67	Alpine Guest House
33	Villa Fern Guest House	68	Sun Shine Guest House
36	Browns Beach Hotel	69	Roman Garden Guest House
37	Golden Beach Hotel	71	New Rest House
40	BG Guest House	73	Lagoon View Rest House
42	Sana's Restaurant & Guest House		
45	Nilwala Guest House	▼ PLACES TO EAT	
46	Blue Horizon Guest House		

▼ PLACES TO EAT			
6	Oyesters Restaurant	19	Bijou Restaurant
9	Sherry Land Restaurant	21	Stanley's Restaurant
11	Silvester's Restaurant	22	Restaurant Europa Treff
13	Sea Side Restaurant	23	Araliya Restaurant
14	Alt Saarbrucken German Restaurant	26	Regency Beach Restaurant
15	Restaurant Fish & Lobster	27	Pri-kin Restaurant
		29	Sea Food Restaurant
		30	Seven Hills Restaurant
		31	Vasana Restaurant
		32	Ocean Fish Restaurant
		34	Picco Bello Restaurant
		35	Marshal Wolfgang Restaurant
		38	Oriental Seafood Restaurant
		41	Sea View Restaurant
		43	Mandarin Restaurant
		44	Jaya Restaurant
		48	Honky Tonk Two
		51	Pancake House
		55	Bolonghe's Restaurant
		57	Mandingo Lotus Tourist Restaurant
		63	Join Us Restaurant
		74	Coronation Hotel

OTHER		
28	Tourist Police
39	Nishal Tours
52	Alma Tours
70	Fish Market
72	Fort
75	Bank of Ceylon
76	Bus Station

Still further south at 67 Parakrama Rd, Kurana, which is between Negombo and the airport, *Mr Srilal Fernando's* (☎ 031-2481) has been highly recommended by a reader for its clean rooms with fans and attached bath at Rs 125/150, good meals, and friendly family who'll pick you up for free from the airport if you ring. You can also get there by a No 240 Colombo-Negombo bus.

Places to Stay – top end

Negombo probably has more hotels (as opposed to guest houses) than any other beach resort in Sri Lanka, though they're mostly not as big as elsewhere. Several of the large hotels have equipment and facilities for watersports – sailing, windsurfing and waterskiing. Biggest, best known, and probably best of the bunch is *Browns Beach Hotel*, but the new *Royal Oceanic Hotel* runs fairly close.

Most top-end places are at the far north of the beach strip in Ethukala and Waikkal. But the *Blue Lagoon Hotel*, about eight km from Negombo, is reached by the small coast road over the lagoon bridge (probably the easiest way to get there from Negombo is by three-wheeler). Prices quoted here are generally room only but many of the hotels also have prices inclusive of meals. They include:

Blue Lagoon Hotel (☎ 031-3004/5), Talahena, 28 rooms, singles/doubles US$17/21, air-con US$7.50 extra

Blue Oceanic Beach Hotel (☎ 031-2377, 2642), Ethukala, 75 rooms, singles/doubles US$22/25, air-con US$5 extra

Browns Beach Hotel (☎ 031-2031/2, 2076/7), 175 Lewis Place, 132 rooms plus 10 beach bungalows, singles/doubles US$34/40

Goldi Sands Hotel (☎ 031-2021, 2348), Ethukala, 75 rooms, singles/doubles US$25/30

Hotel Dolphin (☎ 031-3129), Waikkal, 76 rooms, singles/doubles US$36/48

Ranweli Holiday Village (☎ 031-2136), Waikkal, 84 chalets, singles or doubles Rs 1000, air-con Rs 200 extra

Royal Oceanic Hotel (☎ 031-2377, 3098/9), Ethukala, 85 rooms, singles or doubles US$35

Places to Eat

There are numerous restaurants, including several seafood specialists, along and just off Lewis Place. Wander along and see which ones are getting regular custom.

The majority are up the north end of the strip to cream off business from the big hotels, with one concentration just north of Browns Beach Hotel and along the road inland there. Here the *Ocean Fish Restaurant* does tasty prawns and noodles for Rs 80, while the slow but good *Vasana Restaurant* is good value for more expensive things like whole lobster in garlic sauce (Rs 300). Also here, the *Pri-kin Restaurant* has a chef from Beijing concocting real Chinese fare. The prawns with cashew and chilli and the giant bowls of soup are meals in themselves. A steamed grouper will cost Rs 160.

Further south, the Hotel Silver Sands has been recommended for good if not cheap food, while the restaurant at *Dephani Guest House*, 189/15 Lewis Place, serves good food at reasonable prices – rice and vegetable curry Rs 50, pancakes Rs 25 to Rs 40, prawn and fish dishes around Rs 95. The *Lagoon View Rest House* does good rice and curry.

If you need to really fill up, try the Rs 220 all-you-can-eat Sunday lunch buffet at *Browns Beach Hotel*, which includes free use of the hotel pool. In the evenings this hotel serves buffets of varying international cuisines at Rs 300.

In town you'll find quite a selection of the standard rice and curry places plus the *Coronation Hotel* which offers various rice dishes and good short eats.

Getting There & Away

To/From the Airport One of Negombo's most useful roles is as a transit point to/from the Colombo airport, and airport transport is cheaper from Negombo than from Colombo. Buses (Rs 5) run every 15 to 30 minutes from about 4.30 am to 10 pm. A taxi costs about Rs 200 from the bus stand, Rs 250 from Lewis Place, Rs 300 or Rs 350 from a hotel. A three-wheeler is about half those prices.

Bus & Train Private buses between Colombo (Saunders Place) and Negombo are frequent. The last go about 10 pm. There are CTB services (No 240) too. Long queues form at Negombo bus station on weekend evenings as day-trippers return to the capital. The trip is about an hour. There are also trains for Rs 8.25 (3rd class), but they're slower and rarer than the buses.

Taxi You could get a taxi between Negombo and Colombo for Rs 500 or Rs 600.

Car & Motorbike There are a few rental places in Negombo. If you can, test the vehicle before agreeing to rent it. Prices quoted are comparable with those in Colombo, but may be negotiable. Nishal Travels, almost opposite the Golden Beach Hotel, quotes Rs 900 a day plus Rs 40 a day insurance, and US$200 cash deposit, for a Toyota Corolla. Alma Tours, next to the Catamaran Beach Hotel on Lewis Place, has motorbikes from Rs 200 to Rs 450 a day.

Getting Around

There are buses along Lewis Place but three-wheelers are the easiest way of reaching a guest house or hotel from the bus or train station if you don't want to walk. They cost about Rs 50 to the middle of Lewis Place.

A rented bicycle is good transport for a leisurely look around Negombo, along the canal or over the lagoon bridge to the islands. A number of places on Lewis Place, such as Alma Tours next to the Catamaran Beach Hotel, have bikes for Rs 60 a day. Alma's are mostly in quite good condition.

KALUTARA

Kalutara, 43 km south of Colombo, was once an important spice trading centre controlled at various times by the Portuguese, Dutch and British. Today it has a reputation for fine basketware (visit Basket Hall) and for the best mangosteens on the island. Immediately south of the Kalu Ganga Bridge on the main road is the Gangatilaka Vihara, which has a hollow dagoba with an interesting painted interior. By the roadside there's a small shrine and bo-tree where drivers often stop to make offerings to ensure a safe journey.

Places to Stay

Kalutara and Wadduwa, a few km north, have beaches and a number of middle and top end places to stay. But there's little to halt the individual traveller en route to more laid-back beach spots further south. Hostelries include:

Garden Beach Hotel (☎ 034-22380), 62/9 Sri Sumangala Mawatha, Kalutara North, 12 rooms at Rs 250, air-con Rs 150 extra.
Hibiscus Beach Hotel (☎ 034-22704-6), Mahawaskaduwa, Kalutara North, 50 rooms (no air-con), singles/doubles US$25/28.
Samudra (☎ 034-22229), 77 Sri Sumangala Rd North, Kalutara North, four rooms at Rs 275 including breakfast.
Sindbad Hotel (☎ 034-22537/9), Kalutara, 105 rooms, singles/doubles US$36/48, air-con US$10 extra.
Tangerine Beach Hotel (☎ 034-22295, 22640), Kalutara, 130 rooms (all air-con), singles/doubles US$55/58.
Villa Ocean View (☎ 034-32463), Wadduwa, 84 rooms, singles/doubles US$18/20, air-con US$4.50 extra.

BERUWELA

Together with Bentota, to its south across the mouth of the Bentota River, Beruwela, 58 km south of Colombo, has been developed into Sri Lanka's chief package tour resort, with a long string of middle and top-end hotels along its fine beach, where locals address foreigners initially in German. There's nothing really to attract the independent traveller here.

The first recorded Muslim settlement of the island took place at Beruwela in 1024 AD. The Kechimalai Mosque, on a headland in the town, north of the hotel strip, is said to be built on the site of the landing and is the focus for a major festival at the end of Ramadan.

Places to Stay

The tourist hotels are all very much aimed at the package groups who come to Sri Lanka from the European winter. Bed & breakfast or room-only prices in these hotels range from US$15 to US$72, but the vast majority of the guests are on all-inclusive packages. All the hotels have various jet-set facilities. The Riverina, for instance, boasts floodlit tennis, windsurfing, sailing and minigolf. The Barberyn Reef has an Ayurvedic health centre. The Beruwela hotels are:

Barberyn Reef Hotel (☎ 034-75582), 65 rooms, from US$15/17 bed & breakfast.
Beach Hotel Bayroo (☎ 034-75297), 100 rooms (all air-con), singles/doubles from US$45/55.
Confifi Beach Hotel (☎ 034-75217), 68 rooms, singles/doubles US$30/41.
Hotel Swanee (☎ 034-75208), 52 rooms from US$30 single or double, air-con US$4 extra.
Neptune Hotel (☎ 034-75218), 104 rooms (100 air-con), singles/doubles US$39/51.
Palm Garden Hotel (☎ 034-75263), 120 rooms (all air-con), singles/doubles US$51/57.
Pearl Beach Hotel (☎ 034-75117), 40 bungalows, singles/doubles US$25/28.
Riverina Hotel (☎ 034-75377), 190 rooms (all air-con), singles/doubles US$60/72.
Riviera Beach Resort (☎ 034-75245), 48 rooms at US$11.
Wornels Reef Hotel (☎ 034-75430), 100 rooms, singles/doubles US$32/35.

Getting There & Away
See the Bentota section.

BENTOTA, ALUTHGAMA & INDURUWA
Bentota, like Beruwela, is dominated by big package hotels, but it also has a number of smaller places catering to independent travellers. There are more such places in Aluthgama, a small town on the main road between Beruwela and Bentota. Aluthgama has a raucous fish market, local shops, and the main railway station for the whole resort area. In addition to sea beaches as fine as Beruwela's, Bentota (like Aluthgama) enjoys the beautiful calm waters of the Bentota River, good for sailing, windsurfing and water skiing. A few km inland, on the south bank of the river, is the Galapota Temple, said to date from the 12th century. To reach it, take the Elpitiya turning off the main road a km south of the Bentota River bridge.

Fine beaches continue several km south from Bentota. Induruwa, a hamlet five km down the road, has a small cluster of places to stay on a lovely, quiet length of beach, at the north end of which is one of the turtle hatcheries that you can visit in this area. The beach south of the resort at Kosgoda, five km beyond Induruwa, is reputedly the best in Sri Lanka for turtle viewing, with the island's original hatchery (see Unawatuna for more info on turtle habits).

Orientation & Information
Just south of the middle of Aluthgama the main road crosses the Bentota River into Bentota where, on its seaward side, there's the Bentota resort centre with a post office, Bank of Ceylon branch, tourist shops and a few restaurants, all near the little-used Bentota station. From the river bridge the river turns to flow north, parallel to the coast, for a few hundred yards, divided from the sea only by a narrow spit of land on which are built some of Bentota's top hotels (they're reachable only from the beach or by boat across the river). The river mouth is the dividing line between Bentota and Beruwela.

Places to Stay – bottom end & middle
Aluthgama *Hemadan Tourist Guest House* (☎ 034-75320) at 25A River Ave is one of a handful of guest houses on the inland bank of the river, reached by a lane from the north side of the Bentota River bridge. Its rooms are moderately sized for Rs 550/600, but they're clean and have balconies. There's a restaurant and a free boat across the river for beachgoers.

The *Little Villa Tourist Inn* (☎ 034-75066) is a small place with a lovely riverfront position, just off the main road about 1½ km north of the Bentota River bridge. The sizeable, very clean rooms (Rs 650/800) have big double beds and verandahs opening on to the riverside garden.

Further north, just before Aluthgama becomes Beruwela, *Dulmini Beach Cottages* (☎ 034-75230) has 20 pleasant bungalow-style rooms in a big garden giving on to the beach, just where the river meets the sea, plus a pool and restaurant, for Rs 600 single or double (air-con Rs 150 extra).

Bentota The *Susanta Palm Restaurant* (☎ 034-75324) in Bentota resort centre has moderate rooms with private bath for Rs 380 single or double, but the *Susanta Guest House*, with the same phone number and run by the same people, 200 metres away on a track leading towards the beach, is more secluded. Its rooms are clean and cool with fans and nets, though not huge, and cost Rs 250/350 including breakfast.

The small family-run *Sooriya Tourist Inn* is 300 metres down a track west off the main road, about 1¼ km south from the resort centre. Its clean, cool rooms with fan, net and attached bathroom cost Rs 250 or Rs 300. Meals are available and you're only a hop, skip and a jump from the beach.

Another quarter-km south down the main road is the turning to *The Villa* (☎ 034-75312) – a spacious, elegant 19th-century Dutch-style villa with a big coconut grove garden, two minutes' walk from the beach. The six rooms cost US$20/30. A further half-km or so south on the inland side of the main road is another rambling villa-turned-hotel –

the mock-Tudor *Hotel Warahena Walauwa* (☎ 034-75372), complete with interior courtyards around fish ponds, with 20 aircon rooms at US$15/20.

Induruwa Two hundred metres north of Induruwa station, *Long Beach Cottage* (☎ 01-727602), is the home of a Sri Lankan-German family and has five plain, but clean and pleasant rooms with nets, fans and attached bath for Rs 200/250. Sri Lankan food is available.

Half a km south of the station, *Little Dream Cottage* (no tel, fax 034-75186) is a lovely little guest house with a garden opening on to the beach, run by two Italians and very successfully combining Italian and Sri Lankan style. The half-dozen rooms are very clean, tasteful and sizeable, and come for Rs 550/600 with breakfast. There's delicious Italian and Sri Lankan food too – though it's far from cheap at Rs 250-ish for rice and curry, Rs 100 to Rs 300 for spaghetti. A few minutes' walk either side of the Little Dream Cottage are two bigger hotels, both with pools and large comfortable rooms but much less atmosphere – the *Hotel Whispering Palms* to the north charging Rs 400/500, and the *Emerald Bay Hotel* to the south at Rs 650.

Places to Stay – top end
The top hotel and one of the biggest beach hotels in Sri Lanka is the 133-room *Bentota Beach Hotel* (☎ 034-75176) immediately south of the Bentota River bridge, complete with floodlit tennis, air-conditioning, pool, discotheque and, in case you're not hot enough, squash. It's rivalled by the *Hotel Ceysands* (☎ 034-75073), on the spit of land between river and sea, with 84 rooms, all air-con, at US$55/65 to US$90/100 depending on the season. Immediately south of the Bentota Beach Hotel are the *Hotel Serendib* (☎ 034-75248) with 90 rooms at US$36/48 (air-con US$10 extra), and the *Lihiniya Surf Hotel* (☎ 034-75126) with 92 air-con rooms at US$34/38.

Places to Eat
There's a handful of non-hotel restaurants in the Bentota resort centre, including the *Susanta Palm Restaurant* with fish or steaks at Rs 80 or Rs 90, rice and curry Rs 140, the *Goldi Steak Haus* with steaks around Rs 130, and the *Golden Gourmet* seafood restaurant. A few basic local eateries can be found in Aluthgama.

Getting There & Away
Bentota and Beruwela are both on the main Colombo-Matara railway but Aluthgama, the small town sandwiched between them, is the station to head for. Many trains don't bother to stop at the smaller Beruwela and Bentota stations. Aluthgama has five or six quick (1½ to two hours) trains daily to/from Colombo, and a similar number to/from Hikkaduwa, Galle and Matara. Avoid the other, slower trains. The fares from Colombo to Aluthgama are Rs 10 in 3rd class, Rs 28 in 2nd class. Aluthgama is also the best place to pick up a bus when you're leaving, although there's no trouble getting off one at Bentota or Beruwela when you arrive.

AMBALANGODA
South of Bentota the road and railway run close to the continuously beautiful coast. Ambalangoda, 86 km from Colombo, is a fair-sized but sleepy town, overshadowed as a destination by its more glamorous neighbour Hikkaduwa, 13 km further south, but with a beautiful sweep of sandy beach to its north and some famous mask carvers, whom you will find concentrated on the northern edge of town.

Good mask carvers include M H Mettananda at 142 Patabendimulla, on the Colombo road about 500 metres north of the rail and bus stations, which are on the same main road in the middle of town. Tony bought a mask here when researching the first edition of this book and was pleased to find, on subsequent trips, that Mettananda's masks had become even better. About 300 metres further towards Colombo, the two shops of the famous mask carver Ariyapala and his son are a few steps apart either side of a roundabout. Handwoven cotton is another Ambalangoda craft.

Places to Stay & Eat

Most of the more attractive places are north of the centre. From the bus station, walk a short distance south to a junction where you'll see the railway station a block inland. Go one block west (away from the railway station) to Main St, then turn right (north). After about 200 metres, on the right, is the *Chinese Hotel Restaurant*, a fan-cooled oasis of good food with even a fair attempt at Chinese decor. Rice and four curries is Rs 25, chicken, fish or prawn dishes are Rs 60 to Rs 85. Fried rice or noodle dishes are Rs 40 to Rs 60 and the chicken and egg noodle soup is a tasty meal in itself, liberally endowed with vegetables, garlic and pepper.

The *Sumudu Guest House*, about 500 metres north of the Chinese at 418 Main St, Patabendimulla, is a large, cool, old-style house run by a friendly family, with pleasant clean rooms for Rs 200 a person including good breakfast and dinner. You might be able to get a room-only rate too. Just beyond the house is the roundabout on the Colombo road with the Ariyapala mask shops. There's also a lowland dance school just up the road.

If you turn off Main St down towards the sea soon after the Chinese, then go to the right along Sea Beach Rd, you reach *Shangrela* (☎ 09-27342), a big house facing the sea with three clean rooms at Rs 150/250 with attached bathroom. Breakfast is available for Rs 60. One traveller wrote that, curiously, 'the landlady does not like single travellers'. On the beach at the next corner along Sea Beach Rd is the *Portman Restaurant*, a palm shack serving shark, chips and veg salad for Rs 110, and other good fare. It has a house opposite with two rooms with attached bath, net and fan at Rs 300 double.

About 300 metres south of the centre along Main St – remember that Main St is one block west of the main road – is the *Rest House* (☎ 09-27299). It has a reasonable restaurant, and big rooms with fan, net and attached bath for Rs 300 single or double, but is a bit dilapidated and overlooks a small fishing-boat cove which could be picturesque but is in fact dirty and smelly. Next door to the Rest House, the *Blue Horizon Tour Inn* (☎ 09-27475) at 129 Modera Devale Rd, has dingy singles/doubles at Rs 150/200. *Seaview*, a family house at 14 Hirewatha, the street running down between the Rest House and the Blue Horizon, has a couple of small rooms with fan, net and attached bath for Rs 100/150. In Randomba, three km north of Ambalangoda, the good *Randomba Inn Hotel* has doubles with private bath and verandah overlooking the beach for Rs 250, plus good inexpensive food. At Ahungalla, nine km north of Ambalangoda, the oceanside *Triton Hotel* (☎ 09-54041) is one of Sri Lanka's most luxurious hotels, with lovely grounds and a giant swimming pool that looks like it merges with the ocean. Its 150 air-con rooms start at US$78/98 room only. Buses between Colombo and Ambalangoda pass right by the Triton and the Randomba Inn.

Getting There & Away

Ambalangoda is on the main road and railway from Colombo to Hikkaduwa, Galle and the south. The fares from Colombo are Rs 15 by bus or in 3rd class on the train, Rs 39 in 2nd class on the train. Frequent buses come through to/from Hikkaduwa.

HIKKADUWA

Situated 98 km (61 miles) south of Colombo, Hikkaduwa is the most popular of the beach centres. It's the variety that attracts people. Accommodation ranges from a handful of top-end hotels to dozens of smaller, cheaper guest houses populated by backpackers and other independent travellers. All these are backed up by an equally varied selection of restaurants, snack bars and cafés. Hikkaduwa today has stretched out into the villages south of it and is three or four km long – a strip of houses, shops, restaurants, cafés, guest houses and hotels either side of the road and along the beach. But there are no real high-rise buildings, and particularly towards the southern end it's quite spread out, so that even at the height of the tourist season it stays relaxed.

There's an equally varied choice of beach and sea – coral for snorkellers, waves for board and body surfers, and good wide strips of sand, backed by cafés, if you just want to sit back and relax.

Hikkaduwa can be surprisingly pleasant during the May-to-October monsoon period: prices drop, the crowds disappear, and the weather is often OK – though the waters may be too rough for swimming anywhere except the coral sanctuary.

Orientation

Services like the rail and bus stations, banks, post office and non-tourist-oriented shops congregate in the north end of Hikkaduwa proper, which was the original settlement. A little further south is where the first tourist hotels, guest houses and restaurants opened up, but this area now seems overdeveloped and a bit shabby compared with Wewala and Narigama further south (two to three km from the stations), where most independent travellers stay. These areas are more relaxed and spread out, and with better beaches, than Hikkaduwa proper. South of Narigama the waters tend to be rougher and less safe for bathing – but there are yet further guest houses scattered along the beach and road through Thiranagama and Patuwata, even as far as Dodanduwa, almost half way to Galle.

Information

Money You can change money or traveller's cheques at three banks in Hikkaduwa proper. The People's Bank is the most southerly and has much longer opening hours (from Monday to Friday 8 am to 7 pm, Saturday and Sunday 9 am to 2 pm) than the Bank of Ceylon or the Commercial Bank of Ceylon (both Monday 9 am to 1 pm and from Tuesday to Friday 9 am to 1.30 pm). Exchange rates are pretty well identical between the three banks. You can save the trip to a bank – but lose about 1½ rupees per dollar – by changing at the hotels.

Post & Telecommunications The little Dimasha agency post office on the main road just south of the railway station is open daily 8 am to midnight for mail, telegrams, photocopies and phone calls. The main post office is on the Baddegama road, five minutes' walk inland from the bus station – open from Monday to Saturday 6 am to 8 pm.

Books You can borrow books in numerous European languages from the 'Tourist Library' in Narigama for Rs 20 to Rs 25 a shot, plus a deposit of about the same.

Things to See & Do

Coral Sanctuary Hikkaduwa's 'coral sanctuary', stretching out from the string of 'Coral' hotels to a group of rocks a couple of hundred metres offshore, is a large, shallow area enclosed by a reef, carpeted with colourful corals and populated by countless tropical fish, with fishing and spear fishing banned. You can swim out to the rocks from the Coral Gardens Hotel, where the reef runs straight out from the shore. The water over the reef is never more than three or four metres deep. Turtles also circulate; they lazily glide away from you if you try to pursue them.

If you don't have your own mask, snorkel and fins, there are places near the Coral Rock and Coral Seas hotels which will hire them out for around Rs 30 an hour. There are also two or three enterprises in the same area which will take you out in a glass-bottom boat to see the coral, for around Rs 200 for four people for 45 minutes. However these boats have caused some damage to the reef, especially at low tide, and we even heard from one unhappy pair of snorkellers who complained of nearly being run over by a glass-bottom boat. The best way to see the reef is with a snorkel.

At least in the sanctuary the coral isn't being torn up and burnt to make lime for building, as is happening elsewhere at Hikkaduwa – with the consequence that the beach is being eroded in places.

Scuba Diving The Poseidon Diving Station charges Rs 600 an hour for diving trips

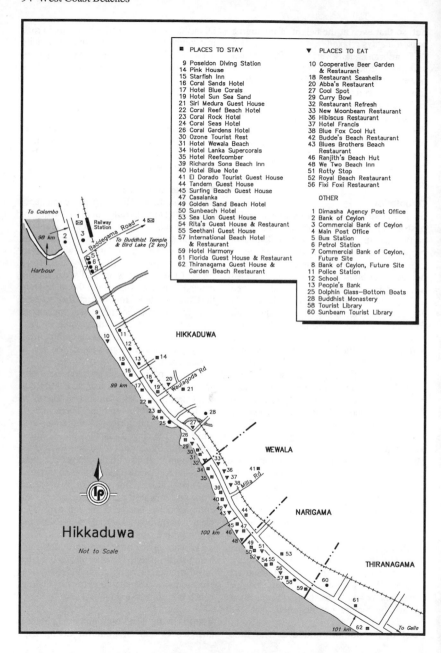

■ PLACES TO STAY

9 Poseidon Diving Station
14 Pink House
15 Starfish Inn
16 Coral Sands Hotel
17 Hotel Blue Corals
19 Hotel Sun Sea Sand
21 Siri Medura Guest House
22 Coral Reef Beach Hotel
23 Coral Rock Hotel
24 Coral Seas Hotel
26 Coral Gardens Hotel
30 Ozone Tourist Rest
31 Hotel Wewala Beach
34 Hotel Lanka Supercorals
35 Hotel Reefcomber
39 Richards Sons Beach Inn
40 Hotel Blue Note
41 El Dorado Tourist Guest House
44 Tandem Guest House
45 Surfing Beach Guest House
47 Casalanka
49 Golden Sand Beach Hotel
50 Sunbeach Hotel
53 Sea Lion Guest House
54 Rita's Guest House & Restaurant
55 Seethani Guest House
57 International Beach Hotel
   & Restaurant
59 Hotel Harmony
61 Florida Guest House & Restaurant
62 Thiranagama Guest House &
   Garden Beach Restaurant

▼ PLACES TO EAT

10 Cooperative Beer Garden
   & Restaurant
18 Restaurant Seashells
20 Abba's Restaurant
27 Cool Spot
29 Curry Bowl
32 Restaurant Refresh
33 New Moonbeam Restaurant
36 Hibiscus Restaurant
37 Hotel Francis
38 Blue Fox Cool Hut
42 Budde's Beach Restaurant
43 Blues Brothers Beach
   Restaurant
46 Ranjith's Beach Hut
48 We Two Beach Inn
51 Rotty Stop
52 Royal Beach Restaurant
56 Fixi Foxi Restaurant

OTHER

1 Dimasha Agency Post Office
2 Bank of Ceylon
3 Commercial Bank of Ceylon
4 Main Post Office
5 Bus Station
6 Petrol Station
7 Commercial Bank of Ceylon,
   Future Site
8 Bank of Ceylon, Future Site
11 Police Station
12 School
13 People's Bank
25 Dolphin Glass—Bottom Boats
28 Buddhist Monastery
58 Tourist Library
60 Sunbeam Tourist Library

To Colombo

98 km

Railway
Station

Baddegama Road

To Buddhist Temple
& Bird Lake (2 km)

Harbour

HIKKADUWA

99 km

Wauragoda Rd

Milla Rd

WEWALA

Hikkaduwa

Not to Scale

NARIGAMA

100 km

THIRANAGAMA

101 km

To Galle

including use of the boat, though you can't rely on facilities being available out of season. There are a number of wrecks in the area. You can also take four or five-day diving courses for about Rs 10,000 here – check whether they lead to the internationally recognised PADI certificate.

Surf & Beach A short distance south of the coral reef, in front of Wewala and Narigama, there's good surf for board riders, and international surfers are here in numbers. Then the beach widens out into a fine strip for sunbathing with, in places, good waves for body surfing. Some of the guest houses and beach cafes towards this south end rent out surfboards and boogie boards (Rs 25 an hour and up). And of course there's the usual parade of beach life – snake charmers, coconut hawkers, elephant rides – to keep you awake.

As anywhere on this west coast, take care in the water at Hikkaduwa – the currents can be tricky and there are no life-saving facilities. There have been drownings.

Inland Life at Hikkaduwa isn't only sea and sand, although it may often feel that way. There are countless shops along the road selling everything Sri Lanka has to offer – masks, gems, jewellery, batik, pirate tapes (about Rs 100 each), antiques. Plus clothes shops making all the usual travellers' gear – skirts, light cotton trousers and so on. Unfortunately a lot of traffic – notably of course private buses – screams through Hikkaduwa far too fast, which makes walking or cycling along the road an unpleasant, sometimes dangerous, occupation. Hikkaduwa is one of the first places south of Colombo where traffic thins out enough for much overtaking to be possible, so other road users just have to get out of the way.

To leave the beach scene completely, just walk or cycle along any of the minor roads inland into the forest. They lead to a calmer, completely different, rural world. Just up the Baddegama road from the bus station is an interesting Buddhist temple with lots of the popular 'comic book' paintings (the work of

one man over nearly a decade) and a couple of beautiful peacocks. After two km there's a lake with a lot of bird life. Several other temples and monasteries are within easy bicycling reach of Hikkaduwa.

Places to Stay – bottom end & middle
Virtually all Hikkaduwa's places to stay are strung out along the main road. The best way to find something to suit is simply to wander down the road and look at a variety of rooms. All bottom-end prices can be bargained over. Those given here are what you'd expect to pay in the peak season – Christmas to February – when a basic guest house room with private bath on the beach side is around Rs 200 to Rs 300. Out of season the same room may go for Rs 100 or maybe even less. For lower prices, ask for rooms with shared bath – or look on the 'jungle side' of the road. Prices also vary according to which stretch of the strip you're on – down where the sands are wider, room rates tend to get higher. In season the best-value smaller places fill up quickly: you may need to make a booking for a few days ahead and meanwhile bide your time elsewhere.

The places that follow are just a cross-section of the wide choice along the strip, starting in Hikkaduwa proper and moving south. If mosquitoes are in season you'll probably find fewer of them on the beach side of the road.

Hikkaduwa Generally the beach is narrower and less attractive, and the buildings closer together, up this northern end, though there are some good-value places to be found. On the beach side *Poseidon Diving Station* (☎ 09-23294) has fair singles/doubles with net and private bath for Rs 250/350. The *Starfish Inn* has a nice little garden overlooking a fishing boat anchorage, and rooms with fan and private bath at Rs 350 single or double which are clean but nothing special.

The much cheaper *Pink House,* inland over the railway tracks, with several buildings in a large garden, is shabby but reasonably clean and spacious. Singles/doubles with fan and shared shower and toilet are Rs 75/80, with private bathroom Rs 100/110. A little further down, the *Hotel Sun Sea Sand* has rooms with private bath for Rs 150/200 or Rs 200/250, and a pleasant garden. Breakfast is Rs 50.

Inland on Waulagoda Rd are a number of places including the cheap *Siri Medura Guest House*, a medium-size family home with a few rooms to let at Rs 50 or Rs 75 with fan and net. The shared toilets are clean. Back on the beach side the *Coral Seas Hotel* is probably the cheapest of the hotels, as opposed to guest houses, at Rs 400 a double including breakfast, but the rooms are nothing special. The *Ozone Tourist Rest* has just a few good clean rooms with fan, mosquito net and private bath for Rs 220 single or double, and a seafront sitting area.

Away from the beach altogether, at Pathana, 2½ km inland along the Baddegama road from Hikkaduwa bus station, the *Bird Lake Lodge* (☎ 09-22018) has 10 rooms with private bath, fan and balconies overlooking a lake which, as the name suggests, has a plentiful bird life. Rooms are Rs 250/350 including breakfast and there's a restaurant too. If you can't find a bus along the Baddegama road, a three-wheeler from Hikkaduwa is about Rs 30.

Wewala *Richards Sons Beach Inn* is a basic little place, but with a beautifully breezy position, a big seafront garden, and run by a friendly family. Rooms are Rs 300 a single or double, with private bath and net. Next along is another good little place, the *Hotel Blue Note*, opening straight onto the beach. The very clean rooms have individual verandahs and are angled to catch maximum sea breeze. They're attractively decorated with batiks and cost Rs 500 each, private bath included.

Along the inland lane opposite the Blue Note, *El Dorado Tourist Guest House* is also very clean, and run by friendly people. Rooms with fan and net, some with private bath, cost Rs 125 to Rs 200. A bit further south on the main road, the *Tandem Guest House* has good, sizeable, clean rooms with

nets and big bathrooms for Rs 350/400 including breakfast.

The *Surfing Beach Guest House* fronts directly on to the best surfing waves in Hikkaduwa. The rooms are basic but the location keeps prices up: bare fanless singles generally cost Rs 100 with common shower, Rs 150 with private bathroom; doubles or triples with attached bathroom are about Rs 300 but can jump to Rs 500 or more in season. The *Casalanka* is another friendly, basic place on the beach side, with doubles around Rs 200 to Rs 250.

Narigama, Thiranagama & Patuwata The *Golden Sand Beach Hotel* and the *Sunbeach Hotel* are slightly upmarket small places with tidy beachside gardens, and clean rooms with private baths at around Rs 400 a double.

Right on the wide beach with good body-surfing waves, *Rita's Guest House & Restaurant* charges Rs 400 for rather dark, muggy rooms with nothing special except the location. *Seethani Guest House* next door has more appealing rooms with net, fan and private bath for Rs 300 in its older ground floor block, and Rs 400 in a newer two-storey block.

On the jungle side of the main road the *Sea Lion Guest House* has smallish rooms with nets and fans round a little yard for Rs 100 with shared bath, Rs 150 with private bath. There's little breeze here but it's cheap and friendly.

Further down on the beach side, the *Hotel Harmony* has good clean spacious rooms with fan, net and private bath for Rs 350 downstairs, and Rs 450 upstairs.

Beyond this, yet more places are scattered down both sides of the road for a couple of km as the built-up area thins out. Prices vary wildly but one fair-value place is the *Thiranagama Guest House* with clean rooms, fan and net included, for Rs 200 with shared bath, Rs 250 with private. Its garden opens on the beach, and rice and curry meals are available. The friendly *Upul's Restaurant & Guest House* in Patuwata, beyond the 102 km marker, has half a dozen clean, decent-

Top: Local children (PT)
Left: Planting rice beside the Colombo-Kandy road (TW)
Right: Monks (PT)

Top: Lion Platform, Sigiriya (JN)
Left: Reclining Buddha, Aluvihara (TW)
Right: Fresco, Sigiriya (TW)

size rooms with fan, net and private bath for only Rs 100 a double, even in high season.

Places to Stay – top end

There are a number of top-end places close together overlooking the coral sanctuary – and just to ensure that you get them nicely confused they all have 'coral' in their names. The most southerly of this group is the *Coral Gardens Hotel* (☎ 09-23023), Hikkaduwa's biggest and best hotel, set on the point of land where the coral reef runs out to the coral sanctuary. The 156 air-con rooms here cost from US$55/60 to US$95/115, plus US$10 extra from mid-December to the end of February. Facilities include disco, gym, pool and squash.

Going north from the Coral Gardens Hotel, there's the cheaper Coral Seas Hotel (see bottom end), then the *Coral Rock Hotel*, nothing special for Rs 800 double; the *Coral Reef Beach Hotel* (☎ 09-22197), with 32 rooms at Rs 520/660 bed & breakfast; the *Hotel Blue Corals* (☎ 09-22679) with 52 rooms at Rs 910/1070; and the *Coral Sands Hotel* (☎ 09-22436) with rooms at US$20/34, also a US$6/9 annex on the inland side of the road. The Blue Corals is probably the nicest of this group, with spacious enough rooms, and some landscaping and palm trees on the beach front, but really none of them is particularly special.

South from the Coral Gardens are the *Hotel Wewala Beach* with sizeable, cool rooms including balcony, fan and net at Rs 800/1200, and a seafront pool; the *Hotel Lanka Supercorals* (☎ 09-23387), more appealing with a fine seafront pool and garden, and 93 rooms that vary in size and outlook but all cost US$21/22; and the *Hotel Reefcomber* (☎ 09-23374), Hikkaduwa's second best, with cool rooms all opening on to sea-view verandahs for US$32/40, and another seafront garden with pool.

Places to Eat

You'll find all the standard travellers' menu items in Hikkaduwa's many eating places. Pancakes, fruit salad, omelettes, banana fritters, yoghurt, fruit drinks, ice cream and all the other necessities of life to turn a place into a food trip. In a few days at Hikkaduwa an awful lot of money seems to get spent on just dropping into some place or other for a quick fruit salad and yoghurt, or something similar.

Many of the travellers' restaurants are remarkably alike, even down to the misspellings on the menus. They're also rather variable – they'll fix you something fresh and beautifully prepared for one meal and then serve up something tired and stale for the next. Seafood figures large on the menus, of course – Hikkaduwan crab, whether it is boiled, roasted, or served with chips, salad or ginger sauce, is a taste treat not to be missed. All sorts of fish (although usually fairly anonymous) are also popular. If fair German-style cooking is what you're in the mood for, head for the little *Abba's Restaurant* on Waulagoda Rd in Hikkaduwa, where neatly prepared omelettes cost Rs 25 to Rs 35, salads Rs 25 to Rs 40, fried rice, noodles or spaghetti Rs 55 to Rs 90, fish and other dishes more.

One of the longest-running places at Hikkaduwa, and still one of the best, is the little roadside *Cool Spot*, opposite the Coral Gardens Hotel. It seems to be busy at almost any time of the day or night. Low prices, good food and friendly service are the secret here. Three veg curries and rice will cost you Rs 30, and there are good hoppers (Rs 18 with curd and honey, Rs 12 with scrambled egg), plus noodles, fish, salads, lassi, juices, cakes, you name it.

On the beach side of the road the *Curry Bowl* is another popular, long-running restaurant with a wide range of medium-price fare. Rice and three veg curries at Rs 45 is reasonably tasty though not as flavoursome as home (or good guest house) cooking. Fish and salad is Rs 50 to Rs 65, omelettes Rs 30, an avocado and prawn cocktail Rs 40.

A little further down the road there's a cluster of places with above-average prices but also above-average food. One is the *Restaurant Refresh*, where fish or prawn dishes cost Rs 80 to Rs 100, vegetable noodles Rs 45, and Chinese dishes around Rs 90.

The *New Moonbeam Restaurant* across the street is good for lobster or devilled crab – Rs 250-worth of the latter, which comes with chips, salad and vegetables, is enough for two – and the clean toilet is a revelation! A couple more doors down, the *Hibiscus Restaurant* also prepares its food with a bit of care – a good prawn curry and rice is Rs 50, noodles or fried rice will cost you around Rs 45, fish and prawn dishes Rs 65 to Rs 85.

The *Blue Fox Cool Hut* opposite the Nippon Villa hotel serves some of the tastier food you'll find along the strip, including respectable rice and curries (Rs 50 to Rs 75). Fish dishes are in the same price range.

A bit further along is a pair of eateries side by side right on the beach with virtually identical menus, both serving up quite acceptable fare: *Blues Brothers Restaurant* (the one with the breezy tower) and *Budde's Beach Restaurant*. Fish, prawn and meat dishes are Rs 70 to Rs 90, crab Rs 160, fried rice or noodles Rs 30 to Rs 50. Budde's Indian-style fish comes in a good spicy coconut sauce. There's also straightforward Western food like spaghetti, mashed potato or omelettes.

Still on the beach, *Ranjith's Beach Hut* is *the* place in Hikkaduwa for hanging out late at night, with rock and reggae music into the early hours and a variety of good munchies like pancakes (Rs 15 to Rs 20), fried rice or noodles (Rs 30-ish), ice cream and fruit salad – along with beer, arrack and soft drinks. You can while away the hours playing backgammon or carrom here.

The *We Two Beach Inn* a little further along the beach has a similar scene and fare to Ranjith's, populated by a mainly German-speaking crowd. Eateries beyond here on the beach tend to be OK for snacks or drinks but disappointing for a main meal. The best place of all to cure the munchies – at any time from late afternoon till you're staggering home from Ranjith's or We Two at 2 or 3 am – is a small, unassuming hut on the main road in Narigama called the *Rotty Stop*, which doles out Hikkaduwa's tastiest rotties to a constant stream of customers. There's a vast range of fillings from veg curry at Rs 10 (which turns out to be mostly hot chilli) to cheese, tomato, onion and garlic at Rs 23.

Getting There & Away

Bus There are frequent buses from Colombo, both private (from the Bastian Mawatha bus yard) and CTB, with fares around Rs 16 for the two to 2½-hour trip. Buses going to Galle or beyond will take you to Hikkaduwa, and will drop you somewhere south of the bus station if you know where you're headed. Buses also operate frequently to nearby Ambalangoda and Galle. Leaving Hikkaduwa, you stand more chance of a seat if you start at the bus station.

Train There are five or six quick (2½ to three hours) trains daily to/from Colombo Fort. The fare is Rs 45.25 in 2nd class, Rs 16.50 in 3rd class. There are also a few slow trains which can take four or five hours, so avoid them. Trains on this route can get very crowded – and also attract a number of touts who try to latch on to you at Fort station or on the train. However persuasive they might sound, you'll thank yourself if you turn them down and check out some places for yourself when you get to your destination. You'll also stand a better chance of negotiating a price when you're on the spot.

There are four to six quick trains daily to/from Matara (1½ hours), and one daily through train to/from Kandy in a scheduled 5½ hours. There's an extra train to Kandy on Saturdays, and from Kandy on Sundays. Of course you can reach Kandy at other times by changing trains at Colombo Fort.

Taxi Many Hikkaduwa taxis are small minibuses able to hold eight or so passengers, so they can be relatively cheap if there's a group of you. Some gather in front of the Hotel Reefcomber if you need to find one. They have fixed prices printed on a card which they should be able to show you, but sometimes you can bargain a couple of hundred rupees off these fares, which include Galle Rs 500, Unawatuna Rs 700, Colombo or Tangalla Rs 1400, Colombo Airport Rs 1800, Yala Rs 3000, Kandy Rs 3500.

Motorbike Motorbikes are readily available to rent in Hikkaduwa, both for local use and further afield. A 125 cc machine costs around Rs 250 to Rs 325 a day, a 250 cc Rs 275 to Rs 350. You can usually get a discount of about 10% if you take it for several days or a week. Of course you have to add the cost of petrol. Few of the operators offer any sort of guarantee or protection, so check the bike out as thoroughly as you can before agreeing on a deal.

Getting Around
A three-wheeler costs about Rs 25 from the rail or bus station to Wewala or Narigama. Once you're settled in, bicycle is a nice way to get around and it's easy to hire a bike here. Daily charges are cheaper at the south end of the strip: in Narigama you can get a bike for Rs 50 a day or Rs 5 'there and back'.

GALLE
The port of Galle – Sri Lanka's fourth biggest town, with 80,000 people – is 115 km south of Colombo and close to Hikkaduwa. Galle is Sri Lanka's most historically interesting living city. Although Anuradhapura and Polonnaruwa are far older they are effectively dead cities – the modern towns are quite divorced from the ancient ruins. Until the construction of breakwaters at Colombo harbour was completed in the late 19th century, Galle was the major port in Sri Lanka and still handles shipping – and cruising yachts – today.

Historians believe Galle may be the Tarshish of Biblical times – where King Solomon obtained gems, spices and peacocks – but it assumed real importance only with the arrival of the Europeans. In 1505 a Portuguese fleet, bound for the Maldives, was blown off course and took shelter in the harbour at dusk. It is said that, on hearing a cock *(galo* in Portuguese) crowing, they gave the town its name. Another story is that

the name is derived from the Sinhala *gala* (rock), of which the harbour has plenty. In 1589, during one of their periodic squabbles with the Kingdom of Kandy, the Portuguese built a small fort which they named Santa Cruz. Later they extended this with a series of bastions and walls but the Dutch, who took Galle in 1640, destroyed almost all traces of the Portuguese presence.

In 1663 the Dutch built the 36-hectare fort which stands in almost perfect repair today, occupying most of the promontory that forms the older part of Galle. By the time Galle passed into British hands commercial interest was turning to Colombo, and old Galle has scarcely altered since. It's delightfully quiet and easy going, with a real sense of being steeped in history.

Galle is an easy day trip from Hikkaduwa or Unawatuna, but there's a variety of places to stay if you want to soak up more of the atmosphere.

Warning
Galle has developed a bad reputation for rip-offs and con artists. Many travellers are approached by people who say the Fort is 'closed' – a patent absurdity since the Fort is a part of the town like any other – or ask you to translate a letter or document for them, or offer to show you crocodiles (in reality water monitors beside the canal on Havelock Place) or offer free or cheap lifts to Unawatuna or Hikkaduwa. These people's real aim is usually to get you into gem shops – where you may be charged absurdly high prices or sold fakes, or asked to buy gems and re-sell them in other countries – the kind of activity that even a gem expert would think twice about co-operating with strangers in. There are also some of the usual scheming accommodation touts.

Orientation & Information
The old town, or Fort, occupies most of a south-pointing promontory. Around where the promontory meets the 'mainland' is the centre of the new town, with the bus and rail stations, shops and services. The main post office is near the market on the Matara road,

though there's also a small, decaying office in the Fort. You can send faxes or telexes, and make photocopies or IDD phone calls at Selaka Communications in a small shopping arcade by the bus station, or one or two similar offices on Havelock Place.

The Fort Walls

One of the most pleasant strolls you can make is the circuit of the Fort walls at dusk. As the daytime heat fades away you can, in an easy hour or two, walk almost the complete circuit of the Fort along the top of the wall. Only once – between Aurora bastion and the old gate – is it necessary to leave the wall.

The main gate in the northern stretch of the wall is a comparatively recent addition – it was built by the British in 1873 to handle the heavier flow of traffic into the old city. This part of the wall, the most heavily fortified since it faced the land, was originally built by the Portuguese with a moat, then substantially enlarged by the Dutch, who in 1667 split it into separate 'Star', 'Moon' and 'Sun' bastions.

Following the Fort wall clockwise you soon come to the 'Old Gate'. On its outer side the British coat of arms tops the entrance. Inside the letters VOC, standing for Dutch East India Company, are inscribed in the stone, flanked by two lions and topped by a cock, with the date 1669. The gate houses the disappointing National Maritime Museum. Just beyond the gate is the 'Zwart' bastion, or 'Black Fort', thought to be Portuguese-built and the oldest of the Fort bastions. Today it houses a police station.

The eastern section of the wall ends at the Point Utrecht Bastion, close to the powder magazine and topped by the modern 18-metre-high lighthouse. The lighthouse keeper *may* magically materialise when visitors arrive and, for a few rupees, show you up to the top.

The rocky point at the end of the next stretch of wall was once a Portuguese bastion. From here the Dutch signalled approaching ships to warn them of dangerous rocks – hence its name: 'Flag Rock'.

Musket shots were fired from Pigeon Island, close to the rock, to alert ships to the danger. On the Triton bastion there used to be a windmill which drew up sea water to be sprayed from carts to keep the dust down on the city streets. This stretch of the wall is a great place to be at sunset. There's a series of other bastions, and the tomb of a Muslim saint before you arrive back at your starting point.

Inside the Fort

Most of the older buildings within the Fort date from the Dutch era and many of the streets still bear their Dutch names, or are direct translations – thus Mohrische Kramer Staat became the Street of the Moorish Traders and Rope Walk Street has remained as Leyn Baan Street, which now contains a Dutch Period Museum in a well-restored Dutch house at No 31-39.

There's another small museum next to the New Oriental Hotel but the hotel itself is more interesting. Originally built in 1684 to house the Dutch governor and officers, it became a hotel in 1863. The maps and prints on its walls reveal much about the town's history. You can imbibe the colonial atmosphere over a lime soda (Rs 45) on its airy verandah. The 'Groote Kerk', or Great Church, next door was originally built in 1640 but the present church dates from 1752-55. Its floor is paved with gravestones from the old Dutch cemetery.

Opposite the church are a 1701 bell tower and the old Dutch Government House, now used as offices by Walker & Sons. Over the doorway a slab bears the date 1683 and the figure of a cock. The old Dutch ovens are still inside and the building is said to be haunted by more than one ghost! The Dutch also built an intricate sewer system which was flushed out daily by the rising and falling tide. With true colonial efficiency they then bred musk rats in the sewers, which were exported for their musk oil.

Places to Stay – bottom end

Mrs Wijenayake's or *Beach Haven* (☎ 09-22663) at 65 Lighthouse St is immaculately

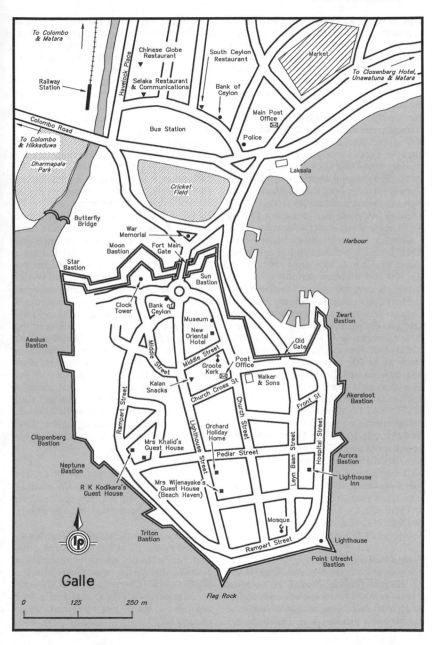

To Colombo & Matara

Railway Station

Chinese Globe Restaurant

South Ceylon Restaurant

Market

To Closenberg Hotel, Unawatuna & Matara

Havelock Place

Selaka Restaurant & Communications

Bank of Ceylon

Colombo Road

To Colombo & Hikkaduwa

Bus Station

Main Post Office

Police

Dharmapala Park

Cricket Field

Laksala

Butterfly Bridge

War Memorial

Harbour

Moon Bastion

Fort Main Gate

Star Bastion

Sun Bastion

Clock Tower

Bank of Ceylon

Museum

Aeolus Bastion

New Oriental Hotel

Zwart Bastion

Middle Street

Middle Street

Old Gate

Groote Kerk

Post Office

Walker & Sons

Kalan Snacks

Church Cross St

Akersloot Bastion

Clippenberg Bastion

Rampart Street

Church Street

Front St

Orchard Holiday Home

Lighthouse Street

Leyn Baan Street

Hospital Street

Mrs Khalid's Guest House

Neptune Bastion

Pedlar Street

Aurora Bastion

Lighthouse Inn

R K Kodikara's Guest House

Mrs Wijenayake's Guest House (Beach Haven)

Mosque

Triton Bastion

Rampart Street

Lighthouse

Galle

Point Utrecht Bastion

0   125   250 m

Flag Rock

kept, though prices have risen a lot with the upgrading of the accommodation here. The excellent guest rooms are in their own section, upstairs at the back, with their own bright sitting room. All have private bath, nets and fan, and range from Rs 300 to Rs 600. Very good meals are available here too – about Rs 100 for a dinner of rice and curry, and dessert. Mrs Wijenayake is a town councillor and her husband the town coroner, so you can find out plenty about local life. A cheaper family-run guest house is the friendly *Mrs Khalid's* (☎ 09-22725) at 106 Pedlar St. Foreign students spending time in Galle often lodge here. Rooms with attached bath and mosquito net are Rs 150 to Rs 250. The food is good, rice and curry costing Rs 55, more if you want fish or meat.

The *Ashrab Brothers Guest House* (☎ 09-23417) at 62 Lighthouse St is a new place found by readers, with eight rooms from Rs 100 and a cheap dormitory. There's family cooking and a bicycle available.

Many other places in Galle are the worse for wear after the late 1980s tourism slump. One friendly place where renovations have at least begun is *R K Kodikara's* (☎ 09-22351) at 29 Rampart St, which is clean and cheap at Rs 100 with shared bath, Rs 125 with attached bath. Rooms have net and fan. There's no sign – look for the number.

The *Orchard Holiday Home* (☎ 09-22370) at 61 Lighthouse St has seven dark, faded rooms with private bathroom at Rs 125 single, Rs 250 double, and a bar that gets noisy at night. The *Lighthouse Inn* (no sign) at 24 Hospital St is similarly shabby with singles/doubles at Rs 175/300 downstairs, doubles at Rs 375 upstairs. There are fans but no nets.

There are 11 *Railway Retiring Rooms* (☎ 09-2271) at Galle station, costing Rs 100 a single, Rs 125 a double.

Places to Stay – top end

The olde worlde *New Oriental Hotel* (☎ 09-32191) at 10 Church St has all the Victorian flavour you could ask for. It's the only upper-notch hotel in the Fort, with an atmospheric old bar and a pleasant pool. The rooms are variable, though mostly spacious. In general the downstairs rooms are bright and clean but with ageing bathrooms, while some of the upstairs ones, many of which have four-posters, have a scent of decay. The 35 rooms range from a few shabby ground floor doubles at US$13, to standard doubles at US$22 and suites at US$30 or US$35. Meals cost from US$3 to US$6 but are nothing to write home about.

On the promontory on the east side of Galle harbour, about three km from the Fort, the *Closenberg Hotel* (☎ 09-23073) at 11 Closenberg Rd was built as a 19th century P&O captain's residence in the heyday of British mercantile supremacy. The 21 elegant rooms have old wooden furniture and those facing away from Galle have pleasant balconies. All have fans, nets and private bath and cost Rs 700 a single, Rs 1000 a double. The restaurant here is a highlight. People trip in from Galle, Hikkaduwa and Unawatuna for the authentic rice and curry – two curries and trimmings is Rs 85 to Rs 95, extra curries Rs 35 to Rs 45, but book it ahead if you're coming in the evening, as the curries may otherwise have run out by then. Fish and most other main dishes are Rs 160-plus. Closenberg Rd is off the Matara road, just before the 119 km marker, and the hotel is at the end, about ¾ km along. Any bus along the Matara road will take you to the Closenberg Rd junction, but if you don't fancy walking the last bit the best bet is a three-wheeler from town.

Places to Eat

See Places to Stay for some of the best places to eat – *Mrs Wijenayake's* and *Mrs Khalid's* guest houses (where outsiders too can dine, if they book ahead), and the *Closenberg Hotel*.

There are good cheap eats at *Kalan Snacks* on Lighthouse St in the Fort. Outside the Fort, beside the bus station, is the excellent *South Ceylon Restaurant*, upstairs from the South Ceylon Bakery. The food is tasty, the drinks good, and it's cheap and friendly. Rice and curry is Rs 20 to Rs 35, fried rice or noodles Rs 30 to Rs 45, whole crab or mandarin fish with rice or salad about Rs 150. There are good breakfasts too. Around the corner in Havelock Place are more eateries including the *Chinese Globe Restaurant.*

Getting There & Away
Bus There are plenty of CTB and private buses running up and down this busy coastal strip. Bus fare to/from Colombo is Rs 20 for about a three-hour trip; to/from Hikkaduwa Rs 5, Unawatuna Rs 3, and Matara Rs 9. There are buses as far afield as Tangalla (two hours), Tissamaharama, Kataragama, Wellawaya (five hours), Ella, Haputale, Monaragala, and Ratnapura via Deniyaya.

Train Trains from Colombo cost Rs 53.75 in 2nd class, Rs 19.50 in 3rd. There are four or five daily 'expresses', taking 2½ to three hours, between Galle and Colombo. There is one daily going on to/from each of Anuradhapura and Kandy. Several trains a day run to/from Matara, another one to two-hour trip.

Boat If you're trying to find a crew position on a yacht sailing from Sri Lanka, ask at the Don Windsor yachting agency on Closenberg Rd or at the Port Office, Ocean Cruising Club, also on Closenberg Rd.

UNAWATUNA
Just a few km south of Galle, Unawatuna is a wide, curving bay with a picturebook sweep of golden beach. Unawatuna is much smaller and quieter than Hikkaduwa, and popular with budget travellers – though nothing like as small, quiet or cheap as it used to be. Still, the fine beach, clear water, good reef and relatively calm and peaceful atmosphere make this one of the most pleasant beach spots in Sri Lanka.

Things to See & Do
You can hire snorkelling equipment from some of the beachfront places – or borrow it from guest houses – to explore the reef a short distance out from the west end of the beach.

There are several wrecks about 20 minutes

offshore by boat, and Unawatuna Beach Resorts (UBR) can provide scuba gear for US$15 a dive, and take you there and back for US$15 per boatload (up to six people). You can also do five-dive courses leading to the PADI certificate for US$125 at UBR.

Back on land, UBR holds a disco on Saturday nights. And on a higher plane, the South Ceylon Restaurant runs meditation classes. It also has a travellers' notice board and a visitors' book with a mixture of very useful tips and incoherent ramblings.

You can take some interesting walks over the rocks rising from the west end of the beach or along the tracks back past the Strand guest house and up the hill.

Sea turtles lay their eggs on Unawatuna beach at night around full moon from October to March, and can often be seen by snorkellers inshore from the reef. The Strand guest house has a turtle hatchery in its garden. The eggs are bought from locals who collect them (they used to sell them for eating), and are allowed to hatch (about 60 days). The baby turtles are then kept in a small pond for seven to 10 days before being set loose in the sea.

Places to Stay
Unless the much-delayed Aldiana Club resort development goes ahead towards the west end of the beach, Unawatuna has only two top-end places, and those on a modest scale. But there's a big variety among the guest houses, some of which are extremely comfortable. You can save a lot of money by staying a few minutes' walk from the beach instead of right on it. Prices given here are high-season (from November/December to about March). Out of season you can get a third or so off most of them.

Unawatuna Village Beach
The top-end *Unawatuna Beach Resorts (UBR)* (☎ 09-22147) is the first place you reach if you walk along the village beach from the main road. It's been improved into a comfortable place, with rooms on three

floors round a small garden. They're clean, with balconies and nice tiled bathrooms, and simply but tastefully decorated. Most prices range from Rs 450/500 to Rs 650/700 for singles/doubles, room only, but there are a few top floor rooms, with the best bay views, for Rs 950/1000. Air-con is Rs 150 extra.

Just beyond the UBR are a few smaller hotel-type places – the *Rumassala Hotel* (☎ 09-23027), charging Rs 225 to Rs 300 for ordinary rooms with net, fan and attached bath; the three-storey *Sandy Lane*, with rooms at Rs 450 including a good breakfast;

and the *Sunny Beach Hotel* with quite comfortable rooms, especially those upstairs with the big verandah area, at Rs 300/350 including breakfast. Buckets of fresh water are provided if you don't like the salty stuff that comes out of the showers.

Just along the beach the *Happy Banana Restaurant* has two nicely furnished rooms out the back, with verandahs, attached baths, fans and nets for Rs 450/500. Combined with the *Moon Shadow Restaurant* is the *Full Moon Guest House*, a cheapie as beach prices go, charging Rs 200 or Rs 250 for

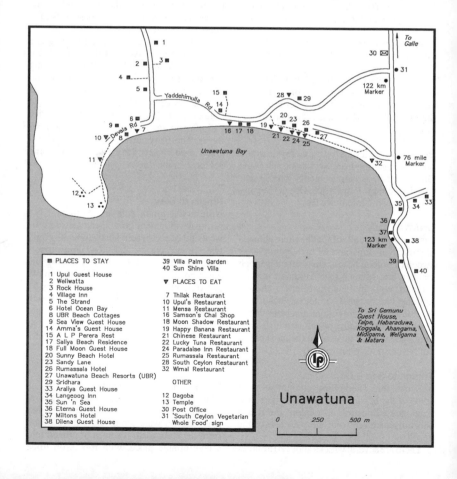

PLACES TO STAY

1 Upul Guest House
2 Weliwatta
3 Rock House
4 Village Inn
5 The Strand
6 Hotel Ocean Bay
8 UBR Beach Cottages
9 Sea View Guest House
14 Amma's Guest House
15 A L P Perera Rest
17 Saliya Beach Residence
18 Full Moon Guest House
20 Sunny Beach Hotel
23 Sandy Lane
26 Rumassala Hotel
27 Unawatuna Beach Resorts (UBR)
29 Sridhara
33 Araliya Guest House
34 Langeoog Inn
35 Sun 'n Sea
36 Eterna Guest House
37 Miltons Hotel
38 Dilena Guest House

39 Villa Palm Garden
40 Sun Shine Villa

▼ PLACES TO EAT

7 Thilak Restaurant
10 Upul's Restaurant
11 Mensa Restaurant
16 Samson's Chai Shop
18 Moon Shadow Restaurant
19 Happy Banana Restaurant
21 Lucky Tuna Restaurant
22 Lucky Tuna Restaurant
24 Paradaise Inn Restaurant
25 Rumassala Restaurant
28 South Ceylon Restaurant
32 Wimal Restaurant

OTHER

12 Dagoba
13 Temple
30 Post Office
31 'South Ceylon Vegetarian Whole Food' sign

Unawatuna

0   250   500 m

To Galle

122 km Marker

76 mile Marker

123 km Marker

Unawatuna Bay

Yaddehimulla Rd

Devala Rd

To Sri Gemunu Guest House, Talpe, Habaraduwa, Koggala, Ahangama, Midigama, Weligama & Matara basic rooms with fan and attached bath. The *Saliya Beach Residence* next door also has bare, basic rooms, again with fan, net and attached bath, for Rs 150/200. *Samson's Chai Shop* has two very basic cabanas, each with two single beds, right on the beach for Rs 150. There's a toilet on the spot but you have to go to a well behind a nearby house to wash.

Near the west end of the beach, opposite the Sea View guest house, *UBR Beach Cottages* are two 'two-room apartments' (bedroom, sitting room, bathroom and verandah), costing Rs 600 or Rs 750 a night – ask at the UBR.

Yaddehimulla Rd

Several more places are dotted along Yaddehimulla Rd, the track which leaves the main road just north of the 122 km marker, then wiggles along behind the beach. One of the first is *Sridhara*, a private house letting out a couple of rooms, with mosquito nets, for Rs 100 single or double. Bath and toilet are shared but like the rest of the place they're clean. Next door there are a few bare box-like rooms at the *South Ceylon Restaurant* (see Things to See & Do) for Rs 100/125. They have nets but no fans.

Where Yaddehimulla Rd runs close to the beach, a little path leads a short distance inland to the *A L P Perera Rest*, where a number of variable basic rooms, with nets and mostly hard beds, are just Rs 60/100. Toilets and shower are shared. Rice and four curries including fish costs Rs 50 here.

Further on, Yaddehimulla Rd turns inland to one of Unawatuna's best guest houses, *The Strand* (fax 09-32045, 'Attention Strand'), an attractive early 20th-century southern family house. The four best rooms, all with attached bath, fans, nets and verandahs or balconies, are Rs 500. There are also two cheaper rooms at Rs 250, and a separate bungalow for Rs 750. The family here is friendly and the atmosphere very relaxed. Advance bookings are taken for a minimum of two weeks.

The *Village Inn* immediately behind the Strand is run by another hospitable family,

with clean rooms from Rs 150 with net and shared bath, to Rs 350 with net, fan and attached bath. *Weliwatta*, next along Yaddehimulla Rd, is an interesting old, airy house, with clean rooms at Rs 200 or Rs 250 with nets, fans and clean shared bath. Food is good at both these places – a rice, curry and dessert dinner at Weliwatta costs around Rs 75. Opposite Weliwatta is *Rock House*, with rooms from Rs 75/100 with shared bath, to Rs 250 with private bath. Again meals are available. There's a quarry behind the house.

Further up Yaddehimulla Rd and along branch tracks are yet more places to stay, some of them charging as little as Rs 40 or Rs 50 a room. A few hang out signs, others are private homes that will let out a room or two if approached. A rice and curry meal will only be about Rs 35 in these places. Ask around.

Devala Rd

Devala Rd runs off Yaddehimulla Rd towards the west end of the beach. A short distance along, the *Hotel Ocean Bay* was still under construction when we visited, but the completed rooms have fan, net and attached bath for Rs 350. Those upstairs at the front have good views and catch the breeze.

The *Sea View Guest House* (fax 09-32045, 'Attention Yatawara family') is, like the nearby Strand, another of Unawatuna's longest-running and best guest houses, now expanded to over a dozen comfortable rooms, set in a large garden just back from the beach. It's a relaxed place run by a friendly family. The very clean rooms are all ground-floor with nets, fans and attached bathrooms, and most have their own spacious verandahs. Some bathrooms even have their own indoor flower beds! Prices for bed & breakfast are from Rs 500/550 to Rs 700/800 depending on the size of the room. There's also a spectacular two-storey bungalow, with two bedrooms and its own kitchen area, at Rs 1600 bed & breakfast. The food at the Sea View is very good, with rice and curry in the Rs 75 region.

Along the Main Road

There are more possibilities on and off the main road as it heads out of Unawatuna. Some private houses along the road will let out rooms for Rs 50, but they are likely to be noisy Up an inland track not far past the 76 mile marker, the friendly *Araliya Guest House* has five clean, cool rooms with attached baths, fans and four-poster beds with all-round mosquito nets, for Rs 350 double. Half a dozen even better rooms are being added – and there's a good little restaurant here, doing among other things veggie burgers or vegetables au gratin for Rs 65, and a variety of Chinese main dishes for Rs 55 to Rs 80. Further down the main road, *Sun Shine Villa* on the inland side charges Rs 250 or Rs 300 for clean doubles of reasonable size with fan, net and attached bath. Some have their own verandahs, and food is available.

A little further out, on the beach side 100 metres past Dalawella police station, the excellent *Sri Gemunu Guest House* (☎ 09-53202) is set in lovely gardens at the start of an idyllic little stretch of coast, with calm water for swimming in the lee of a reef close offshore, and good snorkelling – altogether ideal for a spot of relaxed seaside sun-drenching. Sri Gemunu's eight clean rooms go for Rs 250 single, Rs 300 double, and there's a lovely upstairs verandah. A rice and curry dinner is Rs 65, fish chips and salad Rs 80.

Places to Eat

The food in some guest houses is excellent value (see Places to Stay) but there are plenty of places to eat out too. The *UBR* restaurant isn't cheap, but serves good food in generous portions – fish with chips and veg for about Rs 140, rice and curry Rs 60 to Rs 120, baked crab Rs 250, and steaks Rs 200-plus. Some nights there's an all-you-can-eat buffet. Among the smaller eateries just along the beach, the *Happy Banana* is one of the best if also one of the most expensive. Devilled crab, which comes with rice and a bit of salad, is a speciality – a one kg crab, enough for two people, costs around Rs 250. There

are cheaper options including fish dishes at Rs 90 or Rs 100, and good noodles or fried rice for as little as Rs 30 or Rs 40. There's also good food, at reasonable prices, at the *Chinese Restaurant* in front of the Sunny Beach Hotel – good battered prawns for Rs 80. The *Lucky Tuna* draws crowds for its cheaper prices but we found the fish disappointing.

Further along and right on the sands, the *Moon Shadow Restaurant* does good fish, chips and salad for Rs 90, also fried rice for Rs 35 to Rs 55, and a typical eggs breakfast for Rs 40. *Samson's Chai Shop* is cheap and popular with rice and curry or fish dishes at Rs 50 to Rs 75, fried rice or noodles at Rs 35 to Rs 50. You can linger over a Rs 15 pot of tea till late. *Thilak Restaurant* has Sri Lankan fare such as string hoppers or rotty and curry (both Rs 30), along with travellers' offerings like omelettes, fruit salad (both Rs 15) and pancakes (Rs 25).

Inland on Yaddehimulla Rd the *South Ceylon Restaurant* does vegetarian food that's both filling and nutritious – though slow in arriving and not exactly elegantly prepared. Tofu, hummus, beansprouts and muesli are all here. The excellent nachos, or the veggie burger with chips, salad and fried egg are both Rs 60. A Rs 50 meal from a different part of the world is lined up each night of the week – based on lasagne one night, gado gado the next, and so on.

Getting There & Away

You hardly notice Unawatuna from the main road, so make sure you don't miss the stop if you're coming by bus. It's only 10 or 15 minutes from Galle to Unawatuna – take any bus heading east from Galle. The fare is Rs 3. From Colombo, a Matara bus is the best bet. Leaving Unawatuna, probably the easiest place to get a bus to stop is a couple of hundred metres towards Galle from the Yaddehimulla Rd junction, near the few shops. A three-wheeler to or from Galle costs Rs 50.

UNAWATUNA TO WELIGAMA

Beyond Unawatuna the road runs close to the coast most of the 23 km to Weligama, and

Stilt Fishermen

beyond. There are numerous beautiful stretches of beach, picturesque coves and tiny bays – and a number of attractive, secluded places to stay.

Things to See

This is the part of the coast, particularly at Ahangama, where you will see **stilt fishermen** if the sea is running right. Each fisherman has a pole firmly embedded in the sea bottom close to the shore. When the sea and fish are running in the right direction, they perch on their poles and cast their lines out. Stilt positions are passed down from father to son and are highly coveted.

Just before Koggala there's a WW II airstrip, beside which a small road turns inland to a large lake. Near the Hotel Horizon at Koggala, a little inland from the road and railway (a sign directs you), there's the **Martin Wickramasinghe Museum of Folk Art & Culture**, open 9 am to noon and 1 to 5 pm except on Mondays and poya days.

Just beyond Koggala is the interesting old **Purvaramaya Temple**, with some recently restored murals. The turn-off is in Kataluwa – past the 82-mile and 132-km posts, and across the river. You have to go a couple of km off the road and take the right turn – ask

for directions. A monk will open the building up if you ask. Some of the Jataka scenes painted here are said to be 200 years old. Notice the European figures in their 19th-century attire.

Places to Stay & Eat

Talpe These places share the same lovely stretch of coast as Sri Gemunu Guest House in Unawatuna. Just past the Club Point de Galle at 654 Matara Rd, Mihiripena, Talpe, two km beyond the south end of Unawatuna, there's a pair of comfortable wooden *Cabanas* (☎ 09-53321), large and with their own bathrooms, set in a beachside garden. The costs are Rs 450 a double, breakfast Rs 55 and dinner Rs 70. Readers have also mentioned some cheaper brick cabanas, apparently just on the Unawatuna side of the Club Point de Galle.

Also at Talpe, between the 125 and 126-km markers, is the 25-room *Hotel Beach Haven* (☎ 09-53362), right by the beach and with a swimming pool. Smallish but clean rooms with fans, nets and attached bath cost Rs 350, and there's one bigger room, with the best view, for Rs 450. There's good food there too – lunch or dinner being about Rs 100.

Habaraduwa & Koggala About three km further along, just before Koggala, the *Sunny South Hotel* stands in a large garden by the beach. Singles/doubles with private bathroom cost Rs 300/350. Not far beyond, on the inland side of the road, the *Bon Bon Hotel* is a good seafood restaurant – fish and chips are Rs 100, crab Rs 150. It also has 10 clean, recently built rooms at Rs 350 double.

Koggala itself is little more than two large hotels for package tourists, with a third hotel converted into a garment factory, but it has a fine stretch of beach. The *Hotel Horizon* (☎ 09-53229) has 74 rooms, for which it asks US$20/22 room only (air-con US$5 extra). The *Koggala Beach Hotel* (☎ 09-53244) has 200 rooms at US$20 single or double (air-con US$6 extra).

Ahangama *Hotel Club Lanka* (☎ 09-2587) on the beach at Ahangama has clean but not huge rooms for US$13 single or double, room only, and a big pool in nice gardens. There's a restaurant too.

Midigama Soon after the 137 km post, at Midigama, is a small point with a little beach and good surf when the waves are right. It's a low-key, relaxed place where some surfers and a few others find cheap rooms and meals with local families. *Sugath's House* behind Midigama railway station has no sign, but is friendly with four clean, sizeable rooms at Rs 50 per person. There are no fans or mosquito nets, and water is from the well. Excellent meals are cooked up at *Jai & Sumana's House* 100 metres from Sugath's – all you can eat for Rs 20 at breakfast and Rs 40 at dinner. There's also the *Relax* guest house on the road at the 137 km marker, with singles/doubles at Rs 150/200.

Getting There & Away

There are frequent buses along this stretch of coast from Galle, Unawatuna, Weligama, Matara and other points. Bus No 350 from Galle costs Rs 6 to Midigama. The main rail stations are Talpe and Ahangama, where some trains from Colombo stop. Only a few local trains stop at lesser stations like Midigama.

WELIGAMA

About 30 km south of Galle, the town of Weligama has a fine sandy sweep of bay – just as its name, which means 'sandy village', might suggest. Very close to the shore, so close in fact that you could walk out to it at low tide, is a tiny island known as Taprobane. It looks like an ideal artist's or writer's retreat, which indeed it once was. The novelist Paul Bowles wrote *The Spider's House* here in the 1950s. Currently it is leased to two German families.

Orientation & Information

The main road divides to go through Weligama, with one branch running along the coast, the other running parallel through the town centre, a short distance inland. The bus station and Bank of Ceylon are on the inland road in the middle of town. To reach the centre from the coast road, turn in half a km east of Taprobane.

Things to See & Do

Scenic though the bay is, Weligama beach is close to the main road and none too clean in the vicinity of the town centre.

A turning inland, off the inland road west of the centre, takes you over the railway to a small park with a large rock-carved figure known as the *Kustaraja*. It's been variously described as a king who was mysteriously cured of leprosy, or as Avalokitesvara, a disciple of the Buddha. Nearby there's a temple with a large modern standing Buddha. Weligama is famous for its lacework; local entrepreneurs may rush out to try to sell you some.

Places to Stay

At 484 New By Pass Rd, where the coast and town roads meet (or divide depending which way you look at it) at the Matara end of town, about 700 metres from the centre, the friendly *Sam's Holiday Cabanas* have a pretty garden beside a relatively secluded stretch of beach. Singles/doubles with breakfast, in rooms with attached bath, fan, net and verandah, cost Rs 150/300. It's a pleasant, unhurried place with good food (dinner Rs 100).

Weligama has two rest houses. The attractive *Weligama Bay Inn* (☎ 041-5299) on the coast road 200 metres west of Taprobane, has a wide verandah, pleasant green gardens and a fine view across the beach. There are 12 sizeable rooms at US$9/10. Breakfast is US$2, lunch or dinner US$3. The smaller *Rest House*, about half a km towards Galle from the Weligama Bay Inn, is also pleasant. Doubles are Rs 350 and again meals are available.

There are cheaper places on the coast road just east of the Weligama Bay Inn, none of them very clean. Try for a room away from the road in these places. The *Dilkini Tourist Inn* has rooms for Rs 125/200 with private bath. Close by, the *Udula Beach Inn* charges Rs 150 a room, again with private bathroom. There's also the *Weligama Bay Tourist Inn*. Better is the *Ruhunu Guest House* (☎ 041-5228), which is back from the coast at 12 D M Samaraweera Mawatha. A signpost points the way at the Weligama Bay Tourist Inn – you then turn left at the first junction and right at the second. Rooms cost Rs 200. The drawback is that it's next to a school – noisy at certain times of the day.

Back in the town at 245 Main St, a large old house on the north side of the inland road about 300 metres west of the centre, *Raja's Guest House* has no sign or number, but it has rooms at Rs 75 or Rs 100 with shared bath. The people who run it are reputedly friendly.

Getting There & Away

Weligama is on the Colombo-Matara railway line, three to 3½ hours from Colombo, and there are frequent buses in both directions along the coast.

MIRISSA

Mirissa, four km from Weligama on the Matara road, has a beautiful curve of sandy beach with calm, clear waters that are a delight to swim in or lie in front of. At the west end is a headland which you can walk up on for views over Weligama Bay. At the east end is a rocky outcrop good for sunset-watching.

Places to Stay & Eat

In between are two very relaxed places to stay, with gardens right on the beach. Towards the east end of the beach the *Mirissa Beach Inn* has rooms in the house from Rs 75 to Rs 150, some with attached bath, and three garden cabanas for Rs 100 with shared bath or Rs 250 with private bath. Meals are available too. A few hundred metres further towards Weligama, a track leads off the road (which is further from the beach at this point) to the *Paradise Beach Club* which has 11 cabanas for Rs 100 with outside squatter toilet and shower, or Rs 250 with private bath and fan, and a few rooms at Rs 300 with verandah, attached bath and fan. The restaurant here serves good food, though slightly on the pricey side. If you ask around along the track that continues past the Paradise Beach Club, or inland from the main road, you may be able to find rooms in private houses for as little as Rs 50 to Rs 75.

Getting There & Away

The bus fare from Weligama is Rs 2; a three-wheeler is Rs 60.

MATARA

Matara, 160 km from Colombo, is at the end of the southern railway and, with 40,000 people, Sri Lanka's eighth biggest town. There's a long stretch of beach and though most people wouldn't choose it for a get-away-from-it-all holiday, Matara is both historic and lively enough to make a visit worthwhile.

Things to See & Do

Matara has two fine **Dutch forts**; the larger one, occupying most of the promontory dividing the Nilwala River from the sea, contains much of old Matara, which is quiet and picturesque. The other fort, the small 1763 Star Fort, has a most attractive and unusual gateway. It's about 350 metres from

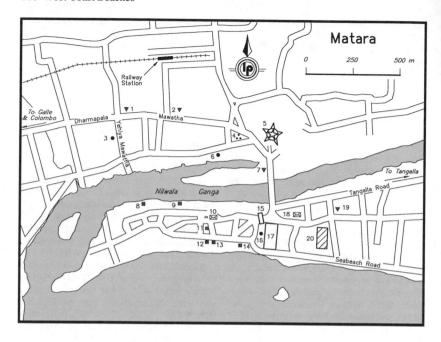

the main fort gate – across the river on the Colombo road – and now contains a **Museum of Ancient Paintings**. A little further along the Colombo road, Dharmapala Mawatha, a few metres after the temple at the junction, there's a factory making high quality drums for temples and drum schools – a good place to buy genuine instruments or observe the drum-making process. The building is orange. If you're interested in batik, drop into **Jez Look Batik** at 12 Yehiya Mawatha.

Polhena, a quiet village three km towards Colombo, has a good coral reef that you can walk to at low tide. At the time of researching this edition Matara and Polhena were the stamping grounds of a plausible group of con men who befriend travellers then try to sell them gems and fairly ordinary batik at inflated prices.

Places to Stay
Matara In the Matara Fort, about 100 metres from the bus station, you'll find *Matara Rest House* (☎ 041-2299) which, as usual, is beautifully situated right by the beach. It's said to be built on a site where captured elephants were corralled. Rooms are comfortable, with attached bathrooms, and cost Rs 275 single or double.

Further into the fort the *River Inn Guest House* (☎ 041-2215), by the river down a little lane at 96A Wilfred Gunasekera Mawatha, has good rooms with private baths and verandahs overlooking the river for Rs 150/225 single/double. At 38 Wilfrid Gunasekera Mawatha, *Blue Ripples* (☎ 041-2058) is peacefully situated in a riverside garden. Prices with net, fan and attached bath range from around Rs 125/150 to Rs 150/190. The better rooms are right on the riverbank with their own verandahs. There's no sign outside but you can find it by the street number. Touts are unwelcome here.

Also in the fort, the *SK Guest House* has very basic rooms at Rs 100/200 with

■ PLACES TO STAY

8	River Inn Guest House
9	Blue Ripples
11	Victory Press
12	SK Guest House
13	Befriend Guest House
14	Rest House

▼ PLACES TO EAT

1	Chamin Restaurant & Guest House
2	GOB Restaurant
7	Richcurd Restaurant & Bakers
19	Hotel Wijeyagiri

OTHER

3	Jez Look Batik
4	Temple
5	Star Fort
6	Bank of Ceylon
10	Post Office
15	Fort Gates
16	Clock Tower
17	Bus Station
18	Post Office
20	Market

attached bathroom. Next door is the *Befriend Guest House* with good, clean rooms with attached bath for Rs 250 a double. Nearby the self-styled 'former imperial lighthouse keeper' who now runs the *Victory Press* offers dingy but reasonably clean rooms for Rs 75/100 with shared bath.

Polhena Polhena is a short ride by the No 350, 356 or 260 bus from Matara bus station, but there is only a handful of buses right to the beach each day – otherwise you have to get off at the main road junction and walk the one km to the beach. (To reach the beach with the reef, turn right at the T-junction half a km from the main road, then left at the next junction.)

The *TK Guest House* (☎ 041-2603), a long-running semi-budget place, now has three locations. To reach its newest building near the beach, at 116/1 Polhena Beach Rd,

turn right at the T-junction, right again at the next junction, and left at the third. There are three decent rooms here, with private bath, for Rs 250/300, plus a dining room – but 'far too many staff and hangers-on,' complained one pair of travellers. For the original TK building, which has reasonably sized rooms for Rs 200/250, turn right instead of left at the third junction. The third building, which is by the TK sign at the second junction, has both basic rooms using an open-air shower for Rs 50/75 and two better ones at Rs 250/300. A rice and curry dinner at TK costs Rs 80. You can rent snorkel gear at Rs 150 for a couple of hours or so.

The exaggeratedly named *Holiday Resort Sepalika*, just back from the beach half a km west of the Reef Gardens Hotel, opposite Polhena school, is friendly with basic rooms for Rs 50.

Polhena Reef Gardens Hotel (☎ 041-2478), across the road from the seafront facing the reef, has 20 rooms costing Rs 400/450. They're quite big, with fan, net, attached bath and verandah, but some are a bit rundown. To reach it turn right, left and then left again as you come from the main road. Food here is fairly dear – fish main courses, for instance, are about Rs 130.

Places to Eat

Matara *Rest House* does good meals, with breakfast around Rs 60 and lunch or dinner about Rs 100. Outside the Fort there's a cluster of small rotty, hopper and rice and curry places, as well as the slightly smarter *Richcurd Restaurant & Bakers*, along the roadside just north of the bridge. Also here are some very well-stocked fruit stalls. Another 400 metres towards Galle, along Dharmapala Mawatha, the popular *Galle Oriental Bakery (GOB) Restaurant* does rice and curry for Rs 25, also cakes and short eats.

Getting There & Away

Matara is at the end of the railway from Colombo, with four or five fast trains each way daily making the trip in four hours. Fares from Colombo are Rs 74 in 2nd class,

Rs 26.75 in 3rd. A new line from Matara to Tangalla and Kataragama is supposed to open by 1995.

Buses travel to/from Colombo and intermediate coastal points about half-hourly on average through the day. Colombo is a 3½ to four-hour trip, costing Rs 25. The one-hour trip on to Tangalla is Rs 7.50. There are also direct buses up to Ratnapura and the hill country. If you miss the direct ones you can get to Wellawaya and take a connection from there if you don't leave it too late in the day.

MATARA TO TANGALLA

At Medawatte, on the main road a few km east of Matara, is the impressive new Ruhuna University campus. There are also several places of interest just off the 35 km of road from Matara to Tangalla, including two superb examples of what one visitor labelled 'neo-Buddhist kitsch'.

Weherehena Temple

Just as you leave Matara, a turn inland will take you to the Weherehena temple, where an artificial cave is decorated with about 200 comic-book like scenes from the Buddha's life. There's also a huge Buddha figure here. You can get there on a 349 bus.

At the time of the late November/early December full moon, a perahera is held at the temple to celebrate the anniversary of its founding. During the evening there's a big procession of dancers and elephants from all the surrounding villages. There's also a smaller 'preview' procession the day before.

Dondra

Only five or six km out of Matara you come to Dondra, the southernmost point of Sri Lanka. It's a pleasant walk out to the lighthouse, which marks the extremity of the island. From here you get a superb view of the fishing boats riding the waves. There's good snorkelling here too.

Wewurukannala Vihara

If the Weherehena temple is 'Marvel Comics

meets Lord Buddha', then here it's Walt Disney who runs into him. At the town of Dikwella, 22 km from Matara, a road turns inland towards Beliatta. About 1½ km along you come to a huge, 50-metre-high, seated Buddha figure – the largest in Sri Lanka.

The temple has three parts. The oldest is about 250 years old but of no particular interest. Larger and newer, a second shrine room has a quite amazing collection of life-size, vibrantly coloured figures depicting the Buddha doing everything from taking his first steps (immediately after birth) to leaving his family to seek enlightenment, finding it, passing on the message and finally achieving nirvana. There are also models of devils, monsters, Veddahs, disciples, 24 of the Buddha's previous incarnations, and everything else you could ask for, including a long, dingy corridor with hundreds of gory paintings of crimes, with the relevant punishment in the next life shown below them. Finally there is the gigantic seated figure which was constructed in the 1960s. As if to prove that it really is as high as an eight-storey building, what should be right behind it but an eight-storey building? You can climb up inside to look over his shoulder at the surrounding rice paddies. 'I couldn't work out the significance of the ice cream cone on his head', wrote one highly impressed visitor.

Furthermore, the walls of the backing building have been painted with yet more comic-strip representations of events in the Buddha's lives. 'Our favourites', two travellers wrote, 'were a man in combat with a Gonzala styled ape and a man questioned, then whipped, then arms and legs sawn off and then going to nirvana. So far they're only down to the fourth floor so the lower three have yet to reveal their stories'. It's all quite a contrast to the supremely tasteful Buddhist art of the ancient cities. There's one other thing to see here, an interesting clock in the adjoining building – made by a prisoner 65 years ago.

Mawella

About six km beyond Dikwella, at the 117

milestone, a path leads off the road to the spectacular Ho-o-maniya blowhole on the coast. You may need to ask directions to find it and children will probably accompany you the last few hundred metres to call up a big 'blow'. During the south-west monsoon (June is the best time) high seas can force water through a natural chimney in the rocks 23 metres up and then spout out up to 18 metres in the air.

Places to Stay

The top-end, Italian-built *Dikwella Village Resort* (☎ 041-2961) stands on a headland on the Matara side of Dikwella. It should be a good place for a spaghetti! There's also the cheaper *Manahara Beach Cottages* on Mahawela Rd, Moraketiyara at Mawella.

TANGALLA

Situated 195 km (122 miles) from Colombo, Tangalla (also spelt Tangalle, Tengalle and Tengalla but usually pronounced 'Ten-gol') is one of the nicest places along the coast – particularly if you just want somewhere to laze and soak up the sun. Accommodation is relatively cheap. The town itself is an easy-going place with several reminders of Dutch days, including a Rest House which was once home for the Dutch administrators.

Tangalla's series of bays are the modern attraction. To the east of the Rest House the long white sands of Medaketiya beach shimmer away into the distance, while to the west is a whole series of smaller bays. But beware: some of the beaches, including Medaketiya, shelve off very steeply, and the resulting waves make them dangerous for poor swimmers if there is any sort of wind or tidal current.

The bay just on the town side of the Tangalla Bay Hotel is probably the most sheltered, although right beside the Rest House there's a tiny bay which is very shallow and generally flat calm. The point in front of the Rest House is also popular with snorkellers. By the Palm Paradise accommodation is a picturesque and fairly secluded bay popular with seekers of an overall

suntan. It's also far enough from the town to minimise worries about cleanliness.

Places to Stay

Most accommodation is in small, laid-back travellers' guest houses with just a few simple rooms, typically with attached bath, fan and mosquito net. Prices given here are for the high season. The town has its share of persuasive touts waiting for travellers at the bus stop. Avoid them if possible. Most of the places that follow are an easy walk from the bus stop – though if you're coming from the west and want to stay at Palm Paradise or anywhere else on that side of town, try to get your bus to drop you on the way in.

Near the Town Centre *Santana Guest House* at 55 Parakrama Rd has good clean singles/doubles from Rs 75/100, with shared bath, to Rs 175 with attached bath. The friendly owner – who not only likes but looks like Carlos Santana – has added a lovely airy little restaurant on stilts out over the lagoon, with a bamboo bridge leading to the beach. He won't pay touts. Next door to the Santana is the cheap *Deepa Pension*, and down a path beside the Deepa there's *Sethsiri* which has reasonable doubles for Rs 150 and good, well priced food.

The *Rest House* is pleasantly situated on the promontory above the harbour. It's one of the oldest rest houses in the country, originally built – as a plate on the front steps indicates – by the Dutch in 1774. bed & breakfast is Rs 320/400. *Diana Travellers Lodge*, about 300 metres from the bus station along the road towards Matara, has large, clean rooms set back from the road for Rs 100 single or double.

East of the Centre If you head east from the bus station over the river bridge, then take the first road on the right, you'll find yourself going towards Medaketiya, the long beach stretching two or three km east of the town. Several guest houses dot the beachfront track and they get gradually cheaper as you go along. *Namal Garden Beach Hotel* fronting right on to the beach has good, sizeable

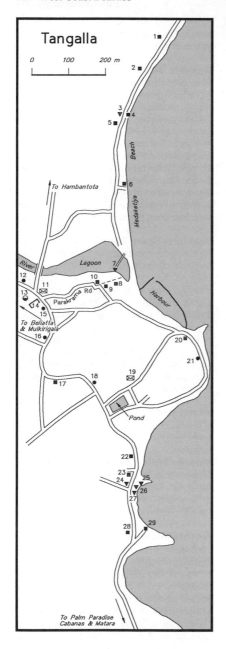

Tangalla

0   100   200 m

To Hambantota

River

Lagoon

Beach

Medaketiya

Harbour

Parakrama Rd

To Beliatta
& Mulkirigala

Pond

To Palm Paradise
Cabanas & Matara

■ PLACES TO STAY

1   Blue Horizon Guest House
2   German Lanka Ranjith
     Guest House
4   Gayana Guest House
5   Nila Beach Inn
6   Namal Garden Beach Hotel
8   Sethsiri
9   Deepa Pension
10   Santana Guest House
17   Diana Travellers Lodge
20   Rest House
22   Sea View Tourist Inn
23   Touristen Gasthaus
28   Tourist Guest House
29   Tangalla Bay Hotel

▼ PLACES TO EAT

3   Saman's Restaurant
7   Santana Guest House Restaurant
24   Sea Food Restaurant
25   Lobster Inn
26   Turtles Landing Restaurant
27   The Chalet Restaurant

     OTHER

11   Agency Post Office
12   Petrol Station
13   Bus Station
14   Market
15   Bank of Ceylon
16   Petrol Station
18   Southern Bakers
19   Post Office
21   Navy Station

singles/doubles at Rs 200/250. On the inland side of the track the modern, clean *Nila Beach Inn* charges Rs 200 a double, with private bath, while *Saman's Restaurant* nearly next door has eight moderately clean rooms with private bath, at Rs 100/150. *Gayana Guest House* opposite Saman's has rooms for Rs 150 on its road side or Rs 200 on the beach side, and is also OK. *German Lanka Ranjith Guest House* charges Rs 75/100 for small rooms and Rs 125/150 for bigger ones, all with attached bath, and down at the end the *Blue Horizon Guest House* has just two rooms at Rs 100 a double

– one's big with a four-poster bed, the other smaller with a roofless shower. There's no electricity and no mosquito nets, but there are few mosquitoes either and it's a friendly place with good food.

West of the Centre Ten to 15 minutes' walk in the Matara direction from the bus station, the *Tourist Guest House/Touristen Gasthaus* is friendly with good, very clean rooms from Rs 200/300 to Rs 450 a double. A second *Tourist Guest House*, opposite the big Tangalla Bay Hotel, also has clean, sizeable rooms from Rs 250 single with shared bath, to Rs 400 a double with attached bath. Both places stand alone and are shielded from the road by gardens.

The *Tangalla Bay Hotel* (☎ 047-40346), built in the early 1970s, is meant to look like a boat, and each room has a balcony over the room below. It's showing serious signs of decay and was trying to attract custom with 'budget prices' about a third lower than the regular US$17.50/20 when we last checked.

In that sort of price bracket, *Palm Paradise Cabanas* (☎ 01-717517, fax 047-40401 'Attention Palm Paradise Cabanas, Tangalle') are far more appealing. Fifteen large, clean wooden cabanas are scattered around a secluded beachside palm grove at Goyambokka, down a half-km track from the main road, three km from the town centre (buses in the Matara direction from Tangalla will drop you at the turn-off for Rs 4). They're solidly built on stilts and all have their own sleeping-living area, bathroom (with shower and sit-down toilet) and breezy verandah. There's electricity too, and an open-air bar and restaurant. Breakfast and a three-course dinner – sometimes Sri Lankan, sometimes Western – are included in the price of Rs 520/790, though you might be able to get a room-only or bed & breakfast price if you want. There's a lovely little beach immediately in front of the palm grove – all in all this is a great get-away-from-it-all spot.

Places to Eat

As you'd expect from the number of fishing boats, there's good seafood to be found in Tangalla. Several guest houses have their own restaurants and the food at *Saman's*, *Santana* and the *Blue Horizon* is particularly good. You don't have to be staying at these places to eat at them. Service at Saman's is slow but the wait is worthwhile – a tasty grilled fish, chips and salad will cost Rs 140, noodles or fried rice Rs 45 to Rs 65, a string hopper breakfast Rs 35. Santana's restaurant has the advantage of being set on stilts over the lagoon to catch the beach breeze. An excellent grilled fish, rice and salad will cost you Rs 100 here. The Blue Horizon is a bit of a walk down Medaketiya beach but the food justifies it – fish or prawn dishes are Rs 80 or Rs 90, rice and curry, fried rice or noodles Rs 45 to Rs 65.

The food at the Rest House is fairly good – rice and curry Rs 90, grilled fish Rs 225. In the town centre there are a number of small local eateries across the road from the bus station. *Gamini Hotel*, recommended for rice and curry, and the *New Perlyn Hotel* are two of the more popular.

The Chalet is a more expensive beachside seafood restaurant about a km out of town towards Matara, just before the Tangalla Bay Hotel. Two readers wrote that a big boiled crab at Rs 200 was enough for two, but that lobster ('actually crayfish') was not good value at Rs 700 each! The beers here are '*really* cold', they added more happily.

Getting There & Away

The railway from Colombo terminates in Matara but there are regular buses from Matara (Rs 7.50, one hour). You can of course travel all the way from Colombo (five hours) or elsewhere on the coast by bus. There are also regular buses from Tangalla east to Hambantota (Rs 8, 1¼ hours), Tissamaharama and Kataragama, and some going north to Wellawaya, Haputale and the hill country.

MULKIRIGALA

Mulkirigala rock temple about 16 km north of Tangalla has a little of Dambulla and

Sigiriya about it. Steps lead up to a series of cleft-like caves in the huge rock. Like Dambulla they shelter large reclining Buddhas, together with wall paintings and other smaller sitting and standing figures. You can then continue on your barefoot way to a dagoba perched on the very top of the rock, where there is a fine view over the surrounding country.

Manuscripts discovered here in a monastic library by a British official in 1826 were the key which scholars used to translate the *Mahavamsa* from the Pali script. You will be asked for a Rs 100 donation to enter.

Getting There & Away

Mulkirigala can be reached from Tangalla either via Beliatta or Wiraketiya. By bus take a Middeniya bus (check that it will go via Beliatta) and ask to be let off at the Mulkirigala junction. Or take a bus just to Beliatta and then another on to the Mulkirigala junction. You can even get there by bicycle from Tangalla – the jeweller's by the post office hires them out – although it's a rather rough ride at times. A three-wheeler from Tangalla costs about Rs 250 for a return trip.

HAMBANTOTA

Between Tangalla and Hambantota, 237 km from Colombo, you move from a wet zone into a dry zone, which continues right across Yala West National Park. Hambantota is not the best place along the coast if you are in search of sand and sea, although there are magnificent sweeps of beach both east and west of the small promontory in the town. A large collection of outriggered fishing boats is often beached on the sands. Hambantota has a high proportion of Malay Muslims in its population, many of whom speak Malay as well as Tamil and Sinhalese. A major industry in Hambantota is the production of salt by the age-old method of evaporating sea water from shallow salt pans. You will see these pans alongside the road on the east side of Hambantota, as you turn inland from the coast. Between Hambantota and Tissamaharama there are a number of road-side stalls selling delicious curd and honey or treacle – definitely worth a stop if you can manage it.

Bundala Sanctuary

Bundala bird sanctuary stretches nearly 20 km along a coastal strip starting just east of Hambantota. The main road east passes along Bundala's northern boundary. Birds apart, around March and April, the end of the dry season here, there are often more elephants to be seen in Bundala than in Yala West National Park. Bundala is also good for crocodile-spotting – and it's less visited than Yala. A four-hour jeep trip to Bundala from Hambantota should cost about Rs 650 for four people. Bundala is unsupervised so there are no entry or tracker fees to be paid. Hambantota has a number of touts angling to take you to Bundala or to Yala, but the most reliable places to organise a trip include the Peacock Beach Hotel, which sends out safari wagons, the Sunshine Tourist Rest and the Rest House. There's little advantage in going to Yala from Hambantota rather than from Tissamaharama.

Places to Stay

Hambantota Rest House is nicely situated on top of the promontory overlooking the town and the long sweep of beach. It is fairly modern (by rest house standards) and quite large, but two readers complained they had 'no mosquito net but lots of mozzies'. Singles/doubles cost Rs 250/350.

The *Sunshine Tourist Rest* (☎ 047-20129) at 47 Main St, five minutes' walk from the bus station in the Tissamaharama direction, has good, clean rooms priced up to Rs 200 for a double with attached bathroom. Mrs Nihar, who runs this place, is an excellent cook. The traffic noise quietens down after about 8 pm.

A short distance from the bus station, also in the Tissa direction, at 33 Terrace St, *Mr Hassim's* guest house offers rooms from Rs 50 to Rs 150. Some have fan, net and attached bath.

The *Sea Spray Guest House* in Galwala, about a km along the Tissa main road from the bus station, is a well-maintained but expensive place with air-con rooms at Rs 840 for a double with bed & breakfast. A new three-storey beachside block with balconies facing the sea is being built. Next door the large, plush *Peacock Beach Hotel* (☎ 047-20377) has 80 rooms at US$35 room only single or double – plus a fine swimming pool which non-residents can use for Rs 50.

Getting There & Away

Hambantota is about six hours from Colombo by bus. To/from Tissamaharama takes an hour and costs Rs 7; Tangalla is Rs 8 for a 1¼-hour trip. There are also buses between Hambantota and Ratnapura via Embilipitiya (3½ hours, Rs 33), and others heading north to Wellawaya and the hill country.

TISSAMAHARAMA

From Hambantota the main road runs northward to the crossroad town of Wellawaya (see the Hill Country chapter). The main turn-off to Tissamaharama is at Wirawila, 20 km from Hambantota, on the south side of the Wirawila tank. There's a second turning just north of the tank.

Yala West National Park is the main reason most visitors come to Tissa, which as a result is something of a cowboy town with 'safari' touts lurking at guest houses and bus stops, jeep drivers racing round looking for customers, and everybody else trying to get *their* cut of the safari business too. See the following Yala West National Park section for info on visiting the park – but meanwhile there are a few other places of interest in the Tissa vicinity.

Orientation

The two turn-offs from the Hambantota-Wellawaya road converge after a few km at the clocktower in the village of Deberawewa. Deberawewa is a couple of km from Tissa itself – despite the signs announcing 'Tissamaharama' as you enter it and accommodation touts who board buses and advise travellers to get off because 'this is Tissa'.

Tissa itself is the best place to organise a Yala trip.

The bus station is the focal point of Tissamaharama's main street, which continues eastward to become the road to Yala and Kirinda. To reach the rest house area, where most of the accommodation is found, take the first left as you go east along the main street from the bus station. The road winds through rice paddies and past the main Tissa dagoba. After the rest house area it becomes the Kataragama road.

Tissawewa & Dagobas

The tank in Tissa, the Tissawewa, is thought to date from the 3rd century BC and has an active birdlife. There are several ancient dagobas in the Tissa area. The large white restored dagoba between Tissa town centre and the tank is credited to Kavantissa, a king of the ancient southern kingdom of Ruhunu centred on Tissamaharama. Next to the dagoba is a statue of Queen Viharamahadevi who, according to legend, landed at Kirinda, about 10 km south of Tissa, after being sent to sea by her father King Kelanitissa as a penance for his killing a monk. The daughter landed unharmed and subsequently married Kavantissa. Their son Dutugemunu was the Sinhalese hero who, starting from Ruhunu, liberated Anuradhapura from Indian invaders in the 2nd century BC. The Sandagiri Wehera, another dagoba near the Tissa one, is also credited to Kavantissa. By the roadside between Tissa and Deberawewa is the Yatala Wehera, built 2300 years ago by King Yatala Tissa, who fled Anuradhapura after a palace plot and founded the Ruhunu kingdom.

Wirawila Tank

Between the northern and southern turn-offs to Tissamaharama, the Hambantota-Wellawaya road runs on a causeway across the large Wirawila Wewa. This extensive sheet of water is a bird sanctuary and the best time for watching is early morning. From Hambantota or Tissamaharama you can get a bus to Wirawila junction on the south side of the tank and walk north, or from Tissa you can go to Pandegamu on the north side and walk south. You may also see crocodiles, monkeys or even (west of the tank) elephants.

Kirinda

On the coast, about 10 km south of Tissa, the village of Kirinda has a fine beach and a small Buddhist shrine on the rocks. Kirinda was used as a land base by Arthur C Clarke's party when diving for the Great Basses wreck – see Clarke's *The Treasure of the Reef*. The Great and Little Basses reefs have some of the most spectacular scuba diving around Sri Lanka but only on rare occasions are conditions suitable for diving. For much of the year fierce currents sweep across the reefs. A lighthouse was erected on the Great Basses in 1860.

Places to Stay & Eat

Tissamaharama The *Tissa Rest House* (☎ 047-37299) is delightfully situated right on the banks of the Tissawewa tank, about a km from the bus station along the Kataragama road (Rs 20 by three-wheeler). It has comfortable rooms, a pool and a pleasant open-air restaurant and bar, but it's not cheap at Rs 650/740 for bed & breakfast. Lunch and dinner are US$3 or US$4. There are 62 rooms, but they don't all face the lake. This is the number one choice for groups so don't rely on getting a room in season.

A number of alternatives are nearby. To find the pleasant little *Singha Tourist Inn* (☎ 047-37090), continue a short distance along the Kataragama road past the rest house and take the first left, Tissawewa Mawatha. The Singha has just a few rooms, all air-con with private bathrooms, at Rs 450/500 for bed & breakfast. Other meals are available. Its garden goes down to the lake. A km past the rest house on the Kataragama road, the 12-room *Priyankara Tourist Inn* (☎ 047-37206) charges Rs 550 for good clean bed-and-breakfast doubles with attached bath, net and fan. A rice and curry dinner will cost you Rs 110, a Western dinner up to Rs 190.

The *Sandakumari Guest House*, indicated by a sign pointing down a track almost opposite the rest house, will give you a room for Rs 150 or so if you arrive without a tout. Follow the track round to the left for about 10 minutes. One or two other houses in the rest house area put out signs when they want to let out rooms.

A minute's walk back towards the town from the rest house, still in view of the tank, the *Lake Side Tour Inn* (☎ 047-37216) has rooms for Rs 350/450 with net, fan and attached bath – but they should be shinier for the price. Dinner is Rs 110 to Rs 190.

A reader has recommended the *Siriketha Safari Inn* on Yala Rd, Kasingama, for its large clean rooms at Rs 250/300 with private bath, good food and very helpful family. A three-wheeler from Tissa bus station is Rs 25. On Tissa main street, almost opposite the bus station, the new-looking *Hotel Tissa* is worth checking out. The *Lakshmi Restaurant* next to the post office is reportedly friendly, with reasonable prices.

Deberawewa A lot of travellers end up at the *Tissa Inn* (☎ 047-37233) on Wellawaya Rd, Polgahawela, 1½ km along the northern road from the Deberawewa clock tower. It has some very active touts working for it. Rooms with net and fan are Rs 100/150 with shared bath, Rs 200/250 with attached bath. They're clean enough, and meals are available, but there are fewer jeep operators than in Tissamaharama: some travellers have reported having to pay over the odds for a jeep to Yala from Deberawewa. On the other hand, at a busy guest house it's easier to find other travellers to share a jeep with.

A km nearer the clock tower along the same northern road is the *Riverside Inn*, friendly with clean, if dingy, rooms for Rs 150 single or double with shared bath, Rs 200 with private bath.

Amaduwa & Kirinda Close to the entrance to Yala West National Park, about 20 km from Tissa, on a rather desolate stretch of coast at Amaduwa, are two hotels you can't reach by bus. *Browns Safari Beach Hotel* (☎ 047-20326) has just eight rooms at

US$10.50 a single or double, room only. Meals are US$2 to US$3.50. Even if you're not staying, you could come here for lunch and a pool swim after a morning visit to Yala. *Yala Safari Beach Hotel* (☎ 01-698819) has 54 rooms at US$15, room only. At Kirinda there's the new *Kirinda Beach Resort* with doubles at Rs 350 or Rs 500.

Getting There & Away

A bus from Colombo to Tissa costs Rs 45 and takes six to seven hours. To/from Hambantota is one hour for Rs 7. Only a few buses go direct to or from the hill country, and if you can't get one you'll need to change at either or both of Wirawila junction and Wellawaya. Wirawila to Tissa is Rs 4. From Tissa you can reach Kirinda by bus, but not Yala park itself.

YALA WEST NATIONAL PARK

Yala West, or Ruhuna National Park, Sri Lanka's most visited national park while Wilpattu is closed, covers 966 sq km, beginning 10 km east of Tissamaharama and including a long coast and a hinterland up to 45 km deep. Only 133 sq km in the southwest of the park are open for game watching. Yala West is closed in September and usually part of August and October too – though it's still possible to visit the nearby Bundala sanctuary (see Hambantota) during these months.

Yala West is a mixture of scrub, plains, brackish lagoons and rocky outcrops. It's particularly known for its elephants, best seen from October to December. Solitary males may provide your first glimpses (a far cry from a century ago when professional 'sportsmen' were very active, with one man claiming to have shot 1400). Yala also has occasional leopards and bears, lots of deer, crocodiles, wild boars, monkeys and buffalo, and a multitude of birds including wild peacocks and jungle fowl. Particularly around the waterholes you can often see groups of several different species together, which gives Yala the feel of a real kingdom of the animals! Some people are disappointed by

Yala: to be sure, it's not in the same league as Africa's safari parks, and not everyone would want to make a special trip all the way from Kandy or even Hikkaduwa to visit Yala alone. But anyone with some kind of interest in wildlife is likely to find it well worthwhile as part of a longer trip to this region of Sri Lanka.

Visiting Yala

Most people visit Yala West in a half-day trip from Tissamaharama. At the time of writing private vehicles are allowed into the park, so if you have one you can just trundle up to the park entrance – nine km down a rough track off the Tissamaharama-Kirinda road, about 20 km from Tissa itself – pay the park entrance fee of Rs 50 per person, plus Rs 50 or Rs 75 for a tracker to accompany you, and a few minor extras for insurance and so on, amounting to about Rs 50, then have a drive round the tracks to see what you can see. Four-wheel drive is an advantage though not essential unless it's muddy.

What most people have to do, however, is hire a jeep and driver in Tissamaharama to take them into and around the park. You can usually fix this up through where you're staying. If not, go to the Tissa rest house where jeeps and drivers congregate, or hail some passing jeeps – there are lots of them around – on the street. The price for the one-hour drive from Tissa, two to three hours in the park, and the drive back is Rs 750 to Rs 850 for the jeep (which can usually take six people) – to which must be added at least some of the same extras as in the previous paragraph. When negotiating your jeep price, try to establish exactly what extras will need to be added.

The best times to see the wildlife are around dawn or dusk, so you leave Tissa either before dawn (when it's cold, so take some warm clothing) or about 3 pm. At times it can resemble Piccadilly Circus in the park, with a dozen or two jeeps all searching the same small area where elephants are thought to be! Some people take both morning and evening trips and relax at an Amaduwa or Kirinda hotel in between.

At certain times the Bundala sanctuary can be a better place for seeing elephants, and a trip to Bundala from Tissa should be cheaper than to Yala since it's nearer. But one trick the Deberawewa and Tissa jeep cowboys have been known to work on people wanting to visit Yala is to claim that Bundala is part (sometimes 'block three') of Yala. Another is to say they'll take you to Yala – and charge you for that – then take you to Bundala instead. Bundala has its merits, but it is *not* part of the national park, and if it's Yala you want to go to, don't be misled.

If you want to avoid haggling on the spot, some hotels, travel agents or taxi drivers in Bentota, Hikkaduwa, etc, will take you all the way for an inclusive price. Or contact Upali Travels (☎ 01-20465) of 34 Galle Rd, Colombo 3, which advertises half-day jeep safaris for Rs 850, full days for Rs 1600, also Bundala trips for Rs 750.

Places to Stay

For a more prolonged experience of Yala West you can try to book one of the seven park bungalows or two campsites in the park. The bungalows at Buttawa or Mahsilawa are on the coast. The Wildlife & Nature Protection Society of Sri Lanka also has a bungalow just outside the park where visitors can lodge. See Parks & Reserves in Facts about the Country for more info on these possibilities.

KATARAGAMA

Fifteen km north of Tissa is Kataragama, along with Adam's Peak the most important religious pilgrimage site in Sri Lanka. It is a holy place for Buddhists, Muslims and Hindus, and across the Menik Ganga River from the small residential part of the town is a sprawling religious complex containing buildings of all three religions. There is a tradition that King Dutugemunu built a shrine to the Kataragama Deviyo (resident god) here in the 2nd century BC, and the Buddhist Kirivehera dagoba dates back to the 1st century BC. The most important shrine is the untidy-looking Maha Devala,

supposedly containing the lance of the six-faced, 12-armed Hindu war god Skanda, who is identical here with the Kataragama Deviyo. Followers of all three religions make offerings here at the three daily *pujas* (4.30 am, 10.30 am and 6.30 pm).

In July and August the predominantly Hindu Kataragama festival draws thousands of devotees over a two-week period. See the introductory festivals section for more details on the fire-walking and other acts of ritual masochism which take place here.

There's an interesting small museum, including a scale model of the town, near the Maha Devala. Several other Hindu gods are worshipped at Kataragama, including the elephant-headed Ganesha, who helps people in intellectual pursuits. Apart from festival time, the town is busiest with pilgrims at weekends and on poya days.

Places to Stay

The *Kataragama Rest House*, just off the Sithulpahuwa road, has rooms at Rs 300 and does good cheap Sri Lankan vegetarian meals. A few metres away is the *Kataragama New Rest House* (☎ 047-20349) which charges Rs 250/450 for bed & breakfast, singles/doubles.

The *Bank of Ceylon Rest House* has very clean twin-bedded rooms with shower for Rs 150. Book for the good rice and curry dinner (Rs 25). For rooms you're supposed to have booked ahead in Colombo but there are often on-the-spot vacancies. Nearby, the *MCW (Matara Cycle Works) Rest House* behind the police station – not to be confused with the MCW Rest House on Main St near the bus stop – also has decent rooms with attached bath for Rs 200.

Another place you could try is the very cheap *Government Pilgrim's Rest* (locally known as the Dutugemunu), opposite the bus stand.

Getting There & Away

Buses from Tissamaharama are fairly frequent and the fare is Rs 6.50. There are some direct buses to/from Colombo and places on the south coast and in the hill country.

The Hill Country

The hill country in the centre of Sri Lanka is totally different from anywhere else on the island. The altitude dispels the often sticky heat of the coastal regions or the dry air of the central and northern plains, producing a cool, perpetual spring. Everything is green and lush and much of the region is carpeted with the glowing colour of the tea plantations.

The Kingdom of Kandy resisted European takeover for over 300 years after the coastal regions had succumbed, and the city of Kandy remains the Sinhalese cultural and spiritual centre – one of the top attractions in Sri Lanka. It's a relaxed place with a delightful lakeside setting, where it's very easy to find the days just drifting by. Higher up into the hills are many more towns worth a visit and an abundance of pleasant walks and climbs, refreshing waterfalls and historic sites. Since the 19th century there has been a large population of Tamils in the hill country, brought from India by the British to labour on the tea estates.

Hill Country Trains

A railway from Colombo winds up through the hill country to Badulla, with stops including Hatton, Nanu Oya (near Nuwara Eliya), Haputale and Ella, and a short branch line into Kandy. This is a good way to travel the hill country, a bit slower than the buses, but less crowded and enabling you to enjoy the marvellous scenery. Three main daily trains in each direction run the length of the line between Colombo and Badulla (a trip of eight to 12 hours). Two are daytime trains with 1st-class observation saloons; the other is the Night Mail, which has sleeping accommodation and gets heavily booked at weekends and holidays.

The daytime trains are the Podi Menike leaving Colombo at 5 am and Badulla at 8.50 am, and the Udarata Menike leaving Colombo at 9.45 am and Badulla at 5.55 am. The Podi Menike detours into Kandy to pick up/drop off people there. The Night Mail – not particularly useful for travellers, who mostly take the hill country in relatively short hops and like to see the scenery! – leaves Colombo at 8.15 pm and Badulla at 5.45 pm. There are several other trains daily just between Colombo and Kandy.

COLOMBO TO KANDY

The Henerathgoda Botanic Gardens near Gampaha, off the Colombo-Kandy road about 30 km from Colombo, are overshadowed by the better known Peradeniya gardens near Kandy, but it was here that the first rubber trees planted in Asia were carefully grown and their potential proved. Some of those original rubber trees are still here today.

Kegalle, 77 km from Colombo, is the nearest town to the Pinnewala Elephant Orphanage. Sometimes if you can't get a bus all the way through between Colombo and Kandy, you can get one to Kegalle and change there. At Kadugannawa, just after the road and railway make their most scenic climbs, with views south to the large Bible Rock, is a tall pillar in memory of Captain Dawson, the English engineer who built the Colombo-Kandy road in 1826.

Pinnewala Elephant Orphanage

The government-run Pinnewala Elephant Orphanage near Kegalle, set up to save abandoned or orphaned wild elephants, is about the most popular 'elephant attraction' in Sri Lanka – and with good reason, for nowhere else except at peraheras are you likely to see so many elephants at close quarters. They're controlled by their keepers to make sure they feed at the right times and don't endanger anyone, but otherwise roam freely around the sanctuary area.

There are about 35 young elephants here and some are surprisingly small; this must be one of the few places where an elephant can step on your foot and you might walk away with a smile! The orphanage is open daily (Rs 60 for adult non-Sri Lankans) and bathing times for the babies are 10 am to noon and 2 to 4 pm, with meal times (the little ones gulp down several huge bottles of milk!) at 9.15 am, 1.15 and 5 pm. Most of the elephants become working elephants once they are grown up. Occasionally one of the older female elephants produces a baby to add to the herd.

There are also a couple of purely tourist-oriented 'elephant parks' on the road from Kegalle to Pinnewala.

Getting There & Away The orphanage is on a minor road, quite passable for cars and buses, a few km north of the Colombo-Kandy road. The turn-off is just out of Kegalle on the Kandy side. You can reach the orphanage by bus, train-and-bus, or car, en route between Colombo and Kandy, or as an outing from Kandy, or even as an outing from Colombo (though that's twice as far). From Kandy you can take a private bus or CTB bus No 662 to Kegalle (Rs 8), then another to Pinnewala (Rs 4). It's about an hour from Kandy to Kegalle, 15 minutes Kegalle to Pinnewala. There are also numerous buses between Colombo and Kegalle.

Rambukkana station on the Colombo-Kandy railway is about three km north of the orphanage. From Rambukkana get a bus going towards Kegalle. The 10 am train from Kandy (Rs 17.50 in 2nd class, Rs 6.50 3rd class) will get you to the orphanage in time for the lunchtime feeding.

KANDY

Only 115 km inland from Colombo, but climatically a world away due to its 500-metre altitude, Kandy is Sri Lanka's second biggest city, with 100,000 people, and the easygoing 'capital' of the hill country. It was also the capital of the last Sinhalese kingdom, falling to the British in 1815 only after three centuries of defying the Portuguese and Dutch.

Kandy is particularly famed for the great Kandy Esala Perahera over the 10 days leading up to the full moon in the month of Esala (July or August by the Gregorian calendar), but it has enough attractions to justify a visit at any time of the year. The town itself and the countryside around are lush and green and there are many pleasant walks both from the town itself or further afield. The town centre, close to Kandy's picturesque lake set in a bowl of hills, is a delightful jumble of old shops, antique and gemstone specialists, a bustling two-storey market and a good selection of hotels, guest houses and restaurants – though it becomes pretty quiet at night.

Locally Kandy is known as Maha Nuwara (Great City) or even just Nuwara (City), which is what some Kandy-bound bus conductors call out.

Orientation

The focus of Kandy is its lake, with the Temple of the Tooth on its north side. The city centre is immediately north and west of the lake, with the clock tower a handy reference point and the railway station, market and the various bus stands just a short walk from the lake. The city spreads into the surrounding hills, where many of the places to stay are perched, looking down on the town.

Information

Tourist Office On the lakeside road, a short distance from the temple, is the small Tourist Office – helpful on transport and things to do in the Kandy area, also with some info on places to stay – which is open Monday to Friday from 8.30 am to 4.45 pm and on Saturday from 8.30 am to 1 pm. In the same building is the Kandyan Art Association & Cultural Centre.

Money Most of the banks are on Dalada Vidiya and are open for foreign exchange Monday to Friday from 9 am to at least 2 pm, and for a few hours on Saturday morning. The Hatton National Bank offers the friendliest and generally the quickest service.

Post & Telecommunications The main post office is over the road from the railway station, open Monday to Friday from 8.30

am to 4.30 pm, and on Saturday 8.30 am to noon. There are a few more central sub-post offices including one next door to the Olde Empire hotel – and the Seetha agency post office on Kotugodalle Vidiya.

Cultural Centres The British Council (☎ 08-22410) at 178 D S Senanayake Vidiya (formerly Trincomalee St) has a library with back copies of British newspapers, cassettes and videos; sometimes it has film nights or exhibitions. Non-members are not particularly encouraged but you'll get beyond the security staff if you're keen – ask to speak to the head librarian. Some travellers have reported having to pay the Rs 275 annual membership fee for use of the facilities. It's open Tuesday to Saturday from 8.30 am to 6 pm.

Books You can buy and/or exchange books at Cindy's Bookstall in Torrington Lane, a side street near the clock tower. K V G de Silva at 86 D S Senanayake Vidiya has a few dozen books in English. *Kandy* by Dr Anuradha Seneviratna is an excellent and authoritative guide to the temples and monuments of the city. It's published by the Ministry of Cultural Affairs. If you're interested in books on Buddhism, visit the Buddhist Publication Society towards the east end of the lake.

Kandy Esala Perahera

The big night of the year in Kandy is the culmination of 10 days of increasingly frenetic activity. A perahera is a parade or procession and Kandy's, held to honour the sacred tooth enshrined in the Dalada Maligawa, the Temple of the Tooth, peaks at the time of the full moon in Esala (July/August). The first six nights are relatively low-key; on the seventh things start to take off as the route lengthens, the procession becomes more and more splendid – and accommodation prices go right through the roof. The procession is actually a combination of five separate peraheras. Four come from the four Kandy *devales* – shrines to deities who protect the island and are also devotees and servants of the Buddha. Natha is a Buddha-to-be of special importance to Kandy. Vishnu is the guardian of Sri Lanka and an indicator of the intermingling of Hindu and Buddhist beliefs since he is also one of the three great Hindu gods; the others being Skanda, the god of war and victory, and Pattini, the goddess of chastity. The fifth and most splendid perahera is that of the Dalada Maligawa itself.

The procession is led by thousands of Kandyan dancers and drummers beating thousands of drums, leaping with unbounded energy, cracking whips and waving colourful banners. Then come long processions of elephants, 50, 60 or more of them. The brilliantly caparisoned Maligawa Tusker is the most splendid of them all – decorated from trunk to toe he carries a huge canopy which shelters, on the final night, a replica of the sacred relic cask. A carpetway of white linen is laid in front of the elephant so that he does not step in the dirt. In 1988 the old Maligawa Tusker died after 50 years of faithful service, and was replaced by a Thai-born youngster specially trained for the task. You can view the taxidermied remains of the elder in the Temple of the Tooth.

The Kandy Esala Perahera is the most magnificent annual spectacle in Sri Lanka and one of the most famous in Asia. It has been an annual event for many centuries and is described by Robert Knox in his 1681 book *An Historical Relation of Ceylon*. There is also a smaller procession on the full moon day in June and special peraheras may be put on for important occasions. It's essential to arrive early for roadside seats for the perahera – by 2 pm for the final night. Earlier in the week you can get seats about half way back in the stands quite cheaply. Midway between the Temple of the Tooth and Queen's Hotel is a good place to take photographs because there's an area floodlit for Sri Lankan TV.

The Lake

Kandy's lake, a lovely centrepiece to the town, is artificial and was only created in 1807 by Sri Wickrama Rajasinha, the last ruler of the Kingdom of Kandy. Several small-scale local chiefs who protested because their people objected to labouring on the project were put to death at stakes in the lake bed. The island in the centre was used by Sri Wickrama Rajasinha's personal harem – to which he crossed on a barge. The less romantically inclined British used it as an ammunition store – but they did add the fortress-style parapet around the perimeter of the lake.

The perimeter road makes a very pleasant stroll – it's also used by a steady procession of learner drivers. From the west end of the lake you can take short cruises on small motor boats. On the south shore, in front of the Malwatte monastery, there's a circular enclosure which is the monks' bathhouse. They may invite males inside to see how a monk takes a fully clothed bath!

Dalada Maligawa (Temple of the Tooth)

Close to the lake, the Temple of the Tooth houses Sri Lanka's most important Buddhist relic. The sacred tooth of the Buddha was said to have been snatched from the flames of his funeral pyre in 543 BC, and was smuggled into Ceylon during the 4th century AD, hidden in the hair of a princess. At first it was taken to Anuradhapura, but with the ups and downs of Sri Lankan history it moved from place to place before eventually ending at Kandy. For a short period from 1283 it was actually carried back to India by an invading army but then brought back again to Ceylon by King Parakramabahu III.

Gradually the tooth came to assume more and more importance but in the 16th century the Portuguese, in one of their worst spoilsport moods, captured what they claimed was the tooth at Jaffna, took it away and burnt it with Catholic fervour in Goa. 'Not so' is the Sinhalese rejoinder; they were fobbed off with a replica and the real incisor remained safe.

The present Temple of the Tooth was constructed mainly under Kandyan kings from 1687 to 1707, and 1747 to 82. It is an imposing pink-painted structure, surrounded by a deep moat. The octagonal tower in the moat

was built by Sri Wickrama Rajasinha, the last king of Kandy, and houses an important collection of ola-leaf (palm-leaf) manuscripts. The eye-catching gilded roof over the relic chamber is a recent addition by President Premadasa.

The temple has a constant flow of worshippers and flocks of tourists. It's open 24 hours daily (at a charge of Rs 15 for non-Sri Lankans and Rs 50 to take photos or make tape-recordings). Shorts are not acceptable attire and it is required that you remove your shoes. There are morning and evening pujas (5.30 to 6.30 am, 9.30 to 10.30 am and 6.30 to 7.30 pm) when the heavily guarded room housing the tooth is open to devotees – and to tourists. (Travellers have recommended avoiding the 6.30 pm puja due to the tour bus crowds who come here before a 7.30 pm Kandy dance performance.) Of course you don't actually see the tooth – just a gold casket said to contain a series of smaller and smaller caskets and eventually the tooth itself. Or perhaps a replica, nobody seems too sure. The casket is behind a window and two decidedly mean-looking monks stand heavily on either side. To see the stuffed remains of the Maligawa Tusker who died in 1988, take a left after ascending the first steps up to the temple, and after passing security.

Around the Temple of the Tooth

The small but excellent National Museum beside the Temple of the Tooth, once quarters for the Kandyan royal concubines, houses royal regalia and reminders of Sinhalese life before the arrival of the Europeans. It contains a copy of the agreement, made in 1815, handing over the Kandyan provinces to British rule. This worthy document announces that the 'cruelties and oppressions of the Malabar ruler, in the arbitrary and unjust infliction of bodily tortures and pains of death without trial, and sometimes without accusation or the possibility of a crime, and in the general contempt and contravention of all civil rights, have become flagrant enormous and intolerable'. Sri Wickrama Rajasinha was therefore declared, 'by the habitual violation of the chief and most sacred duties of a sovereign', to be 'fallen and deposed from office of king' and 'the dominion of the Kandyan provinces' was 'vested in the sovereign of the British empire'.

The museum is open from 9 am to 5 pm, except on Fridays. Admission is Rs 40. The National Museum, the less interesting Archaeological Museum behind the temple, the old royal courtyard, royal audience hall and queen's chamber in the temple precincts, and other temples around Kandy – but not the Tooth Temple itself – together make up one of Sri Lanka's Cultural Triangle sites, and you can get a US$7 ticket at the National Museum which lets you into them. You can also buy the US$20 Cultural Triangle round tickets here (see the Cultural Triangle section in the Ancient Cities chapter for more detail on this scheme). The audience hall, notable for the tall pillars supporting its roof, was the site for the convention of Kandyan chiefs which ceded the kingdom to Britain in 1815.

The courts around the back of the Temple of the Tooth are open to the public, even when in session. Sometimes you can see lawyers openly bargaining with each other to reach a settlement for their clients.

Monasteries

Kandy's principal Buddhist monasteries have considerable importance – the high priests of the two best known monasteries, Malwatte and Asgiriya, are the most important in Sri Lanka. They also play an important role in the administration and operation of the Temple of the Tooth. The Malwatte monastery is directly across the lake from the Temple of the Tooth, while the Asgiriya is on the hill off D S Senanayake Vidiya, to the north-west of the town centre, and has a large reclining Buddha image.

Elephants

Elephants can be seen frequently around Kandy, both in the town and surrounds. Working elephants might be spotted anywhere and you may catch the Tooth Temple elephants hanging around in front of the temple or, about 4 pm, being bathed at their quarters on Anagarika Dharmapala Mawatha or down near the bridge over the Mahaweli at Lewella.

From Kandy it's a fairly easy trip to the Pinnewala Elephant Orphanage (see the Colombo to Kandy section).

Scenic Walks

There are many walks almost in the centre of Kandy, such as up to the Royal Palace Park, also constructed by Sri Wickrama Rajasinha, overlooking the lake. It closes at dusk. Further up the hill on Rajapihilla Mawatha there are even better views over the lake, the town and the surrounding hills, which disappear in a series of gentle ranges stretching far into the distance. There are paths on up from Rajapihilla Mawatha if you're in the mood.

You can reach the big new concrete Buddha overlooking the town centre from the west by walking 20 minutes uphill from the tourist police station on Peradeniya Rd.

Udawattakelle Sanctuary North of the lake you can take a longer stroll around this cool and pleasant forest close to the heart of Kandy. There are plenty of huge trees, much bird and insect life and more than a few monkeys, but visitors are advised to be a little careful in this secluded woodland if they're alone. Muggers are rare in Sri Lanka but not unknown. The odd leech is almost certain to accompany you after rain. Entrance to the sanctuary is officially Rs 10 and only through the gate, which you reach by turning right after the post office on D S Senanayake Vidiya (there's a sign at the junction). There are clear paths but it's worth paying attention to the map at the entrance.

Arts & Crafts

The Kandyan Art Association & Cultural Centre beside the lake has a good display of local lacquerwork, brassware and other craft items. There are some craftspeople working on the spot. The beautiful, miniature 'batik' elephants make good little presents for children back home. Next door to the centre there's a fine auditorium for dance and other performances.

Botanic Gardens

The Peradeniya Botanic Gardens are six km out of Kandy towards Colombo. Before the British came this was a royal pleasure garden: today it's the largest botanic garden in Sri Lanka, covering 60 hectares and bounded on three sides by a loop of the Mahaweli River.

There is a fine collection of orchids and a stately avenue of royal palms planted in 1905. A major attraction is the giant Javan fig tree found on the great lawn – it covers 1600 sq metres. The gardens are open daily, from 7 am to 6 pm, and admission is Rs 50 for foreign visitors, Rs 25 for students, Rs 5 for locals. Bus Nos 652 or 724 from beside Kandy market will take you to the gardens for Rs 3. A three-wheeler from the market to the gardens will set you back around Rs 75.

There is a Royal Gardens Cafeteria about 100 metres from the entrance, to the left, with a good set lunch, but sometimes slow service. Shoestringers can always take their own picnic. You can easily spend a whole day wandering around the gardens. Keep your eyes open for an oxen-drawn lawn mower!

A Temple Loop from Kandy

Visiting some of the many temples around Kandy gives you a chance to see a little rural life as well as observe Sri Lankan culture. One particularly pleasant loop will take you to three temples and back via the Botanic Gardens.

The first stop is the Embekke Devale, for which you need a bus from beside Kandy market, or from Railway Approach Rd past the Colombo bus stand. The buses only run about once an hour and the village of Embekke is about seven twisting and turning km beyond the Botanic Gardens. From the village you've got a pleasant countryside stroll of about a km to the temple, built in the 14th century. Its carved wooden pillars, thought to have come from a royal audience hall in the city, are said be the finest in the

Kandy area. The carvings include swans, double-headed eagles, wrestling men and dancing women. There's a small entry charge to the temple. A miniature version of the Kandy perahera is held here in late August.

From here to the Lankatilake Temple is a 1½-km stroll along a path through the rice paddies until the temple looms up on the left. From Kandy you can go directly to the Lankatilake Temple on a Kiribathkumbara or Pilimatalawa bus from the same stops as Embekke buses. Built on a rocky outcrop, the temple is reached by a long series of steps cut directly into the rock. It's a mainly Hindu temple with a Buddhist annexe which houses a fine Buddha image and Kandy period wall paintings. Outside there are stone elephant figures.

It's a further three-km walk from here to the Gadaldeniya Temple, or you can catch a bus – No 644, among others, will take you there. This Buddhist temple with a Hindu annexe is also constructed atop a rocky outcrop, and dates from a similar period to Lankatilake and the Embekke Devale. A moonstone marks the entrance to the main shrine. There's a small entry charge here too.

From Gadaldeniya the main Colombo-Kandy road is only about a km away; you reach it close to the 65th milestone. It's a pleasant stroll and from the main road almost any bus will take you to the Botanic Gardens or on into Kandy.

Swimming

It costs Rs 30 (including a towel) for non-residents to use the pool at the Hotel Suisse, set in a fine garden overlooking the lake. Buy a ticket from the reception. Several other top end hotels allow non-residents to use their pools but generally charge more than the Suisse. The Hotel Hilltop's pool (Rs 60) is large, clean and not too busy. There are some stunningly sited pools in Kandy including the Hotel Thilanka's, on a terrace looking down on the lake, but perhaps the most spectacular of all is the Hotel Citadel's, which overlooks a big sweep of the Mahaweli River.

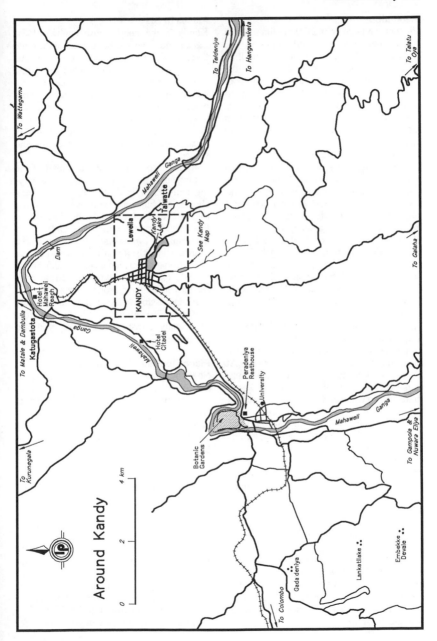

Around Kandy

Meditation

Visitors can learn or practise meditation and study Buddhism at several places in the Kandy area. You can ask at the Buddhist Publication Society (☎ 08-23679) by the lake in Kandy, open Monday to Friday from 9 am to 4 pm, Saturday from 8.30 am to noon, or at the Buddhist Information Centre in Colombo (see the Information section in the Colombo chapter), for details of some courses.

The *Nilambe Meditation Centre* near Nilambe Bungalow Junction, reached by bus via Galaha is, in the words of one traveller, 'an extraordinary oasis of tranquillity and beauty (also good food)'. You can stay for a suggested but negotiable price of Rs 150 a day, and you need a sleeping bag and blanket. Casual visitors not intending to learn meditation are not encouraged. There is a large library of books and a tape library here. To reach Nilambe from the Bungalow Junction you have a steep 1½-km walk through tea plantations. Follow the white arrows.

Rockhill Hermitage (☎ 08-52593) at Wegirikanda, Hondiyadeniya, reached via Gampola on bus No 645, and *Uduwela* are other meditation centres near Kandy. At Uduwela guests are asked to make a donation for food or to work in the garden. To get there take an Uduwela bus from Kandy clock tower to the last bus halt, Ooragalla Leafshed, from where it's just a 20-minute walk along the estate road towards Ongurugolle.

The *Sri Jamieson Hermitage* at Samadhi Mawatha, Ampitiya is a further meditation centre near Kandy catering for foreigners. It's about three km from the town centre along the Ampitiya-Talatu Oya Road. To get there, catch an Ampitiya bus from near the clock tower. The centre has four cottages for visitors.

Finally, the *Siyane Vipassana Meditation Centre* at Kanduboda, Delgoda, about an hour by bus from Colombo, is a working monastery which welcomes Westerners who seriously want to learn or practise. Food and lodging are free.

Places to Stay

Kandy is the guest house capital of Sri Lanka, and at the low-budget end of the scale there are quite a few popular places. In the middle and top brackets there are some lovely, more luxurious houses and an increasing number of good hotels. Many places are set on the hills surrounding the town – in some cases two or three km from the centre, but worth the effort of reaching because of their outstanding locations and views.

Kandy also used to be the capital of the touting business with numerous very annoying touts. Happily these creeps have been cleaned out but some taxi drivers are trying to step into the breach. At the time of the Esala Perahera, room prices in Kandy treble, quadruple, or even worse – if you can find a room at all that is. If you're intent on coming to see the perahera then be prepared for what it will cost you. Booking far ahead may secure you a more reasonable price.

It's impossible to list all the places to stay in Kandy. The following is just a selection. The Kandy tourist office can help you find places too.

Places to Stay – bottom end

Near the Town Centre At the very cheapest end, the *Burmese Rest* is about five minutes' walk along from the Queen's Hotel at 270 D S Senanayake Vidiya. It's part of a Buddhist monastery and has four large clean double rooms at Rs 50 per person, including a light breakfast. The common bathroom isn't too inviting.

More congenial, the *Pink House* is 10 minutes' walk from the town centre at 15 Saranankara Rd near the lake. The rooms are Rs 40 or Rs 50 per person and basic, but it's clean with good food, a stream running through the garden and a menagerie of birds and animals. The owners are very friendly and helpful – and they refuse to deal with touts, so don't arrive with one. Filling breakfasts and dinners are available, each at Rs 70 per person. To get there turn off Sangaraja Mawatha shortly before the Hotel Suisse. If the Pink House is full, the owners can direct

Top: Cave Temple, Dambulla (JN)
Left: Mosque, Galle (PS)
Right: Jami-Ul-Alfar Mosque, Pettah, Colombo (TW)

Top: Tea pluckers, Hali Ella (RI'A)
Middle: Outrigger fishing boats on beach, Hambantota (TW)
Bottom: Buddhist Monks at Kumara Pokuna (or Prince's Bathing Pool),
Polonnaruwa (JN)

you to other places nearby that take in guests for much the same price.

Right in the town centre, close to the big Queen's Hotel, is one of Kandy's best value hotels, with plenty of old colonial atmosphere – the *Olde Empire* (☎ 08-24284) at 21 Temple St. Singles/doubles, all with common bath, are Rs 110/154. Some of the rooms at the back are a little dingy but there's a pleasant balcony at the front, overlooking the lake, and a good, reasonably priced restaurant.

Kandy has a YMCA and a few similar hostels. None is particularly inviting but they may be worth trying at peak times, such as during the perahera. The *YMCA* (☎ 08-23529) on Kotugodalle Vidiya has doubles with fans, attached toilet and common bath at Rs 182. Singles are Rs 91, while a bed in a three-bed dorm costs Rs 50. All rooms are very clean but the bathroom is grotty.

Along Anagarika Dharmapala Mawatha
This road, which goes up the hill past the Temple of the Tooth, leads to a number of popular guest houses on the edge of the town. Bus Nos 654, 655 and 698 will get you to this area and beyond. There's a handful of small places on Sangamitta Mawatha, the road up to the left off Anagarika Dharmapala Mawatha at the top of the hill. At the bottom of a steep drive *Jingle Bells* has good food, a lovely garden and a friendly owner. Rooms are Rs 150/175 with common bath or Rs 200 with attached bath. Further up Sangamitta Mawatha at No 34A, *Green Woods* is a quiet house with a jungle atmosphere on the edge of the Udawattakelle Forest Sanctuary. Doubles are Rs 150 with common bath or Rs 200 with private bath, and the food is excellent. Next door is the *Little Nest* which costs Rs 150 per person with breakfast and dinner included; the food is reputedly excellent but the common bathroom not.

At 18 First Lane, Dharmaraja Rd (turn right off Anagarika Dharmapala Mawatha a fraction past Sangamitta Mawatha), *Mrs Clement Dissanayake's* (☎ 08-25468) receives good reports from many travellers. Rooms are from Rs 150 with common bath

to Rs 300 with attached bath. The family is friendly and helpful and the area quiet and rather upmarket. Breakfast and dinner can be had for Rs 60 and Rs 75 – the food is very good. If you phone from the main post office when you arrive in Kandy, they'll come and pick you up. They have a motorbike for hire at Rs 300 per day. Two further family houses rent out rooms on First Lane. At No 12 is *Mrs Lionel Galahitiyowa* with two rooms from Rs 200. *No 39*, at the far end, is a big house on a hill with fantastic views; it has two detached rooms with all facilities and verandahs.

The *Travellers Nest* (☎ 08-22633) at 117/4 Anagarika Dharmapala Mawatha, slightly to the left off the road a few hundred metres after Dharmaraja Rd, caters for a variety of budgets. At the shoestring end there are small ground-floor rooms at Rs 75 or Rs 100 a single, Rs 100 or Rs 150 a double, some with common bath, some with private bath. The price of food and drinks here can mount up very quickly. See also Places to Stay – middle.

Continue along the main road about a km beyond the Travellers Nest and you'll come to a sign directing you left down a steep track to *Prasanna Tourist Inn* (☎ 08-24365) at 53/29 Hewaheta Rd, Talwatta. This is a popular place with helpful owners. Its four rooms, each with attached bath, cost Rs 200. The house is clean, with good food (breakfast Rs 40, dinner Rs 50) and close to the Mahaweli River. The owner refuses to pay touts, and if you telephone on arrival in the town he will pick you up. Alternatively you can get a No 698 Haragama bus for Rs 2 to Talwatta, from beside the central market.

A few more small guest houses are situated down in Lewella, close to the Mahaweli and reached by turning left down Lewella Rd soon after the Travellers Nest. Bus No 655 from Kandy clock tower goes down here. A short walk downhill from the milk bar, the friendly *Charm Inn* (☎ 08-25650) at 30/34 Bangalawatta has singles/doubles with private bath at Rs 100/200. On the same loop road are several other houses which will let out rooms for Rs 75/100, usually again with

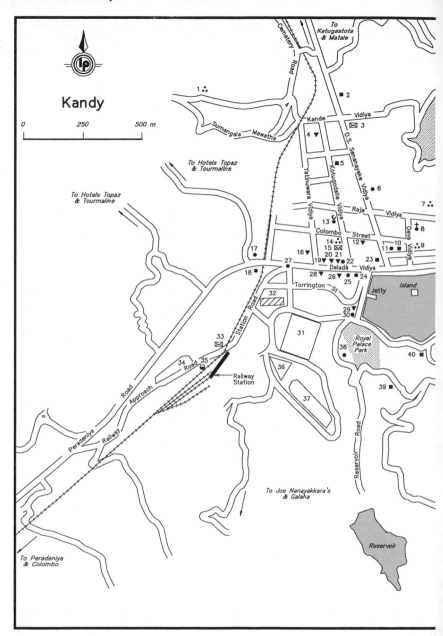

Kandy

0   250   500 m

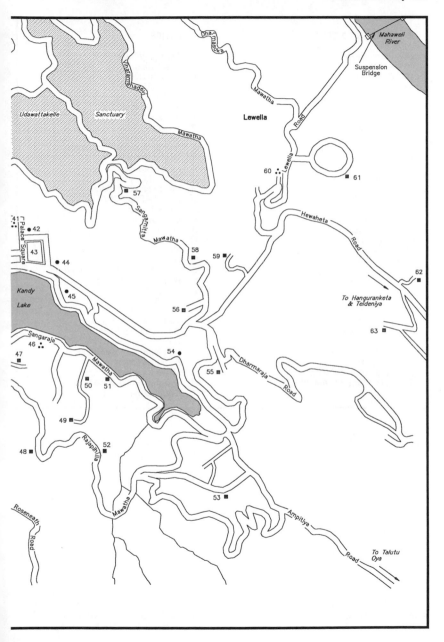

■ PLACES TO STAY		OTHER	
2	Burmese Rest	1	Asgiriya Vihara
5	YMCA	3	Post Office
10	Olde Empire	6	KVG de Silva
23	Queen's Hotel	7	Vishnu Devale
39	Castle Hill Guest House	8	St Paul's Church
40	Devon Rest	9	Pattini Devale
47	Lake Round	11	Air Lanka
48	The Chalet	13	Mosque
49	Sharon Inn	14	Skanda Devale
50	Pink House	15	Seetha Agency Post Office
51	Hotel Suisse	17	Tourist Police
52	McLeod Inn	18	Police Station
53	Hillway Tour Inn	22	Bank of Ceylon
55	Mrs Clement Dissanayake's	24	Hatton National Bank
56	Hotel Thilanka	25	Cargill's Food City
57	Green Woods	27	Clock Tower
58	Jingle Bells	30	Laksala
59	Travellers Nest	31	Prison
61	Charm Inn	32	Market
62	Prasanna Tourist Inn	33	Main Post Office
63	Gem Inn II	34	Goods Shed Bus Yard
		35	Colombo Private Bus Stand
▼ PLACES TO EAT		36	Bogambara Bus Yard
		37	Stadium
4	Flower Song Chinese Restaurant	38	YMBA
12	Victory Hotel	41	Natha Devale
16	Paiva's Moghul Restaurant	42	Archaeological Museum
19	Impala Hotel	43	Temple of the Tooth
20	Bake House	44	National Museum
21	East China Restaurant	45	Kandyan Art Association
26	Devon Restaurant		& Tourist Office
28	White House Restaurant	46	Malwatte Vihara
29	Lake Front Restaurant	54	Buddhist Publication Society
		60	Gangarama Vihara

attached bath – among them the clean and friendly *Linton Lodge* at No 30/61, *Lucky House* at 30/40, and *Mr Illankone's* at 30/26.

Places to Stay – middle

Some of the most pleasant places to stay in Kandy fall in this category.

Near the Town Centre There are several places up Saranankara Rd past the Pink House. At the top the *Sharon Inn*, No 59 (☎ 08-25665), is the pick of the bunch. It's clean, friendly and spacious with a good view and singles/doubles at Rs 200/250, some with private baths but all with access to hot water. The food is excellent, there is a

garden and the owners will arrange international calls for you. Next door, the *Lakshmi* (☎ 08-22154) at No 57 is clean at Rs 250/350 with attached bath. A few metres down the hill, the *Lake Inn* (☎ 08-22208) at No 43 has singles/doubles/triples at Rs 350/450/550 including breakfast. Some rooms have hot water.

Slightly back towards the centre and just over the road from the lake at 4E Sangaraja Mawatha, the modern *Devon Rest* (☎ 08-32392) has large, clean doubles with balconies and attached baths at Rs 550, or Rs 450 without the view. Also overlooking the lake, at 8/5 Sangaraja Mawatha, the *Lake Round* (☎ 08-22689) has been recommended with singles/doubles at Rs 250/350 including attached bath, fan and net. Just past the east end of the lake at Sangaraja Mawatha 52, opposite the tennis club, is *Ivy Banks* (☎ 08-22434) with very clean rooms from Rs 350/450, including private bath and hot water.

The *Travellers Nest* (☎ 08-22633) at 117/4 Angarika Dharmapala Mawatha has comfortable rooms beside its upstairs balcony at Rs 250/350/450 a single/double/triple with private bathroom and hot water. The food can be good but slow in coming – breakfast is Rs 50 and dinner of rice and curry Rs 60. There are also cheaper rooms (see Bottom End).

Further Out The excellent *Gem Inn II* (☎ 08-24239) at 102/90 Hewaheta Rd, Talwatta is about 2½ km east of the town centre, perched on a hillside with wonderful views over the Mahaweli River and the Knuckles Range. This spacious, relaxed home is good value with just a handful of doubles at Rs 250 or Rs 300, and a four-bed family room at Rs 350. The rooms are very clean, simple but comfortable with verandahs, nets, fans and private bath – and the cooking is some of the best you'll find in Sri Lanka (dinner usually Rs 60 to Rs 75). It's not so easy to find: as one amused guest wrote in the visitors' book: 'The path to enlightenment is not easy; nor is the path to Gem Inn II'. Try ringing first for directions and you may be offered a lift. Otherwise get a three-wheeler or taxi (Rs 60 or Rs 70 and don't believe any driver who tries to tell you Gem Inn II is closed), or catch a No 698 Haragama or Gurudeniya bus, from beside the central market, to Talwatta. The track to Gem Inn II is up to the right off Hewaheta Rd, just before the Kandy municipal limit sign. Follow it round its first hairpin, but at the second hairpin continue straight on: Gem Inn II is the house at the end.

Joe Nanayakkara's at 29 Gemunu Mawatha, Public Servants Housing Scheme, Hantana Place, has superb views over the town and surrounding hills. Mr and Mrs Nanayakkara are a friendly, lively pair of teachers only too happy to impart their knowledge of Sri Lankan life to their visitors. Double rooms with private baths are Rs 250. Go up Hospital Rd (off Station Rd) past the space-capsule-like former Hantana Hotel, then take the first road up to the left and keep left until you reach the house, about a km from Station Rd. An Uduwela bus from near the clock tower will take you some of the way, or you could get a taxi for Rs 60 to Rs 70. Once there, you'll be shown a short cut which will have you down in town in 10 minutes.

There are several good middle-range guest houses close together on Rajapihilla Mawatha, high above the south side of the lake, all with good views. They include the *Lake View Rest* (☎ 08-32034) at No 71, which has 20 rooms at Rs 400/450 a single/double. The owners will pick you up from the station. *McLeod Inn* (☎ 08-22832) at No 65A has six rooms at Rs 450. The food here is reportedly delicious with rice and curry plus dessert at Rs 100. *Blinkbonnie* is yet another recommended guest house close by, with nine doubles at Rs 450 including breakfast.

Lucktissme (☎ 08-22725) at 125 Pitakanda Rd, Mahayaya is about two km north of the town centre, up the hill from the Katugastota road. It has 10 pleasant doubles with attached tiled bathrooms and verandahs at Rs 350. The garden and views are lovely, the owners friendly and the location quiet and peaceful. Take bus No 625 and get off at Pitakanda Rd, from where it's a km or so walk uphill (there is a short cut once you've got there), or phone from town for a lift. A taxi from town costs Rs 75 to Rs 100.

Places to Stay – top end
Kandy has a couple of hotels in colonial-era style, plus several modern luxury places and a number of better-quality guest houses.

Near the Town Centre On the south side of the lake at 30 Sangaraja Mawatha, the old-style *Hotel Suisse* (☎ 08-22637, 22672) has 100 rooms at US$26/30/37 a single/double/triple, room only. It's secluded and quiet but not too far to stroll around the lake to the town centre. Balcony rooms are very clean, spacious and restful. There are spacious public areas, including a snooker room, and a fine garden and swimming pool overlooking the lake.

The *Hotel Thilanka* at 3 Sangamitta Mawatha (☎ 08-22060, 25497), is a pleasant place surrounded by trees and overlooking the lake. Singles/doubles are from US$22/23. Those facing the front are the best. There's a pleasant terrace bar and a good restaurant, plus a pool with a great view over the town and lake.

The colonial-style *Queen's Hotel* (☎ 08-22121/2), right in the town centre overlooking the lake, has 100 rooms with singles/doubles/triples at US$22/28/33, US$10 extra with air-con. The rooms are OK but nothing very special, and the beds certainly aren't the greatest – one reader discovered an old door put between his mattress and the springs, another described his bedding as 'rough and torn'. There's a restaurant and garden with pool and bar.

Further Out In Anniewatte, way up on top of a hill overlooking the town centre from the west, about two km up from Peradeniya Rd, the *Hotel Topaz* (☎ 08-23062, 24150) has 65 rooms at US$25. Next door, the more modern and sparkling *Hotel Tourmaline* has 25 rooms with air-con, bathtubs and balconies at US$30. Both hotels have swimming pools and you can even play floodlit tennis. Some readers have experienced difficulty getting transport to town from up here.

Also on this side of Kandy, the *Hotel Hilltop* (☎ 08-23892, 24162) at 200/21 Bahirawakanda, a five-minute walk up to the right off Peradenaya Rd, has commanding views over the town and surrounding hills, and a peaceful garden with a good-sized, clean swimming pool. Singles/doubles are US$23/25. Five km west of the town centre at 124 Srimath Kuda Ratwatte Mawatha is the modern and expensive *Citadel* (☎ 08-22020), built beside the Mahaweli River. All rooms (US$66 double) have balconies overlooking the river. The swimming pool is worth a visit! Take a three-wheeler or taxi to get there.

Overlooking the lake from the slopes to its south, the *Castle Hill Guest House* (☎ 08-24376) at 22 Rajapihilla Mawatha is a top-end guest house with just four doubles at Rs 960 for bed & breakfast. Good for a luxury stop, reported one visitor – 'the immense rooms with their low art deco-like furniture, French doors to the gardens and stylised flower arrangements could almost be hotel stage-sets from a Fred Astaire movie!' The view from the lovely garden is stunning. The *Chalet* (☎ 08-24353) at 32 Rajapihilla Mawatha has 30 singles/doubles at Rs 750/850 including breakfast. 'The views are magnificent and the service excellent', reported one visitor, though others have been disappointed with the food. It has a small swimming pool and a resident troupe of monkeys.

About six km north of the centre near the Katugastota bridge, the *Mahaweli Reach* (☎ 08-32062/3) is at 35 Siyambalagastenne Rd and also has a well-sited swimming pool. It has 50 rooms at US$30 and even boasts a helipad.

Finally, one of Kandy's most modern hotels is 27 km out of Kandy. higher up in a tea estate at Elkaduwa. The *Hunas Falls Hotel* (☎ 08-76402/3) has 29 very modern rooms with air-conditioning and all other mod-cons including swimming pool, tennis court, a well-stocked fish pool above the Hunas waterfalls and plenty of walks in the surrounding hills. Count on around Rs 600 for a double, Rs 1310 with all meals.

Places to Eat
Many people eat mostly in their guest houses, where some of Kandy's tastiest food is to be had. *Gem Inn II, Sharon Inn, Green Woods* and *Mrs Clement Dissanayake's* are just a few of the guest houses with excellent food. You can eat cheaper in town but you'll miss out on many of the local specialities, particularly at poya or other special occasions.

Cheaper Restaurants There are a number of popular cheaper places in central Kandy but they all seem to yo-yo between acceptable and awful! Several of them are on Dalada Vidiya, the street running down from the lake to the clock tower, where the *Devon Restaurant* has received better reviews than most of late. A good curry spread is Rs 55 and beers go for Rs 55. The chicken soup and the hamburgers have also been recommended. There's also a take-away counter for lunch packs, bread, cakes and short eats. Just down the street, the cool *White House Restaurant* is not open in the evenings but is good for lunch and popular for quick snacks, drinks or ice cream ('delicious strawberry ice cream' reported one traveller). Sometimes it does the best coffee in town. Sausages, mash, tomato and salad cost Rs 65 while noodles, fried rice or curries are Rs 30 to Rs 40. On the other side of Dalada Vidiya, the *Bake House* is a big, two-level place with good short eats and a comprehensive menu with Western dishes at around Rs 60, noodles, omelettes and soups for Rs 30. Quality is typically variable, but the upstairs balcony provides an entertaining if noisy view of this part of town. The counters out the front sell reasonable bread, cakes and short eats. A few doors up the street, the *East China Restaurant* stays open until 9.30 or 10 pm and has variable meals from Rs 40 to Rs 80, with sometimes slow service. Down towards the clock tower, the scruffy but very cheap *Impala Hotel* (biriyanis a speciality) does a really refreshing mixed-fruit drink and good kottu rotty. Three hot curries and rice cost only Rs 15. Just around the corner on Yatinuwara Vidiya, the upstairs *Paiva's Moghul Restaurant* does good north Indian dishes from Rs 15 to Rs 80.

There are several ordinary local eateries on Kotugodalle Vidiya. The *Green Cafe* is good value and quiet and has good bread. Further up the street, the *Sri Lanka Soya Project*, beside the YMCA, is busy over lunch hour selling cheap nutritious food such as soya ice cream and short eats at reasonable prices. The *Kandy City Mission* at 125 D S Senanayake Vidiya has good short eats and plates of rice and curry. The *Victory Hotel* on Colombo St, open till 11 pm, has a variety of food including Chinese and Western dishes for Rs 60 to Rs 70, and rice and curry for Rs 25.

The *Olde Empire*, between the Queen's Hotel and the Temple of the Tooth, may look a little grey and dreary, but the food is consistently good. Come for a good rice and curry for around Rs 60 and try their excellent ice cream.

On the south side of Peradeniya Rd, straight on past the clock tower and after the police station, the *Lyons Café* is clean, with quick service and good, cheap food. It also does good coffee and sports a photograph of a civic reception it once laid on for President Tito of Yugoslavia!

The *Lake Front Restaurant* next to the Laksala shop at the town end of the lake has a café section upstairs, with some good little snacks, and a reasonable Chinese restaurant downstairs – fried rice or noodles Rs 30 or Rs 40, most mains Rs 80, beefsteak or chicken with veg, potato and salad Rs 70 or Rs 80.

More Expensive Restaurants At the top end of Kotugodalle Vidiya is a top-end surprise – the *Flower Song Chinese Restaurant*, a clean, classy, air-conditioned place that even has a substantial wine list. The 'small' dishes on the menu, mostly in the Rs 100 to Rs 120 range, are enough for one person, and tasty; the 'large' dishes serve two or more. Otherwise, if you want to splash out there's little to choose from except hotel dining rooms. The *Hotel Suisse's* fixed-price buffet lunches and dinners are Rs 220 per person, while the *Queen's Hotel's* four-course dinners are Rs 150. Both get mixed reviews. The restaurant at the *Hotel Thilanka* has good Moghul, Chinese and Sri Lankan specialities.

Entertainment
Kandyan Dancers & Drummers The famed Kandyan dancers are not principally a theatrical performance, but you can see them go through their athletic routines every night at one or more locales around Kandy. The most popular and probably the best show at the

time of writing is at the Red Cross Building next door to the Kandyan Art Association & Cultural Centre. The performance starts at 7.30 pm and lasts about 1½ hours, ending with a fire dance. Other shows nightly at the same time, and with much the same programme, are at the Cultural Centre itself, Kandy Lake Club a couple of km up Sangamitta Mawatha, which is also a casino, and the YMBA which has perhaps the least professional troupe. Tickets for all performances are officially Rs 150 but you may be able to get one at a discount from your hotel or guest house. Beware the price of drinks at the Lake Club – soda water is Rs 35, Coca-Cola Rs 30.

You can also hear Kandyan drummers every day at the Temple of the Tooth – their drumming signals the start of the daily pujas.

Other There's not a great deal else to go out

to at night in Kandy. Unlike those in the beach resorts, the restaurants are fairly quiet, as many visitors eat in their guest houses or hotels. There are occasional concerts at the Kandyan Art Association auditorium by the lake, and regular local bands on at the Hotel Citadel. For a drink, check out some hotel bars. The Queen's Hotel has a pub-like side section called the Queen's Cafe & Bar. You can buy beer to take away at Cargill's Food City supermarket on Dalada Vidiya. The Hotel Suisse has a big, well-kept snooker table where you can play billiards for Rs 30 per half hour, or snooker for Rs 60 per 45 minutes. One traveller reported that his game was attended by a compulsory referee called Francis who would make comments like 'That was a very bad miss, sir.'

Things to Buy

There's a government-run Laksala arts and crafts shop at the town end of the lake with cheaper prices than at the Art Association, but it has nothing on the big Laksala in Colombo.

Central Kandy is packed with shops selling antique (and instant-antique) jewellery, silver belts, and other items in abundance. Some travellers have recommended Da Silva at 3 Temple St, the street where the Olde Empire hotel is located, for antiques. You can also buy crafts in and around the colourful covered main market on Station Rd.

Kandy also has a number of batik manufacturers. For individual and truly artistic but quite pricey batiks, find your way to Upali Jayakodi, Jayamali Batiks Studio, 178 Dharmasoka Mawatha, Lewella. It's worth a trip to simply have a look!

Getting There & Away

Air Kandy has no airport, but Air Lanka has an office (☎ 08-32494) at 19 Temple St, next to the Olde Empire Hotel.

Bus There are many private and CTB bus services available.

To/From Colombo The fare for the 2½ to three-hour trip is Rs 25, and there are both private buses (from Colombo's Bastian Mawatha bus yard) and CTB. Services thin out after about 8 pm but there are supposed to be some private and CTB buses right through the night. The Colombo terminus in Kandy is on Railway Approach Rd, a short distance past the railway station. Express buses with numbered seats, costing Rs 50, leave Kandy station for Colombo at 6 and 6.30 am, returning from the capital at 4 and 4.30 pm.

To/From Colombo Airport There is a daily direct bus leaving the Olde Empire Hotel at 5 pm. The trip takes about three hours: get there half an hour early for a seat. The fare is Rs 24. In the opposite direction, the bus stops on the road outside the airport at approximately 8 am. Get help to identify it as there are a lot of buses around at this time.

To/From Other Places There are plenty of buses for other up-country places – though for Haputale you need to change in Nuwara Eliya and probably again in Welimada. Buses to Hatton and Nuwara Eliya leave from beside St Paul's Church near the Olde Empire. The Nuwara Eliya trip takes three hours, and the last bus from Kandy leaves at about 5 pm.

Buses to/from Dambulla, Sigiriya, Polonnaruwa, Anuradhapura, Badulla, Mahiyangana, Trincomalee and Monaragala use the big Bogambara bus yard near the prison. There's an 8 am CTB bus direct to Sigiriya, taking 2¾ hours for Rs 16. Buses to Polonnaruwa (Rs 25) and Anuradhapura (Rs 26), both three to four hours, leave up to late afternoon. Buses to all these three places go through Dambulla.

Buses to/from Matale gather beside the central clock tower. CTB buses to/from Kegalla and Kurunegala stop at the top of Railway Approach Rd near the post office. Some other CTB and private buses use the Goods Shed bus yard a little further down the same road.

Train Trains in and out of Kandy offer excellent views of surrounding areas.

To/From Colombo There are eight or nine daily trains each way, the first from Colombo Fort at 5 am and the last at 8.15 pm. Some people say the right-hand side has the best views on the way up, others the left. Either way it's a nice view. On most trains the trip takes three to 3½ hours and costs Rs 57 in 2nd class, Rs 20.75 in 3rd; the two daily inter-city expresses each way take only 2½ hours and all seats on them are reserved, costing Rs 60 (return tickets valid for 10 days cost Rs 90). The inter-city expresses leave at 6.55 am and 3.35 pm from Colombo, 6.30 am and 3 pm from Kandy – there are special ticket windows (Nos 17 and 18) for them at Colombo Fort station. You can book in advance if you wish.

To/From the West & South Coasts One Colombo-Kandy train in each direction, each day, continues on to/from Matara, providing a direct link with west coast resorts like Bentota, Hikkaduwa and Galle. Departure from Kandy to Matara – a scheduled seven-hour trip – is at 5 am daily, with an extra train at 1.10 pm on Sundays; and from Matara to Kandy at 1.25 pm, with an extra train at 7 am on Saturday.

To/From the Hill Country The Podi Menike from Kandy at 9 am goes through Hatton (three hours), Nanu Oya (four hours, for Nuwara Eliya), Haputale (six hours) and Ella (seven hours) to Badulla, where it arrives at 5 pm. Four seats in the 1st-class observation saloon are available from Kandy and should be booked in advance. (The other observation seats are reserved for passengers from Colombo.) The Podi Menike in the reverse direction leaves Badulla at 8.50 am, reaching Kandy about 4.30 pm. The Udarata Menike stops at Peradeniya – just six km and an easy bus ride west of Kandy – on the way between Colombo and Badulla, around midday or 1 pm in both directions.

Taxi It's easy to get long-distance taxis to or from Kandy. The official fare from the airport is Rs 1600, from Hikkaduwa Rs 3500, but you may be able to bargain these down a bit. Many Kandy taxi drivers are happy to take you on tours of the Ancient Cities or the high hill country – price to be negotiated.

Getting Around

Buses to outlying parts of Kandy and nearby towns like Peradeniya, Gampola and Gampaha mostly leave from from the stands around the market and clock tower. A taxi costs about Rs 50 from the railway station to the Pink House, Sharon Inn, Hotel Suisse or other places towards the east end of the lake, Rs 60 or Rs 70 to places a bit further out like the Travellers Nest or Gem Inn II. A three-wheeler is about half those prices.

KANDY TO THE EAST COAST

Most travellers from Kandy go west to Colombo, north to the ancient cities or south to the rest of the hill country. It's also possible – though in troubled times there's little incentive – to go east to Mahiyangana, beyond which are Gal Oya National Park, Badulla on the south-east edge of the hill country, Batticaloa on the east coast and Monaragala on the way to Arugam Bay.

The Buddha is supposed to have preached at Mahiyangana and there's a dagoba to mark the spot. On the way from Kandy are the Mahiyangana bends, where the road winds hair-raisingly down from the hill country to the dry-zone plains, through 18 hairpins. From the top you have a magnificent view of the Mahaweli development scheme – but don't attempt the trip if you're of a nervous disposition or familiar with the maintenance standards on Sri Lankan buses! On the way up you worry about overheating, on the way down you worry about the brakes. You usually pass at least one jeep or truck which didn't make it and lies in the jungle beneath.

Travellers from Mahiyangana to Monaragala may need to change buses at Bibile.

ADAM'S PEAK

Whether it is Adam's Peak (the place where Adam first set foot on earth after being cast out of heaven), Sri Pada ('sacred footprint'),

or Samanalakande (the 'butterfly mountain', where butterflies go to die), Adam's Peak is a beautiful and fascinating place. Not all faiths believe the huge 'footprint' on the top of the 2224-metre (7300-foot) peak to be that of Adam – some claim it belongs to the Buddha, St Thomas the early apostle of India, or even Lord Shiva.

Whichever legend you care to believe, the fact remains that it has been a pilgrimage centre for over 1000 years. King Parakramabahu and King Nissanka Malla of Polonnaruwa provided *ambalamas* or 'resting places' up the mountain to shelter the weary pilgrims.

Today the pilgrimage season begins on Poya day in December and runs until the start of the south-west monsoon in April. At other times the temple on the summit is unused, and between May and October the peak is obscured by cloud for much of the time. During the season a steady stream of pilgrims (and the odd tourist) makes the climb up the countless steps to the top from the small settlement of Dalhousie, 33 km by road south-west of the tea town of Hatton, which is on the Colombo-Kandy-Nuwara Eliya railway and road. The walk is lit in season by

a string of lights, which look very pretty as they snake up the mountainside, but at other times you need a torch. Many pilgrims prefer to make the longer, much more tiring – but equally well marked and lit – seven-hour climb from Ratnapura via the Carney Estate, because of the greater merit thus gained.

It is not only the sacred footprint that pilgrims climb to see. As the first rays of dawn light up the holy mountain you're treated to an extremely fine view – the hill country rises to the east, while to the west the land slopes away to the sea. Colombo, 65 km distant, is easily visible on a clear day. It's little wonder that English author John Stills described the peak as 'one of the vastest and most reverenced cathedrals of the human race'.

Interesting as the ascent is, and beautiful as the dawn is, Adam's Peak saves its pièce de résistance for a few minutes after dawn. The sun casts a perfect shadow of the peak onto the misty clouds down towards the coast. As the sun rises higher this eerie triangular shadow races back towards the peak, eventually disappearing into its base. As you scramble back down the countless stairs to the bottom you can reflect on how much easier the ascent is today than it was 100 years ago – as described in a Victorian guidebook to Ceylon:

...others struggle upwards unaided, until, fainting by the way, they are considerably carried with all haste in their swooning condition to the summit and forced into an attitude of worship at the shrine to secure the full benefits of their pilgrimage before death should supervene; others never reach the top at all, but perish from cold and fatigue; and there have been many instances of pilgrims losing their lives by being blown over precipices or falling from giddiness induced by a thoughtless retrospect when surmounting especially dangerous cliffs.

The Climb

You can start the seven-km climb from Dalhousie soon after dark (in which case you'll need at least a good sleeping bag to keep you warm overnight at the top) or you can wait till the early hours of the morning. The climb is up steps most of the way and with plenty of rest stops you'll get to the top in three or four hours. 'I spent one hour 45 minutes getting to the top', reported one athlete! A 2 am start will easily get you there before dawn, which is usually around 6 or 6.30 am.

From the car park the slope is gradual for the first half hour or so. You pass under an entrance arch, then by the Japan-Sri Lanka Friendship Dagoba, construction of which started in 1976. From here the path gets steeper and steeper until it is simply a continuous flight of stairs. In season there are teahouses for rest and refreshment all the way to the top, some of which are open through the night.

Since it can get pretty cold and windy on top, and you'll work up quite a sweat on the climb, there's no sense in getting to the top too long before the dawn and then having to sit around shivering. Bring warm clothes in any case, including something extra to put on when you get to the summit. Some pilgrims wait after sunrise for the priests to make a morning offering – 'Buddha's breakfast' as one irreverent witness put it.

One traveller wrote that at holiday times, climbing the peak can be much more difficult: 'I climbed it on a full moon holiday – along with 20,000 pilgrims – it took 11 hours'. Another suggestion was: 'While waiting for the sun to rise at the top, why not write a letter? There is a post box up there and I can vouch that letters sent from there will reach their destination'. 'Why all the emphasis on rushing up in the dark?' was another suggestion. 'The walk up, with stops to wash in the stream, to take tea with the Japanese monks at the beautiful Peace Pagoda, and rest and chat at the chai shops, was as good as the time spent on the top – on Christmas morning'. 'Tremendous view – the best thing I've seen in a year's travelling', was another comment.

An ascent beginning at dawn, or one in the afternoon to catch the sunset, would require a full night in Dalhousie before or after.

Places to Stay & Eat

Dalhousie In the pilgrimage season Dalhousie has a few tea shops, some of which stay open all night, where you can get something to eat, buy provisions for the climb, or get a place to sleep (part of the night). The *Wijitha Hotel*, where the buses stop, charges Rs 150 for small rooms holding up to four people. At the *Pilgrims' Rest* at the foot of the ascent, it's Rs 100 for a mat on the floor and you can leave baggage for Rs 10.

Maskeliya The *Old Post Office* has doubles for Rs 150 including breakfast. Ask in the post office next to the bus station. Maskeliya is a friendly, little-touristed town.

Hatton The *Ajantha Guest House*, a seven-minute walk from the station, has reasonable doubles for Rs 300 with attached bath. The *Hatton-Dickoya Rest House* is poorer value at Rs 400 double.

Getting There & Away

Reaching the base of Adam's Peak is quite simple and if you're making a night ascent you've got all day to arrive. Buses run to Dalhousie from Kandy (the Nuwara Eliya bus stand), Nuwara Eliya and Colombo in the pilgrimage season. Otherwise you need to get first to Hatton or to Maskeliya, which is about 20 km along the road from Hatton to Dalhousie. If you're really running late, taxis from Nuwara Eliya will take you to Hatton or Dalhousie.

To/From Hatton or Maskeliya The Podi Menike train from Colombo and Kandy reaches Hatton about noon. The Podi Menike in the other direction passes through Haputale at 10.50 am and Nanu Oya about 12.30 pm, reaching Hatton about 2 pm. There's also a 10 am down train from Hatton: you can change at Gampola for Kandy. Or there are buses from Colombo, Kandy or Nuwara Eliya to Hatton – from Kandy they take three hours for about Rs 12, with the last departure about 4 pm. The last bus from Nuwara Eliya is about 5 pm.

There are also some direct buses from Nuwara Eliya and even Colombo to Maskeliya, enabling you to avoid a stop in Hatton if you wish.

Hatton or Maskeliya to Dalhousie There are some direct buses from Hatton to Dalhousie in the pilgrimage season for Rs 12. The trip takes nearly two hours. Otherwise you have to take one bus from Hatton to Maskeliya (Rs 7, last departure about 7.30 pm), then another to Dalhousie (also Rs 7, last departure about 8.30 pm). It's a rather hair-raising ride – plenty of unguarded sheer drops on tight corners.

KANDY TO NUWARA ELIYA

The 80 km of road from Kandy to Nuwara Eliya is an ascent of nearly 1400 metres but you start to climb seriously only after about half way. At Pussellawa, 45 km from Kandy, there's a well-sited four-room *Rest House* (☎ 08-78397) with fine views. Singles/doubles are US$6/7. A little further up the road you can look down to the large Kothmale Reservoir created as part of the Mahaweli Development Programme, and partly blamed by some locals for unusual climatic conditions in recent years.

On up towards Nuwara Eliya, the road takes a number of long zig-zags at one point to get up a fairly steep section of mountain. Child flower-sellers wait at the top of the zig-zags for descending motorists and if a driver passes without stopping they hurtle off at breakneck pace down a path to appear before the car again at the next hairpin...and the next...and the next, losing perhaps 400 or 500 metres height in the end if their increasingly distressed expressions don't extract some charity from the driver.

About 15 km before Nuwara Eliya, the Labookellie high-grown tea factory is a convenient one to visit as it's right on the roadside and they'll willingly show you round. You can buy boxes of good tea cheaply here – Rs 40 for 200 grams.

NUWARA ELIYA

At 1889 metres Nuwara Eliya (pronounced 'nu-REL-iya', meaning 'City of Light') was the favourite hill station of the British, who kitted it up like some misplaced British village. The old pink-brick post office, the English country-house-like Hill Club with its hunting pictures, mounted hunting trophies and fish, and the 18-hole golf course (said to be one of the finest in Asia) all cry out 'England'.

Nuwara Eliya has a fair assortment of other British country-style houses with large gardens – many now turned over to vegetables to make this one of Sri Lanka's main market gardening centres – and a well-kept central park which comes alive with flowers around March to May and August to September, plus the pleasant Gregory's Lake just south of the town, encircled by a variety of walking paths. The trout hatcheries are still maintained and, all in all, a retired tea planter would feel absolutely at home. Come prepared for the evening cool – Nuwara Eliya is much higher than Kandy. In January and February you may find yourself needing to sleep with two blankets and all your clothes on.

The town is in the middle of the tea-growing country and there are occasional outbreaks of tension between Sinhalese and Tamils – the new-looking blocks of shops in the town centre have filled gaps left by the 1983 anti-Tamil destruction – but the hill country Tamils have kept out of the campaign for a separate Tamil state which has turned other parts of the country into a war zone.

Nuwara Eliya is the 'in place' for Sri Lankan socialites in April, around the Sinhalese New Year. At that time the cost of accommodation – if you can find any – goes through the roof. They hold horse races on the picturesque semi-derelict racecourse then too.

The town attracts its share of touts, who work overtime in search of rake-offs from guest houses. You'll very likely be approached by some of them when you step off the train at Nanu Oya (the station for Nuwara Eliya), or emerge from the bus station. As usual they're nothing but a nuisance.

Sports & Crafts

The golf course, wrote one traveller, 'is a real beauty for Asia. I played 11 holes in the pouring rain after being given a caddy (who had a handicap of seven and always played in bare feet), four golf balls and some pretty good clubs'. According to the club's dress code, players must wear not only shoes but also socks, a shirt and slacks or shorts. Green fees are Rs 600 (though you can play six holes after 3.30 pm for Rs 200), hire of clubs Rs 150 or Rs 250, and a caddy Rs 75.

There are tennis courts at the Hill Club which some hotels and guest houses can arrange for you to play on. The Grand, St Andrew's and Glendower hotels have snooker rooms and non-residents can usually play for a fee – Rs 30 for half an hour at the Grand, for instance. You can take pony rides on the racecourse or up into the hills.

Viskam Nivasa, the Small Industries Department saleroom 250 metres from the Windsor Hotel, is worth a visit.

Pidurutalagala

Mt Pedro, as it is also known, is the highest mountain in Sri Lanka at 2524 metres, and topped by the island's main TV transmitter. It rises immediately to the north of the town and since Nuwara Eliya is already at a considerable height, getting to the top is not so much a climb as a stiff walk along well-marked paths. 'A tough scramble up muddy trails', wrote one less-than-convinced climber! It takes less than two hours to walk to the top but you'll probably be pretty tired by the time you get there. The path starts from Keena Rd, close to the Roman Catholic church, and there are marker stones at 7500 and 8000 feet.

Hakgala Gardens

The second hill country botanic gardens (after the Peradeniya Gardens near Kandy) were originally a plantation of cinchona – from which is derived the anti-malarial drug quinine. Later they were used for experiments in acclimatising temperate-zone plants to life in the tropics, and were run by the same family for three generations, up to the 1940s.

Today they're a delightful small garden, famed for its roses and ferns, about 10 km out of Nuwara Eliya (and about 200 metres lower) on the road to Welimada and Bandarawela. The name means 'jaw-rock' and derives from the legend that the Hakgala rock, to which the gardens cling, was carried from the Himalaya by Hanuman, the monkey god, in his jaw. He had been sent there by Rama to bring back a medicinal herb but, forgetting which one it was, decided to simply carry back a representative chunk of mountain hoping that the particular herb would be growing on it!

About a km before the gardens you pass the Sita Eliya temple on the left-hand side of the road. It's said to mark the spot where Sita was held captive by the demon king Rawana, and daily prayed for Rama to come and rescue her. On the rock face across the stream are a number of circular depressions said to be the footprints of Rawana's elephant. The Hakgala Gardens are a couple of rupees' bus ride from Nuwara Eliya, and there is a Rs 50 admission charge for non-Sri Lankans (Rs 25 for students).

Day Trips to Horton Plains

Nuwara Eliya touts and guest houses may do their best to persuade you to take a car or jeep day trip to Horton Plains and World's End. The standard price for up to six passengers is Rs 1500, and the Alpen Tour Inn is the easiest place to arrange such a trip – but it will involve five or six hours of bumping along rough tracks for a much shorter time on the plains themselves, and is a much less enjoyable way of visiting the plains than staying up there overnight or doing a rail-and-foot day trip from Haputale. Anyone who tells you that these other ways of reaching Horton Plains are closed, or dangerous, or whatever, is lying. You can also rent trail bikes but they would only shatter the plains' special, unearthly quietness.

Places to Stay

Nuwara Eliya is not a great place for cheap accommodation, although prices in many places come down at the slacker times of the year. During the 'season', around the Sinhalese New Year in April, rooms are three to five times their normal cost. Prices may also increase at long-weekend holidays.

Almost any time of year you need blankets to keep warm at night, owing to the altitude. Hot water can be very welcome too and some places to stay only have it a few hours a day, while others don't have it at all – so this is something worth asking about before you take a room. Another way of keeping warm is to get a fire lit in your room, for which you may have to pay Rs 50 or so.

Places to Stay – bottom end & middle

South End of Town *Molesworth* (☎ 052-2501), a ramshackle, sprawling old house near the Grand Hotel, has lumpy dorm beds for Rs 40 or Rs 50 and a couple of single/double rooms, sharing one bathroom with cold water, for Rs 100/150. It's friendly. Breakfast is Rs 40.

The main grouping of guest houses is along Badulla Rd opposite the racecourse. This is where most of the better value accommodation is to be found. The first place you reach coming from the town is the rather run-down but clean enough *Ascot Guest House* (☎ 052-2708) with triple rooms at Rs 350 but no meals. The *Carlton Hotel* (☎ 052-2404) next door at 122 Badulla Rd is a step up with 24-hour hot water, doubles sharing a bathroom at Rs 400, bigger rooms with attached bath at Rs 500 or Rs 700, and meals available, including roast beef dinner for Rs 110!

Up Unique View Rd, off Badulla Rd just past the Carlton, the clean, friendly *Sun Hill Tour Inn* at No 18 has doubles from Rs 200 to Rs 350. The dearer are sizeable and have hot water. Meals are available. Further up at No 24, the *Unique View Guest House* (☎ 052-2404) is also OK with doubles/triples at Rs 400/600 for bed & breakfast. There's a little balcony overlooking the valley.

Back on Badulla Rd, the very clean *Kamal's New Country House* (☎ 052-2368)

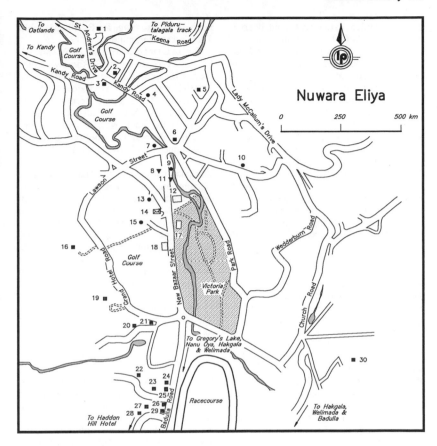

Nuwara Eliya

■	PLACES TO STAY
1	St Andrew's Hotel
2	Mr Perera's
3	Pedro Hotel
5	Wattles Inn
6	Windsor Hotel
16	Hill Club
19	Grand Hotel
20	Molesworth
21	Glendower
22	Unique View Guest House
23	Sun Hill Tour Inn
24	Ascot Guest House

25	Carlton Hotel
26	Kamal's New Country House
27	Alpen Tour Inn
28	Grosvenor Hotel
29	Travelodge
30	Priory Guest House

▼	PLACES TO EAT
8	Milano Restaurant
11	New Royal Hotel

	OTHER
4	Cargill's
7	Bank of Ceylon
9	Market
10	Viskam Nivasa
12	CTB Bus Station
13	Bank
14	Post Office
15	Golf Club
17	Public Library
18	Private Bus Station

has a nice garden, its own restaurant, doubles at Rs 500 or Rs 600, and an 'apartment' of two doubles with its own sitting area for Rs 1200. The *Travelodge* (☎ 052-2233) is an old-fashioned colonial bungalow-style place, with mostly spacious rooms all with private bathroom. There's one single (with a separate toilet) for Rs 200, a double at Rs 300, two triples at Rs 400, and 'family rooms' for four people at Rs 500. A dinner of rice, curry and dessert is Rs 90.

Just off Badulla Rd at 4 Haddon Hill Rd, the *Alpen Tour Inn* (☎ 052-3009) is one of the busiest guest houses year-round, as it succeeds in pulling in a high proportion of international travellers. There's a wide range of rooms, from small and cheap at Rs 100 a single or double with shared bath, up to Rs 350 or Rs 450 a double, some quite old-fashioned and comfortable, with attached bath. You may need to ask specifically about the separate building at the back if you want the cheapest rooms. Both local and Western food is available – rice and curries Rs 65, roast beef, fish or steak Rs 110.

Next door to the Alpen, the well kept *Grosvenor Hotel* (☎ 052-2307) at 6 Haddon Hill Rd has good, big, clean rooms with hot water at Rs 500 a single or double, with breakfast. The *Haddon Hill Hotel*, about half a km further up the same road, charges around Rs 600 a double.

Over on Upper Lake Rd on the south-east side of town, the *Priory Guest House* (☎ 052-2676/8) is much faded from its 1950s heyday when it was one of the top places in town, but it does offer large doubles with hot water for Rs 250.

North End of Town *Mr Perera* at 9 Chapel St, off Kandy Rd, has basic single, double and family rooms to let out, and he won't deal with touts. The single is up to Rs 150 depending on the season. The *Pedro Hotel* on Kandy Rd is a bar with four cubicle-like rooms upstairs for Rs 60 a single, Rs 120 a double. The shared toilet is none too clean.

Wattles Inn (☎ 052-2804) at 13 Srimath Jayatillake Rd has clean but not huge rooms with attached bath, and hot water for 1½

hours in the morning, for Rs 400 a double. There's a restaurant too.

Oatlands (☎ 052-2572) at 124 St Andrew's Drive, just behind the big St Andrew's Hotel, is a spacious, comfortable, very well kept old British bungalow with five rooms, all different, at Rs 500 a single or double with attached bath. There are also a couple of rooms at the back with shared bath for Rs 250. The friendly owner prepares good food: dinner Rs 150, breakfast Rs 75.

Hakgala Just beyond the Hakgala Botanic Gardens entrance *Humbugs* is a pleasant small restaurant/snack bar with a modern chalet at the back where you can get a room with pine double bed and floor-to-ceiling windows on a stunning view for Rs 500 double including breakfast. If you like you can take your shower in a waterfall at the bottom of the garden. In season the café even has strawberries and cream.

Places to Stay – top end
The 114-room *Grand Hotel* (☎ 052-2881, or for reservations 01-422518), right by the golf course, is very much in the old English style, with wood-panelled billiard room, table tennis, a large lounge, etc, and costs US$20/22.50 for room-only singles/doubles. Though the Grand is now much populated by European and Asian tour groups, it's still hard to imagine anything more redolent of the British colonial era – until you see the *Hill Club* (☎ 052-2653), almost next door. Once a preserve of the British male, the Hill Club now admits both Sri Lankans and women but remains very much in the colonial tradition, with one bar still reserved for men. It welcomes lots of 'temporary visitors from overseas' to keep the till ringing. There are 31 rooms at US$30/35/40 a single or double, plus two suites. The billiard room, dating from 1876, is the oldest part of the building. If you're cold at night they'll bring you a hot-water bottle! The rooms are generally comfortable, though one or two visitors lately have complained that the Hill Club's prices didn't include 24-hour hot water or post-colonial bed springs.

The *Glendower* (☎ 052-2749) at 5 Grand Hotel Rd is a recently renovated colonial house with sizeable, comfortable doubles at Rs 1000 for bed & breakfast (only marginally cheaper than the Grand itself), and suites with their own sitting areas for Rs 1500 – it's a pity they haven't much to look out on. There's a restaurant and billiard room.

In the centre of town, at 2 Kandy Rd, the modern 48-room *Windsor Hotel* (☎ 052-2554) has tastefully decorated rooms, in good condition, for Rs 650/750, or large luxury rooms for Rs 1150, and a Sri Lankan-cum-Western-cum-Chinese restaurant. *St Andrew's Hotel* (☎ 052-2445), in the north of the town on a rise overlooking the golf course and town at 10 St Andrew's Drive, resembles a 19th-century Scottish manse. Its 49 singles/doubles cost US$17/20.

Places to Eat

Hotels and guest houses provide some of the best food, and you're welcome to sample places other than where you're staying. The *Grand Hotel* often does a Rs 150 lunch buffet if you're in the mood for a big fill-up. There are a few restaurants on New Bazaar St in the centre of town including the *New Royal Hotel*, which makes good tea and short eats. The best of the bunch is probably the *Milano Restaurant*, with rice and curry at Rs 22 to Rs 37, Chinese dishes Rs 35 to Rs 60, beefsteak, fish or chicken Rs 65 to Rs 90.

At the other end of the price scale, a meal at the *Hill Club* is an experience not to be missed, at least as regards style. Dinner is served at 8 pm. You get a full five-course meal – soup, fish, main course, dessert, tea or coffee – for US$7, and the whole process is accomplished with considerable panache. If you have opted for a pre-dinner drink (in either the 'men's bar' or the 'mixed bar') you'll be summoned to the dining room when the meal is ready. At your candlelit table you'll be served by white-uniformed (and white-gloved) waiters. You can retire to the lounge, with its open fire, for your after-dinner tea or coffee. You may get away with less than US$7 if you opt for the á la carte

menu – but you'll pay more if you decide to sample the wine cellar where bottles of European wine run into the high figures. Corkage if you bring your own bottle of wine is Rs 150.

You must be properly dressed – no jeans allowed in this august establishment. Men must wear ties. If, like most travellers, you do not possess such an arcane piece of attire they'll loan you one. One traveller wrote of the embarrassment of having to return his tie, to get back the deposit on it, before he could pay the bill!

With all this etiquette and paraphernalia you could almost forget that you were there to eat. But have a good look at the menu before deciding on the Hill Club. Not everybody has been happy with what they were served of late. One British traveller wrote: 'I sent the starter back as the 'fish' didn't actually appear on my plate – only the salad garnish! The main course was a revolting mixture of meat in a barbeque sauce (but actually there was no sauce, just something stuck to the meat like congealed sauce), roast potatoes, salad and – even worse than my memories of school dinners – cabbage mornay (also rather dry, if not rubbery). This was followed by an orange dessert that looked like it had escaped from a toddlers' tea party – it was *bright* orange, sponge-like, and had a lump of artificial cream on it. Roll on the coffee!!' The same writer also strongly advised travellers to ask for the drinks price list before ordering in the bar.

The Rest, the old Municipal Rest House on Badulla Rd, a kind of Sri Lankan Fawlty Towers, has been 'closed awaiting renovation' for so long that no one believes it will ever open again. Which is (in some respects) a great loss, as shown by the following classic episode reported by an early 1980s visitor, who one evening opted out of meat loaf (!) at the Hill Club:

The waiters are in great form – on our commenting that the price of rum omelette was high our waiter promised to be liberal with the rum. Some 20 minutes later we guessed something was happening when one of the staff turned off and on the dining room lights!

Yes; in came the omelette, flambé-style from the kitchen as the room was plunged into darkness. Our waiter had indeed been generous with the rum for the flames rose some two feet above the plate, apprehensively placed on our table. No amount of blowing would extinguish the pyre by which time the omelette was getting black at the edges.

The lights-waiter attempted to illuminate the scene again to regain control, threw all the switches together and fused the dining room, which a few seconds later blew the hotel fuse and (inevitably?) caused something that put all Nuwara Eliya in darkness for the next 20 minutes! By the time candles had been brought and the omelette extinguished with a soup tureen a charred, smouldering lump remained to the delighted comments of the waiters. This is an experience to replace no end of meat loaf dinners.

Getting There & Away

Bus The bus trip from Kandy is about three hours for around Rs 22. It's a fairly spectacular climb, covered by several buses a day, the last in each direction leaving about 5.30 pm. There are also buses to/from Colombo (Rs 50, 4½ hours, about hourly up to 7.30 pm), other places in the hill country – though for Haputale you usually have to change at Welimada – and even Matara on the south coast, for which a CTB bus is scheduled to leave at 8.30 am, but sometimes departs a few minutes earlier.

Train Nuwara Eliya does not have its own railway station but is served by Nanu Oya, about nine km along the road towards Hatton and Colombo. Buses (Rs 5) and taxis (about Rs 120) connect with the trains. The 5 am Podi Menike from Colombo (via Kandy) reaches Nanu Oya about 1.15 pm. The 9.45 am Udarata Menike from Colombo, but not Kandy, reaches Nanu Oya about 3.30 pm. The 8.15 pm Night Mail from Colombo arrives in Nanu Oya at 3.47 am. Downward, the Udarata Menike leaves Nanu Oya about 9.50 am, the Podi Menike about 12.50 pm

---

Tea

Tea remains a cornerstone of the Sri Lankan economy and a major export, although there are worries that many plantations are degrading through insufficient care, and that the quality of Ceylon tea has declined too far after growers turned to lower-grade bushes in response to a late 1980s world tea slump that cut the profits out of high-grade tea.

Tea came to Sri Lanka as an emergency substitute for coffee when the extensive coffee plantations were all but destroyed by a devastating disease in the 19th century. The first Sri Lankan tea was grown at the Loolecondera estate, a little south-east of Kandy, by one James Taylor in 1867. Today the hill country is virtually one big tea plantation, for tea needs a warm climate, altitude and sloping terrain – a perfect description of the Sri Lankan hill country.

Tea grows on a bush; if not cut back it would grow up to 10 metres high and would require some very tall people to pick the leaves! As it is, tea bushes are pruned back to about a metre in height and squads of Tamil tea pluckers, all women, move through the rows of bushes picking the leaves and buds. These are then 'withered' – de-moisturised by blowing temperature-controlled air through them – either in the old-fashioned multi-storey tea factories, where the leaves are spread out on hessian mats, or in modern mechanised troughs. The partly dried leaves are then crushed, which starts a fermentation process. The art in tea production comes in knowing when to stop the fermentation, by 'firing' the tea to produce the final, brown/black leaf. Tea plantation and factory tours are readily available all over Sri Lanka.

There is a very large number of types and varieties of teas which are graded both by size (from cheap 'dust' through fannings and broken grades to 'leaf' tea) and by quality (with names like flowery, pekoe or souchong). Tea is further categorised into low-grown, mid-grown or high-grown. The low-grown teas (under 600 metres) grow strongly and are high in 'body' but low in 'flavour'. The high-grown teas (over 1200 metres) grow more slowly and are renowned for their subtle flavour. Mid-grown tea is something between the two. Regular commercial teas are usually made by blending various types – a bit of this for flavour, a bit of that for body.

Unfortunately, as in India, the Sri Lankans may grow some very fine tea but most of the best is exported. Only in a small number of hotels, guest houses and restaurants will you get a quality cup. But you can buy fine teas from plantations or shops to take home with you. ■

(reaching Kandy about 4.30 pm), and the Night Mail about 10 pm. Fares from Colombo to Nanu Oya are Rs 170.75 in 1st class, Rs 98 in 2nd, and Rs 35.50 in 3rd.

HORTON PLAINS & WORLD'S END

The Horton Plains form an undulating plateau over 2000 metres high, about 20 km south of Nuwara Eliya and 20 km west of Haputale. They consist mainly of grasslands interspersed with patches of forest, with some unusual high-altitude vegetation. From them rise Sri Lanka's second and third highest mountains – Kirigalpotta (2387 metres) and Totapola (2361 metres).

The plains are a beautiful, silent, strange world with some excellent walks. The most famous and stunning feature is World's End, where the southern Horton Plains come suddenly to an end and drop almost straight down for 700 metres. It's one of the most awesome sights in Sri Lanka, but unfortunately the view is often obscured by mist, particularly during the rainy season, April to September. Dawn or very early morning usually offers the best chance of a glimpse of this scenic wonder – which, if you can afford it, is a good reason to spend the previous night on the plains, rather than arrive later in the day on a day trip.

Farr-Inn, a former rest house and now a pleasant though not cheap guest house, is a convenient central landmark on the plains, reachable by rough vehicle tracks from various directions or by a couple of hours walking from the railway. Horton Plains are now a national park, with park fees of Rs 50 for non-Sri Lankans and Rs 10 for Sri Lankans collected by the park rangers, whose office is at the start of the four-km track from Farr-Inn to World's End.

Wildlife

Herds of elephant used to roam the plains but most of them were shot by colonial hunters. The last few departed in the first half of the 20th century. But there are still a few leopards, and any droppings you see containing animal fur are likely to be leopard droppings. The big, shaggy bear monkey, with its purple face and white beard, is often seen in the forest on the 'motorable' track up from Ohiya, and sometimes in the woods around World's End (its call is a wheezy grunt). Sambar emerge from the forest onto the edge of the grasslands around Farr-Inn in the evening.

Walks

Walking is the most worthwhile way to get on to the plains (see Getting There & Away). Once you're up there, the trail to World's End is the most frequented. Another interesting spot is Baker's Falls, down a river off the Farr-Inn-World's End track, also accessible by continuing round from World's End. Kirigalpotta and Totapola are both about seven km from Farr-Inn. The park rangers can tell you how to reach these and other goals on the plains. There's a wall map of sorts at Farr-Inn.

Places to Stay & Eat

In the evenings the Horton Plains get cool and you need long trousers and a sweater. *Farr-Inn* has eight clean, sizeable rooms, with attached bathrooms and warm water, for Rs 504 a single or double, Rs 630 a triple. Outside Sri Lankan holidays you'd be unlucky to find the inn full but you can call 01-23501 or 20194 for a reservation if you like. A fairly good dinner is Rs 160, lunch Rs 120, breakfast Rs 80. You don't have to be staying at the inn to eat there. You can also call in for tea, chocolate, beer (Rs 80) or mineral water (Rs 55 a litre).

Anderson Lodge, scenically sited three km from Farr-Inn along the track to Ohiya, is a Wildlife Conservation Department bungalow, with showers, accommodating eight people. See Parks & Reserves in the Facts about the Country chapter for booking info. A couple of small shops at Ohiya sell a few very basic foods and drinks.

Getting There & Away

Train & Foot Despite what some jeep operators in Nuwara Eliya might try to tell you (see the section on that town), the walk up to the plains from Ohiya station is enjoyable, easy and quite popular. Ohiya is two stops and 40 minutes by train from Haputale, and 1¼ hours from Nanu Oya (the station for Nuwara Eliya). The walk from Ohiya to Farr-Inn is three to four hours by the 'motorable' track, or an hour less by the short cut, and amply rewarding either way.

Five trains a day in each direction stop at Ohiya. The 7.55 am from Haputale (Rs 3 in 3rd class, Rs 8 in 2nd), reaching Ohiya at 8.35, enables you to make a day trip to the plains (and World's End) from Haputale. From Ohiya you can return to Haputale on the 4.38 pm train, or go on down towards Nanu Oya and Colombo on the 8.47 pm. You can't do a day trip from Nuwara Eliya by rail unless you're game to catch the 3.47 am train from Nanu Oya.

From Ohiya on foot, the 'motorable' track is the easier route to follow and gentler graded; the short cut is quicker but to be absolutely certain of not getting lost you'd need to find a guide in Ohiya – although in

fact if you follow the major path at each fork in the forest you'll be right. For the short cut you start by walking 10 minutes along the railway tracks from Ohiya station, then branch up to the left at the 5 kp/h limit sign immediately before a tunnel. You climb through the forest for about 45 minutes before emerging for an hour's walk across the plains to Farr-Inn.

You can also walk to Farr-Inn from Pattipola, the next rail station north of Ohiya (a walk of about 10 km along a jeep track), or – easier downhill than up! – Belihul Oya on the Ratnapura-Haputale road, about four hours downhill from the plains (see the Belihul Oya section).

Road So-called motorable tracks reach Farr-Inn from Boralanda (10 km south of Welimada, 20 km from Farr-Inn) via Ohiya, and from Nuwara Eliya via Pattipola off the Nuwara Eliya-Welimada road, or via the Diyagama estate in Agrapatana off the

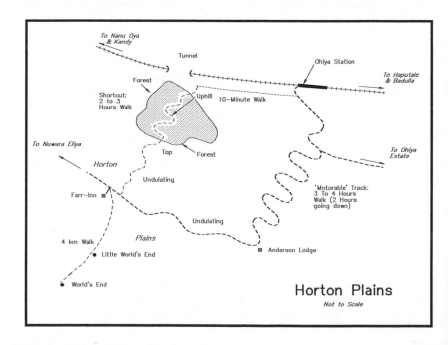

Horton Plains

Not to Scale

Nuwara Eliya-Hatton road. The track from Ohiya has some very steep, rough patches of dubious passability but the three-hour drive to Farr-Inn from Nuwara Eliya is possible in the dry season even without 4WD. For info on semi-organised jeep trips see the Nuwara Eliya section.

HAPUTALE

The village of Haputale is perched right at the southern edge of the hill country. It lies along a ridge with the land falling away steeply on both sides, and almost has the feeling of being up in the sky! As you come in from Bandarawela, the road rises up to the ridge, crosses the railway, dips down the main street – then suddenly sails off into space! Actually it makes a sharp right turn at the edge of town and runs along just beneath the ridge, but at first glance it looks as if it simply disappears into thin air. On a clear day you can see from this ridge all the way to the south coast, and at night the Hambantota lighthouse may be visible.

Haputale is a pleasant place with some good cheap accommodation, and makes a very good base for visiting Horton Plains, exploring other places in the area, or simply taking pleasant walks in the cool mountain air.

Information

The town isn't too small to have a Bank of Ceylon branch, open Monday from 9 am to 1 pm, Tuesday to Friday to 1.30 pm, where you can change money and travellers' cheques, and which also has one-inch/one-mile maps of the surrounding area on its wall. Bawa Guest House has another one-inch map in its dining room, and Highcliffe guest house has a good collection of printed material on the area.

Diyaluma Falls

Heading down from Haputale towards Wellawaya, you pass the 170-metre-high Diyaluma Falls, one of Sri Lanka's highest waterfalls, just five km beyond the town of Koslanda. By bus, take a Wellawaya service from Haputale and get off at Diyaluma – the

ride takes 1¼ hours. The falls leap over a cliff face and fall in one clear drop to a pool below – very picturesque and clearly visible from the road.

If you're feeling energetic you can climb up to the beautiful rock pools and a series of mini-falls at the top of the main fall. Walk about a ½ km down the road from the bottom of the falls and take the estate track which turns sharply back up to the left. From there it's about 20 minutes' walk to a small rubber factory, where you strike off left uphill. The track is very indistinct, although there are some white arrows on the rocks – and if you're lucky, people in the rubber factory will shout if they see you taking the wrong turn! At the top the path forks: the right branch (more distinct) leads to the pools above the main falls, the left fork down to the top of the main falls. The pools above the second set of falls are a good spot for a cool swim.

You could make an interesting day circuit from Haputale by going down to the Diyaluma Falls, taking another bus from there to Wellawaya, going up to the Rawana Ella Falls, continuing up to Ella and the gap and finally going back through Bandarawela to Haputale.

Adisham

This is a Benedictine monastery about an hour's walk from Haputale. You start along Temple Rd and there's a sign at the Adisham turn-off. The monastery is an old British planter's house, a replica of the planter's Yorkshire home. It's open to visitors from 9 am to noon and from 3 to 5 pm. Often a monk will show you round. It's possible to stay here, but you should call or write in advance for a reservation. There's lots of stonework around here – stone walls, stone steps, stone terracing, all done by hand. Bus No 327 from Haputale will get you most of the way.

Other Attractions

Idalgashinna, eight km along the railway from Haputale and with a view perhaps even more spectacular since the land falls away steeply for a great distance on both sides, the

Tangamalai nature reserve, and the scattered traces of the Portuguese Katugodella Fort (a reminder of one of their attempts to capture the hill country), are all within easy reach of Haputale.

Places to Stay & Eat

The *Bawa Guest House* (☎ 057-8021) is on the hillside with a great view down to the coastal lowlands, and has a range of rooms from bare singles/doubles at Rs 60/75 with tolerable shared bathrooms, up to Rs 150 double with private bath and a small sitting area overlooking the best view. Unexciting vegetarian meals are served (breakfast Rs 45, dinner of rice, three curries and fruit salad Rs 75). Walk along the railway tracks about 300 metres in the Kandy direction from the railway station, then turn left up a steep little path just past the petroleum depot, onto Temple Rd. Walk to the right, and the guest house (which has no signs) is down a small path on the left after about 250 metres.

Further along Temple Rd are the *Green House* at No 94, with rooms at Rs 50/75 and reportedly good, cheap food, and Mrs Daniel's *Hyacinth Cottage* where you pay Rs 50 per person in shared two or four-bed rooms. The shared toilets and showers are clean (though the water is cold), the food is good, and Mrs Daniel is a terrific scrabble player. She refuses to pay touts, who respond by leading travellers to a number of fake 'Mrs Daniel's' around town.

In the centre of town, next to the railway crossing, *Highcliffe* was one of the first budget travellers' stops in town, and it has maps, a book describing interesting walks, and other information on the area. There are dorm beds at Rs 40, singles at Rs 50 and doubles at Rs 100 and Rs 120, but the rooms are cramped and the facilities fairly primitive. A rice and curry dinner costs around Rs 40.

The newer *Milky Way* guest house, just below the Colombo road as it slopes down out of town, has two clean rooms, sharing a clean bathroom, for Rs 150/200. But one pair of travellers wrote that the beds were hard and there was no hot water. At 180 Colombo Rd the friendly *Rose Mount* (☎ 057-8001) has doubles with attached bathroom at Rs 120, and reportedly good food.

The *Old Rest House*, across the railway from the Highcliffe, is a bit bare but has adequately comfortable singles/doubles with attached bath at Rs 137/275. There's a bar here and the restaurant stays open later into the evening than the others in the town. The newer *Rest House* a few hundred metres along the Bandarawela road charges Rs 440 for doubles with attached bath, but most people find it less appealing than the old one.

There are a few basic local eateries around the town centre where you can get short eats, rice and curry, etc, cheaper than in the guest houses. For instance an adequate meal of rice, curries, egg and fish will cost around Rs 25 at the place down on the Colombo road shortly before the turning to Temple Rd.

Getting There & Away

Bus There are a couple of direct buses to/from Nuwara Eliya daily – one private direct bus is supposed to leave Haputale at 7.30 am – but more often you have to change at Welimada (which has a Rest House on the north-east side of town). Haputale-Welimada and Welimada-Nuwara Eliya both cost Rs 9. To/from Bandarawela there are frequent buses for Rs 5 into the early evening. There are also express buses to Colombo (Rs 50, 5½ hours) and a few direct buses to/from the south coast (including an 8.30 am bus from Matara) and other towns like Monaragala and Kataragama, but normally for the south coast you have to change at Wellawaya, 1½ hours down the hill from Haputale. The last bus from Haputale to Wellawaya in the afternoon is usually about 4 to 4.30 pm.

Train Haputale is on the Colombo-Badulla line, so you can travel direct by train to/from Kandy or Nanu Oya (the station for Nuwara Eliya). It's 7½ to 10 hours from Colombo, six hours from Kandy, two hours from Nanu

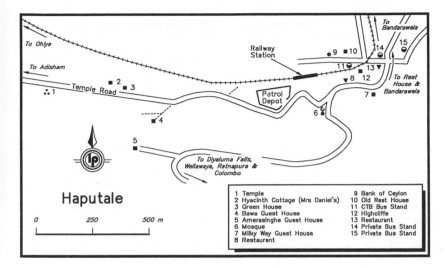

Haputale

1 Temple	9 Bank of Ceylon
2 Hyacinth Cottage (Mrs Daniel's)	10 Old Rest House
3 Green House	11 CTB Bus Stand
4 Bawa Guest House	12 Highcliffe
5 Amerasinghe Guest House	13 Restaurant
6 Mosque	14 Private Bus Stand
7 Milky Way Guest House	15 Private Bus Stand
8 Restaurant	

Oya, 40 minutes from Ohiya, half an hour on to Bandarawela and two hours to Badulla. The main daily departures are, in the Badulla direction, at 5.35 am, 3.09 and 5.13 pm, and in the Colombo direction 7.55 and 10.52 am and 8.03 pm. Only the middle of the three trains goes via Kandy. Fares to/from Haputale in 1st/2nd/3rd class include: Colombo Rs 203.50/116.75/42.25; Kandy Rs 114/65.50/23.75; Nanu Oya Rs 33.75/19.50/7; Ohiya Rs 14/8/3; Badulla Rs 37/21.25/7.75.

BANDARAWELA

Bandarawela, 10 km north of Haputale but noticeably warmer at only 1230 metres high, is a busy market town and an up-country resort popular with Sri Lankans at holiday times, though less so with foreign travellers.

About five km out of Bandarawela, on the road to Badulla, the little Dowa Temple is pleasantly situated close to a stream on the right-hand side of the road, with a beautiful four-metre-high standing Buddha cut in low relief into the rock face below the road. The temple is very easy to miss so ask the bus conductor to tell you when to get off.

Orientation & Information

The focal point of town is the busy junction outside the railway station. From here Haputale Rd goes south-west; Welimada Rd goes north then, just past the post office, turns fairly sharply left by a mosque; and Badulla Rd, with the main bus stands, heads downhill to the east. Main St, with most of the shops and town restaurants and a Bank of Ceylon branch where changing money is fairly easy, forks left off Badulla Rd after a few metres and rejoins it further down the hill.

Places to Stay – bottom end

Two of the better cheaper places are along a short signposted track to the right off Welimada Rd, a couple of hundred metres after the mosque bend. The first you come to, the *Red Lantern Guest House* (☎ 057-2212), has clean and fair-sized, if dark, rooms with attached bath and hot water for Rs 125 per person. It also has a restaurant with a variety of Western, Sri Lankan and Chinese dishes. Its address is 125 Welimada Rd. A little further along the track, the *Hill Side Holiday Inn* is also clean with fair-sized but bare rooms at Rs 150 a single or double with cold water, Rs 200 with hot water available if you say when you need it. Some rooms have balconies.

You can reach two more places by going straight on where Welimada Rd turns left by the mosque. The first fork to the right then brings you to the *Chinese Union Hotel* (☎ 057-2502) on the right, at 8 Mt Pleasant. Its five rooms, mostly with attached bathroom (but only cold water), have fans but are a bit dingy, and cost Rs 100/200 for singles/doubles. If you pass that first fork but go on down about 400 metres, past the People's Bank, and take the right fork which climbs above the sports oval, you reach the *Isuru Guest Inn* (☎ 057-2328) at 46/3 Esplanade Rd, a pleasant bungalow-style house with rooms around Rs 150/200 with attached bath, and quite spacious lounge and dining areas.

The friendly *Hotel Seasons*, about 15 minutes' walk from the centre on Heeloya Rd, has clean, sizeable doubles with attached bath and hot water for around Rs 250, and some with shared bath for less. To get there, follow Badulla Rd from the town centre and turn right into Kinigama Rd, then left into Heeloya Rd. There are signs at both turnings.

Places to Stay – middle & top end

Near the town centre, just beyond the Chinese Union Hotel (see bottom end), is the *Orient Hotel* (☎ 057-2407) at 10 Dharmapala Mawatha, a modernish 50-room hotel with comfortable enough, but not huge, singles/doubles for Rs 650/850. You might be able to bargain these prices down at quiet times. There's a restaurant (dinner Rs 160) and billiard room and, wrote one pair of travellers, 'the four-poster room is very pleasant'. A little further on past the Orient, the *Rest House* (☎ 057-2298/9) is a good choice if you can get in. It has nine typically spacious rooms at Rs 450/500, all with nets, fans, attached bath, and balcony or verandah. The food is good (breakfast Rs 75, dinner Rs 120) and there's a very pleasant lounge jutting into the garden to catch any breeze.

The top hostelry in town, the *Bandarawela Hotel* (☎ 057-2501) is at 14 Welimada Rd: its drive runs up opposite the mosque. This former tea planters' club, a large chalet-style building still kitted out with the furniture and fittings of a bygone era – vast easy chairs to sink into in the lounge, equally vast bath tubs with lots of hot water in spacious rooms – charges US$20/23 with verandah.

Getting There & Away

Bus Buses for the 35 km from Nuwara Eliya cost about Rs 15. They take about 1¼ hours unless you have to change at Welimada. There are regular buses between Bandarawela and Haputale (Rs 5), Ella (Rs 5.50), and Badulla (Rs 7 or Rs 8). Long-distance services include runs to Colombo, Tissamaharama, Tangalla and Galle. If there are no direct buses to Tissa or the south coast you can change at Wellawaya.

Train Bandarawela is on the Colombo-Badulla railway, half an hour from Haputale, with three main trains a day in each direction.

ELLA

Sri Lanka is liberally endowed with beautiful views, and Ella has one of the best. To fully appreciate it, walk up through the village to the rest house and into the garden, where the world suddenly drops away at your feet. Through the gap in the hills in front of you, you look down from Ella's 1100-metre altitude to the coastal plain nearly 1000 metres below. Ella also has a handful of guest houses and makes a good last stop in the hill country before heading down to the coast.

The road down through the Ella Gap to Wellawaya, 27 km south, was only completed in 1969. Coming uphill from Wellawaya can be quite a struggle for a rickety CTB bus.

Rawana Ella Falls

These spectacular falls are about five km down the gap from Ella towards Wellawaya. Buses from Ella are Rs 4. The water comes leaping down the mountainside in what is claimed to be the wildest-looking fall in Sri

Lanka. Naturally they are connected with the Ramayana saga; the demon king Rawana was said to have held Sita captive in a cave, which you can visit, in the cliff facing the rest house.

Places to Stay & Eat

A great many of Sri Lanka's rest houses are blessed with attractive settings but the *Ella Rest House* (☎ 057-2636) tops the lot. The front lawn and four of the six rooms look out over the Ella Gap. The price for singles/doubles in all rooms is Rs 510. It's a pleasant place. Breakfast is Rs 85 and dinner Rs 170, but the food is only fair.

There are a number of other places right around the centre of the small village. Immediately behind the Rest House, the *Rock View Guest House* (☎ 057-2661) has good, big, clean rooms at Rs 200 to Rs 350. Some have attached bath, some share, but there's no hot water. Three new rooms are being built on the hillside with views possibly even better than the rest house. Meals are available but not specially good at Rs 100 to Rs 150 for dinner, Rs 75 for breakfast. Across the road the *Ella Gap Tourist Inn* (☎ 057-2628) has hot water and smaller rooms at Rs 200/250 with shared bath, Rs 300/350 with attached bath. It's a friendly place with very good food, but no view. Just behind the Rock View is the simple *Ella Rest Inn* with rooms from Rs 125 to Rs 200, some with attached bath.

Going back from the village centre towards the railway, a track leads 300 metres up to the right to the *Lizzie Villa Guest House*, where Rs 175/250 is asked for smallish rooms with shared bath and no hot water, but the price will come down. A couple of basic eateries in the village centre are the alternatives to the rest and guest house meals.

Getting There & Away

Bus The road to Ella diverges from the Bandarawela-Badulla road about nine km out of Bandarawela. A bus from Bandarawela to Ella costs Rs 5.50. The road continues down through the Ella Gap to Wellawaya, where you can go on south to Tissamaharama or the south coast, or east to Monaragala and Pottuvil. There's a handy 7.45 am CTB bus that goes all the way round the south coast to Galle. For Tissamaharama you normally need to change buses at Wirawila, Rs 19 and three hours from Ella.

Train Ella is an hour from each of Haputale and Badulla on the Colombo-Badulla railway. The stretch from Haputale (through Bandarawela) is particularly lovely. About 10 km north of Ella at Demodara the line performs a complete loop around a hillside and tunnels under itself at a level 30 metres lower. There's a model of this spectacular piece of colonial railway engineering in the National Museum in Colombo.

BADULLA

Standing at about 680 metres, Badulla marks the south-east extremity of the hill country and is a gateway to the east coast. It's a pleasant little town, capital of the Uva province and neatly ringed by mountains. The railway through the hill country from Colombo and Kandy terminates here and if you come by bus you will probably have to change buses here. From Bandarawela or Welimada you can get off in the centre of town rather than carrying on to the bus station, which is over the river on the edge of town.

St Mark's Church in Badulla was built in memory of the British administrator Major T W Rogers, who has been described as a 'sportsman'. Whether that is a correct label to apply to a man whose chief purpose in life seemed to be to wipe out the elephant population of Sri Lanka single-handedly, is questionable. What is more certain is that some protector of elephants finally decided that enough was enough and Rogers was struck dead by a bolt of lightning while sitting on the verandah of the Haputale rest house!

Dunhinda Falls

About six km out of Badulla are the 60-metre-high Dunhinda waterfalls – said to be the most awe-inspiring in Sri Lanka, well worth a visit and a fine spot for a picnic – but watch out for the monkeys who'll grab your food if you're not looking! Bus No 314, about hourly, will take you close to the falls. From the bus stop it's about a km along a clearly defined, sometimes rocky, path. There's a good observation spot at the end of the path and you can see a lower falls on the walk.

Namunukula
You can climb this 1850-metre peak, about 10 km south-east of Badulla, by taking a Spring Valley bus (No 318) from Badulla. Spring Valley is in the centre of the tea estates, and is an interesting place to walk around with fine views.

Places to Stay & Eat
Smack in the centre of town, the *Badulla Rest House* has singles/doubles at Rs 150/225. The Rs 40 rice and curry lunch here is good value. The *Dunhinda Falls Inn* (☎ 055-2406) at 35/11 Bandaranaike Mawatha, about a km from the town, is pleasant, fairly modern, and has good food. There are 12 rooms at Rs 100 to Rs 200 a single, Rs 150 to Rs 350 a double, which is good value.

Apart from these, there are a number of rather basic cheap guest houses and small hotels. Try *Mrs Jayakody's* at 7 Race Course Rd, or *Richard & Astrid Fernandez* at 26 Old Bede's Rd, just out of town. Rooms should cost Rs 50 to Rs 100.

Centrally located, five minutes' walk from the railway and bus stations (which are 10 minutes east of the town centre), the *Castle Hotel* (☎ 055-2334) at 134 Lower St has doubles at Rs 100, but it's none too clean and doesn't do meals.

Nearer the rail and bus stations, the shabby, rambling *Uva Hotel* has rooms from singles at Rs 40, to a four-bed room with bath at Rs 225. No food here either. The *Riverside Holiday Inn* (☎ 055-2090) at 27 Lower King St, 300 metres from the bus station, has doubles all the way from Rs 50 to Rs 200. It isn't beside the river.

Getting There & Away
Bus Buses run every half hour or so from Nuwara Eliya to Badulla (two hours, Rs 16). There are also regular buses to/from Haputale, Bandarawela and Ella, and services to/from Colombo and Kandy. One convenient CTB service leaves at 7.15 am for Ella, Wellawaya, Matara and Galle.

From Badulla to the east coast there are just a few buses each day – sometimes direct but more often the trip involves a change at Monaragala, where you meet the Wellawaya-Pottuvil road. The first half hour down from Badulla is very scenic.

Train The three main daily services to Colombo leave Badulla at 5.55 am, 8.50 am (via Kandy), and 5.45 pm. The first two have observation cars and the third has sleeping accommodation.

WELLAWAYA
At Wellawaya you have left the hill country and descended to the plains. Apart from the nearby Buduruvagala carvings, Wellawaya is just a small crossroads town. Roads run north up past the Rawana Ella Falls and through the spectacular Ella Gap to Ella and the hill country, south to the coast at Hambantota, east through Monaragala to Arugam Bay on the east coast, and west through Ratnapura to Colombo with a branch up to Haputale in the hill country.

Buduruvagala
About five km south of Wellawaya a small track branches west off the Hambantota road to the huge rock-cut Buddha figure of Buduruvagala. A small signpost points the way along a four-km unsurfaced road, which is in good enough shape to get a car along. If you don't have one, the walk is well worthwhile – this is one of the quietest, most peaceful and secluded historic sites in the country. As you walk, notice the scattered pillars and the mound of an old dagoba to the right. The pillars are said to be the remains of an old palace. At one point walkers can take a boat across an irrigation tank which the road skirts. At the end of the track you

cross a small footbridge and suddenly a sheer rock face rises before you with a 15-metre standing Buddha flanked by six smaller figures.

The figures are thought to date from around the 10th century AD, and are of the Mahayana Buddhist school, which enjoyed a brief heyday in Sri Lanka. The gigantic standing Buddha still bears traces of its original stuccoed robe and a long streak of orange suggests it was once brightly painted. The central of the three figures to the Buddha's right is thought to be the Buddhist mythological figure, the bodhisattva Avalokitesvara.

To the left of this white-painted figure is a female figure in the 'thrice bent' posture, thought to be his consort Tara. The three figures on the Buddha's left appear to an inexpert eye to be of a rather different style. One of them is holding up the hourglass-shaped Tibetan thunderbolt symbol known as a *dorje* – an unusual example of the Tantric side of Buddhism in Sri Lanka. One of them is said to be Maitreya, the future Buddha, while one is Vishnu. Several of the figures hold up their right hands with two fingers bent down to the palm – a beckoning gesture. It is worth obeying; the effort of getting to this uncommercial and unfrequented spot is amply repaid.

Buduruvagala means Buddha *(Budu)*, images *(ruva)*, of stone *(gala)*.

Places to Stay

If you take the Old Ella Rd from the central crossroads in the middle of Wellawaya to where it merges with the New Ella Rd running north to Ella, then continue a little further, you reach the fairly well kept *Wellawaya Inn Rest House*, with doubles with attached bath for Rs 250. On the way out to the Rest House are the *Surlander Holiday Inn*, near the centre, with a restaurant, air-con rooms at Rs 500, and other doubles at Rs 150 with shared bath or Rs 250 with private bath, and the friendly *Wellawaya Rest Inn* with doubles at Rs 150 including attached bath.

Getting There & Away

Wellawaya is a major staging point between the hill country and the south and east coasts. If you can't find a through bus you can usually find a connection in Wellawaya – but don't leave it too late in the day. The last bus up to Haputale leaves about 4 pm.

MONARAGALA

This small town, known as 'Peacock Rock', is a junction point on the road to the east coast. Here the roads from Badulla and Wellawaya meet. If you get stuck here there are a number of places to stay – though it can get very busy on Mondays when gem dealers converge on the town for a nearby fair.

Maligawila

At Maligawila, about 20 km south of Monaragala via Okkampitiya, stand two huge, ancient statues which, combined with Buduruvagala, make this corner of Sri Lanka fertile ground for monument hunters. One of the statues, an 11-metre Buddha, is reckoned to be the world's largest in-the-round Buddha figure. The other, a km away, is a 10-metre-high Avalokitesvara. Thought to date from the 6th or early 7th century AD and attributed to King Aggabodhi, they had lain fallen for centuries before being unearthed in the 1950s, and raised and restored during 1989-91. The Avalokitesvara had been broken into over 100 pieces. Both are made of crystalline limestone.

Places to Stay & Eat

The pleasant *Wellassa Inn Rest House* is Rs 300 a double including breakfast. Opposite is the *De Silva Guest House* charging about Rs 80. Other small guest houses will cost you Rs 50 or so a night. The friendly former YMCA on the Wellawaya road, also known as *Kandaland*, is in this category.

There are several small curry and rice places down towards the bus stand.

Getting There & Away

There are buses from Wellawaya and Badulla to Monaragala. There are also a few

Gems

Ratnapura is the gem centre of Sri Lanka; every second person you meet on the street is likely to whisper that they have the bargain of your lifetime wrapped up in their pocket. If you're no expert on gemstones the bargain is 100% likely to be on their side of the line, not yours.

Gems are still found by an ancient and traditional mining method. Gem miners look for seams of *illama*, a gravel-bearing stratum likely to hold gemstones. It's usually found in lowland areas – along valley bottoms, riverbeds, and other, usually very damp, places. On the Colombo-Ratnapura road you'll see countless gem-mining operations in paddy fields beside the road – but there are many more off in the hills and fields all around.

Gem mining is a co-operative effort: you need someone to dig out the illama, someone to work the pump to keep water out of the pit or tunnel, someone to wash the muddy gravel and an expert to search through the pebbles for the stone that may make all their fortunes. If a stone is found, the profit is divided between all the members of the co-op, from the person who supplies the finances to the one up to his neck in mud and water, clad only in a tiny loincloth known as an *amudes*. The mines can be vertical or horizontal depending on which way the illama runs.

It's a peculiarity of Sri Lankan gemming that a variety of different stones is almost always found in the same pit. A stone's value depends on a number of factors including rarity, hardness and beauty. Gems are still cut and polished by hand, although modern methods are also coming into use. Some stones are cut and faceted *(en cabochon)*, while others are simply polished. The division between precious and semi-precious stones is a purely arbitrary one – there is no clear definition of what makes one stone a precious stone and another only semi-precious. For more information on gems, see Things to Buy in the Facts for the Visitor chapter. Some of the more popular types of stone are listed below.

Corundrums This group includes sapphires and rubies, both precious stones and second only to the diamond in hardness. The best and most valuable rubies are red and are not found in Sri Lanka in commercial deposits. You will, however, see pink rubies, which are equally correctly called pink sapphires. Rubies and sapphires are the same kind of stone, with gradations of colour depending on the precise proportions of the chemicals in their make-up. Other sapphires can be yellow, orange, white and, most valuable, blue. Beware of people trying to pass off pink or blue spinels as sapphires. You can often find corundrums which contain 'silk', minute inclusions which give the stone a star effect, particularly with a single light source.

Chrysoberyl Cat's-eye and Alexandrite are the best known in this group. Cat's-eyes, with their cat-like ray known as *chatoyancy*, vary from green through a honey colour to brown; look for translucence and the clarity and glow of the single ray. Alexandrite is valued for its colour change under natural and artificial light. One rip-off to watch for is tourmalines, which are very much less valuable, being sold as cat's eyes.

Beryl The best known stone in this group, the emerald, is not found in Sri Lanka. The aquamarine, which is found here, is quite reasonably priced since it is not so hard or lustrous as other stones.

Zircon The appearance of a zircon can approach that of a diamond although it is a comparatively soft stone. It comes in a variety of colours, from yellow through orange to brown and green.

Quartz This stone can vary all the way from transparent to opaque and is usually quite low priced. Quartz can also vary widely in colour, from purple amethyst to smoky quartz, right through to brown stones so dark they look almost black.

Feldspar The moonstone is Sri Lanka's special gem. Usually a smooth, grey colour, it can also be found with a slight shade of blue although this colouring is rarer.

Other Spinels are fairly common but also quite hard and rather attractive. They come in a variety of colours and can be transparent or opaque. Garnets are a sort of poor person's ruby; light brown garnets are often used in rings in Sri Lanka. Topaz is not found in Sri Lanka – if someone offers it to you it'll probably be quartz. ■

direct services from Kandy, Haputale, Galle and elsewhere. From Kandy they go via Mahiyangana and Bibile, and take about six hours.

BELIHUL OYA

From Belihul Oya, 35 km from Haputale on the Ratnapura road, you can walk up to Horton Plains – or, perhaps better(!), down from them, which takes about four hours – and you can also reach the Bambarakanda Falls, at 240 metres the highest in Sri Lanka, which are uphill from Kalupahana, about 12 km back along the road towards Haputale.

Places to Stay

Belihul Oya has another exquisitely situated *Rest House* (☎ 045-7200), perched beside a stream that rushes down from Horton Plains. Out front you can sit on the verandah, sipping afternoon tea, admiring the huge tree and watching the occasional bus cross the stone bridge. The 10 single/double rooms with private bath are Rs 370/410 – try to avoid those nearest the stream, where the water noise is tremendous. The *Pearl Inn* overlooking the village centre is another good place: very clean doubles with attached bath cost Rs 250, and there's good food.

RATNAPURA

The gem centre of Sri Lanka, Ratnapura (the name means 'City of Gems') is 100 km from Colombo. There is beautiful scenery in abundance from Ratnapura to Haputale, which makes this an interesting alternative route to/from the hill country; you skirt round the southern edge of the hill country and then ascend into the hills at Haputale. You soon realise just how abruptly the hills rise from the plain.

The scenery around Ratnapura is magnificent and this is reputed to be the best place for views of Adam's Peak, since here you view the mountain from below while from the other side you're looking at it from about the same level. Ratnapura is also the starting point for the 'classical' (read 'hard') route up Adam's Peak via Gilimale and Carney Estate. There are less arduous walks much

closer to town, even right from the Rest House. There's a full-size replica of the Aukana Buddha on top of a hill overlooking the town, and a river bathing pool near the Rest House.

Museums

A visit to the Gem Museum (admission free) at Getangama is worthwhile, although it's mainly just gem polishing you see. There's an interesting collection of gemstones from Sri Lanka and all over the world. You can inspect a wide range of gems for sale but here, as elsewhere in Ratnapura, gem merchants sell only the stones. There are no stones available in settings as there are in Kandy or elsewhere, and some travellers have reported that prices are not competitive with Colombo's. The Gem Museum does, however, have a fine art gallery of mostly silver objects designed by the owner. The objects are 'top class; he uses traditional elements in a very creative manner', wrote one traveller. To get to the museum take a bus from the railway station to Getangama; it's only a few stops.

There's another gem museum 1½ km on the Badulla road out of town – the Gem Bank Gemmological Museum at 6 Ehelapola Mawatha, Batugedera. Several other 'gem museums' have sprung up in the town, but many of them would be more aptly described as salerooms.

Ratnapura's other small museum, on the Wellawaya side of town opposite the CTB bus depot, has a collection of prehistoric fossil skeletons of elephants, hippopotamuses and rhinoceroses – all found in caves or gem pits in the area. It's open from 9 am to 5 pm, except on Fridays and Saturdays.

Places to Stay

The CTB bus station is just off the centre of town, on the rise that culminates in the Rest House. Half way up the hill towards the Rest House you will find *Travellers' Rest* at 66 Inner Circular Rd (or Rest House Rd). It's very basic but doubles are Rs 200. Right beside it, at No 60, is the *Star Light Tourist Rest* (☎ 045-2831) where rooms, some with common bath, some with attached bath, cost from Rs 100 to Rs 175.

At the top of the hill, beautifully situated overlooking the town, Ratnapura's *Rest House* (☎ 045-2299) has once again grabbed the best site in town. From up here you can overlook the town and surrounding country-side, well above the noise and heat down below. There are 11 rooms, a spacious veran-dah and a small grassy garden in the back. Airy rooms with attached bath upstairs are Rs 265/530 for singles/doubles including breakfast and dinner. There are also some more basic rooms downstairs.

Polhengoda Village (signposted from the CTB station) is about two km from the town centre, and is the personal estate of the owner of the Gem Museum, Purandara Sri Bhadra Marapana. It has a three-acre herb garden and the *Hotel Kalawathie*, full of fine antique furniture and specialising in 'indigenous herb baths', courses of which include such exotica as one hour's relaxation on banana leaves, mouth wash and gum massage with 21 varieties of tooth powder, face wash with pomegranate, shampoo with dill seeds, and medical smoke with margosa oil, followed by a vegetarian lunch at a table decorated with frangipani and orchids. Rooms at this establishment cost around Rs 500 a double.

Places to Eat
In the town the *Ratnaloka Hotel* is a good place for a tasty, inexpensive curry and rice – go upstairs. Along Main St from the central clock tower, then up a small road to the left, is the cool, clean and rather more expensive *Nilani Tourist Restaurant* – it's signposted. The *Rest House* has good food with the usual graciously old-fashioned service. At the Gem Bank Gemmological Museum you'll find the pleasant but rather pricey *Chamber Restaurant*.

Getting There & Away
Buses cost Rs 15 for the two to three-hour trip from Colombo. A CTB express bus from Colombo to Haputale stops at Ratnapura about 8 am, costing Rs 23 for the spectacular three-hour ride to Haputale. There are also buses to/from Kandy, Galle, Matara and Hambantota. The private bus stand is a few metres from the central clocktower; the CTB station is on the rise topped by the Rest House.

RATNAPURA TO THE SOUTH
At Pelmadulla between Ratnapura and Haputale, a road splits off to the south, leading to the coast at Galle, Matara or Ham-bantota. The Galle and Matara branch goes through a southern spur of the hill (and tea) country, where there's a *Rest House*, and at least one guest house, at Deniyaya (90 km from Ratnapura).

Uda Walawe National Park
Thimbolketiya, just a few km north of Embilipitiya on the Ratnapura-Hambantota road, is the entrance to Uda Walawe National Park. The park's 310 sq km include a large reservoir whose catchment area it was created to conserve. Elephant herds can be seen in the dry season (May-September) along the Walawe River, and deer are common. There's little forest owing to exten-sive slash-and-burn farming, but tall pohon grass growing in the wake of the burning makes wildlife-watching difficult except during the dry months.

In the dry season 30 km of track in the park are passable for cars. You need to get a permit and pick up a tracker from the rangers' office at Thimbolketiya before entering the park. There are two campsites in the park, or you could find accommodation in Embilipitiya. For regulations on park entry and informa-tion on camping contact the Department of Wildlife Conservation (☎ 01-567083), 82 Rajamalwatte Rd, Battaramulla, Colombo.

The Ancient Cities

The ancient city region of Sri Lanka lies north of the hill country, in one of the driest parts of the island. During the golden age of Sinhalese civilisation, which reached its peak over 1000 years ago, the Sinhalese overcame continual harassment from invading south Indian forces to build two great cities (Anuradhapura and Polonnaruwa) and create many other magnificent reminders of the strength of their Buddhist culture – only to abandon them all. For 1000 years the jungle did its best to reclaim them, but major archaeological excavations over the past century have restored them to some of their past glory.

Apart from the 1985 Anuradhapura massacre, the civil war has not reached the main ancient city sites, though killings have sometimes come alarmingly close to Polonnaruwa. Outlying sites such as Medirigiriya or Dimbulagala may be borderline cases. Check before venturing too far north or east.

Kandy is a good starting point for a visit to the ancient city region. The two highlight sites apart from Anuradhapura and Polonnaruwa are Sigiriya and Dambulla.

Cultural Triangle

The Sri Lankan government and UNESCO (the United Nations Educational, Scientific and Cultural Organisation) are carrying out a number of restoration projects within the 'cultural triangle' formed by the old Sinhalese capitals Kandy, Anuradhapura and Polonnaruwa. There are now admission charges for large areas of the ancient cities at Anuradhapura and Polonnaruwa (each US$7 for non-Sri Lankans); the rock and water gardens at Sigiriya (US$7); the cave temple at Dambulla (US$7); the National Museum together with other buildings near the Temple of the Tooth at Kandy, and other temples around the town (but not the Temple of the Tooth itself) (US$7); and the Nalanda Gedige (US$4).

The ticket you get for your US$7 or US$4 is valid only on the day of issue. A US$20 'round ticket', allowing you to visit each site once is available, which will save you money if you're going to visit three or more of the main sites. It can be bought at the first five sites, and possibly at Nalanda too. Generally it's valid for a month but some readers have reported that round tickets issued at Kandy were only valid for two weeks. It's also possible, but hardly worth bothering, to get a round ticket at the Cultural Triangle Fund office at 212 Bauddhaloka Mawatha, Colombo 7.

The six main Cultural Triangle restoration projects cover the Jetavanarama and Abhayagiri Dagobas in Anuradhapura; the water gardens at Sigiriya; the Alahana Pirivena at Polonnaruwa; some rock paintings at Dambulla; and the area within the four devales at Kandy. Not all the work has met with universal approval – there have been some complaints about incompetent work damaging ancient structures.

KANDY TO DAMBULLA
Matale

This small, busy town 24 km north of Kandy is encircled by hills, with a pleasant park at the foot of which is a monument to the leaders of the 1848 Matale Rebellion – one of the less famous contributions to history's Year of Revolutions!

Aluvihara

The rock monastery of Aluvihara is beside the Kandy-Dambulla road eight km north of Matale – about 40 km before Dambulla. The monastery caves are situated in rocks which have fallen in a jumble from the mountainsides high above the valley. It's an extremely picturesque setting – in fact it has even been described as 'theatrical'. Some of the caves have fine frescoes, there is a 10-metre-long reclining Buddha image and one cave is dedicated to the Indian Pali scholar

Buddhagosa, who is supposed to have spent several years here. It is said that the doctrines of the Buddha were first recorded here, in Pali script, around the 1st century BC. The monks today are inscribing Buddhist scriptures in ola (palm) leaf books and you

Architecture & Ruins

Sri Lanka's ancient cities have a real lost city storyline. After the abandonment of first Anuradhapura and then Polonnaruwa, they gradually reverted to the jungle. At times efforts were made to restore them or at least slow the decline: Parakramabahu I, the great king of Polonnaruwa, tried to maintain a foothold in Anuradhapura, even building the Brazen Palace with bits and pieces purloined from other buildings, and a king of Kotte and one from Kandy made feeble attempts at minor restoration as late as the 18th century. But overall the ancient cities were little more than a legend when the British arrived.

Their systematic study began in 1890 with the first Government Archaeologist, H C P Bell, whose truly inexhaustible energy lives on even today. The discovery of some new ruin will still be initially labelled a *bel kalla* or 'Bell Fragment'.

The ruins display a number of set forms. First there are dagobas – in other countries these might be called stupas, pagodas or chedis but everywhere the basic form is the same: a solid hemisphere rising to a point or spire. The Sinhalese variation on this simple pattern is that the 'relic chamber' is sometimes raised up above the hemisphere, rather than being buried in its centre. This chamber contains more than just a relic of the Buddha; it is also supposed to represent a model of the Buddhist cosmos. You can see the contents of an excavated relic chamber in the Anuradhapura Archaeological Museum. The solidity of a dagoba sometimes surprises Westerners accustomed to hollow churches designed to hold congregations. A dagoba is a focus, not an enclosure – meditation and worship take place out in the open. You should always walk around a dagoba in a clockwise direction.

A more uniquely Sinhalese architectural concept is the *vatadage*, or circular relic house. Today you can see vatadages in Anuradhapura and Polonnaruwa, and perhaps the finest at Medirigiriya. They consist of a small central dagoba, flanked by Buddha images and encircled by rows of columns. Long ago these columns held up a wooden roof, but in the ancient cities all traces of wooden architecture have long disappeared and you must get your imagination into top gear to picture how things really were. Only important religious buildings were built of stone – everything else, from the king's palace to the monks' monastery, was made at least partly of wood, so what we see today is a very incomplete picture. You can see a complete model of the Thuparama Vatadage in the Anuradhapura Museum.

Another peculiarly Sinhalese style is the *gedige* – a hollow temple with extremely thick walls topped by a 'corbelled' roof. Often the walls are so thick that a stairway can be built right into the wall. There are a number of gediges in Anuradhapura and Polonnaruwa but almost all their roofs collapsed long ago.

Some of the most interesting Sinhalese designs are found in the little artistic embellishments to the buildings. Moonstones, no relation to the semi-precious stones, are a recurring element that you can study at both main cities. They're essentially semi-circular stones at the base of stairways or the entrance doors to buildings – like a rock doormat. Their design follows a set pattern representing the Buddhist view of life with its pain of birth, disease, old age and death. The outermost band is a ring of fire symbolising the state of the world. The next band of animals – elephants, horses, lions or bulls – symbolises the vitality of the world despite its problems and pains. The band of geese symbolises those who leave home in search of the meaning of life and finally, in the central half-lotus, those who continue the search find enlightenment.

Guardstones are another design element one sees frequently – they generally flank entrances or doorways with sculptures of cobra kings holding auspicious objects or similar themes. Other interesting figures may be included in the guardstones, including the ever-present dwarves who add a touch of humour to so many ancient buildings. Another element of Sinhalese art and architecture impossible to miss is the extraordinary quality of rock-cut figures. It has been said in Burma that the Burmese are unable to see a hill without plonking a pagoda on top of it. Well the Sinhalese seemed, at one time, to be unable to see a rock without cutting a Buddha into it. Some of the best figures include the Gal Vihara in Polonnaruwa, the gigantic Aukana image and the impressive Buduruvagala group near Wellawaya. ∎

Top: Seated Buddha, Gal Vihara, Polonnaruwa (PS)
Bottom: Carving at entrance to Temple of the Tooth, Kandy (JN)

Top: Sunset, Hikkaduwa (PS)
Bottom: Fishing boats on the beach, Beruwela (PT)

can see their workshop. There are official guides here (not demanding commissions) and some friendly English-speaking monks.

One of the monastic caves contains a horror chamber reminiscent of the Tiger Balm Gardens in Singapore. Ask the monks to unlock it for you. Colourful statues of devils and sinners show the various forms of punishment handed out in the afterlife. One writer 'particularly liked the punishment of a sexual sinner who had his skull cut open and was having his brains ladled out by two demons while he wept bitterly'. Another exhibit shows the gory drawing and quartering of a prostitute.

There are many spice gardens and several batik showrooms along the road near Aluvihara. According to readers, the International Spice Walk just north of Aluvihara has 'really friendly people with free loads of info, plus spice tea and cake; and good prices for spices if you want to buy', while Batik Fair at Thotagamuwa, Polapathwela, also just north of Aluvihara, has a 'huge selection of themes, designs and sizes'.

Nalanda

The 8th century gedige at Nalanda, 25 km north of Matale and only 20 km before Dambulla, is a rare example of mixed Buddhist and Hindu architecture, though to some eyes it looks oddly like a Mexican Mayan temple! It has Tantric carvings with sexual subjects. The entrance fee is US$4. The site is beside a tank one km east of the main road – a sign marks the turn-off.

Places to Stay

At Matale there is a *Rest House*, beautifully situated as usual on the south side of the town centre, between the lower and upper roads from Kandy, with doubles at Rs 300 with private bath.

Readers have recommended the *Clover Grange Hotel* (☎ 066-3124) at 95 King's St, with two doubles at Rs 500 in a big colonial house with a friendly owner.

Getting There & Away

There are frequent buses to Matale from just below the clock tower in Kandy. Dambulla or Anuradhapura buses from Kandy or Matale will drop you at Aluvihara, spice gardens or the Nalanda turning.

DAMBULLA

The great cave temple of Dambulla is 100 to 150 metres above the road in the southern part of the village of Dambulla, which consists of two separate areas divided by about one km of unbuilt-up country. The walk up to the temple begins along a vast, sloping rock face. The temple is open from 6 am to 7 pm and the entrance fee for non-Sri Lankans is US$7. The ticket office is at the foot of the rock, near the road, some distance from the cave temple itself. From the level of the caves you have superb views over the surrounding countryside; Sigiriya is clearly visible to the north-east, only 19 km away.

The caves' history is thought to date back to around the 1st century BC when King Valagam Bahu, driven out of Anuradhapura, took refuge here. When he regained his throne he had the caves converted into a magnificent rock temple. Later kings made further improvements, including King Nissanka Malla who had the temple interior gilded, earning it the name of Ran Giri – the 'Golden Rock'.

There are five separate caves containing 150 Buddha images, the largest cave being over 50 metres long and about six metres high. The first cave you come to has a 15-metre-long reclining Buddha. The second cave has many large images of Hindu gods. All the caves are full of Buddha images in a variety of positions and are decorated in glowing colours with frescoes showing scenes from the Buddha's life, and events in Sinhalese history. The frescoes are comparatively modern and not of particular significance. As dusk draws in, hundreds of swallows swoop and dart around the cave entrance.

Places to Stay & Eat

Most places to stay are in the southern part of town on the Kandy road, fairly close to the cave temple. Apart from the Rest House nearly everything is bottom-end. If you're

seeking greater comforts and more mod cons
you should head for Sigiriya.

About 150 metres down the road beside
the bus stop, almost opposite the cave temple
entrance, the friendly *Sunflower Inn* is clean
and well kept, with singles/doubles at
Rs 100/200. The rooms have private bathrooms, nets and fans; those nearer the road
are generally better. There's a pleasant
garden and meals are available. Further out
towards Kandy there are rooms for
Rs 100/150 at the little *Sena Tourist Inn* and
Rs 150/200 at the *Hotel Laxapana*. Meals
are available at both.

A short distance north from the cave
temple is Dambulla's real cheapie, the
grandly named *Oasis Tourist Welfare Centre*.
It's a basic (no electricity) but friendly,
helpful and fairly clean place where you pay
Rs 40/75. Food is cheap too.

The *Dambulla Rest House* (☎ 066-8299)
half a km north of the Oasis has just four
huge rooms at Rs 250/300. The price is good
by rest house standards. There's a garden, a
cool verandah where you can sip an evening
drink, and a dining room serving good meals
(dinner Rs 130, breakfast Rs 85). The
Chamara Tourist Inn and the *Healey Tourist
Inn* are two cheaper places just north of the
rest house, both asking Rs 150 for reasonable rooms with private shower, toilet, net
and fan. They'll probably come down from
this price when they're not busy.

The turn-off towards the police station
between the Rest House and the Chamara
leads to *Freddies Holiday Inn*, where large,
good rooms with private bathroom, net and
fan cost Rs 100/150 including dinner. You
may have to bargain a bit to get this price.

About a km beyond the Colombo junction, on the north edge of town, is the good
Gimanhala Transit Hotel (☎ 066-8364) with
rooms at Rs 250/350 including private bath.
The staff are helpful and the food good.

Getting There & Away

Dambulla is 72 km north of Kandy on the
road to Anuradhapura. The Colombo-
Trincomalee road meets this road two km
north of the cave temple, then splits off from

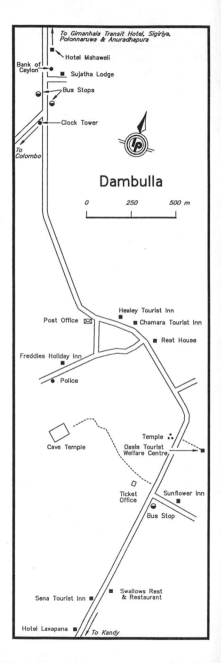

Polonnaruwa. Because Dambulla is on so many major routes, plenty of buses pass through it with inconsistent frequency, but the nearest railway station is at Habarana, 22 km north. Some buses go from the stop in the southern part of Dambulla near the cave temple entrance, but more go from the stops by the Colombo junction.

It takes two to 2½ hours to Polonnaruwa (66 km) or Anuradhapura (64 km) and the fare is Rs 14, to Sigiriya (30 minutes) is Rs 5, to Kandy it takes two hours for Rs 15. From Colombo, it's Rs 28 and four hours. There are frequent buses between the two parts of Dambulla.

SIGIRIYA

The spectacular rock fortress of Sigiriya, 19 km north-east of Dambulla, is one of Sri Lanka's major attractions. In 473 AD King Dhatusena of Anuradhapura was overthrown and, so one legend goes, walled up alive by Kasyapa, his son by a palace consort. Moggallana, Dhatusena's son by his true queen, fled to India swearing revenge, so Kasyapa, fearing an invasion, decided to build an impregnable fortress on the huge rock of Sigiriya. When the long-expected invasion finally came in 491, Kasyapa didn't just skulk in his stronghold but rode out at the head of his army on an elephant. In attempting to outflank his half-brother, Kasyapa took a wrong turn, became bogged in a swamp, was deserted by his troops, and took his own life.

Sigiriya later became a monastic refuge but eventually fell into disrepair, and was only rediscovered by archaeologists during the British era. Describing it as merely a fortress does Sigiriya no justice. Atop the 200-metre-high rock (377 metres above sea level) Kasyapa built a wet-season palace – a kind of 5th-century penthouse. It is hard to imagine Sigiriya at the height of its glory but it must have been something akin to a European chateau, plonked on top of Australia's Ayers Rock! If you would like to know a lot more about Sigiriya, including the many points of interest on the route up the rock, try to find a copy of R H de Silva's booklet *Sigiriya*, published by the Department of Archaeology in Colombo, 1976.

The admission charge for foreign visitors is US$7. Sigiriya is open daily from 6.30 am to 5.30 pm. An early or late ascent of the rock avoids the main crowds and the fierce midday heat.

Water Gardens

The approach to the rock from the ticket office is through Kasyapa's beautiful water gardens, which extend from the western foot of the rock, with royal bathing pools, little moated islands which acted as dry-season palaces, and trees framing the approach to the rock. The rock rises sheer and mysterious from the jungle: a switchback series of steps leads up through the boulders at its foot to the western face, then ascends it steeply.

Frescoes – the Sigiriya Damsels

About half way up the rock a modern spiral stairway leads up from the main route to a long, sheltered gallery in the sheer rock face. Painted in this niche are a series of beautiful women – similar in style to the rock paintings at Ajanta in India. These 5th-century pin-ups are the only non-religious old paintings to be seen in Sri Lanka. Although there may have been as many as 500 portraits at one time, only 22 remain today – several were badly damaged by a vandal in 1967. Protected from the sun in the sheltered gallery, they remain in remarkably good condition, their colours still glowing. They're at their best in the late afternoon light.

Mirror Wall with Graffiti

Beyond the fresco gallery the pathway clings to the sheer side of the rock and is protected on the outside by a three-metre-high wall. This wall was coated with a mirror-smooth glaze on which visitors of 1000 years ago felt impelled to note their impressions of the women in the gallery above. The graffiti were principally inscribed between the 7th and 11th century, and 685 of them have been deciphered and published in a two-volume edition – *Sigiri Graffiti* by Dr S Paranavitana (Oxford University Press, 1956). They are of

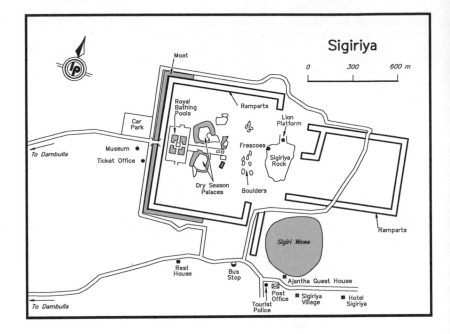

great interest to scholars for their evidence of the development of the Sinhalese language and script. One typical graffito reads:

The ladies who wear golden chains on their breasts beckon me. As I have seen the resplendent ladies, heaven appears to me as not good.

Another, by a female scribbler, goes:

A deer-eyed young woman of the mountain side arouses anger in my mind. In her hand she had taken a string of pearls and in her looks she has assumed rivalry with us.

Lion Platform

At the northern end of the rock the narrow pathway emerges on to the large platform from which the rock derives its name of Sigiriya – the lion rock. In 1898 H C P Bell, the British archaeologist responsible for an enormous amount of discovery in Ceylon, found two enormous lion paws when excavating here. At one time a gigantic brick lion

sat at this end of the rock and the final ascent to the top commenced with a stairway which led between the lion's paws and into its mouth! For a short, slightly adventurous, detour here, you can clamber down to a rock-cut lily pond visible down the side of the rock to the left as you face the lion's paws.

Today the lion has disappeared, apart from the first steps and the paws. To reach the top means clambering up across a series of grooves cut into the rock face. Fortunately there is a stout metal handrail but vertigo sufferers are strongly advised not to look down. Still, sari-clad Sri Lankan women manage it, even on windy days, so it can't be that bad. Beware, however, of the Sigiriya wasps which sometimes appear here.

The Summit

The top of the rock covers 1.6 hectares and at one time must have been completely covered with buildings, only the foundations of which remain today. The design of this rock-top palace, and the magnificent views it enjoys even today, make one think that Sigiriya must have been much more palace than fortress. A pond scooped out of the solid rock measures 27 metres by 21 metres. It looks for all the world like a modern swimming pool, although it may have been used merely for water storage.

The king's stone throne, also cut from the solid rock, faces the rising sun. You can sit here and gaze across the surrounding jungle, as no doubt Kasyapa did 1500 years ago, and watch for an invading army, complete with elephants.

Places to Stay & Eat

The *Rest House* (☎ 066-8324) has an all but unbeatable location, directly opposite the side of the rock, about 400 metres away. There are 15 big, clean rooms at a nightly cost of Rs 380 a single or double and they're equipped with mosquito nets (which Sigiriya's top-end hotels lack), fans and private baths (though water is sometimes limited to just a few hours a day). Meals are available at Rs 85 for breakfast, Rs 125 for lunch and Rs 165 for dinner (you don't have to be staying here to eat here). This is one of the nicest rest houses and on the spacious verandah you can sit and study the rock.

The cheapest place is the *Ajantha Guest House* on the track from the rest house to the top-end hotels and beside the Sigiri Wewa, a lake that's often so overgrown with vegetation that no water is visible. The asking price for rooms with mosquito nets is Rs 100 a single with shared bath, Rs 150 a double with private bath, but you can usually bargain these down a bit.

Sigiriya's two upper-bracket hotels are close together about a km beyond the rest house, separated only by their extensive gardens. The first you reach is the 100-room *Sigiriya Village* (☎ 066-8216), the second is the 50-room *Hotel Sigiriya* (☎ 066-8311). Both are modern and pretty well designed. The Hotel Sigiriya is marginally more laid-back (though both are relaxed) and has splendid views of the rock from its dining room and pool, while the rooms and grounds at the Sigiriya Village are a bit bigger. Bed-and-breakfast singles/doubles in high season are US$22.50/30 (air-con US$7.50 extra) at the Hotel Sigiriya, US$21/25 (air-con US$5) at the Sigiriya Village, but these figures often go down at other times. You can usually use the hotels' pools for Rs 50 if you're a non-resident, or for nothing if you have a meal there.

There is a number of drink and snack stalls in the car park by the main entrance to the rock, and a couple more on the road through the village.

Getting There & Away

Sigiriya is about 10 km east of the main road between Dambulla and Habarana. The turn-off is at Inamaluwa. There are buses from Dambulla about hourly in the morning from 6.30 am (Rs 5, half-hour trip), less often in the afternoon. The last bus back to Dambulla leaves at 6.30 pm. There's a direct CTB bus to Sigiriya from Kandy (Bogambara bus yard) at 8 am, returning at 12.15 pm. It takes 2¾ hours for Rs 16. The paved road does not continue beyond Sigiriya, although there is a dirt road that eventually meets the Habarana-Polonnaruwa road quite close to Habarana.

POLONNARUWA

It was the south Indian Chola dynasty that first made its capital at Polonnaruwa, after conquering Anuradhapura in the late 10th century AD. Polonnaruwa was a more strategic place to guard against any rebellion from the Ruhunu Sinhalese kingdom in the south-east. It also, apparently, had fewer mosquitoes! When the Sinhalese king Vijayabahu I drove the Cholas off the island in 1070, he kept Polonnaruwa as his capital. Parakramabahu I (1153-86) raised Polonnaruwa to its heights, erecting huge buildings, planning beautiful parks and, as a crowning achievement, creating a 2400-hectare tank – so large that it was named the Parakrama Samudra – the 'Sea of Parakrama'. The present lake incorporates three older tanks, so it may not be the actual tank he created.

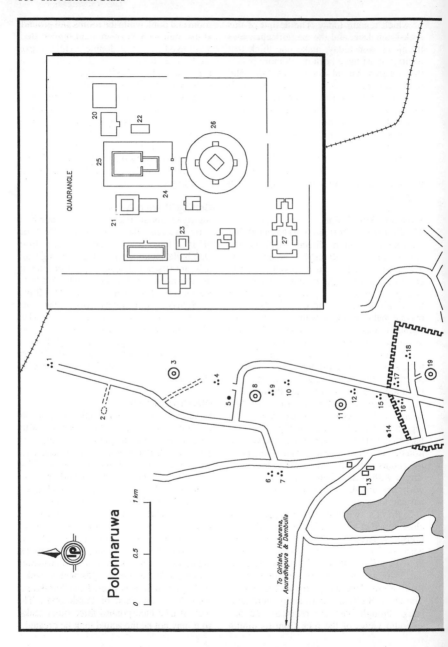

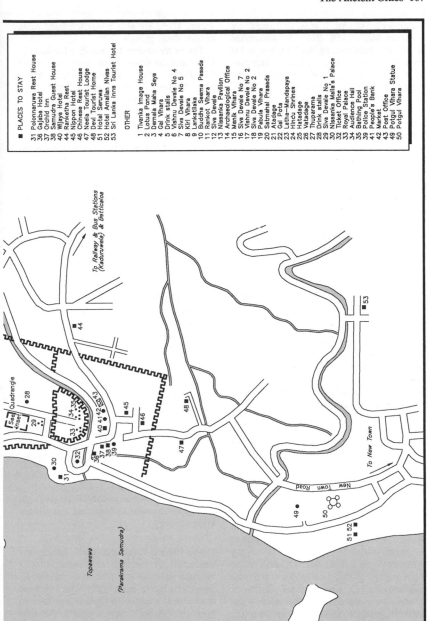

■ PLACES TO STAY

31 Polonnaruwa Rest House
36 Gajaba Hotel
37 Orchid Inn
38 Samudra Guest House
40 Wijaya Hotel
44 Ranketha Rest
45 Nippon Hotel
46 Chinese Rest House
47 Neela Tourist Lodge
48 Devi Tourist Home
51 Hotel Seruwa
52 Hotel Amalian Nivas
53 Sri Lanka Inns Tourist Hotel

OTHER

1 Tivanka Image House
2 Lotus Pond
3 Demala Maha Seya
4 Gal Vihara
5 Drink stalls
6 Vishnu Devale No 4
7 Siva Devale No 5
8 Kiri Vihara
9 Lankatilaka
10 Buddha Seema Pasada
11 Rankot Vihara
12 Siva Devale
13 Nissanka Pavilion
14 Archaeological Office
15 Menik Vihara
16 Siva Devale No 7
17 Vishnu Devale No 2
18 Siva Devale No 2
19 Pabula Vihara
20 Satmahal Prasada
21 Atadage
22 Gal Pota
23 Latha–Mandapaya
24 Hindu Shrines
25 Hatadage
26 Vatadage
27 Thuparama
28 Drink stalls
29 Siva Devale No 1
30 Nissanka Malla's Palace
32 Royal Palace
33 Ticket Office
34 Audience Hall
35 Bathing Pool
39 Police Station
41 People's Bank
42 Market
43 Post Office
49 Potgul Vihara Statue
50 Potgul Vihara

Parakramabahu I was followed by Nissanka Malla (1187-96), who succeeded in virtually bankrupting the kingdom in his attempts to match his predecessors' achievements. By the early 1200s Polonnaruwa was beginning to prove as susceptible to Indian invasion as Anuradhapura, and despite a further century of efforts to stand strong, eventually it too was abandoned and the Sinhalese capital shifted to the west of the island.

Polonnaruwa stands 140 km north-east of Kandy and 104 km south-east of Anuradhapura. Although nearly 1000 years old, it is much younger than Anuradhapura and generally in much better repair. Furthermore, its monuments are arranged in a more compact area and their development is easier to follow. All in all, if you're something less than a professional archaeologist you'll probably find Polonnaruwa the easier of the two ancient capitals to appreciate. By bicycle is the ideal way to explore it and you can rent one at several places in the town.

Orientation & Information

Polonnaruwa has both an old town and a spread-out new town to the south. The main areas of ruins start on the north edge of the old town and spread north. Accommodation is mostly in and around the old town. The main bus and railway stations are, inconveniently, in neither the old town nor the new town but in Kaduruwela, a few km east of the old town on the Batticaloa road. However, buses from anywhere except the east go through the old town on their way in, so you can get off there anyway.

The Polonnaruwa ruins can be conveniently divided into five groups: (1) a small group near the Rest House on the banks of the tank; (2) the royal palace group a little to the east of the Rest House; (3) a very compact group a short distance north of the royal palace group, usually known as the quadrangle; (4) a number of structures spread over a wide area further north – the northern group; (5) a small group far to the south towards the new town – the southern

group. There are also a few scattered ruins outside these groups.

The entry charge for non-Sri Lankans is US$7 and the ticket office is just east of the Rest House – tickets are sold from 7 am to 5 pm. Officially the site closes at 6 pm but in practice you can stay till dark. Tickets are not checked at the Rest House group or the southern group, but the other three groups are within a single big enclosure and you have to enter at the official entrance on the Habarana road, just north of the Royal Palace.

Solo women should exercise a little caution when wandering around the more remote ruins.

Rest House Group

The Rest House, situated on a small promontory jutting out into the Topawewa, is a delightful place for a post-sightseeing drink. Concentrated a few steps to the north of the Rest House are the ruins of Nissanka Malla's royal palace, which aren't in anywhere near the same state of preservation as the Parakramabahu palace group.

The royal baths are nearest the Rest House. Furthest north is the King's Council Chamber, where the king's throne in the shape of a stone lion once stood – it is now in the Colombo Museum. Inscribed into each column in the chamber is the name of the minister whose seat was once beside it. The mound nearby becomes an island when the waters of the tank are high – on it are the ruins of a small summer house used by the king.

Royal Palace Group

This group of buildings dates from the reign of Parakramabahu I. There are three main things to see.

Royal Palace Parakramabahu's palace was a magnificent structure. It measured 31 by 13 metres and is said to have had seven storeys. The three-metre-thick walls certainly have the holes to receive the floor beams for two higher floors but if there were a further four levels they must have been made of wood.

The roof in this main hall, which had 50 rooms in all, was supported by 30 columns.

Audience Hall The pavilion used as an audience hall by Parakramabahu is particularly notable for the frieze of elephants around its base – every elephant is in a different position. There are fine lions at the top of the steps.

Bathing Pool In the south-east corner of the palace grounds the Kumara Pokuna, or Prince's Bathing Pool, still has one of its crocodile-mouth spouts remaining.

Quadrangle

Only a short stroll north of the Royal Palace ruins, the area known as the Quadrangle is literally that – a compact group of fascinating ruins in a raised-up area bounded by a wall. It's the most concentrated collection of buildings you'll find in the Sri Lankan ancient cities.

Vatadage In the south-east of the quadrangle, the Vatadage, or circular relic house, is typical of its kind. Its outermost terrace is 18 metres in diameter and the second terrace has four entrances flanked by particularly fine guardstones. The moonstone at the northern entrance is reckoned the finest in Polonnaruwa, although not of the same standard as some of the best at Anuradhapura. The four entrances lead to the central dagoba with its four seated Buddhas. The stone screen is thought to be a later addition to the Vatadage, probably by Nissanka Malla.

Thuparama At the southern end of the quadrangle the Thuparama is a gedige, an architectural style which reached its perfection at Polonnaruwa. This is the smallest gedige in Polonnaruwa but also one of the best, and the only one with its roof intact. The building shows strong Hindu influence and is thought to date from the reign of Parakramabahu I. There are several Buddha images in the inner chamber.

Gal Pota The 'Stone Book', immediately east of the Hatadage, is a colossal stone representation of a palm-leaf *ola* book. It measures nearly nine metres long by 1½ metres wide, and from 40 to 66 cm thick. The inscription on it, the longest such stone inscription (of which there are many!) in Sri Lanka, indicates that it was a Nissanka Malla production. Much of it extols his virtues as a king but it also includes the footnote that the slab, weighing 25 tonnes, was dragged from Mihintale, nearly 100 km away!

Hatadage Also erected by Nissanka Malla, this tooth-relic chamber is said to have been built in 60 days.

Latha-Mandapaya The busy Nissanka Malla was also responsible for this unique structure. It consists of a latticed stone fence, a curious imitation of a wooden fence with posts and railings, surrounding a very small dagoba surrounded by stone pillars. The pillars are shaped like lotus stalks topped by unopened buds. Nissanka Malla is said to have sat within this enclosure to listen to chanted Buddhist texts.

Satmahal Prasada This curious building, about which very little is known, has apparent Cambodian influence in its design. It consists of six diminishing storeys (there used to be seven) like a stepped pyramid.

Atadage This tooth-relic temple is the only surviving structure in Polonnaruwa dating from the reign of Vijayabahu I. Like the Hatadage, it once had an upper wooden storey.

Siva Devale No 1 Immediately south of the quadrangle, this 13th century Hindu temple indicates the Indian influence that returned after Polonnaruwa's Sinhalese florescence. It is notable for the superb quality of its stonework, which fits together with unusual precision. The domed brick roof has collapsed but when this building was being excavated a number of excellent bronzes were discovered and these are now in the museum in Colombo.

Close to the Quadrangle

Continuing along the road north from the quadrangle, a gravel road branches off to the right, just before you reach the city wall. It leads to the following structures.

Siva Devale No 2 Similar in style to Siva Devale No 1, by the quadrangle, this is the oldest structure in Polonnaruwa and dates from the brief Chola period when the invading Indians established the city. Unlike so many buildings in the ancient cities, it was built entirely of stone, so the structure today is seen much as it was when built; one does not have to imagine missing wooden components.

Pabula Vihara Also known as the Parakramabahu Vihara, this is a typical dagoba from the period of Parakramabahu. It is the third largest stupa in Polonnaruwa.

Northern Group

You will need a bicycle or other transport to comfortably explore these very spread-out ruins, which are all north of the city wall. They include the Gal Vihara, probably the most famous group of Buddha images in Sri Lanka, and the Alahana Pirivena group, which is the subject of a Cultural Triangle restoration project.

Rankot Vihara After the three great dagobas at Anuradhapura this is the next biggest in Sri Lanka. Built by Nissanka Malla in clear imitation of the Anuradhapura style, it stands 55 metres high. This building, the Lankatilaka, the Kiri Vihara, the Buddha Seema Pasada and other structures around them form the Alahana Pirivena monastic college group – the name means 'crematory college' since it stood in the royal cremation grounds established by Parakramabahu.

Buddha Seema Pasada This, the tallest building in the Alahana Pirivena group, was the monastery abbot's convocation hall. There is also a fine *mandapaya* (raised platform with decorative pillars) on this south side of the Lankatilaka.

Lankatilaka Built by Parakramabahu, and later restored by Vijayabahu IV, this huge gedige has walls still standing 17 metres high although the roof has collapsed. The cathedral-like aisle leads to a huge, but now headless, standing Buddha. The outer walls are decorated with bas reliefs showing typical Polonnaruwa structures in their original state.

Kiri Vihara This dagoba is credited to Subhadra, Parakramabahu's queen. It was originally known as the Rupavati Cetiya but the present name means 'milk-white', since when the overgrown jungle was cleared, after 700 years of neglect, the original lime plaster was found to be still in perfect condition.

Gal Vihara Across the road from the Kiri Vihara you come to a group of Buddha images which probably mark the high point of Sinhalese rock carving. They are part of Parakramabahu's northern monastery. The Gal Vihara consists of four separate images, all cut from one long slab of granite. At one time each was enshrined within a separate enclosure – you can clearly see the sockets cut into the rock behind the standing image, into which wooden beams would have been inserted.

The standing Buddha is seven metres tall and is said to be the finest of the series. It stands with the arms in an unusual position and this, plus the sorrowful expression on the face, led to the theory that it was an image of the Buddha's disciple Ananda, grieving for his master's departure for nirvana since the reclining image is next to it. The fact that it had its own separate enclosure, and the later discovery of other images with the same arm position, has discredited this theory and it is now accepted that all the images are of the Buddha.

The great reclining image of the Buddha entering nirvana is 14 metres long and the beautiful grain of the stone of the image's face is to many people the most impressive part of the Gal Vihara group. Notice also the subtle depression in the pillow under the head and the sun-wheel symbol on the pillow end. The other two images are both of the seated Buddha; one is smaller and of inferior craftsmanship within a small cavity in the rock.

Demala Maha Seya Not far north of the Gal Vihara is the huge Demala Maha Seya, which looks like a flat-topped hill but is in fact an unfinished attempt by Parakramabahu I to build the world's biggest dagoba. It was largely overgrown but has now come in for some Cultural Triangle restoration work.

Lotus Pond A track to the left from the northern stretch of road leads to the unusual Lotus Bath, nearly eight metres in diameter. You descend into the empty pool by stepping down five concentric rings of eight petals each.

Tivanka Image House The northern road ends at this image house, which, with the lotus pond, is one of the few surviving structures of the Jetavanarama monastery. Its name means 'thrice bent' and refers to the fact that the Buddha image within is in a three-curved position normally reserved for female statues, as opposed to the more upright male form. The building is notable for the energetic dwarves who cavort around the outside and for the fine frescoes within. Some of these date from a later attempt to restore Polonnaruwa by Parakramabahu III, but others are far earlier.

Southern Group

The small southern group is close to the compound of 'top-end' hotels. By bicycle it's a pleasant ride along the bund of the Topawewa.

Potgul Vihara Also known as the library dagoba, this unusual structure is a thickwalled, hollow, stupa-like building which may have been used to store books. It's effectively a circular gedige, and four smaller solid dagobas arranged around this central

dome form the popular Sinhalese *quincunx* arrangement.

Statue The most interesting other structure in the southern group is the statue at the northern end. Standing nearly four metres high, it's an unusually lifelike human representation, in contrast to the normally idealised or stylised Buddha figures. Exactly whom it represents is a subject of some controversy. Some say that the object he is holding is a book and thus the statue is of the Indian religious teacher Agastaya. The more popular theory is that it is a rope representing the 'yoke of kingship' and that the bearded stately figure is Parakramabahu I.

Places to Stay & Eat – bottom end

There are several cheaper places in and around the old town, and a couple of others out near the new town which are fine if you have a decent bicycle. At some of the underpopulated guest houses you can bargain the prices down. Polonnaruwa has a tout problem and you'll probably hear the usual lies about rival hostelries being dirty, closed or whatever.

One of the better places is the *Devi Tourist Home* at Lake View Watte, New Town Rd, about a km south of the old town centre and down the track that's signposted 'Devi Tourist House'. The friendly owner, Mr Johoran, is one of Sri Lanka's small Malay population and a retired chief of the Polonnaruwa police. He has dorm beds at Rs 25 and rooms from Rs 75 to Rs 135 with attached bath. The rooms are fairly clean and there's reasonably priced food.

The *Nippon Hotel* (☎ 027-3205) in the old town centre has some pretty pushy individuals trying to attract custom, but travellers who have lodged there report it to be a good place, with friendly management. Doubles are Rs 125 to Rs 175 and fairly clean, with nets, fans and private bathrooms. There's a small interior garden. The *Orchid Inn* is the other better bet at the cheaper end in the town centre, asking Rs 200 a double for reasonably sized, clean enough rooms with private bathroom. Nearby are the *Wijaya Hotel*, asking Rs 150 for small, dirty doubles with no nets and shared bathrooms, and the *Samudra Guest House* where similarly unclean rooms with private bath are Rs 100.

Also in the old town is the *Chinese Rest House* with rooms at the rear of a large open courtyard which could be lovely if someone was minded to make it so. Meanwhile it's a very basic place charging Rs 75/100 for bare singles/doubles with fan and private bathroom but no net.

On the Batticaloa road the *Ranketha Rest* has moderately clean and spacious rooms with fan, net and attached bath for Rs 250 a single or double. It's used by quite a lot of Sri Lankan tourists and business travellers. A rice and curry dinner is Rs 140.

Places to Stay & Eat – middle & top end

The *Polonnaruwa Rest House* (☎ 027-2299) is on a promontory right by the tank, with superb views north, south and west over the waters, and just a short distance from the heart of the ancient city. There's a fine terrace overlooking the lake where you can sip tea or a cool drink. The rooms are enormous and well enough kept, and cost Rs 400/520 for singles/doubles with breakfast – but there are only 10 of them and they can get fully booked during the tourist season. If you want to make a reservation you have to do it through the Ceylon Hotels Corporation at 63 Janadhipathi Mawatha, Colombo (☎ 01-23501). The restaurant is reasonably good and lunch costs Rs 120, dinner Rs 160.

Also in the centre of things, near the ruins and the middle of the old town, is the friendly and good *Gajaba Hotel* (☎ 027-2392) at Kuruppu Gardens, across the road from the sluice where water runs out from the tank. There are 10 clean rooms with fan, net and attached bath at Rs 200/300. There's also a restaurant doing Sri Lankan, Western and Chinese food, with most main dishes at Rs 60 to Rs 90, and breakfast Rs 60 to Rs 75.

Another good place, peacefully but distantly placed three km from the old town on Second Channel Rd, New Town, is the *Sri Lankan Inns Tourist Hotel* (☎ 027-2403). It's

a lovely cool spacious house with an attractive restaurant in the front, a small fish pond, and good rooms round a grassy courtyard. They cost Rs 275/350 and have fans, nets and attached bath. A car or a bike is distinct advantage here – otherwise bus No 847 from the railway station or the old town passes within about a km.

Finally there are two government-built air-conditioned tourist hotels in a lakeside compound just over two km south of the old town. Both are adequately comfortable and well enough run but under-used. The better bet is the *Hotel Seruwa* (☎ 027-2411) all of whose rooms have balconies or terraces overlooking the lake, which laps the hotel garden. The *Hotel Amalian Nivas* (☎ 027-2405) behind the Seruwa has rooms round a central courtyard or in bungalows. Doubles in either place are Rs 400. Singles in the Seruwa are Rs 400, in the Amalian Nivas Rs 350. A third hotel in the compound is, for the moment at least, closed.

Places to Stay – Giritale

At Giritale, 12 km west of Polonnaruwa on the Habarana road and on the fringe of Minneriya-Giritale Sanctuary, are two more government-created top-end hotels plus a couple of cheaper places, any of which could be used as a base for visiting Polonnaruwa and possibly other places in the ancient cities region if you are motorised. The cheaper places, both on the main Polonnaruwa Road in Giritale, are the small 15-room *Hotel Hemalee* (☎ 027-6257) with singles/doubles at Rs 200/250, and the *Wood Side Inn* at Rs 125/175. The *Royal Lotus Hotel* (☎ 027-6316) overlooking the large Giritale Tank is the most luxurious place in the whole district, with 54 air-con rooms at US$34/38 for bed & breakfast. The 42-room *Giritale Hotel* (☎ 027-6311), also beside the tank, charges Rs 680/910 for bed & breakfast. It too is air-conditioned.

Getting There & Away

Bus Polonnaruwa's main bus station is actually in Kaduruwela, a few km east of the old town on the Batticaloa road. Buses to and from the west pass through the old town centre, but if you're leaving Polonnaruwa and want to make sure of a seat, it's best to start off at Kaduruwela (see Getting Around for transport to/from Kaduruwela).

To and from Kandy there are several buses a day, the last departing at 6 or 7 pm. The route is via Dambulla and Habarana, and the trip takes four hours for Rs 25. There are more buses just to/from Dambulla. For Anuradhapura there are three direct buses daily (three hours, Rs 20), the last leaving Polonnaruwa at 12.15 pm; alternatively you can go to Habarana and pick up another bus there, but a lot of people do this and seats are rare if you board a through-bus at Habarana. There are also daily buses to/from Colombo (six hours).

Train Polonnaruwa is on the Colombo-Batticaloa railway, about 30 km south-east of where it splits from the Colombo-Trincomalee line. Like the bus station, the rail station is at Kaduruwela. Violence in the east at one time had virtually closed this line but by mid-1992 there were three trains a week in each direction. However, in July 1992 a reported 40 passengers were killed in a particularly senseless massacre down the line in the Batticaloa district, for which Tamil Tigers were blamed, and as this book was going to press we heard that the line was closed again – for how long, who knows? Trains take six to nine hours from Colombo to Polonnaruwa, for Rs 122 in 2nd and Rs 44 in 3rd.

Getting Around
There are frequent buses between the old town and Kaduruwela, where the bus and rail stations are located. Bus No 847 runs between the rail station, the old town and the new town.

Bicycles are the ideal transport for Polonnaruwa's not too widely scattered monuments. Some guest houses in the old town centre, like the Orchid Inn and the Wijaya Hotel, hire out bikes for usually Rs 60 a day. Some of the bikes are the usual Sri Lankan old nails; try them out before

committing yourself to hours on their saddles. The Devi Tourist Home has good-condition bikes for Rs 75; the Rest House also hires out reasonable machines. Bikes from H S Weerasinghe's (Uncle Weera's) opposite the public library have also been recommended.

A car and driver can be hired for about three hours for around Rs 200, long enough to have a quick look around the ruins.

MEDIRIGIRIYA
The Mandalagiri Vihara near Medirigiriya, a vatadage virtually identical in design and measurement to that of Polonnaruwa, is about 30 km north of Polonnaruwa. You may find the effort of getting there worthwhile, for while the Polonnaruwa vatadage is crowded among many other structures, the vatadage here stands by itself on top of a low hill. This remote site has an eerie, lost-city feel.

An earlier structure may have been built around the 2nd century AD, but the one that stands there today was constructed in the 8th century. A granite flight of steps leads up the hill to the vatadage, which has concentric circles of 16, 20 and 32 pillars around the central dagoba. Four large seated Buddhas, one of which is still in good condition, face the four cardinal directions. The vatadage is noted for its ornamented stone screens. Look for the medicine bath shaped like the bottom half of a coffin. People added herbs to the water and lay down in it if they were sick.

Getting There & Away
Without your own transport, getting to Medirigiriya can be a little time consuming and, as usual on Sri Lankan buses, tiring. Medirigiriya is about 24 km north-east of Minneriya, which is on the Polonnaruwa-Habarana road, north-west of Giritale. To reach Medirigiriya from Polonnaruwa, Habarana or Dambulla by bus involves at least one change at Giritale or Minneriya, where you can catch a bus – or maybe a three-wheeler or taxi – to Medirigiriya. The vatadage is 15 minutes' walk from the bus stop.

DIMBULAGALA

Off the Polonnaruwa-Batticaloa road, about eight km south of Mannampitiya, a rock called Gunners Quoin or Dimbulagala stands out of the surrounding scrub. There are hundreds of caves cut out of the rock in a Buddhist hermitage which has been occupied almost continuously since the 3rd century BC. The inhabitants are not totally devoid of worldly considerations, however: one traveller reported being asked for a totally spurious Rs 100 'entry fee' by a young monk waiting at the foot of the rocks.

HABARANA

This small crossroads village is centrally placed between all the main ancient city sites and has a hotel complex principally for package tourists, although some better-heeled independent visitors also use it. There are a couple of cheaper accommodation alternatives and Habarana also has the nearest railway station to Dambulla and Sigiriya.

Places to Stay

The Village (☎ 066-8316) has 100 rooms available at US$45 a single or double from mid-December to mid-March, US$35 the rest of the year. There's a fine open-air dining area and bar, a swimming pool and extensive grounds. The whole complex is done with considerable taste; the white-painted rooms are functional but comfortable, with fan. Sharing the same compound, *The Lodge* (☎ 066-8321) has 150 rooms at US$60 mid-December to mid-March, US$50 other times. The rooms here are rather more luxurious and have air-con, though the food, one traveller wrote, is unrelentingly German.

Habarana also has a *Rest House* (☎ 066-8355) with rooms at Rs 200/250. It's just to the north of the new hotel complex, while just to the south is the very pleasant little *Habarana Inn* with singles/doubles at about Rs 275/350 including breakfast.

ANURADHAPURA

For over 1000 years Sinhalese kings, with occasional south Indian interlopers, ruled from the great city of Anuradhapura. It is the most extensive and important of the Sri Lankan ancient cities, but its size and the length of its history, and equally the length of time since its downfall, make it more difficult to assimilate than younger, shorter-lived Polonnaruwa. If you allow more than one day to investigate it, the effort is amply repaid!

Anuradhapura first became a capital in 380 BC under Pandukabhaya, but it was under Devanampiya Tissa (260-210 BC), in whose reign Buddhism reached Sri Lanka, that it first rose to great importance. Soon Anuradhapura became a great and glittering city, only to fall before a south Indian inva-

---

Tanks

A casual glance at a map of Sri Lanka would indicate that the island is dotted with lakes, even in the dry northern area. It's a false impression, for lake-like though they may be, most of them are in fact artificial 'tanks'. Many of them are around 2000 years old, and virtually all of them are older than 1000 years. Even today they would be quite considerable engineering projects – for their time they are simply fantastic.

The tanks were constructed by the great kings of ancient Ceylon to provide irrigation water for the growing of rice, particularly in the dry northern region. They are in many ways a more lasting reminder of their power and ability than the great cities they also built; for the cities reverted to the jungle, whereas the tanks have become part of the landscape.

Useful though the tanks may have been, and indeed still are, one suspects that building them was not purely an altruistic activity for the great kings. Like many other dry-region rulers the Sinhalese kings seem to have taken a considerable interest in water and its enjoyment – as the many pools and ponds at Anuradhapura and Polonnaruwa testify. Two of the greatest tank builders were Mahasena (276-303 AD) and Dhatusena (459-477 AD). The latter is better known for his death at the hands of his son Kasyapa, the architect of Sigiriya. ■

sion – a fate that was to befall it repeatedly for over 1000 years. But before long the Sinhalese hero Dutugemunu led an army from a refuge in the far south to recapture Anuradhapura. The 'Dutu' part of his name, incidentally, is from 'Duttha' meaning 'undutiful', for his father, fearing for his son's safety, forbade him to attempt to recapture Anuradhapura. His son disobeyed him – sending his father a woman's ornament to indicate what he thought of his courage.

Dutugemunu, who ruled from 161 to 137 BC, set in motion a vast building programme which included some of the most impressive monuments in Anuradhapura today. Other important kings who followed him included Valagambahu, who lost his throne to another Indian invasion but later regained it, and Mahasena (276-303 AD) who built the colossal Jetavanarama dagoba and is thought of as the last 'great' king of Anuradhapura. He also held the record for tank construction, building 16 of them in all, plus a major canal. Anuradhapura was to survive for more than another 500 years before finally being replaced by Polonnaruwa, but it was again and again harassed by invasions from south India – invasions made easier by the cleared lands and great roads which were a product of Anuradhapura's importance.

Orientation & Information

The ancient city lies to the west and north of the modern town of Anuradhapura, which has a population of about 30,000. The main road from Kandy, Dambulla and Polonnaruwa enters the town on the north-east side then travels south to the centre, which is a spread-out affair with two bus stations – the old bus station near the market, and the new bus station two km further south. Buses heading for the new bus station usually call at the old one on the way through, and will also let you off anywhere else along their route – so you can minimise the walk to your accommodation.

The ancient city is spread out and has few concentrations of related structures like Polonnaruwa. Nevertheless there is one important starting point for exploring it, and

that is the sacred bo-tree, or Sri Maha Bodhi, and the cluster of buildings around it. As at Polonnaruwa, a bicycle is the ideal vehicle for exploring Anuradhapura.

A US$7 entry ticket (or a Cultural Triangle round ticket) is needed by non-Sri Lankans visiting the northern areas of the ancient city: both types of ticket can be bought at the ticket office by the archaeological museum on the west side of the city. Opening hours for the areas covered by the tickets are 6 am to 6 pm. Spots where you don't need a ticket include the sacred bo-tree, the Ruvanvelisaya dagoba and the Isurumuniya temple.

Around the Sacred Bo-Tree

The sacred bo-tree is central to Anuradhapura in both a spiritual and physical sense. The huge tree has grown from a sapling brought from Bodh Gaya in India by the Princess Sangamitta, sister of Mahinda who introduced the Buddha's teachings to Sri Lanka, so it has a connection to the very basis of the Sinhalese religion. It serves as a reminder of the force that inspired the creation of all the great buildings at Anuradhapura and is within walking distance of many of the most interesting monuments. The whole area around the Sri Maha Bodhi, Brazen Palace and Ruvanvelisaya dagoba was once probably part of the Maha Vihara – the 'Great Temple'.

Sri Maha Bodhi The sacred bo-tree is the oldest historically authenticated tree in the world, for it has been tended by an uninterrupted succession of guardians for over 2000 years, even during the periods of Indian occupation. The steps leading up to the tree's platform are very old but the golden railing around it is quite modern. Thousands of devotees come to make offerings at weekends and particularly on poya days.

Brazen Palace So called because it once had a bronze (brazen) roof, the ruins of the Brazen Palace stand close to the bo-tree. The remains of 1600 columns are all that is left

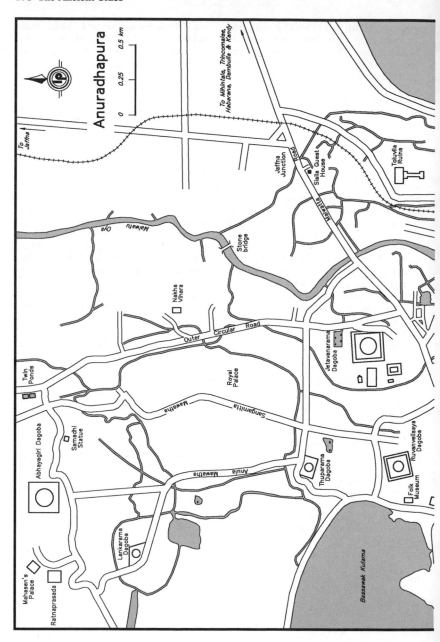

Anuradhapura

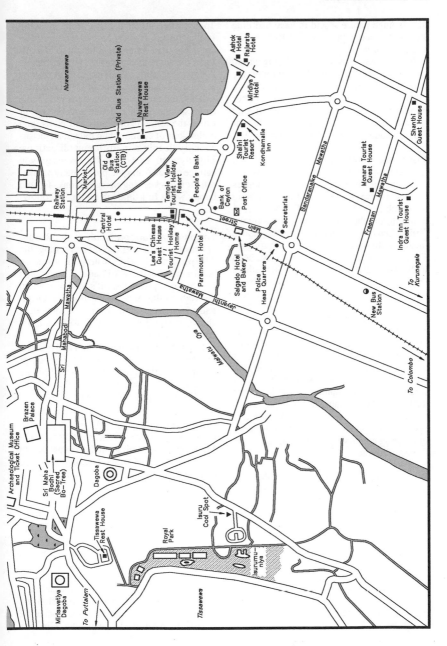

of this huge palace – said to have had nine storeys and accommodation for 1000 monks and attendants.

It was originally built by Dutugemunu over 2000 years ago but down through the ages was rebuilt many times, each time a little less grandiosely. The current, rather nondescript jumble of pillars is all that remains from the last rebuild – that of Parakramabahu around the 12th century AD.

Museums Anuradhapura's archaeological museum, open from 8 am to 5 pm except Tuesdays and public holidays, also houses the ticket office for the ancient city. Among the exhibits are a restored relic chamber, as found during the excavation of the Kantaka Cetiya Dagoba at nearby Mihintale, and a large-scale model of Anuradhapura's Thuparama Vatadage, as it would have been with its wooden roof. Amusing items include the carved squatting plates from Anuradhapura's Western Monasteries, whose monks had forsaken the luxurious monasteries of their more worldly brothers. To show their contempt for these luxury-loving effetes they carved beautiful stone squat-style toilets – with their brother monks' monasteries represented on the bottom! Their urinals illustrated the god of wealth, showering handfuls of coins down the hole. A short distance north of the archaeological museum there's a folk museum, open from 9 am to 5 pm except Fridays, illustrating country life in Sri Lanka's North Central Province.

Ruvanvelisaya Dagoba Behind the folk museum, this fine white dagoba is guarded by a wall of hundreds of elephants standing shoulder to shoulder. Apart from a few beside the western entrance, most of them are modern replacements.

The Ruvanvelisaya is said to be Dutugemunu's finest construction, but he didn't live to see its completion. However as he lay on his deathbed, his brother organised a false bamboo-and-cloth finish to the dagoba, so that Dutugemunu's final sight could be of his 'completed' masterpiece.

Today, after much damage from invading Indian forces, it rises 55 metres, considerably less than its original height. Nor is its form the same as the earlier 'bubble' shape. A limestone statue south of the great dagoba is popularly thought to be of Dutugemunu.

The land around the dagoba is rather like a pleasant green park, dotted with patches of ruins, the remains of ponds and pools, and collections of columns and pillars, all picturesquely leaning in different directions. Slightly south-east of the Ruvanvelisaya you can see one of Anuradhapura's many monks' refectories – keeping so many monks fed and happy was a full-time job for the lay followers.

Thuparama Dagoba North of the Ruvanvelisaya in a beautiful woodland setting, the Thuparama is the oldest dagoba in Anuradhapura, if not Sri Lanka. Constructed by Devanampiya Tissa, it's said to contain the right collar-bone of the Buddha. Originally in the classical 'heap of paddy rice' shape, it was restored in 1840 in a more conventional bell-shape.

It stands only 19 metres high and at some point in its life was converted into a vatadage or circular relic house. The circles of pillars of diminishing height around the dagoba would have supported the conical roof.

Northern Ruins

Quite a long stretch of road, starting as Anula Mawatha, runs north from the Thuparama to the next clump of ruins. Coming back you can take an alternative route and visit the Jetavanarama dagoba.

Abhayagiri Dagoba This huge dagoba – confused by some books and maps with the Jetavanarama – was the centrepiece of a 5000-monk monastery created in the 1st century BC. The name means 'fearless Giri' and refers to a Jain monk whose hermitage was once at this spot. When Valagambahu fled the city before an Indian invasion, he was taunted by the monk and so, when he regained the throne 14 years later, Giri was promptly executed and this great dagoba was built over his hermitage.

After a later restoration by Parakramabahu the dagoba may have stood over 100 metres high but today it is 75 metres. The dagoba has some interesting bas-reliefs, including an energetic elephant pulling up a tree near the western stairway. A large slab with a Buddha footprint can be seen on the north side of the dagoba and the eastern and western steps have unusual moonstones made of concentric stone slabs.

Mahasen's Palace North-west of the Abhayagiri, this ruined palace is notable for having the finest carved moonstone in Sri Lanka – photographers will be disappointed that the railing around it makes an unshadowed picture almost impossible. This is a peaceful wooded area full of butterflies, and makes a good place to stop and cool off during a tour of the ruins.

Ratnaprasada Follow the loop road a little further and you will find the finest guardstones in Anuradhapura. These of the 8th century AD, illustrating a cobra-king, were the final refinement of guardstone design. You can see examples of much earlier guardstone design at the Mirisavatiya dagoba.

Towards the end of Anuradhapura's supremacy the Ratnaprasada ('Gem Palace') was the scene of a major conflict between its Buddhist monks and the king of the day. Court officials at odds with the king took sanctuary in the Ratnaprasada but the king sent his supporters in to capture and execute them. The monks, disgusted at this invasion of a sacred place, departed en masse. The general populace, equally disgusted, besieged the Ratnaprasada, captured and executed the king's supporters and forced the king to apologise to the departed monks in order to bring them back to the city and restore peace.

South of the Ratnaprasada is the Lankarama, a 1st-century BC vatadage.

Samadhi Buddha Statue Returning from your guardstone and moonstone investigations, you can continue east from the Abhayagiri to this 4th-century AD seated statue, regarded as one of the finest Buddha statues in Sri Lanka. This is a site visiting dignitaries and heads of state are inevitably brought to admire.

Twin Ponds The swimming pool-like Kuttam Pokuna, or 'twin ponds', the finest ponds in Anuradhapura, are a little further along this road, on the other side. They were probably used by monks from the monastery attached to the Abhayagiri. Although they are referred to as twins, the southern pond, 28 metres in length, is smaller than the 40-metre northern pond. Water entered the smaller pond through a *makara's* (dragon-demon's) mouth and then flowed to the larger through an underground pipe. Notice the five-headed cobra figure close to the *makara*.

Royal Palace If you return towards the Samadhi Buddha statue but turn south down Sangamitta Mawatha, you'll pass after about 1½ km through the Royal Palace site. This palace was built by Vijayabahu I in the 12th century AD, after Anuradhapura's fall as the Sinhalese capital, and is indicative of the attempts made to retain at least a foothold in the old capital.

Close to it is a deep and ancient well and the Mahapali, a monks' refectory notable for its immense trough, nearly three metres long and two wide, for the lay followers to fill with rice for the monks. You can also find in the Royal Palace area a tooth-relic temple, the Dalada Maligawa, which may have been the first Temple of the Tooth. The sacred Buddha's tooth originally came to Sri Lanka in 313 AD.

Jetavanarama Dagoba

The huge dome of the Jetavanarama dagoba rises from a clearing back towards the centre of the ancient city. Built in the 3rd century AD by Mahasena, it may have originally stood over 100 metres but today is about 70 metres – a similar height to the Abhayagiri with which it has been confused. It has been under reconstruction for several years. The Jetavanarama is made solidly of bricks, and an early British guidebook to Ceylon calculated there were enough of them to make a three-metre-high wall stretching all the way from London to Edinburgh. Behind it stand the ruins of the monastery it formed part of, which housed 3000 monks. One building has door jambs still standing, over eight metres high, with another three metres underground. At one time massive doors opened to reveal a large Buddha image.

Buddhist Railing A little south of the Jetavanarama, and on the other side of the road, there is a stone railing built in imitation of a log wall. It encloses a site 42 metres by 34 metres but the building within has long disappeared.

Along the Banks of the Tissawewa
Three very interesting sites can be visited in a stroll or ride along the banks of the Tissawewa tank.

Mirisavatiya Dagoba This huge dagoba, the first built by Dutugemunu after he captured the city, is almost across the road from the Tissawewa Rest House. Legend has it that building began after Dutugemunu went for a bathe in the tank leaving his sceptre, which contained a relic of the Buddha, implanted in the ground. When he returned he found it impossible to pull his sceptre out, and taking this as an auspicious sign had the dagoba built. At the time of writing it's being rebuilt. To its north-east was yet another monks' refectory, complete with the usual huge stone troughs into which the faithful poured boiled rice.

Royal Park If you start down the Tissawewa tank bund from the Mirisavatiya, you soon come to these extensive royal pleasure gardens, known as the 'Park of the Goldfish'. They cover 14 hectares and contain two ponds skilfully designed to fit around the huge boulders in the park. The ponds have fine elephant reliefs on their sides. It was

here that Prince Saliya, son of Dutugemunu, was said to have met Asokamala, a commoner, whom he married, thereby forsaking his right to the throne. Atop the rocks was once a platform intended for looking out over the tank.

Isurumuniya This rock temple, dating from the reign of Devanampiya Tissa (3rd century BC), has some very fine carvings. One or two of these – including one of elephants playfully splashing water – remain in their original place on the rock face beside a square pool fed from the Tissawewa, but most of them have been moved into a small museum within the temple, where you'll be asked for a donation. Best known of the sculptures is the 'lovers', which dates from around the 5th century AD and is of the Gupta school (the artistic style of the Indian Gupta dynasty of the 4th and 5th centuries). It was probably brought here from elsewhere, since it was carved into a separate slab. Popular legend holds that it shows Prince Saliya and Asokamala.

One bas-relief shows a palace scene – said to be of Dutugemunu with Saliya and Asokamala flanking him and a third figure,

The Lovers

possibly a servant, behind them. There is also a fine sculpture showing a man and the head of a horse. The image house south of the pond has a reclining Buddha cut from the rock. The view over the tank from the top of the temple is superb at sunset.

South of the Isurumuniya are extensive remains of the Vessagiriya cave monastery complex, which dates from much the same time.

The Tanks

Anuradhapura has three great tanks. Nuwarawewa on the east side of the city, covering about 1200 hectares, is the largest. It was built around 20 BC and is well away from most of the old city. The 160-hectare Tissawewa is the southern tank in the old city. The northern tank – and the oldest, probably dating from around the 4th century BC – is the 120-hectare Bassawak Kulama (the Tamil word for tank is *kulam*). Off to the north-west of the Bassawak Kulama are the ruins of the Western Monasteries, where the monks dressed in scraps of clothing taken from corpses and lived only on rice (see Museums, earlier in this section, for more on them).

Places to Stay

Nothing, apart from one of the two rest houses, is very convenient for the ancient city. Nor are many places very near the bus stations. Anuradhapura accommodation touts tend to hang around the old bus station, even boarding buses coming into town to try to funnel travellers towards their pet hostelries.

Places to Stay – bottom end & middle

There's nowhere of specially good value at the bottom end. One place that at least has lots of experience with budget travellers is the *Shanthi Guest House* (☎ 025-2515) in the south of town at 891 Mailagas Junction, 1½ km east of the new bus station. They'll pick you up from the town if you phone, and there's a 15% discount on room rates if you arrive without a tout. The Shanthi has a whole range of basic rooms with net and fan,

from small singles with shared bath for Rs 100, to sizeable doubles with attached bath for Rs 200. There's good food available but it's Rs 80 or so for noodle or fried rice dishes, more for other choices. They have motorbikes (Rs 300 a day) and bicycles (Rs 70) for rent, and will give you a three-hour car tour of the ancient city for Rs 300. The owner's lovely 1931 Austin 7 is still going strong!

The *Monara Tourist Guest House* at 63 Freeman Mawatha on the way from the new bus station to the Shanthi has bare, unloved rooms with fan and net for Rs 150 a single, Rs 225 a double – not very good value. Better, according to reports, is the *Indra Inn Tourist Guest House* at 745 Freeman Mawatha, actually down a side road south from Freeman Mawatha shortly past the Monara. It's a clean family house with just three rooms at Rs 120 a double, Rs 150 a triple. Fans and nets are included. A good dinner is Rs 60.

The other main group of relative cheapies, none very enticing, is along a short street just north of the roundabout at the top of Main St. The *Tourist Holiday Home* has rooms at Rs 150/200 downstairs, Rs 175/225 upstairs. They have mosquito net, fan and attached bathroom, but aren't very clean. The *Temple View Tourist Holiday Resort* is even more basic. Singles/doubles are Rs 150/200. And there's no view of any kind of temple! In the same street are the tatty *Paramount Hotel*, and, round the corner, the better-looking *Lee's Chinese Guest House*.

If you can afford Rs 350 for a single or double (with private bath), the *Shalini Tourist Rest* (☎ 025-2425) at 41/388 Harischandra Mawatha, a km from the old bus station (but close to the route buses take between the old and new stations), is a very well kept home with good-size doubles. There's good food too but some dishes – like mixed noodles at Rs 75 – are expensive. If you stay you can rent a good bicycle for Rs 75 a day. Next door at 42/388 Harischandra Mawatha, the *Kondhamalie Inn* charges Rs 200/250 for reasonable rooms with net, fan and attached bath.

Cheaper meals (lunch or dinner Rs 75, breakfast Rs 50) and bikes are again available.

Set among fields in the north of town at 260/34 Malwatta Rd, Jaffna Junction, *Sisila Guest House* has rooms at Rs 75/100 with shared bath and Rs 150/200 with attached bath. It's clean enough and there's good food and bikes for hire, but it's out of the way unless your bus enters Anuradhapura from the east (which many do). From the town centre take a bus or walk two km north to Jaffna Junction then walk a couple of hundred metres towards the ancient city. The guest house is off the road, to the left.

Places to Stay – top end

The *Tissawewa Rest House* (☎ 025-2299) is one of those elderly places with class that the Sri Lankans can do so well, and has the considerable advantage of being right in there with the ruins. But since it is in the 'sacred area' it can't provide alcohol – although you can bring your own with you. A big verandah looks out on gardens with lots of monkeys, and close behind the rest house is the Tissawewa tank. The 25 rooms cost Rs 410 to Rs 490 for singles and Rs 490 to Rs 575 for doubles and are mostly enormous – but there are a couple of minuscule ones, so look before signing in. Food is expensive (Rs 200 for a rice and curry dinner).

Guests at the Tissawewa can use the good clean swimming pool in the garden at Anuradhapura's other rest house – the *Nuwarawewa Rest House* (☎ 025-2565) in the new town, backing on to the Nuwarawewa tank. The Nuwarawewa too is pleasant in its own way – even if the atmosphere at dinner is rather stiff. Of the 60 rooms, the 35 with air-con mostly face the tank and cost Rs 660/740 for singles/doubles, while the fan-cooled 'economy rooms' on the landward side are Rs 360/440.

A clump of newer tourist hotels sits on Rowing Club Rd, further round the south side of the Nuwarawewa, and less conveniently situated. The best is the 41-room *Miridiya Hotel* (☎ 025-2112, 2519) with a pool and a garden running down to the tank. Some of the rooms are recently modernised and the best, with good tank views, air-con and bathtubs, are Rs 740/820. The cheapest, with shower and fan, are Rs 450/535. Across the road the *Rajarata Hotel* (☎ 025-2578) charges Rs 535/615 for moderately sized rooms with shower and air-con. Only a few have tank views but there's a pleasant garden with a pool. The nearby *Ashok Hotel* (☎ 025-2753) is more down-at-heel but a fair bit cheaper at Rs 300 a single or double for large rooms with fan, net and, upstairs, balconies overlooking the tank.

Places to Eat & Drink

There's little in the way of eating places apart from the places to stay. King coconut vendors lurk in strategic spots to quench your thirst while you're touring the ruins. Just east of the Isurumuniya, the *Isuru Cool Spot* is a reasonable place for refreshments. The *Tissawewa Rest House* is also a good place to cool off with a (non-alcoholic) drink. The *Central Hotel* near the market is a large bar with lots of tables and chairs to sit at – about as close to a pub as you'll find anywhere in Sri Lanka's ancient cities!

Getting There & Away

Bus Buses to/from Kandy via Dambulla start from the old bus station and take about four hours: there are about a dozen daily each way and the last leaves Anuradhapura at about 3 or 4 pm. The fare is Rs 26. Dambulla-only services may run a little later. There are three direct buses to Polonnaruwa from the new bus station, between 7 and 9.30 am – a three-hour trip costing Rs 20. If you've missed the direct buses you can get a bus to Kekirawa or Habarana and change – but you may end up standing much of the way.

There are plenty of Colombo-Anuradhapura buses each day; the trip takes about five hours for Rs 32. Departures in Anuradhapura are from the old bus station and the last is about 8 pm. Trincomalee buses go from the new bus station.

Train Schedules are affected by the security situation in the north. At the time of writing there are departures from Colombo Fort to Anuradhapura daily at 5.45 am (usually very crowded) and 2.05 pm, and from Anuradhapura to Colombo at 5.05 and 9.14 am. The trip takes 4¼ to five hours and costs Rs 96.50 in 2nd class, Rs 35 in 3rd. It's usually more comfortable than a bus, if you get a seat. One of the trains in each direction daily goes all the way to/from Matara. You can also travel between Anuradhapura and Kandy by train, changing at Polgahawela.

Getting Around

Like Polonnaruwa the city is too spread out to investigate comfortably on foot. A three-hour taxi or three-wheeler tour costs Rs 250 or Rs 300 but a bicycle (normally Rs 50 a half day, Rs 75 a day) is the nicest way to explore the ruins in a leisurely fashion. Prices depend on where you hire them; the rest houses and several guest houses can provide them.

Numerous buses run between the old and new bus stations, via Main St.

MIHINTALE

Eleven km north-east of Anuradhapura on the road to Trincomalee, Mihintale is of enormous spiritual significance to the Sinhalese because it is where Buddhism originated in Sri Lanka. In 247 BC King Devanampiya Tissa of Anuradhapura, while deer hunting around the hill at Mihintale, met Mahinda, son of the great Indian Buddhist-Emperor Ashoka, and was converted to Buddhism. Each year a great festival is held at Mihintale on the Poson full moon night (usually June). Exploring Mihintale involves quite a climb so you are wise to visit it early in the morning or late in the afternoon to avoid the midday heat. Mihintale village itself is a peaceful place.

The Stairway

A ruined 'hospital' and the remains of a quincunx of buildings, laid out like the five dots on a dice, flank the roadway before you reach the base of the steps. In a series of flights, 1840 ancient granite slab steps lead majestically up the hillside. The first flight is the widest and shallowest. Higher up the steps are narrower and steeper.

Kantaka Cetiya

At the first landing a smaller flight of steps leads off to the right, to this partly ruined dagoba. Twelve metres high and 130 metres around its base, it was built some time before 60 BC. It is particularly notable for its altar-piece panels with their excellent sculptures of dwarves, geese and other figures. The dagoba, which at one time was probably over 30 metres high, was only discovered in the mid-1930s. You can see a reconstruction of its interior design in the museum in Anuradhapura.

South of the Kantaka Cetiya, where a big boulder is cleft by a cave, if you look up you'll see what's thought to be the oldest inscription in Sri Lanka, predating Pali. Through the cave, ledges on the cliff face acted as meditation posts for the thousands of monks once resident here.

Monks' Refectory

At the top of the next flight of steps, on the second landing, is the monks' refectory with huge stone troughs which the lay-followers were responsibile for keeping filled with rice for monks. There are also two 10th-century AD stone slabs inscribed with the rules and regulations of the monastery. They were erected during the reign of King Mahinda IV. Looking back from here you get an excellent view of Anuradhapura.

Ambasthale Dagoba

The final narrow, steep stairway leads to the place where Mahinda and the king met. The Ambasthale Dagoba is built over the spot where Mahinda stood. Nearby stands a statue of the king where he stood. On the opposite side of the dagoba from the statue is a cloister and behind that a very large, recently constructed white sitting Buddha. The name Ambasthale means 'mango tree' and refers to a riddle about mango trees which Mahinda

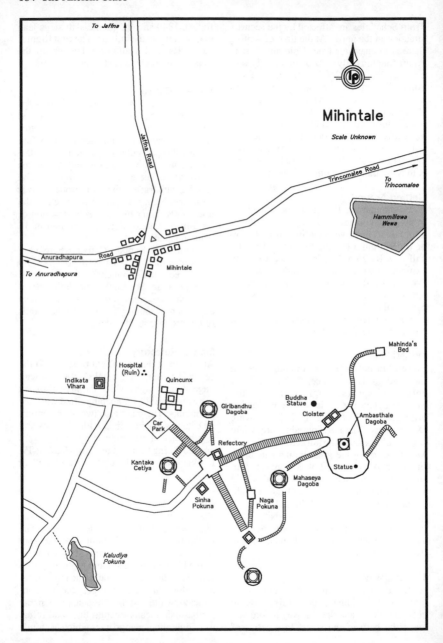

used to test the king's intelligence. There's a Rs 20 entry fee for this area.

Mahaseya Dagoba
A path from the Ambasthale Dagoba leads to a higher dagoba thought to contain relics of Mahinda, with another excellent view of Anuradhapura.

Mahinda's Bed
Above the Ambasthale Dagoba is the huge rock said to be the 'bed' on which Mahinda waited for his meeting with the king.

Naga Pokuna
Halfway back down the steep flight of steps from the Ambasthale Dagoba, a path leads off to the left, around the side of the hill topped by the Mahaseya Dagoba. Here you will find the Naga Pokuna, or 'snake pool' – so called because of the five-headed cobra carved in low relief on the rock face of the pool. Its tail is said to reach right down to the bottom of the pool. If you continue on from here you can eventually loop back to the second landing.

Sinha Pokuna
Just below the monks' refectory on the second landing is this small pool, surmounted by a rampant lion reckoned to be one of the best pieces of animal carving in the country. Anyone placing one hand on each paw would be right in line for the stream of water from the lion's mouth. There are some fine friezes around this pool.

Kaludiya Pokuna
If, instead of returning to the second landing from the Sinha Pokuna, you continue along the gently sloping track down to the road, then walk a little southward, you soon reach the turn-off to the Kaludiya Pokuna or 'dark-water pool'. This artificial pool was carefully constructed to look like a real one, and features a rock-carved bath-house and the ruins of a small monastery. It's a peaceful, quiet and beautiful little escape. Back towards the village of Mihintale you could search for the

hermit caves in the 'royal cave hill' or divert into the ruins of the Indikatu Vihara.

Getting There & Away
It's a fairly short bus ride, costing Rs 5, from Anuradhapura out to Mihintale. A taxi there and back, with two hours to climb the stairs, is about Rs 300.

Places to Stay
There's a small *Rest House* near the junction of the Trincomalee and Jaffna roads.

WILPATTU NATIONAL PARK
Wilpattu, covering 1085 sq km west of Anuradhapura, is Sri Lanka's biggest national park, and used to be the most visited until the ethnic violence closed it in 1985. There has been intermittent talk of a reopening but nothing has happened up to the time of writing.

When open, Wilpattu offers the best chance in Sri Lanka of seeing leopards. Among the many other animals are spotted deer, wild boar, buffalo and mongoose. You have a good chance of spotting crocodiles in the *villus* – small seasonal lakes which dot the generally dry landscape and from which the park's name is derived. Some of the lakes are alive with birds during the November to January nesting season. Between the lakes the park is generally grassy plains, sand dunes and, in the east, forest.

Approximately 240 km of jeep track loop confusingly through the park. When the park was open, you either had to hire a jeep from the park authorities or go on one of their minibus tours. You are likely to see more wildlife in a jeep. Wilpattu is always closed to visitors during September, when it's dangerously dry.

Places to Stay
At the last count there were seven wildlife bungalows in the park, as well as a Wildlife & Nature Protection Society bungalow, great for bird-watching, just outside it. The bungalows at Kali Villu and Manikepola Uttu, towards the northern end of the park, are handy for the larger lakes near Portugal Bay

and for the coast. There were a couple of hotels on the approaches to the park, but Anuradhapura is also a convenient day-trip base.

Getting There & Away

The seven-km road to the park entrance at Hunuwilagama starts at the hamlet of Thimbiriwewa, about 30 km from Anuradhapura on the Puttalam road. There used to be buses from Anuradhapura to the park twice daily.

AUKANA

The magnificent 12-metre-high standing Buddha of Aukana is believed to have been sculpted during the reign of Dhatusena in the 5th century AD. The Kalawewa Tank, one of the many gigantic tanks he constructed, is only a couple of km from the statue, and the road to Aukana from Kekirawa runs along the tank bund for several km. Aukana means 'sun-eating' and dawn is the best time to see it – when the sun's first rays light up the huge statue's finely carved features.

The image stood out in the open for many years but now an ugly (even if authentic) brick shelter has been constructed over it. Note that although the statue is still narrowly joined at the back to the rock face it is cut from, the lotus plinth on which it stands is a separate piece.

The Aukana Buddha is well known and frequently visited despite its isolation. Few people realise, however, that at Sasseruwa, 11 km west, on the site of an ancient cave monastery in the jungle, is another image, also 12 metres high although incomplete and of inferior workmanship. A legend relates that the two images were carved at the same time in a competition between master and pupil. Carving them took several years but it was the finer Aukana image, the work of the master, which was finished first and the Sasseruwa image was abandoned by the pupil.

Getting There & Away

There is a direct bus to Aukana leaving Dambulla in mid-morning. Alternatively

you can get any bus to Kekirawa and take an Aukana bus (a few daily) from there. Aukana is also fairly close to the railway from Colombo to Trincomalee and Polonnaruwa. There is an Aukana railway halt only a short walk from the statue but it's unlikely that express trains will halt there. Kalawewa station is, however, only about four km away and trains do stop there. A taxi from Kekirawa will set you back about Rs 250 for a Kekirawa-Aukana-Kalawewa or back-to-Kekirawa circuit.

YAPAHUWA

This rock fortress rising 100 metres from a plain is similar in concept to the much better known Sigiriya. It's four km from Maho railway junction, where the Trincomalee line splits from the Colombo-Anuradhapura line, and about seven km from the Kurunegala-Anuradhapura road, but a long way from anywhere else.

Yapahuwa, the 'excellent mountain', was originally constructed in the early 1200s as a fortress against the invading Kalingas of south India. Between 1272 and 1284 it was the Sinhalese capital and it is believed that it was from Yapahuwa at that time that invading Indians carried away the sacred tooth-relic (now in Kandy), only for it to be recovered in 1288 by Parakramabahu I. A building to the east of the main fortifications is possibly the tooth temple.

Yapahuwa's magnificently carved ornamental staircase, which led up to the ledge holding its royal palace, is its best point. The porch on the stairway had very fine pierced-stone windows, one of which is now in the museum in Colombo.

PANDUVASNAVARA & DAMBADENIYA

About midway between Chilaw on the west coast (north of Negombo) and Kurunegala, the ruins at Panduvasnavara are in unusually good condition but somewhat difficult to find. There's a picturesque village next to the ruins, and a pleasant tank. Panduvasnavara was a Sinhalese capital in the 13th or 14th century but only excavated after WW II. Its citadel with walls 300 metres long contains an interesting Royal Palace area surrounded by a fine moat. One of the most unusual items in the palace is the site of an external flame which was fuelled by the excreta of the palace residents!

Dambadeniya, 30 km west of Kurunegala, was the Sinhalese capital after Polon- naruwa's fall in the 13th century. There's little more than a former Dalada Maligawa (Tooth Temple), a bo-tree and a dagoba left, but it's a secluded and beautiful spot.

Kurunegala has two *Rest Houses* – one finely situated by its lake, and sometimes full; the other in the town with doubles at Rs 200 including private bathroom.

East Coast Beaches

Sri Lanka's east coast has some of the country's most attractive beaches, some interesting towns, and two national parks just inland. It was always much less developed for tourism than the west and south coasts and conveniently, it's at its best climatically from about May to September, when the monsoon is making things unpleasant on the west coast. Sadly, most of the east has been off-limits to travellers since the ethnic violence took a grip in the mid-1980s. At the time of writing it is possible to reach – with no guarantees of safety – Trincomalee, the nearby beaches at Uppuveli and Nilaveli, and, sometimes, Arugam Bay towards the south of the east coast. Batticaloa has been retaken by government forces after having been fairly firmly under Tamil Tiger control at one stage – but the region around it remains the main centre of Tiger activity apart from the north of the island, and is definitely not worth straying into for the moment. In one incident in the Batticaloa district in July 1992, for which the Tigers were thought responsible, Muslims were ordered off a Batticaloa-Colombo train, and when no one budged, the passengers were attacked with grenades and automatic rifles, leaving a reported 40 dead.

The situation could develop either way – new troubles might close Trincomalee again or, who knows, peace might even break out along the whole coast – so if you're thinking of heading to the east, talk to locals and travellers elsewhere in Sri Lanka to find out the latest picture. If you're the type of person who likes to go where there may be risks, consider registering with your embassy in Colombo first.

At present, the few places you can reach are a shadow of what they once were, with only a few accommodation places open and much visible damage from the fighting. But a reliable peace would undoubtedly lead many old places to reopen and new ones to be built.

TRINCOMALEE

Trincomalee (or 'Trinco') really didn't stand a chance of peace when Sri Lanka's ethnic jigsaw started to fall apart. For one thing, it's highly strategic as it has one of the world's finest harbours. For another, the population of the town and surrounding district before the troubles began was almost equally divided between Sinhalese, Tamils and Muslims. By 1992, after several years of sporadic horrors during which travellers could only occasionally get through to it, the town was controlled by government troops, and travellers curious enough to make the effort were usually allowed through the various roadblocks en route. Even so, there was still the occasional bombing such as one which reportedly killed 10 people at Trinco bus station in August 1992. The countryside round Trinco was also under government control, though perhaps less securely.

The town looks a mess, with many buildings wrecked or boarded up, but it's still lively enough and the locals seem pleased to see tourists. There may still be curfews.

History

Trinco has the most convoluted colonial history of any place in Sri Lanka. The Dutch (or rather the Danes because the Dutch-sponsored visit actually used Danish ships!) first turned up here in 1617, but their visit was a brief one. At that time the Portuguese were the dominant European power in Ceylon but they did not arrive in Trinco until 1624, when they built a small fort. The Dutch took it from them in 1639 but promptly handed it over to the King of Kandy with whom they had a treaty. In 1655, treaties conveniently forgotten, they took it back, but in 1672 they abandoned it to the French who promptly handed it back to them. Finally it was the turn of the British, who took it from the Dutch in 1782 but promptly lost it to the French – who gave it back to the Dutch a year later!

Much of this back-and-forth trading was

a result of wars and political events in Europe, of course. In 1795 the British were back again and the Dutch, months away from the latest news in Europe, were totally uncertain whether to welcome them as allies in their struggles with the French or to fend them off as enemies of themselves and their friends, the French. After a bombardment lasting four days the British kicked the Dutch out and Trincomalee was once again the first British possession in Sri Lanka.

Fort Frederick
Originally built by the Portuguese, Fort Frederick, on the spit of land pointing east into the sea, is used by the military but usually, it seems, visitors are allowed in. Close to the gate is a stone slab inscribed with the double-fish emblem of the south Indian Pandyan empire, and a prediction of the 'coming of the Franks'. You've got to search to find it, as it is built into the fort entrance arch on the right-hand side. If you follow the road through the fort, about 100 metres from the gate a large building with a verandah stands on your right. This is Wellesley Lodge (although nobody in Trinco seems to know it!) where the Duke of Wellington, the 'Iron Duke' of Waterloo fame, recovered from an illness in 1799 after taking on Tippu Sultan in India. The boat he would have taken, if he hadn't been ill, went down with all hands in the Gulf of Aden – so his poor health was fortunate for him but not so for Napoleon.

Swami Rock
At the end of the road through the fort is Swami Rock. The end of the spit is occupied by a Hindu temple so you must leave your shoes at the gate house. When the Portuguese arrived here in 1624 there was an important Hindu temple perched atop the rock, so with typical religious zeal they levered it over the edge. Scuba divers have found traces of the temple under the waters over 100 metres below, and recovered the temple lingam which is now mounted in the new temple precincts.

Swami Rock is also known as 'lover's leap', from the story of a Dutch official's daughter who, watching her faithless lover sail away, decided to make the fatal leap. In fact, eight years after her supposed romantic demise, she married for the second time. Her father erected the pillar at the time simply because he was rather fond of her.

Koddiyar Bay
The Mahaweli Ganga, Sri Lanka's largest river, which starts near Adam's Peak and flows through Kandy, reaches the sea on the south side of Koddiyar Bay, about 12 km south of Trinco. Near Mutur, which stands beside one of the Mahaweli's mouths, a stone at the foot of an old tree announces:

This is the White Man's Tree, under which Robert Knox, Captain of the ship *Ann* was captured AD 1660. Knox was held captive by the Kandyan king for 19 years. This stone was placed here in 1893.

In fact it was Robert Knox's father (Robert Knox Senior) who was captain of the *Ann* and Robert Knox Junior who spent 19 years in Kandy – see the introductory Books section for more information. There is a reasonably regular launch service from Trinco to Mutur, taking 1½ hours for Rs 14. The ferries depart from the pier at the end of Customs Rd. The road south from Mutur is closed at the time of writing.

Other Attractions
Somewhere in **St Stephen's Cemetery** on Dockyard Rd is the grave of P B Molesworth, the first manager of Sri Lanka's railway system who, in his spare time, dabbled in astronomy, and while living in Trinco discovered the famous Red Spot on Jupiter – didn't know that did you?

Dutch Bay at Trinco can suffer from a very dangerous undertow so take great care if swimming there. The best beaches in the Trinco area are north of the city, particularly at Nilaveli.

At **Kanniyai**, eight km north-west of Trinco, are some hot wells which legend relates were created by Vishnu to distract the demon king Rawana, who named them after

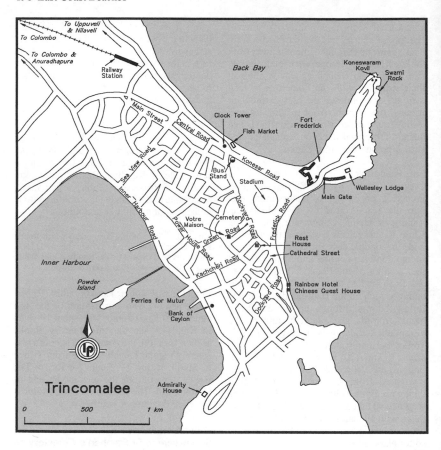

To Uppuveli & Nilaveli
To Colombo
To Colombo & Anuradhapura
Railway Station
Back Bay
Koneswaram Kovil
Swami Rock
Main Street
Central Road
Clock Tower
Fish Market
Fort Frederick
Konesar Road
Sea View Road
Inner Harbour Road
Bus Stand
Stadium
Dockyard Road
Frederick Road
Wellesley Lodge
Main Gate
Votre Maison
Power House Road
Green Road
Cemetery
Rest House
Cathedral Street
Inner Harbour
Kachcheri Road
Dockyard Road
Rainbow Hotel
Chinese Guest House
Powder Island
Ferries for Mutur
Bank of Ceylon
Trincomalee
Admiralty House
0   500   1 km

his mother, thinking that she had died. There's no place to soak here but you can slosh with buckets of hot water.

Places to Stay & Eat

The few places open at the time of writing include the basic but very hospitable *Votre Maison* at 45 Green Rd, which seems to have bravely stayed open all through the troubles. Rooms are from Rs 40 a single to Rs 100 a double, with good food at Rs 45 to Rs 50 for dinner. One traveller particularly recommended the crab and fish. The *Rutz' Inn* at 96 Main St, also friendly with good cheap food,

reopened in 1992 after five years. Singles are Rs 75. The *Rest House* on Dockyard Rd is open too, with rooms at Rs 250 a double and meals available. The *Chinese Guest House* at 312 Dyke St is hanging on too, as is the *Rainbow Hotel* also on Dyke St. Both charge about Rs 150 to Rs 200 a room, and the Rainbow's food gets good reports. Other places on Dyke St can be expected to reappear if tourism takes off in Trinco again. A recently opened place discovered by one traveller is *The Villa* at 22 Orr's Hill Rd. Singles/doubles with fan are US$10/14, and there's an air-con room for US$20. All have private bathrooms and prices include breakfast.

Several rice-and-curry 'hotels' provide alternatives to guest house food.

Getting There & Away

Bus There are buses to Trinco from as far afield as Colombo (seven hours, Rs 55) and Kandy (five hours). Most travel in the morning, to arrive before dark. Expect several checkpoints along the way. To/from Dambulla takes three hours for Rs 25. The Anuradhapura-Trincomalee road was reopened in 1992, only to be quickly closed again. Habarana is the junction town 80 km south-west of Trinco from where roads lead to Anuradhapura, Dambulla, Colombo, Kandy, and Polonnaruwa. If you can't get a through bus, you'll likely be able to pick up a connection in Habarana.

Train To reach Trinco by train you must normally change at Gal Oya, where the Trinco line branches off from the Colombo-Batticaloa line. There are supposed to be two connecting services a day from Colombo, taking 7½ and nine hours to Trincomalee, but schedules are affected by the security situation. The jungle for some distance either side of the track on the approach to Trinco has been cleared to remove cover for any would-be attackers. Fares from Colombo are Rs 50.50 in 3rd class, Rs 139.75 in 2nd.

UPPUVELI & NILAVELI

In 1992 the military would let people through from Trinco to these two beach areas to the north. Uppuveli, just three to six km from town, doesn't have as nice a beach as Nilaveli but it's not bad and it's certainly convenient. You can even walk there from Trinco.

Nilaveli village is 15 km north of Trincomalee but the beautiful beach goes on to the lagoon mouth about four km further north. Beware of the currents near the lagoon mouth, in fact all along the beach. You can hire a boat for a trip out to Pigeon Island, not far north of the Nilaveli Beach Hotel, where there's good skin diving and snorkelling. Please don't souvenir the coral.

Places to Stay

Before the troubles, both Uppuveli and Nilaveli had quite a collection of places to stay, all the way up to and beyond the bridge over the lagoon mouth at the north end of Nilaveli, and including some top-end hotels at Nilaveli. But Nilaveli was a major battleground at one stage, and to our knowledge very few places were functioning in 1992. One reader recommended the *Shahira Hotel* (☎ 01-685730), half a km off the road, signposted just north of a garishly painted mosque near the 10th milepost. Doubles are Rs 200 with fan, and cabanas are being renovated. Meals are available (dinner Rs 125 or more). The beachfront *Nilaveli Beach Hotel* is about 16 km from Trinco. The road is quite some way inland at this point so it's about 1½ km to the hotel from the turn-off near the 11th milepost. The hotel (☎ 01-422518 for reservations) has 80 rooms and costs US$7.50/10 for singles/doubles, less than half its old prices, with air-con US$2.50 extra. A third place reportedly open is the *Blue Lagoon Hotel*, a couple of km further north just before the road crosses the lagoon mouth. The Blue Lagoon has the beach out front and the calm waters of the lagoon to one side. Rooms are – or at least used to be – comfortable, with big, mosquito-netted beds (Nilaveli has powerful mosquitoes), verandahs and private bathrooms. The *Hotel Club Oceanic* at Uppuveli has also been renovated.

Getting There & Away

Bus Nos 867 and 900 from Trinco go to Uppuveli. There are buses to Nilaveli too, and taxis available in Trinco.

KALKUDAH-PASSEKUDAH

The major tourist development on the east coast before the troubles was at Passekudah, about 65 km south of Trincomalee and 30 km north of Batticaloa, where there's a wide, calm, blue, shallow, reef-protected bay with a sweep of golden sand. In addition to the three high-class hotels designed for package tourists, a couple of dozen budget places sprang up too – mainly in Kalkudah, immediately south of Passekudah, with its own beach separated from Passekudah by the Kalkudah headland.

The troubles have completely killed off tourism in this area, with the region around Batticaloa being the biggest centre of Tamil Tiger activity apart from the north of the island. If the violence comes to an end, no doubt Kalkudah-Passekudah will rise again.

Getting There & Away

Kalkudah and Passekudah are about five km east of Valaichchenai, which is on the Polonnaruwa-Batticaloa road and the terminus for many buses. There are turnings to Kalkudah-Passekudah both in Valaichchenai and a couple of km south of it. An interesting route, if it ever becomes safe, would be to start with the 1½-hour ferry trip from Trincomalee to Mutur, then take a bus (three to four hours, often with a change at Vakarai) to Valaichchenai, then a local bus.

The main railway station for Kalkudah and Passekudah is Valaichchenai, on the Colombo-Polonnaruwa-Batticaloa line, but there's also a small Kalkudah station a couple of km east on the same line, nearer to the resorts, so it's worth getting off there if your train is stopping at it.

BATTICALOA

The east coast has many lagoons and Batticaloa (Batti to its friends) is virtually surrounded by one of the largest. You must cross bridges and causeways to enter or leave the town. Batticaloa was a chief centre of Tamil Tiger control until the government retook it in 1991. So secure did the Tigers feel here at one time that they even started building their own monuments, one of which has now been turned into a clock tower. Though the town is peaceful at the time of writing, the region around it remains a hotbed of Tiger activity, which makes it unsafe to try to reach Batti.

Batti has an interesting little Dutch fort, but is most famous for its 'singing fish'.

Between April and September a distinct, deep note – described as the type of noise produced by rubbing a moistened finger around the rim of a wine glass – can be heard from the depths of the lagoon. It is strongest on full moon nights. Theories of its cause range from shoals of catfish to bottom-lying shellfish.

There is not a lot to see or do in Batti, and most travellers used to pass straight through on their way between Passekudah-Kalkudah and Arugam Bay. Places to stay included a *Rest House* beside the old Dutch Fort on the east (bus stand) side of the river, a few other places on the far side of the river, more or less directly across from the bus halt, and a couple more on Bar Rd which leads to a lighthouse.

Getting There & Away

The troubles closed the railway to Batticaloa completely at one time, but by mid-1992 there were three trains a week making the eight to 11 hour trip from Colombo and back. However they continued to come under attack and the future of the service must be very much in question. Bus passengers too in this region have been subject to some grisly massacres. For the interest of those heading for Batti if the region ever becomes safe again, buses run inland as well as up and down the coast. It's only a couple of hours to Polonnaruwa. Direct from Kandy takes about 4½ hours – a very scenic trip.

ARUGAM BAY

Arugam Bay, a fishing village 2½ km south of the small town of Pottuvil at the remote south end of the east coast, with probably the best surf in Sri Lanka off a low promontory a little further south, had developed into a low-budget travellers' centre before the troubles. There's a wide, sweeping beach in front of the village itself, good for swimming; and south of the surf promontory a long, deserted beach leading down to 'Crocodile Rock', from where wild elephants can quite often be seen.

Since the troubles began, Arugam Bay has been on and off the 'safe' list, not only

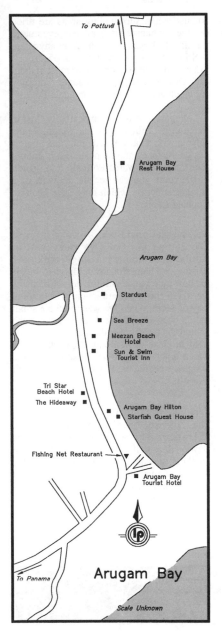

To Pottuvil

Arugam Bay
Rest House

Arugam Bay

Stardust

Sea Breeze

Meezan Beach
Hotel

Sun & Swim
Tourist Inn

Tri Star
Beach Hotel
The Hideaway

Arugam Bay Hilton
Starfish Guest House

Fishing Net Restaurant

Arugam Bay
Tourist Hotel

To Panama

Arugam Bay

Scale Unknown

because of incidents in Arugam Bay itself and Pottuvil, but also because vehicles on the road leading there through Monaragala have been attacked at times. The army usually turns back travellers when they consider the area dangerous, but that doesn't guarantee it's safe at other times. You have to ask around carefully about the latest situation and judge for yourself.

Places to Stay

Arugam Bay is separated from Pottuvil by a lagoon which at certain times of year has a large waterbird population. One or two places to stay, including a *Rest House*, existed north of the lagoon bridge, but many more, including all those which opened in the 1991 season, according to travellers, were south of the bridge. One fairly reliable place when Arugam Bay is open is the attractive *Hideaway*, on the inland side of the road, with pleasant airy rooms upstairs in the house and double bungalows in the garden. A few other places south of here, some of them very cheap cabanas with minimal facilities, often without electricity and with water from a well, are likely to open up at times when travellers can reach Arugam Bay.

Getting There & Away

Badulla and Wellawaya are the best starting points for reaching Arugam Bay. You may be able to get a bus direct to Pottuvil – otherwise go to Monaragala, where there are morning buses to Pottuvil, a trip of about three hours. There are fairly frequent buses from Pottuvil to Arugam Bay for a couple of rupees. At times there may be direct buses from Monaragala to Arugam Bay, or to Pottuvil from further afield.

The 107-km road from Batticaloa to Pottuvil has been closed for ages, but if it should ever reopen it's quite an interesting route, hugging the coast and at times running along narrow sand spits between the sea and vast lagoons. There are a number of small villages, a fair-sized town (Akkaraipattu) and some wide open stretches of beach along the way.

August, when surrounding areas are dried out, the elephants start to move in, eventually forming the largest concentrations anywhere in Sri Lanka. A good viewing time is from 3 to 5 pm. With the October rains most of them drift back to their regular haunts. You may see elephants from the Monaragala-Pottuvil road.

Lahugala also has an evocatively 'lost in the jungle' ruin called the Magul Maha Vihara, with a vatadage, dagoba and numerous guardstones and moonstones. It's about four km back towards Pottuvil; a km south of the ruins you can see the remains of a circular structure which may have been an elephant stable.

Gal Oya National Park

The 260 sq km Gal Oya park, west of Ampara, surrounds a huge tank, the Senanayake Samudra. From March to July is the best time to see wildlife here. Elephants are again the main attraction. The normal way of seeing Gal Oya was to take a small motor boat around the lake, watching the animals on the shore or the birds, and drifting right in close to herds of elephants. There was a hotel at Inginiyagala and a wildlife bungalow beside the Ekgal Aru tank, east of the park.

Yala East National Park

The 180 sq km Yala East, entered at Okanda, 25 km down the coast track south of Arugam Bay via the small town of Panama, has large numbers of water birds, particularly in the Kumana mangrove swamp, where many nest in June and July, plus elephants and the occasional leopard.

EASTERN NATIONAL PARKS

None of the three main eastern national parks is open at the time of writing – although the Monaragala-Pottuvil road passes right through Lahugala – so again the following info is provided in case things change.

Lahugala National Park

Only 15 km inland from Pottuvil, tiny (15 sq km) Lahugala has a superb variety of birdlife and lies on the 'elephant corridor' connecting Yala with Gal Oya. The pastures watered by the Mahawewa and Kitulana tanks attract elephants at any time of year, but around

Jaffna & the North

The north of Sri Lanka, with an overwhelmingly Tamil population, has been the hub of the Tamil rebellion and consequently off the travel map ever since the mid-1980s, except for a brief spell right at the end of the '80s when the Indian Peace Keeping Force held trouble to a minimum and a few travellers visited Jaffna. At the time of writing the north has become a war zone again and it's unlikely you'll be allowed much north of Anuradhapura even if you want to go.

Even before the troubles the north was the least-visited part of the country because of its relative remoteness and dry, flat landscape. For the visitor it meant basically just two areas: the Jaffna peninsula at the northern tip and the island of Mannar, which was the arrival and departure point for the ferry to/from India.

JAFFNA
Before the troubles the population of Jaffna was 118,000, making it the second biggest city in Sri Lanka, and that of the whole Jaffna Peninsula was about 750,000. It was an industrious place with a fairly distinct culture from the rest of Sri Lanka. The population has since been much reduced by war casualties and by many people fleeing the area.

The Portuguese who arrived in Sri Lanka in the 16th century took over the Tamil kingdom centred on Jaffna just as they took over other coastal kingdoms. Jaffna was the longest-lasting Portuguese stronghold on the island and only surrendered to the Dutch after a bitter three-month siege in 1658. The Dutch handed it over to the British in 1795.

During the 1980s and '90s Jaffna has been fought over by Tamil guerrillas, Sri Lankan government troops and planes, and the Indian Peace Keeping Force – a period surely worse than any other in its history. It's now a shadow of its former self. As one traveller who got there in 1989 succinctly wrote: 'There are no places of interest unless you are interested in photographing ruins'.

Jaffna Fort
Jaffna's fort, centrally positioned near Jaffna's lagoon-front, beside the causeway to Kayts Island, was built in 1680 by the Dutch, over an earlier Portuguese fort. It has seen much fighting during the unrest, with government forces often holed up inside it.

Architecturally, it's probably Asia's best example of Dutch fortifications of its period – 22 hectares in area, star-shaped, built on a grass-covered mound, surrounded by a moat, and grander than the Dutch headquarters fort in Jakarta, Indonesia. The outerworks were not built until 1792. Within the fort are the King's House, one-time residence of the Dutch commander and an excellent example of Dutch architecture of the period, plus the 1706 Dutch *Groote Kerk* and, nearby on the outer wall, a small British-period house in which the writer Leonard Woolf, Virginia Woolf's husband, lived for some time. It features in his autobiography *Growing*.

Other Things to See
Jaffna had an interesting little **Archaeological Museum** on Main St, near the old Rest House, which is worth looking for. Most of its Hindu kovils (temples) date from the British era. Their architecture is generally typical of the south Indian Dravidian style. The most spectacular car or *juggernaut* festival is traditionally held from the **Kandaswamy Kovil** on Point Pedro Rd in the Nallur district of the city during July or August. The original Kandaswamy Kovil, torn down by the Portuguese, has been variously described as dating from the 15th, 10th or even an earlier century. Its successor is topped by a typically Dravidian gopuram – the tall 'spire', alive with a technicoloured Disneyland of Hindu characters. Other

important kovils are generally outside the city limits.

Places to Stay

The few places functioning before the Indian Peace Keeping Force left included the *YMCA* on Kandy Rd, about 2½ km east of the fort, which was repaired after apparently being shelled by the Indians, and used to be cheap but restricted to men only. Also open were the two formerly top hotels in Jaffna – the *Hotel Ashok* at 3 Clock Tower Rd, still in good condition and charging from Rs 200 a double, and the *Subhas Hotel* at 15 Victoria Rd, near the railway station, where a basic double sharing common bathroom was Rs 75.

Getting There & Away

The railway tracks into Jaffna were reportedly torn up by the Tamil Tigers: if they are ever replaced there should be trains to/from Anuradhapura and Colombo. In the meantime Anuradhapura, 195 km south, will be an obvious starting point for bus trips.

AROUND THE PENINSULA

The Jaffna Peninsula is actually almost an island; only the narrow neck of land occupied by the Chundikkulam Bird Sanctuary, and the causeway known as Elephant Pass – where once elephants waded across the shallow lagoon, but recently more famous as a battleground – connect it with the rest of Sri Lanka. It's low lying, much covered by shallow lagoons, with a number of islands offshore.

The peninsula looks quite unlike other parts of Sri Lanka. The intensive agriculture – it's famous for its mangoes – is all a result of irrigation, and for the southern coconut palms Jaffna substitutes the stark-looking palmyrah. Popular beaches in peaceful times include **Kalmunai Point** near Jaffna and **Palm Beach** on the north coast – though there were never the sort of beach resorts up here that are found further south. The best known is tranquil **Casuarina** on Karaitivu island, where the water is very shallow and

you have to walk a fair distance out from the shore.

The **Kandaswamy Kovil** at Mavidda-puram, 15 km north of Jaffna near Keerimalai, has a car festival rivalling that of its namesake in Jaffna.

At **Kantarodai**, about three km west of Chunnakam, which is north of Jaffna about half way to Kankesanturai, are nearly 100 curious miniature dagobas crammed into a tiny area of not much over a hectare – the largest is only about four metres in diameter. Discovered in 1916 they are thought to be over 2000 years old.

ISLANDS OFF JAFFNA

Three of the major islands – Kayts, Karaitivu and Punkudutivu – are joined to the mainland by causeways over the shallow waters around the peninsula. Close to the town of Kayts, at the northern tip of Kayts Island, stands the island fort of Hammenhiel which used to be accessible by boat from Kayts. The name means 'heel-of-the-ham' and relates to the Dutch view that Sri Lanka was shaped rather like a ham.

When ferries run, they mostly go from Kayts, including the very short hop across to Karaitivu which is joined to the mainland by a causeway.

Delft

Delft, named after the Dutch town of that name, is 10 km off Punkudutivu and 35 km from Jaffna. Ferries, when they run, go from Siriputu. The island is noted for traces of the Portuguese and Dutch eras (such as the Dutch garrison captain's country-house with a stone pigeon-cote) and for its bleak, wind-swept beauty.

The small Dutch fort is only a short walk from the ferry dock. Behind that is a beautiful beach with many exquisite shells. On the island are hundreds and hundreds of stone walls which, like the Dutch fort, are made of huge, beautiful chunks of the brain and fan coral of which the island is composed.

A 1990 letter indicated that there were two ferries a day from Siriputu to Delft at the time – one in the early morning (seemingly too early to be reachable by bus from Jaffna) and one in the early afternoon, so it was impossible to do a day-trip. The only accommodation possibilities were private houses. The Rest House near the ferry dock was in ruins. From Jaffna to the ferry is a 50-minute bus ride; the ferry crossing is an hour.

MANNAR ISLAND

Mannar is probably the driest, most barren area in Sri Lanka, and the landscape is chiefly notable for the many baobab trees, probably introduced from Africa by Arab traders centuries ago.

Mannar, the major town on the island, is at the landward end, joined to the mainland by a three-km causeway. It's uninteresting apart from its picturesque Portuguese/Dutch fort. Talaimannar, near the west end, is about three km before the pier which was the arrival/departure point of the ferry for India that operated until 1984. A little further west an abandoned lighthouse at South Point marks the start of Adam's Bridge, the chain of reefs, sandbanks and islets that almost connects Sri Lanka to India. This is the series of stepping stones which Hanuman used to follow Rawana, the demon king of Lanka, in his bid to rescue Sita.

There was a handful of places to stay in Talaimannar and Mannar when the ferry was running. But trains to/from Anuradhapura and Colombo connected with the ferry and most travellers went straight through.

Glossary

Adam's Bridge – chain of sand bars and islands that almost connects Sri Lanka to India

ambalamas – wayside shelters for pilgrims

amudes – loin cloths worn by gem miners, very similar to the G-strings worn by tourists at Hikkaduwa!

arrack – distilled toddy, often very potent indeed

Avalokitesvara – one of the Buddha's most important disciples

Ayurvedic – traditional naturopathic medical attention using herbal medicines

baas – skilled workman

banian – long, loose-sleeved, over-shirt

banyan tree – a type of bo-tree

baobab – strange African water-holding, dry-land trees introduced into the northern regions of the island by Arab traders

beedis – small hand-rolled cigars

bel kalla – a 'Bell Fragment', name given to a newly discovered archaeological find, after H C P Bell the first British Government Archaeologist

betel – nut of the betel tree, chewed as a mild intoxicant

Bhikku – Buddhist monk

Bodhisattva – Buddhist 'saint' who refrained from entering nirvana in order to stay in this world and help fellow creatures seek enlightenment

bo-tree – *Ficus religiosa* – large spreading tree under which the Buddha was sitting when he attained enlightenment

bund – built-up bank or dyke around a tank

Burgher – Sri Lankan Eurasian, generally descended from Portuguese-Sinhalese or Dutch-Sinhalese intermarriage

chena – primitive slash-and-burn agriculture; also the fields created in this way

Chola – a powerful, ancient south Indian kingdom which invaded Ceylon on several occasions

choli – short blouse worn with a sari

coir – matting or rope made from coconut fibres

copra – dried coconut kernel, used to make cooking oil

crore – 10 million, of anything but most often rupees

CTB – Central (formerly Ceylon) Transport Board, the state bus network, now being privatised

Culavamsa – the 'Genealogy of the Lesser Dynasty' continues the history of the Mahavamsa right up to 1758, just 60 years before the last King of Kandy, Sri Wickrema Rajasinha, surrendered to the British

curd – buffalo yoghurt

dagoba – Buddhist monument composed of a solid hemisphere containing relics of the Buddha. Known as a pagoda, stupa or chedi in other countries.

devala – temple or shrine, can be Buddhist or Hindu

dhal – a thick soup made of split lentils

Dharma – Buddhist teachings (Sanskrit word, in Pali it is Dhamma)

dorje – hourglass-shaped Tibetan thunderbolt symbol

Dravidian – southern Indian group of peoples and languages which includes Tamils

EPRLF – Eelam People's Revolutionary Liberation Front – a Tamil rebel and political group

ganga – river

gaw – old Sinhalese unit of distance

gedige – ancient Sinhalese architectural style, extremely thick walls and a corbelled roof

gopuram – towering entrance tower to a Hindu temple, a style of Dravidian architecture found principally in south India

Groote Kerk – the old Dutch churches in Jaffna and Galle

guardstone – carved ornamental stones that flank doorways or entrances to temples

gurulu – a legendary bird which preys on snakes

Hinayana – small-vehicle Buddhism, practised in Sri Lanka. Also known as Theravada.

hopper – popular Sri Lankan snack meal – either string hoppers or egg hoppers

howdah – seating structure on an elephant's back

illama – gem-bearing stratum in gem fields

IPKF – Indian Peace Keeping Force – the Indian Army contingent in Sri Lanka from 1987 to 1990

jaggery – hard, brown, sugar-like sweetener made from kitul palm sap

jataka – stories from the Buddha's previous lives

juggernauts – huge, extravagantly decorated temple 'cars', dragged through the streets during Hindu festivals

JVP – Janatha Vimukthi Peramuna, People's Liberation Army – Sinhalese Marxist revolutionary organisation which rose up in the early 1970s and late 1980s

kachchan – a hot, dry wind

kachcheri – government secretariat or residency

Karava – fisherfolk of Indian descent

karma – law of cause and effect (Sanskrit word, in Pali it is Khamma)

kavadi – decorated framework carried in festivals as a form of penance by Hindu devotees

kitul – one of the Sri Lankan palm trees, used to make jaggery and treacle

kolam – masked dance drama

Kotte – the most important Sinhalese capital after the fall of Polonnaruwa – today it is just outside Colombo and the site of the new parliament built by President Jayewardene

kovil – Hindu temple

kul – spicy chowder dish, popular in Jaffna

lakh – 100,000, a standard large unit in Sri Lanka and India

Laksala – government-run arts and handicrafts shop

lamprai – rice and curry wrapped up and cooked in a banana leaf

loris – small, nocturnal, tree-climbing animal

LTTE – Liberation Tigers of Tamil Eelam – the Tamil Tigers, the strongest Tamil rebel group

lunghi – Sri Lankan sarong

Maha – the north-east monsoon season

Mahavamsa – 'Genealogy of the Great Dynasty', a written Sinhalese history running from the arrival of Vijaya in the 6th century BC, through the meeting of King Devanampaya Tissa with Mahinda, and on to the great kings of Anuradhapura

Mahaweli Ganga – Sri Lanka's biggest river, which starts in the hill country near Adam's Peak, flows through Kandy and eventually reaches the sea near Trincomalee. Focus of the Mahaweli Development Scheme in which a series of dams and reservoirs have been built along its length to provide irrigation and hydroelectricity.

Mahayana – large-vehicle Buddhism

Mahinda – son of the Indian Buddhist- Emperor Ashoka, credited with introducing Buddhism to Sri Lanka

mahout – elephant rider/master

Maitreya – future Buddha

mandapaya – raised platform with decorative pillars

mawatha – avenue

moonstone – semiprecious stone or a carved stone 'doorstep' at temple entrances

mouse deer – very small variety of Sri Lankan deer

mudra – hand and body position of a Buddha image

naga – cobra, usually used in a religious sense

naga raksha – (cobra) mask

nibbana – Pali word for nirvana

nirvana – the ultimate aim of Buddhist existence, a state where one leaves the cycle of existence and does not have to suffer further rebirths

Nuwara – city, also used as a name for Kandy

ola – palm leaf used in traditional books

oruva – outrigger canoe

oya – stream or small river

paddy – unhusked rice

padma – lotus flower

pagoda – see dagoba

Pali – the language in which the Buddhist scriptures were originally recorded; scholars still look to the original Pali texts for the true interpretation

palmyrah – tall palm tree found in the dry northern region

panna – one of the three stages in the Buddhist 'eight-fold' path: wisdom and insight

paranibbana – the transition stage to nibbana, as in the reclining Buddha images where the Buddha is in the state of entering nirvana

perahera – procession, usually with dancers, drummers and elephants

Pettah – bazaar area of Colombo

pittu – steamed mixture of rice, flour and coconut

plantain – banana, coming in many varieties in Sri Lanka

pola – special food market on certain day of the week

puja – religious service

potgul – library

poya – full moon holiday

raksha – mask used in processions & festivals

Rakshasas – legendary rulers of Sri Lanka, led by Rawana

Rawana – the 'demon king of Lanka' who abducts Rama's beautiful wife Sita in the Hindu epic the *Ramayana*

relic chamber – chamber in a dagoba housing a relic of the Buddha but also representing the Buddhist concept of the cosmos

Ruhuna – ancient southern centre of Sinhalese power near Tissamaharama, which stood even when Anuradhapura and Polonnaruwa fell to Indian invaders,

sadhu sadhu – 'blessed, blessed', the words pilgrims cry out as they climb Adam's Peak

samadhi – one of the three stages in the Buddhist 'eight-fold' path: equanimity of mind

sambar – species of deer, also called the Indian elk

samudra – large tank or inland sea

Sangamitta – Mahinda's sister, who brought the sapling from which the sacred bo-tree at Anuradhapura has grown

Sangha – the brotherhood of the Buddhist monks

sanni – devil-dancing mask

Sanskrit – ancient Indian language, the oldest known language of the Indo-European family

sari – traditional female garment in Sri Lanka and India

school pen – ballpoint pen, often requested (or demanded!) from tourists by Sri Lankan children

sila – one of the three stages in the Buddhist 'eight-fold' path: known as the precept

Sinhala – language of the Sinhalese people

Sinhalese – majority population of Sri Lanka, principally Sinhala-speaking Buddhists

SLFP – Sri Lanka Freedom Party

sloth bear – large, shaggy, honey-eating Sri Lankan bear

Tamils – people of south Indian origins who comprise the largest minority population in Sri Lanka

tank – artificial water storage lake; many of the tanks in Sri Lanka are both very large and ancient

Tantric Buddhism – Hindu-influenced Buddhism with strong sexual and occult overtones; Tibetan Buddhism

Taylor, James – not the rock singer, this one set up the first tea plantation in Ceylon

thambili – king coconut, makes a very refreshing drink

Theravada – small-vehicle Buddhism, practised in Sri Lanka. Also known as Hinayana.

tiffin – lunch, a colonial English expression

tiffin boys – they pick up the city workers' tiffins from their homes and transport them into the city

toddy – mildly alcoholic drink tapped from the palm tree

toddy tappers – the people who perform acrobatic feats to tap toddy from the tops of palm trees

Tripitaka – the 'three baskets', one of the classical Buddhist scriptures

UNP – United National Party, first Sri Lankan political party to hold power after independence

Vanni – the northern plains, the tank country

vatadage – ancient Sinhalese architectural style; 'circular relic house' with a small dagoba flanked by Buddha images and encircled by rows of columns

Veddahs – the original people of Sri Lanka prior to the arrival of the Sinhalese, still struggling on in isolated pockets

vel – trident, belonging to Skanda, God of War, in Hindu legend

villu – small seasonal lakelet found in Wilpattu National Park and on the Mahaweli Ganga

wewa – irrigation tank, artificial lake

Yala – the south-west monsoon season

Index

MAPS

TEXT

Map references are in **bold** type

Accommodation 44-45
Adam's Peak 138-140
Adisham 149
Ahangama 108
Air Travel 52-54, 80
Akkaraipattu 193
Aluthgama 90-91
Aluvihara 159-161
Amaduwa 118-119
Ambalangoda 91-92
Anuradhapura 174-183, **176-177**
    History 11
    Jetavanarama Dagoba 179
    Northern Ruins 178-179
    Sacred Bo-tree 175
    Tanks 181
Architecture 160
Arts & Crafts 50-51, 79-80, 84,
    125-126
Arugam Bay 192-193, **193**
Aukana 186

Badulla 153-154
Bandaranaike, Sirimavo 16
Bandaranaike, Solomon 15-16
Bandarawela 151-152
Batik 50, 84, 136
Batticaloa 192
Beliatta 116
Belihul Oya 157
Bentota 90-91
Beruwela 89-90
Bicycling 59-60
Bird Sanctuaries see Reserves
Books 28, 36-37, 39, 64
Bo-tree 11, 175
Bowles, Paul 108

Buddhism 26-28, 64
Buduruvagala 154-155
Burghers 26
Bus Travel 55-56, 60, 80-82
Business Hours 33

Car Rental 57-58
Casuarina 196
Ceylon 9-10
Clarke, Arthur C 37, 118
Climate 20, 32
Colombo 61-82, **66-67**, **72-73**
    Books & Bookshops 64
    Cultural Centres & Libraries
        63-64
    Entertainment 79
    Fort 64-65
    Getting There & Away 80-81
    Information 62
    Medical Services 64
    Pettah 65
    Places of Worship 69-70
    Places to Eat 77-79
    Places to Stay 70-77
    Shopping 79-80
Coral Sanctuary, Hikkaduwa 93
Costs 31
Credit Cards 31
CTB 55
Cultural Triangle 159

Dalada Maligawa see Temple of
    the Tooth
Dalhousie 138-140
Dambadeniya 186-187
Dambulla 161-163, **162**
Dance 92, 135-136
Dangers & Annoyances 42-44
Deberawewa 117, 118

Delft 196-197
Departure Tax 54
Dikwella 112-113
Dimbulagala 174
Diyaluma Falls 149
Dondra 112
Drinks 48
Driving 57-59
Dunhinda Falls 153-154
Duwa Island 84

Economy 24
Ekgal Aru Tank 194
Electricity 36
Elephants 121-122, 125, 158,
    194
Ella 152-153
Embassies 30-31, 63
Embekke Devale 126

Fauna 21
    Books 37
Fax 35-36
Ferries 54, 196-197
Flora 21
Food 45-48
Forts 83, 99-100, 109-110, 150,
    189, 195

Gadaldeniya Temple 126
Galle 99-103, **101**
Gangatilaka Vihara 89
Gems 50-51, 156, 157
Geography 20
Giritale 172
Groote Kerk (Great Church) 100

Habaraduwa 108
Habarana 174

202

Thanks

Letter-writers (apologies if we've misspelt your names) to whom thanks must go include:

Wenche Aas (N), Eileen & George Adams (AUS), Peter Allen (AUS), Mick Allen (SL), Sarah & Jeff Allen (UK), Tim Allen (AUS), J Andriessen (NL), Kathleen Aurigemma, Roger Bailey (UK), Geoff & Sharyn Bains (UK), Liam Barrett (UK), Bonnie Baskin (USA), Sophia Baunez (F), Rodney Blakeney (AUS), Emile den Boogert (NL), Mary Boyce (UK), David Bray (UK), Marcel Brevet (NL), Wilma Brillemans (NL), John Brotherton (UK), Aileen Brown (UK), Kate Buckley (UK), Douglas Bullis, Jacob Burger (D), Jamie & Sue Burridge, Rees Campbell (AUS), Rev Bob Campbell-Smith (UK), Bernard Van Cauve (B), Ian Chapman (UK), Dave Clawson, Lis Clegg (UK), David Collins (AUS), Richard Cooper (USA), P & J Crook (AUS), Caroline Cupitt (UK), Bo Danielsen (S), Mark David-Tooze (UK), Kpmatjam Davis (UK), Martin Dichter (D), Robert & Kate Dickson (UK), J Doran, Nathalie Dourneau (F), Peter Doyle (AUS), Katherine Duarte (USA), Hilary Dugdale (UK), Dux Frank (D), Eric Eagle (UK), Ward Edmonds, Ivar Eimon (USA), Ole-Fredrik Einarsen (N), C Ekanayaike (SL), Zohar Elkan (Isr), Mark Ellingham (UK), Manuela Elsasser (D), Ingrid Emonds (NL), Wybo Eric (B), Johnathan Fitzsimmonds (UK), Don Ford (USA), Joachim Franz (D), Gina Geiger (G), Giorgio Genova (D), Richard Glob (DK), Nick Glozier (UK), Lorne Goldman (C), Karl Gorczynski, Andrew Graham (UK), Richard Graves (UK), Guenther Gross (A), Giles Guinen (UK), Katy Haire (AUS), Andres Halas (AUS), Claire Harbour (UK), J Hardash (Isr), Andrew Harmer (UK), Yves Heroux (C), Fredrik Hoglund (S), Fiona Holmes (UK), Joanne Holmes (AUS), Paul Hopson (USA), Jan Hosman (CH), Simon Howarth (UK), patrick Jackson (NZ), Benjamin James (A), Arthur James (AUS), P and H Jayasundara (SL), Sita Jayasundera (SL), D E F Jayasuriya (SL), S Jewitt, J Jeyakumar (SL), Catherine Keats (UK), Malcolm Keir (UK), Jorg Keller (D), Laurence Kelvin (UK), Bob King (AUS), Gerhard Kitschenreuther (D), Anne-Mie Koopmans (NL), Georges Krist (B), Robert Legier (C), Gordon Lidgard (NZ), Amanda Long (UK), Darren Lovell (UK), Chris Lovell (UK), Gesen V Lupke (D), Meredith Maisonneuve (AUS), K Manawadu (SL), David Marks (UK), Gaby Marsch (D), Ross Masterton (UK), Barrie McCormick (NZ), Ted McGraws (UK), Moira McLaughlin (UK), Michael Medzini (Isr), H Meyer (UK), Brenda Miles (UK), Peter Mitchell (AUS), Runmi Mohideen, Mark & Jane Moody (UK), Mike Moxen (UK), Mark Mueller (Kor), Martin & Miriam Murphy (UK), J Neal (AUS), Joe A Neal, Roslyn Nichol (AUS), B Niven (AUS), Terry Norris (UK), Tom Nowak (C), Elizabeth Noyes (UK), Stewart Olney (UK), Marc Osborne (NZ), Stephen Owens (UK), Robert Parker (UK), D Peiris (SL), NJ Perera (SL), Pentti Pohjola (S), Eyal Por (Isr), Linda Reinke, Bill Roberto (AUS), Geoff Rockliffe-King (UK), Paul Rogerson, Yola Ron (Isr), Gisela Rosemann (D), Gilles Rubens (NL), Gerhard Sailer, Jeff Salerno (UK), Martin Sanvarin, Mike Schaffner (CH), E Schawohl, Read Schuchardt (USA), Wendy Schulzc (AUS), Angela Scott (UK), Robin Seedhouse, Frank Slaps (NL), Remco SLUIS (NL), Alister Smith (UK), Barbara Smith (UK), Brian Smith (UK), Richard Smith, Jon Snyder, Erik F Sorensen (DK), Richard Spence (UK), Peter Spittles (UK), Lars Starner (S), Ingeborg & Katryn Steenbeke (B), Lawrence Straus (UK), Helen Stringer (UK), Chris & G'dine Stucki (AUS), E W Swinhoe-Phelan (UK), J Teasdale (UK), Rob. & Marina Tedeschi (I), Eric Telfer (USA), M C Temple (UK), Dave Thomas (AUS), Efi Thomopoulou (G), Kenneth Thompson (USA), Shay Topaz (Isr), Jane Toyota (C), Walt Tynan (USA), John Ullerichs (DK), R H Valentine (USA), Mrs Valentino (I), Thierry Vallois (F), Anthony & Marga van Es (NL), Solveig Velander (CH), Jaap Vossestein (NL), Sarah Wall (UK), Kate Wall (NZ), Frank Waters (UK), Dimitrije Wentner (A), P C Wincote (UK), Alexandra Withell (AUS), Mr & Ms Wolfe (UK), Randall Woltz (USA), George Wright (UK), Marg & Richard Wynne-Jones and Orville Zander

A – Austria, AUS – Australia, B – Belgium, C – Canada, CH – Switzerland, D – Germany, DK – Denmark, F – France, G – Greece, Isr – Israel, I – Italy, Kor – Korea, N – Norway, NL – Netherlands, NZ – New Zealand, SL – Sri Lanka, S – Sweden, UK – United Kingdom, USA – United States of America

PLANET TALK
Lonely Planet's FREE quarterly newsletter

We love hearing from you and think you'd like to hear from us.

When... *is the right time to see reindeer in Finland?*
Where... *can you hear the best palm-wine music in Ghana?*
How... *do you get from Asunción to Areguá by steam train?*
What... *is the best way to see India?*

For the answer to these and many other questions read PLANET TALK.

Every issue is packed with up-to-date travel news and advice including:

- *a letter from Lonely Planet founders Tony and Maureen Wheeler*
- *travel diary from a Lonely Planet author - find out what it's really like out on the road*
- *feature article on an important and topical travel issue*
- *a selection of recent letters from our readers*
- *the latest travel news from all over the world*
- *details on Lonely Planet's new and forthcoming releases*

To join our mailing list contact any Lonely Planet office (address below).

LONELY PLANET PUBLICATIONS
Australia: PO Box 617, Hawthorn 3122, Victoria (tel: 03-819 1877)
USA: Embarcadero West, 155 Filbert St, Suite 251, Oakland, CA 94607 (tel: 510-893 8555)
TOLL FREE: (800) 275-8555
UK: 10 Barley Mow Passage, Chiswick, London W4 4PH (tel: 081-742 3161)
France: 71 bis rue du Cardinal Lemoine – 75005 Paris (tel: 1-46 34 00 58)

Also available: Lonely Planet T-shirts. 100% heavyweight cotton (S, M, L, XL)

Guides to the Indian Subcontinent

Bangladesh - a travel survival kit
This practical guide – the only English-language guide to Bangladesh – encourages travellers to take another look at this often-neglected but beautiful land.

India - a travel survival kit
Widely regarded as *the* guide to India, this award-winning book has all the information to help you make the most of the unforgettable experience that is India.

Karakoram Highway the high road to China - a travel survival kit
Travel in the footsteps of Alexander the Great and Marco Polo on the Karakoram Highway, following the ancient and fabled Silk Road. This comprehensive guide also covers villages and treks away from the highway.

Kashmir, Ladakh & Zanskar - a travel survival kit
Detailed information on three contrasting Himalayan regions in the Indian state of Jammu and Kashmir – the narrow valley of Zanskar, the isolated 'little Tibet' of Ladakh, and the stunningly beautiful Vale of Kashmir.

Nepal - a travel survival kit
Travel information on every road-accessible area in Nepal, including the Terai. This practical guidebook also includes introductions to trekking, white-water rafting and mountain biking.

Pakistan - a travel survival kit
Discover 'the unknown land of the Indus' with this informative guidebook – from bustling Karachi to ancient cities and tranquil mountain valleys.

Tibet - a travel survival kit
The fabled mountain-land of Tibet was one of the last areas of China to become accessible to travellers. This guide has full details on this remote and fascinating region, including the border crossing to Nepal.

Trekking in the Indian Himalaya
All the advice you'll need for planning and equipping a trek, including detailed route descriptions for some of the world's most exciting treks.

Trekking in the Nepal Himalaya
Complete trekking information for Nepal, including day-by-day route descriptions and detailed maps – a wealth of advice for both independent and group trekkers.

Also available:
Hindi/Urdu phrasebook, *Nepal* phrasebook, and *Sri Lanka* phrasebook.

Lonely Planet Guidebooks

Lonely Planet guidebooks cover every accessible part of Asia as well as Australia, the Pacific, South America, Africa, the Middle East, Europe and parts of North America. There are five series: *travel survival kits*, covering a country for a range of budgets; *shoestring guides* with compact information for low-budget travel in a major region; *walking guides*; *city guides* and *phrasebooks*.

Australia & the Pacific
Australia
Bushwalking in Australia
Islands of Australia's Great Barrier Reef
Fiji
Melbourne city guide
Micronesia
New Caledonia
New Zealand
Tramping in New Zealand
Papua New Guinea
Bushwalking in Papua New Guinea
Papua New Guinea phrasebook
Rarotonga & the Cook Islands
Samoa
Solomon Islands
Sydney city guide
Tahiti & French Polynesia
Tonga
Vanuatu
Victoria

South-East Asia
Bali & Lombok
Bangkok city guide
Cambodia
Indonesia
Indonesia phrasebook
Laos
Malaysia, Singapore & Brunei
Myanmar (Burma)
Burmese phrasebook
Philippines
Pilipino phrasebook
Singapore city guide
South-East Asia on a shoestring
Thailand
Thai phrasebook
Vietnam
Vietnamese phrasebook

North-East Asia
China
Beijing city guide
Cantonese phrasebook
Mandarin Chinese phrasebook
Hong Kong, Macau & Canton
Japan
Japanese phrasebook
Korea
Korean phrasebook
Mongolia
North-East Asia on a shoestring
Seoul city guide
Taiwan
Tibet
Tibet phrasebook
Tokyo city guide

Middle East
Arab Gulf States
Egypt & the Sudan
Arabic (Egyptian) phrasebook
Iran
Israel
Jordan & Syria
Middle East
Turkish phrasebook
Trekking in Turkey
Yemen

Indian Ocean
Madagascar & Comoros
Maldives & Islands of the East Indian Ocean
Mauritius, Réunion & Seychelles

Mail Order

Lonely Planet guidebooks are distributed worldwide. They are also available by mail order from Lonely Planet, so if you have difficulty finding a title please write to us. US and Canadian residents should write to Embarcadero West, 155 Filbert St, Suite 251, Oakland CA 94607, USA; European residents should write to 10 Barley Mow Passage, Chiswick, London W4 4PH; and residents of other countries to PO Box 617, Hawthorn, Victoria 3122, Australia.

Indian Subcontinent
Bangladesh
India
Hindi/Urdu phrasebook
Trekking in the Indian Himalaya
Karakoram Highway
Kashmir, Ladakh & Zanskar
Nepal
Trekking in the Nepal Himalaya
Nepali phrasebook
Pakistan
Sri Lanka
Sri Lanka phrasebook

Africa
Africa on a shoestring
Central Africa
East Africa
Trekking in East Africa
Kenya
Swahili phrasebook
Morocco, Algeria & Tunisia
Arabic (Moroccan) phrasebook
South Africa, Lesotho & Swaziland
Zimbabwe, Botswana & Namibia
West Africa

Central America & the Caribbean
Baja California
Central America on a shoestring
Costa Rica
Eastern Caribbean
Guatemala, Belize & Yucatán: La Ruta Maya
Mexico

North America
Alaska
Canada
Hawaii

Europe
Baltic States & Kaliningrad
Dublin city guide
Eastern Europe on a shoestring
Eastern Europe phrasebook
Finland
France
Greece
Hungary
Iceland, Greenland & the Faroe Islands
Ireland
Italy
Mediterranean Europe on a shoestring
Mediterranean Europe phrasebook
Poland
Scandinavian & Baltic Europe on a shoestring
Scandinavian Europe phrasebook
Switzerland
Trekking in Spain
Trekking in Greece
USSR
Russian phrasebook
Western Europe on a shoestring
Western Europe phrasebook

South America
Argentina, Uruguay & Paraguay
Bolivia
Brazil
Brazilian phrasebook
Chile & Easter Island
Colombia
Ecuador & the Galápagos Islands
Latin American Spanish phrasebook
Peru
Quechua phrasebook
South America on a shoestring
Trekking in the Patagonian Andes

The Lonely Planet Story

Lonely Planet published its first book in 1973 in response to the numerous 'How did you do it?' questions Maureen and Tony Wheeler were asked after driving, bussing, hitching, sailing and railing their way from England to Australia.

Written at a kitchen table and hand collated, trimmed and stapled, *Across Asia on the Cheap* became an instant local bestseller, inspiring thoughts of another book.

Eighteen months in South-East Asia resulted in their second guide, *South-East Asia on a shoestring*, which they put together in a backstreet Chinese hotel in Singapore in 1975. The 'yellow bible' as it quickly became known to backpackers around the world, soon became *the* guide to the region. It has sold well over half a million copies and is now in its 7th edition, still retaining its familiar yellow cover.

Today there are over 130 Lonely Planet titles in print – books that have that same adventurous approach to travel as those early guides; books that 'assume you know how to get your luggage off the carousel' as one reviewer put it.

Although Lonely Planet initially specialised in guides to Asia, they now cover most regions of the world, including the Pacific, South America, Africa, the Middle East and Europe. The list of *walking guides* and *phrasebooks* (for 'unusual' languages such as Quechua, Swahili, Nepali and Egyptian Arabic) is also growing rapidly.

The emphasis continues to be on travel for independent travellers. Tony and Maureen still travel for several months of each year and play an active part in the writing, updating and quality control of Lonely Planet's guides.

They have been joined by over 50 authors, 60 staff – mainly editors, cartographers & designers – at our office in Melbourne, Australia, at our US office in Oakland, California and at our European office in Paris; another five at our office in London handle sales for Britain, Europe and Africa. Travellers themselves also make a valuable contribution to the guides through the feedback we receive in thousands of letters each year.

The people at Lonely Planet strongly believe that travellers can make a positive contribution to the countries they visit, both through their appreciation of the countries' culture, wildlife and natural features, and through the money they spend. In addition, the company makes a direct contribution to the countries and regions it covers. Since 1986 a percentage of the income from each book has been donated to ventures such as famine relief in Africa; aid projects in India; agricultural projects in Central America; Greenpeace's efforts to halt French nuclear testing in the Pacific and Amnesty International. In 1994 $100,000 was donated to such causes.

Lonely Planet's basic travel philosophy is summed up in Tony Wheeler's comment, 'Don't worry about whether your trip will work out. Just go!'.